Palgrave Studies in the History of Finance

The study of the history of financial institutions, markets, instruments and concepts is vital if we are to understand the role played by finance today. At the same time, the methodologies developed by finance academics can provide a new perspective for historical studies. Palgrave Studies in the History of Finance is a multi-disciplinary effort to emphasise the role played by finance in the past, and what lessons historical experiences have for us. It presents original research, in both authored monographs and edited collections, from historians, finance academics and economists, as well as financial practitioners.

More information about this series at
http://www.palgrave.com/gp/series/14583

Douglas Kanter • Patrick Walsh
Editors

Taxation, Politics, and Protest in Ireland, 1662–2016

palgrave
macmillan

Editors
Douglas Kanter
Florida Atlantic University
Boca Raton, FL, USA

Patrick Walsh
Trinity College Dublin
Dublin, Ireland

Palgrave Studies in the History of Finance
ISBN 978-3-030-04308-7 ISBN 978-3-030-04309-4 (eBook)
https://doi.org/10.1007/978-3-030-04309-4

Library of Congress Control Number: 2018964566

Cover illustration: De Luan / Alamy Stock Photo
Cover design by Tjaša Krivic

This Palgrave Macmillan imprint is published by the registered company Springer Nature Switzerland AG
The registered company address is: Gewerbestrasse 11, 6330 Cham, Switzerland

Preface

This book explores the politics of taxation in Ireland between 1662 and 2016. It is concerned with both 'high' politics—the world of politicians and policymakers and the calculations that informed their decisions about public finance—and 'low' politics—the popular response to taxation, which included not only compliance but also avoidance, evasion, resistance, and protest. In casting a wide net over a long period of time, this anthology aims to illuminate a neglected aspect of Irish history, and to stimulate further scholarship on a subject that we believe is crucial to an understanding of the early modern and modern Irish experience. To the latter end, this volume does not aim at a comprehensive account of taxation in Ireland over the last 350 years. Rather, it examines key episodes, enduring trends, and recurring themes in the period under consideration. Our hope is that others will elaborate upon the work featured here, expanding upon its insights when appropriate and filling in the gaps where warranted.

An anthology is, by definition, a collaborative affair, and we have incurred a number of debts in producing this book. It is a pleasure to acknowledge them. We wish to extend our thanks to the contributors, whose punctuality in submission, close attention to detail, and patience in the face of many and varied queries have facilitated our work as editors. We are grateful to the team at Palgrave, including Natasha Denby, Aimee Dibbens, Ruth Noble, and Tula Weis, for taking this volume on and assisting in its completion. James Kelly provided crucial support for this project at an early stage of its development. Thanks are also due to the archivists and librarians at those institutions where the contributors have conducted research. Meagan Weisner kindly produced the maps in the chapters by Mel Cousins and Douglas Kanter, while Robert Ellis and Elise Tengs provided excellent research assistance for the chapter by Michelle D'Arcy and Marina Nistotskaya. The latter chapter received funding from the Swedish Research Council (grant agreement D0112101) and the European Research Council (ERC) under the European Union's Horizon 2020 research and innovation programme (grant agreement 339571). Finally, it is a pleasure to thank our families—Faye, Willa, Sadie and Desmond Kanter, and Niamh Cullen and Robin Walsh—who have provided both encouragement for and a welcome distraction from this work.

Boca Raton, FL
Dublin, Ireland

Douglas Kanter
Patrick Walsh

Contents

Notes on Contributors

Robin J. C. Adams is a doctoral candidate in Economic and Social History at St Peter's College, University of Oxford. He has a BBS (Lang) in Business and Russian from Trinity College Dublin (2008) and an MSc in Economic History from the London School of Economics (2013).

Aidan Beatty has a PhD from the University of Chicago and has held fellowships at Concordia University (Montreal) and Trinity College Dublin. He works at the Honors College of the University of Pittsburgh. His peer-reviewed work has appeared in *Éire-Ireland*, *Irish Historical Studies*, the *Journal of Imperial and Commonwealth History*, and the *Journal of Jewish Studies.* His first book, *Masculinity and Power in Irish Nationalism, 1884–1938*, was published in 2016 and was awarded the James S. Donnelly Sr. Prize for Books in History and Social Science by the American Conference for Irish Studies.

Mel Cousins has written extensively about the history of social policy in Ireland, including *Poor Relief in Ireland, 1851–1914* (2011), and articles in journals such as *Irish Economic and Social History*, *Eighteenth Century Ireland*, *History of the Family*, and the *Journal of Ecclesiastical History.* He is working on a broader study of poverty and poor relief in early nineteenth-century Ireland. He is attached to the School of Social Work and Social Policy, Trinity College Dublin.

Michelle D'Arcy is Assistant Professor in the Department of Political Science, Trinity College Dublin. Her research focuses on processes of state building, democratisation, and development in contemporary sub-Saharan

Africa and in Europe historically. She has a particular interest in taxation, having written her PhD thesis on the fiscal contract in sub-Saharan Africa. Her research has been funded by the Swedish Research Council and published in journals including the *European Journal of Political Research*, *Governance*, and *African Affairs*.

James Guilfoyle has a PhD from the University of Chicago and is Lecturer in History at the University of Tennessee, Chattanooga. His research focuses on Ireland in the 'old colonial system' and issues of mercantilism and state formation. He has a particular interest in Restoration Ireland.

Douglas Kanter is Associate Professor of History at Florida Atlantic University and a Fellow of the Royal Historical Society. His publications include *The Making of British Unionism, 1740–1848: Politics, Government and the Anglo-Irish Constitutional Relationship* (2009).

Jason Knirck is Professor of Irish and British History at Central Washington University. His research focuses on the political culture of revolutionary and post-revolutionary Ireland, including topics such as empire, gender, and state building. He is the author of *Women of the Dáil: Gender, Republicanism, and the Anglo-Irish Treaty* (2006), *After Image of the Revolution: Cumann na nGaedheal and Irish Politics, 1922–32* (2014), and recent articles on the Labour Party and the placement of the Irish Revolution in world history. He is working on a monograph about the development of parliamentary opposition in the Free State.

Trevor McCavery graduated from the Queen's University of Belfast in 1981 with a PhD on the subject of finance and politics in Ireland after the British-Irish Act of Union of 1801. He retired in 2013 as Headmaster of Regent House School. He has been chief examiner in 'A' level History for Northern Ireland and has authored a number of books and articles, for which he was appointed a Fellow of the Royal Historical Society.

Charles Ivar McGrath is Associate Professor of History at University College Dublin. He researches and teaches early modern Irish history and the history of the British Empire. His publications include *The Making of the Eighteenth-Century Irish Constitution: Government, Parliament and the Revenue, 1692–1714* (2000) and *Ireland and Empire, 1692–1770* (2012).

Marina Nistotskaya is Associate Professor of Political Science at the University of Gothenburg and Research Fellow at the Quality of Government Institute (Sweden). Her primary research areas are comparative public bureaucracy, state capacity, and public goods production. Her work has appeared in leading international journals in political science and public administration, such as *Governance*, the *European Journal of Political Research*, *Public Administration*, and the *Journal of Public Administration Research and Theory*.

Charles Read is Hong Kong Link Fellow at Corpus Christi College, Cambridge. He is also the editor of the Gulliver blog at the *Economist*. His academic research and teaching interests focus on the economic and business history of the British Isles over the past two centuries. The research for his doctoral thesis at the University of Cambridge, entitled 'British Economic Policy and Ireland, c. 1841–53', won the Thirsk-Feinstein PhD Dissertation Prize, the T. S. Ashton Prize for the best *Economic History Review* article, and the New Researcher Prize of the Economic History Society, as well as the dissertation prize of the International Economic History Association.

Andrew Shields was educated in Ireland and Canada. His research to date has focused on nineteenth-century Irish history and on the history of Anglo-Irish relations. His book, *The Irish Conservative Party, 1852–1868: Land, Politics and Religion,* was published in 2007. Several of his articles on aspects of nineteenth-century Irish history have appeared in various journals and books. He is an adjunct lecturer in the School of Humanities & Languages, Faculty of Arts, at the University of New South Wales.

Patrick Walsh is Assistant Professor of Eighteenth-Century Irish History at Trinity College Dublin. His previous publications include *The South Sea Bubble and Ireland: Money, Banking and Investment, 1690–1721* (2014).

List of Figures

List of Tables

List of Maps

CHAPTER 1

Introduction

Douglas Kanter and Patrick Walsh

The series of austerity budgets passed in Ireland since the onset of the banking and sovereign debt crisis in 2008 have underscored the centrality of taxation to modern Irish politics. Disputes over who should pay, how taxes should be levied, and the mechanisms by which they should be collected have featured prominently in public debate and have influenced popular attitudes towards government and the state.[1] Taxes that have been imposed or collected in what the public has perceived to be an 'unfair' manner—such as the household charge and the water charge—have provoked protest, evasion, and resistance.[2] Most historically informed commentary on the financial crisis has focused on the short and medium terms.[3] But fiscal policy has played a significant role in Irish politics since the middle of the seventeenth century, when Ireland began to make the transition from a 'demesne state'—featuring low levels of taxation, decentralised decision making, and privatised methods of revenue collection—to a modern 'tax state', characterised by high levels of extraction, centralised policymaking, the bureaucratisation of revenue collection, and

D. Kanter (✉)
Florida Atlantic University, Boca Raton, FL, USA
e-mail: dkanter1@fau.edu

P. Walsh
Trinity College Dublin, Dublin, Ireland
e-mail: walshp9@tcd.ie

D. Kanter, P. Walsh (eds.), *Taxation, Politics, and Protest in Ireland, 1662–2016*, Palgrave Studies in the History of Finance,
https://doi.org/10.1007/978-3-030-04309-4_1

the employment of sophisticated financial instruments to facilitate deficit spending.[4] From that time to the present, fiscal policy has shaped the Irish state, informed Irish national identity, and influenced Irish economic activity, electoral preferences, and conceptions of civic morality.[5] Taxation has also served as a node, bringing Irish subjects/citizens into persistent contact with the state and colouring the relationship between taxpayers and their government (whether based in Dublin, London, or Belfast). As such, it has invited conflict as well as compliance. Indeed, the history of Irish taxation connects popular to 'high' politics and Irish peripheries to the centres of power, often exposing fault lines between civil society and the government, and raising enduring questions about equity, consent, and legitimacy.

The present anthology explores these issues over the *longue durée*, in order to identify elements of both continuity and change in the Irish experience of taxation over some 350 years. It takes for its point of departure the Irish Parliament's approval of the 'new' hereditary revenues in 1662, which unwittingly initiated the transformation of the Irish tax system, and it closes with the Dáil's decision to suspend the water charge in 2016 when confronted by widespread public opposition. This volume does not seek to advance a particular ideological perspective or methodological approach but reflects the conviction, expressed by one recent commentator, that 'taxation is first and foremost a political issue'.[6] Accordingly, the chapters featured here foreground policymaking, public debate, and popular protest rather than the sort of economic analysis that conventionally figures in the social scientific study of public finance.[7]

Historiography

The emergence of the tax state was not, of course, a uniquely Irish phenomenon. Nor was the equivocal public reaction to the rise of a more intrusive and extractive government bureaucracy distinctively Irish. Rather, Irish developments mirrored broader European, and ultimately global, trends, which are frequently associated with the advent of modernity. Yet while scholars focusing on other nation-states in Europe and the 'West' have produced a robust interdisciplinary literature on the history of taxation, the subject has remained marginal to Irish studies.[8] The work on Irish fiscal history that has previously appeared is scattered in piecemeal form across a range of unpublished theses, book chapters, journal articles, and monographs, many of which are either outdated or difficult to source.

The earliest scholarly histories of Irish taxation were written in the first decades of the twentieth century and were moulded by the political circumstances of the era. The home rule debates of 1886 and 1893 had called attention to the complex and contested nature of Anglo-Irish financial relations, and by 1896 a royal commission had collated and corrected much of the data necessary for academic appraisal.[9] With expectations for home rule rising as Unionist government faltered after 1900, diachronic inquiry into Irish finance seemed to have immediate policy implications. Between 1903 and 1921, consequently, British Liberals, Irish nationalists, and constructive unionists all composed histories of Irish public finance. Notwithstanding the disparate political views of the authors and relatively minor differences in their findings, these studies generally emphasised the exploitative character of Irish taxation as imposed by British politicians and their Anglo-Irish proxies.[10] Academic interest began to wane, however, following the establishment of Northern Ireland (1920) and the Irish Free State (1922). The latter's conformity to British fiscal norms complicated nationalist criticism of past practice, while the gradual resolution of outstanding Anglo-Irish financial disputes in the 1920s and 1930s finally closed enduring controversies.[11] Though the last major nationalist analysis was published so late as 1930, Irish tax history, deprived of a political *raison d'être*, seemed to have lost its relevance.[12]

Little historical scholarship appeared over the next seventy years. The study of Irish fiscal policy reached a low ebb, with some of the most significant work left unpublished.[13] For the pre-independence period, economic historians shifted their focus from public finance to private enterprise, with important mid-century studies by L. M. Cullen and K. H. Connell examining tax evasion in the eighteenth and early nineteenth centuries.[14] Connell's investigation of illicit distillation, in turn, provided a slight stimulus to work on revenue enforcement.[15] Subsequently, David Dickson and Pauric Travers began to recover a previously obscure history of tax resistance and protest in the late eighteenth and nineteenth centuries.[16] But nationalist allegations of over-taxation, which the first generation of Irish fiscal historians had found persuasive, were given short shrift. The *New History of Ireland*, articulating the historical consensus towards the close of the century, was dismissive of nationalist grievances without devoting close attention to the structure of Irish taxation or the details of the Irish tax code.[17] For the post-independence period, meanwhile, the discussion of southern taxation was mainly confined to institutional histories.[18] Northern public finance received somewhat greater consideration, owing to the unusual arrangements needed to sustain the Stormont regime.[19]

In the twenty-first century, interest in the history of Irish taxation has experienced a modest revival. This development is related, firstly, to the rise of the 'new institutionalism' in political science and sociology, which has provided a conceptual framework for the analysis of the state.[20] It is linked, secondly, to advances in the field of British fiscal history associated with the pioneering studies of P. K. O'Brien, John Brewer, and Martin Daunton.[21] In work that ranged from the seventeenth to the twentieth centuries, Brewer and Daunton, in particular, argued that taxation was constitutive of the British state, traced the political and constitutional ramifications of fiscal policy, and recognised the significant role played by the revenue bureaucracy in connecting central government to society. Because much of the Irish fiscal system was adopted and adapted from Britain, the appearance of their work was perhaps a precondition for the emergence of a more sophisticated approach to the history of Irish taxation. Finally, the Irish manifestation of the global financial crisis that commenced in 2008 has redirected scholarly focus and encouraged a reconsideration of public finance.[22]

The upshot has been renewed attention to Ireland's fiscal history from the mid-seventeenth to the late twentieth centuries. For the early modern period, Ivar McGrath and Neil Johnston have examined the political process by which taxation was approved, along with its implications for Irish governance.[23] David Fleming and Patrick Walsh have linked rising demands for revenue to the evolution of an Irish fiscal-military state and have outlined public responses to this phenomenon.[24] Timothy Watt has underscored the extent to which the growth of the Irish 'Leviathan' provoked protest and resistance.[25] For the nineteenth century, Trevor McCavery and A. P. W. Malcomson have explored the fiscal challenges faced by Irish and British politicians following the passage of the Act of Union (1800), as constraints on taxation imposed by the new constitutional settlement came into conflict with escalating expenditure.[26] Martin McElroy, Douglas Kanter, and Charles Read have assessed the relationship between fiscal policy and popular politics at mid-century, showing that controversies over public finance often excited nationalist disaffection.[27] Other scholars have expanded on earlier studies of illicit distillation and revenue enforcement.[28] Drawing upon many of these works, Theodore Hoppen has composed the first survey of Irish government under the Union to place taxation and expenditure near the centre of the narrative.[29] The study of twentieth-century Irish finance has also proceeded apace. Kieran Coleman and John Considine have demonstrated the persistence of tax protest in the years following the Free State's foundation, while Ryan McCourt has revisited Cumann na nGaedheal's fiscal policy and Dominic de Cogan has explained the origins of Ireland's Corporation Tax.[30] Niamh Hardiman has reviewed the recent history of the Irish tax state in a series of seminal articles, and James Mitchell has offered an astringent account of Stormont finance.[31] Peter Clarke has synthesised much of this material in a brief history of Irish taxation since the pre-Norman era.[32] This volume seeks to build upon this growing body of work.

The Structure of the Book

The modern history of Irish taxation begins in the seventeenth century with the customs and excise legislation introduced into the Irish Parliament after the Restoration of Charles II.[33] As in contemporary England, this legislation drew on innovations made during the Cromwellian period, and it is striking how the administrations in both kingdoms were willing to appropriate the policies of their Commonwealth predecessors.[34] These mid-seventeenth-century developments saw a great increase in Irish revenue beyond that raised by a complex series of medieval measures which had hitherto sufficed. The customs and excise legislation was critical in establishing the mechanisms and the institutions within which Irish revenues were collected. Here, the establishment of the Revenue Commissioners in 1662 was vital, even if the development of a countrywide bureaucracy was delayed until 1682, thanks to a preference for farming Irish revenues to a series of private consortia from 1663 onwards.[35] The importance of the commissioners and their willingness to engage in policy disputes with their English counterparts is the subject of James Guilfoyle's chapter, which explores the negotiations between the revenue administrations in Dublin and London over the application of the Navigation Acts to Ireland. Dublin lost that battle, but his chapter reveals the importance of seeing Irish developments within a wider context. As Patrick Walsh makes clear, Irish revenues throughout the eighteenth century depended on foreign trade. This trade was, however, circumscribed by a legal and institutional framework created to serve London's interests. Nevertheless, as both Walsh and Ivar McGrath show, there was room for Ireland to develop its own version of the fiscal-military state.[36] McGrath's chapter on the debates over the increase in the Irish national debt in 1729 makes clear that Irish parliamentary oversight played a vital role in shaping fiscal developments. Politics was important. Walsh develops this point in his discussion of Grattan's Parliament and the shift in the focus of Irish taxation in the aftermath of the American War of Independence. The significance of Parliament and what happened when there was no longer a local legislature in Dublin forms the backdrop to Trevor McCavery's chapter, which looks at the impact of the Act of Union on the making and implementation of Irish fiscal policy.

Central to Walsh's analysis of the patterns of eighteenth-century taxation is a careful reconstruction of the 'geography of fiscal extraction', which reveals as much as is possible the variegated regional impact of customs and excise taxation and how this might map onto geographies of protest previously identified by Timothy Watt and K. H. Connell.[37] This theme is picked up by Mel Cousins and Douglas Kanter in their respective studies of pre-Famine resistance to the Poor Law and the post-Famine campaign against over-taxation. While some continuities are evident, what each of these chapters stresses is the importance of local factors and the dangers of employing national aggregates even in a small economy like Ireland's.

The theme of Ireland's evolving place in Britain's wider imperial economy, meanwhile, is examined by Andrew Shields in his chapter on Irish attitudes to protection in the second quarter of the nineteenth century. Shields demonstrates that both Conservatives and nationalists were divided over protection, with Conservatives disagreeing about the ends to which protectionist policy ought to be directed, and nationalists conflicted on the issue of free trade. Charles Read's chapter also explores nationalist responses to the liberalisation of trade. Read offers a new interpretation of tax protest during the Famine decade, connecting opposition to British commercial and fiscal priorities with support for Daniel O'Connell's repeal movement and Irish middle-class emigration. These developments, he argues, played an important role in the emergence of post-Famine Irish nationalism. His work adds to a growing body of scholarship which contends that popular protest during the Famine, whether in terms of opposition to local property taxes or food riots, was much greater than many previous historians have suggested.[38] While some scholars might disagree with his conclusions about the links between opposition to changes in taxation and the rise of a new kind of nationalism, it is clear that questions of nationalism and taxation were increasingly entwined from the second half of the nineteenth century onwards. This is even more apparent from

Kanter's study of the 1860s campaign against over-taxation, which connects this important but long-forgotten episode to the emergence of the home rule movement.

Irish nationalism's turn to revolution provides the context for Robin Adams's investigation of the strains put on local taxation by two competing jurisdictions—the old and the new—during the War of Independence. His chapter reveals much about the everyday experience of the Revolution and the ways in which long-established practices and bureaucratic dynasties could be both adapted and extinguished in the tumultuous circumstances of 1919–1923. The challenge of developing fiscal policy for the fledgling Free State is the focus of the chapters by Jason Knirck and Aidan Beatty. Their accounts demonstrate not only that the new state's fiscal policies have been under-explored by historians but also that debates about public finance played a role in shaping the party politics of Ireland's nascent democracy. Both chapters are alert to continuity as well as change in independent Ireland's tax policy—a theme that is addressed more fully in the anthology's final chapter, by Michelle D'Arcy and Marina Nistotskaya, which traces the historical legacies of pre-independence public finance for both formal fiscal institutions and popular attitudes to taxation in the Republic of Ireland.

Directions for Future Research

The chapters in this book point towards the diversity of current research on Irish taxation and its discontents, but this area is still comparatively under-researched. The limits of the existing historiography, combined with our focus on issues of legitimacy, protest, and the interplay between local and national forces, mean that this anthology is not a comprehensive study of the *longue durée* history of Irish taxation. That remains to be written. It is worth highlighting some of the lacunae in our book as well as some directions for future research. Three, in particular, stand out.

Firstly, it is worth stressing that our primary focus is on taxes levied by the state in its various manifestations over the last three-and-a-half centuries. Some attention is paid to the Poor Law by Cousins, Read, and Kanter and to local rates by Adams, but there is much more that can be said about local taxation. We ignore entirely other forms of taxation levied by other authorities, including tolls paid to turnpike trusts in the eighteenth and nineteenth centuries and, much more importantly, tithes paid to the Anglican Church of Ireland.[39] This is a major subject with its own complex historiography, one that at times is interwoven with this history of taxation, especially in the late eighteenth century and during the Tithe War of the early 1830s.[40] The anomaly of a tax on agricultural produce being paid to support a minority religious establishment only ended with the disestablishment of the Church of Ireland in 1871; its impact on perceptions of the legitimacy of all forms of taxation in nineteenth-century Ireland might fruitfully be considered by future scholars.

Local taxation levied at the county level was also a significant and not uncontroversial feature of the Irish fiscal landscape from the eighteenth century onwards. The 'cess' collected and spent by county grand juries was an object of discontent for agrarian protesters in the 1760s, with south Ulster Presbyterians, in particular, objecting to the increasing amounts demanded from them for infrastructural developments.[41] Such complaints about the 'tax for building roads' went back to at least the 1690s, while an early nineteenth-century parliamentary enquiry sought to ameliorate the inequitable local tax 'burthens' created by complex and regionally variant measures of landownership.[42] This was especially important at this juncture because the first half of the nineteenth century saw a substantial increase in the amount of revenue collected by grand juries across the island, with the total rising from £0.4 million in 1803 to £1.3 million in 1840.[43] After that, grand jury revenues remained largely static, though the introduction of the Poor Law into Ireland in 1838 meant that other forms of local taxation were significantly augmented from this date onwards.[44] As Adams clearly demonstrates in this volume, local taxation remained important right through the War of Independence, although the increasing centralisation of independent Ireland culminated in the abolition of local domestic rates by Jack Lynch's populist, if not fiscally prudent, Fianna Fáil government in 1977.[45] The surviving records of grand jury presentments offer a tantalising insight into local government and taxation in Ireland and indicate one way forward for historians interested in charting the regional impact of the state in late eighteenth- and nineteenth-century Ireland.[46] Adams's research, meanwhile, is suggestive of the possibilities provided by in-depth local studies for shedding new light on the complex processes at play between different and competing centres of authority during the violent birth of the new state in southern Ireland.

Secondly, the chapters in this book pay limited attention to issues of gender or, indeed, to the wider cultural ramifications of taxation policy, with the sole exception of Beatty's chapter. With regard to gender, this is both especially regrettable and a consequence of the existing historiography.

There are several avenues that might profitably be explored in the future. E. P. Thompson famously highlighted the role of women as participants in, and indeed leaders of, riots in eighteenth-century England, but the evidence for how well this pattern transferred to Ireland and to tax rioting is frustratingly thin.[47] Occasional examples can be produced, but the detail is insufficient to make any sort of general conclusions. Further research might yield more information and allow us to offer an assessment of the role that gender relations played in fomenting opposition to taxation. Here, it might be worth attending to the role of women as producers of taxable goods, a subject profitably explored by Sarah Meacham in her study of the colonial Chesapeake.[48] Similarly, the interplay between women's roles as consumers and as campaigners for 'free trade' and the abolition of slavery might be usefully connected to wider histories of resistance to taxation.[49] Links between consumption and taxation, and the disproportionate burden of taxation borne by Irish household staples such as sugar and tea,[50] were grist to the mill of late nineteenth-century tax protesters, and might be fruitfully considered from a gendered perspective. Peter Leary's attention to gender in his recent account of smuggling across the Northern Irish border in the twentieth century reminds us that the history of women's participation in tax evasion also merits further consideration.[51]

Finally, more could be productively said using transnational and global perspectives. It is important to stress that the history of Irish taxation, and the reactions to it, cannot be understood solely within an insular, inward-looking framework. As Guilfoyle and, especially, Walsh demonstrate, this has been the case since at least the late seventeenth century, when the great majority of taxes were levied on foreign trade. Disputes over Irish access to imperial markets and how far any preferential status would extend were a matter of controversy following the implementation of the Navigation Acts, with major disputes arising in the 1690s, 1730s, and 1770s. The Irish dimension to the repeal of the Corn Laws and the ushering in of free trade in the mid-nineteenth century is well known, though Shields's chapter in this volume demonstrates that more still remains to be said on this important subject.[52] Some of the same issues arose under a different guise during the 1920s, in the aftermath of independence in southern Ireland and devolution in Northern Ireland.[53] Meanwhile, Kevin O'Rourke has pointed out that the history of twentieth-century Irish protectionism is part of a wider international story, and to fixate on the exceptional nature of the Irish experience is to miss 'something vital'.[54] This observation is worth stressing with regard to the chapters by Knirck and Beatty in this volume, which add significantly to our understanding of the fiscal policies pursued by both major governing parties in the first decades of independence. More research is possible in this area, and it would be interesting to see scholars take up the comparative challenge laid down by O'Rourke. One thinks of his perceptive comments about the similarities between the populist fiscal policies pursued by Fianna Fáil and the Peronists in Argentina, or between developments in Ireland and in other parts of the European periphery, notably Portugal, Greece, and Spain.[55] These after all long predate the emergence of the 'PIGS' in the aftermath of the 2008 Eurozone crisis.[56]

The potential of such comparative research is highlighted in the final chapter in this volume by D'Arcy and Nistotskaya. Their work also shows how some of the major issues in contemporary Irish taxation policy might be historicised. Of particular importance, perhaps, is the way in which successive Irish governments since the 1950s have used low corporate taxation to encourage foreign direct investment and the role that this has played in Irish economic development.[57] Donal Donovan and Antoin Murphy have suggested that a relative lack of industrial development contributed to the transformation of the Irish economy in the late twentieth century—from a donkey-and-cart economy into a modern, globalised, technology-driven one—because there was no significant opposition from indigenous business interests to a fiscal policy that gave preferential treatment to foreign firms.[58] This insight might be extended to explore how the low corporation tax policy was legitimated within Ireland and also justified to outside interests, notably the European Union and its predecessors. Might this be attributed to a 'holier than thou' post-colonial attitude that privileged the need for 'catch up' to make Ireland competitive, even as the morality of its policies increasingly came into question? Here, again, comparative research and an understanding of the interplay of local and global forces is crucial.[59]

The intersection of local and transnational factors can also be seen in the widespread and somewhat successful opposition to new forms of property and water taxation in Ireland since 2008. The austerity policies pursued by successive Irish governments, with their retrenchment of expenditure and increased taxation, were, of course, part of a wider European agenda.[60] But the reaction to these policies, particularly the imposition of the water charge, had a distinctive local flavour, and should perhaps be situated within a wider historical context of resistance to taxation of this type. While it may seem strange to outside observers that many Irish taxpayers are reluctant to pay domestic water charges, the patterns of mistrust of central government and of popular protest against similar rates are familiar to Irish historians. They have parallels, for instance, in previous attempts to levy local taxes on waste disposal. More research is needed, however, to explain why such charges are seen as illegitimate and how successive governments have failed to broaden the tax base in line with European norms. Is this a particular manifestation of the Irish psyche or just evidence of poorly executed policy decisions? Such questions are beyond the scope of this book, but what follows offers a pathway to considering them in historical perspective.

Notes

1. Niamh Hardiman and Aidan Regan, 'The Politics of Austerity in Ireland', *Intereconomics* 48, no. 1 (2013): 9–14; Siobhan O'Sullivan, Amy Erbe Healy, and Michael J. Breen, 'Political Legitimacy in Ireland During Economic Crisis: Insights from the European Social Survey', *Irish Political Studies* 29, no. 4 (2014): 547–72; William K. Roche, Philip J. O'Connell, and Andrea Prothero, eds., *Austerity and Recovery in Ireland: Europe's Poster Child and the Great Recession* (Oxford: Oxford University Press, 2016).
2. Conor McCabe, 'The Radical Left in Ireland', *Socialism and Democracy* 29, no. 3 (2015): 158–65; Rory Hearne, 'The Irish Water War', *Interface: A Journal for and about Social Movements* 7, no. 1 (2015): 309–21; Richard Layte and David Landy, 'Explaining the Belated Emergence of Social Protest in Ireland between 2009 and 2014', *Journal of the Statistical and Social Inquiry Society of Ireland* 46 (2016–17): 132–48.
3. In addition to the works cited above see Michael Lewis, *Boomerang: Travels in the New Third World* (New York: W. W. Norton, 2011), chap. 3; Donal Donovan and Antoin Murphy, *The Fall of the Celtic Tiger: Ireland and the Euro Debt Crisis* (Oxford: Oxford University Press, 2013); Morgan Kelly, 'What Happened to Ireland?', *Irish Pages: A Journal of Contemporary Writing* 6, no. 1 (2013): 7–19; Diarmaid Ferriter, 'Twenty-First-Century Ireland', in *The Princeton History of Modern Ireland*, ed. Richard Bourke and Ian McBride (Princeton, NJ: Princeton University Press, 2016), 170–74, 181–86.
4. For the classic exposition of this transition, see Joseph A. Schumpeter, 'The Crisis of the Tax State' (1918), in *Joseph A. Schumpeter: The Economics and Sociology of Capitalism*, ed. Richard Swedberg (Princeton, NJ: Princeton University Press, 1991), 102–12; for a brief account of the Irish case see

Peter Clarke, 'The Historical Development of the Irish Taxation System', *Accounting, Finance and Governance Review* 21, nos. 1–2 (2014): 5–24, esp. 8–10.

5. For theoretical discussions of taxation upon which the remainder of this paragraph draws, see Isaac William Martin, Ajay K. Mehrotra, and Monica Prasad, 'The Thunder of History: The Origins and Development of the New Fiscal Sociology', in *The New Fiscal Sociology: Taxation in Comparative and Historical Perspective*, ed. Isaac William Martin, Ajay K. Mehrotra, and Monica Prasad (Cambridge: Cambridge University Press, 2009), 3, 14, 18–19; Stephen Smith, *Taxation: A Very Short Introduction* (Oxford: Oxford University Press, 2015), 1–2, 43, 49–50, 83–89.
6. Smith, *Taxation*, 101.
7. See, for example, John Bristow, *Taxation in Ireland: An Economist's Perspective* (Dublin: Institute of Public Administration, 2004).
8. Considerations of space preclude a full bibliography; key works include Sven Steinmo, *Taxation and Democracy: Swedish, British and American Approaches to Financing the Modern State* (New Haven: Yale University Press, 1993); Richard Bonney, ed., *Economic Systems and State Finance* (Oxford: Oxford University Press, 1995); idem, *The Rise of the Fiscal State in Europe, c. 1200–1815* (Oxford: Oxford University Press, 1999); W. Mark Ormrod, M. M. Bonney, and R. J. Bonney, eds., *Crises, Revolutions and Self-Sustained Growth: Essays in European Fiscal History, 1130–1830* (Stamford: Paul Watkins, 1999); Michael Kwass, *Privilege and the Politics of Taxation in Eighteenth-Century France: Liberté, Egalité, Fiscalité* (Cambridge: Cambridge University Press, 2006); José Luís Cardoso and Pedro Lains, eds., *Paying for the Liberal State: The Rise of Public Finance in Nineteenth-Century Europe* (Cambridge: Cambridge University Press, 2010); Bartolomé Yun-Casalilla, Patrick K. O'Brien, and Francisco Comín Comín, eds., *The Rise of Fiscal States: A Global History* (Cambridge: Cambridge University Press, 2012); W. Elliot Brownlee, *Federal Taxation in America: A Short History*, 3rd ed. (Cambridge: Cambridge University Press, 2016); Kenneth Scheve and David Stasavage, *Taxing the Rich: A History of Fiscal Fairness in the United States and Europe* (New York: Russell Sage Foundation, 2016); E. A. Heaman, *Tax, Order, and Good Government: A New Political History of Canada, 1867–1917* (Montreal and Kingston: McGill-Queen's University Press, 2017).
9. Pauric Travers, 'The Financial Relations Question, 1800–1914', in *Ireland, England and Australia: Essays in Honour of Oliver MacDonagh*, ed. F. B. Smith (Canberra: Australian National University, 1990), 43–58.
10. Alice Effie Murray, *A History of the Commercial and Financial Relations between England and Ireland from the Period of the Restoration* (London:

P. S. King and Son, 1903), chaps. 9, 14–15, 17–18; Earl of Dunraven, *The Finances of Ireland before the Union and after: An Historical Study* (London: John Murray, 1912); George O'Brien, *The Economic History of Ireland in the Eighteenth Century* (Dublin: Maunsel, 1918), chaps. 25–26; idem, *The Economic History of Ireland in the Seventeenth Century* (Dublin: Maunsel, 1919), 87–94, 197–203; idem, *The Economic History of Ireland from the Union to the Famine* (London: Longmans, Green and Co., 1921), chap. 11.

11. Ronan Fanning, *The Irish Department of Finance, 1922–58* (Dublin: Institute of Public Administration, 1978), 1, 44, 51–58, 162–64, 297–306.
12. T. J. Kiernan, *History of the Financial Administration of Ireland to 1817* (London: P. S. King and Son, 1930).
13. Simon Kepple, 'A Survey of Taxation and Government Expenditure in the Irish Free State, 1922–1936' (Master's thesis, University College Cork, 1938); Trevor Robert McCavery, 'Finance and Politics in Ireland, 1801–17' (PhD diss., Queen's University Belfast, 1981). For a rare exception, see Patricia Jalland, 'Irish Home-Rule Finance: A Neglected Dimension of the Irish Question, 1910–1914', *Irish Historical Studies* 32, no. 91 (1983): 233–53.
14. L. M. Cullen, 'The Smuggling Trade in Ireland in the Eighteenth Century', *Proceedings of the Royal Irish Academy*, section c, 66 (1967–68): 149–75; K. H. Connell, 'Illicit Distillation', in K. H. Connell, *Irish Peasant Society: Four Historical Essays* (Oxford: Clarendon Press, 1968), 1–50. Neither Cullen nor Cormac Ó Gráda, the two preeminent scholars of pre-independence Irish economic history, have paid much attention to fiscal history; see, for example, the limited coverage of taxation in Cormac Ó Gráda, *Ireland: A New Economic History, 1780–1939* (Oxford: Oxford University Press, 1994).
15. Robert Shipkey, 'Problems in Alcoholic Production and Controls in Early Nineteenth-Century Ireland', *Historical Journal* 16, no. 2 (1973): 291–302; Norma M. Dawson, 'Illicit Distillation and the Revenue Police in Ireland in the Eighteenth and Nineteenth Centuries', *Irish Jurist*, n.s., 12, no. 2 (1977): 282–94.
16. David Dickson, 'Taxation and Disaffection in Late Eighteenth-Century Ireland', in *Irish Peasants: Violence and Political Unrest*, ed. Samuel Clark and James S. Donnelly Jr. (Madison: University of Wisconsin Press, 1983): 37–63; Travers, 'Financial Relations Question'.
17. L. M. Cullen, 'Economic Development, 1691–1750' and 'Economic Development, 1750–1800', in *A New History of Ireland*, vol. 4: *Eighteenth-Century Ireland*, ed. T. W. Moody and W. E. Vaughan (Oxford: Clarendon Press, 1986), 123–58, 159–95; W. E. Vaughan, 'Ireland c. 1870', in *A*

New History of Ireland, vol. 5: *Ireland under the Union, I: 1801–70*, ed. W. E. Vaughan (Oxford: Clarendon Press, 1989), 786–92; H. D. Gribbon, 'Economic and Social History', in *A New History of Ireland*, vol. 6: *Ireland under the Union II: 1870–1921* (Oxford: Oxford University Press, 1989), 327–31. See also David S. Johnson and Liam Kennedy, 'Nationalist Historiography and the Decline of the Irish Economy: George O'Brien Revisited', in *Ireland's Histories: Aspects of State, Society and Ideology*, ed. Seán Hutton and Paul Stewart (London: Routledge, 1991), 18–19; Liam Kennedy and David S. Johnson, 'The Union of Ireland and Britain, 1801–1921', in *The Making of Modern Irish History: Revisionism and the Revisionist Controversy*, ed. D. George Boyce and Alan O'Day (London: Routledge, 1996), 34–70.

18. Fanning, *Irish Department of Finance*; Seán Réamonn, *History of the Revenue Commissioners* (Dublin: Institute of Public Administration, 1981).
19. R. J. Lawrence, *The Government of Northern Ireland: Public Finance and Public Services, 1921–1964* (Oxford: Clarendon Press, 1965); Arthur J. Green, *Devolution and Public Finance: Stormont from 1921 to 1972* (Glasgow: Centre for the Study of Public Policy, 1979).
20. Theda Skocpol, 'Bringing the State Back in: Strategies of Analysis in Current Research', in *Bringing the State Back in*, ed. Peter B. Evans, Dietrich Rueschemeyer, and Theda Skocpol (Cambridge: Cambridge University Press, 1985), 3–37.
21. Patrick K. O'Brien, 'The Political Economy of British Taxation, 1660–1815', *Economic History Review*, 2nd ser., 41, no. 1 (1988): 1–32; John Brewer, *The Sinews of Power: War, Money and the English State, 1688–1783* (Cambridge, MA: Harvard University Press, 1988); Martin Daunton, *Trusting Leviathan: The Politics of Taxation in Britain, 1799–1914* (Cambridge: Cambridge University Press, 2001); idem, *Just Taxes: The Politics of Taxation in Britain, 1914–1979* (Cambridge: Cambridge University Press, 2002).
22. Patrick Walsh, 'Writing the History of the Financial Crisis: Lessons from the South Sea Bubble', *Working Papers in History and Policy*, no. 3 (2012).
23. Charles Ivar McGrath, *The Making of the Eighteenth-Century Irish Constitution: Government, Parliament and the Revenue, 1692–1714* (Dublin: Four Courts Press, 2000); idem, 'Central Aspects of the Eighteenth-Century Constitutional Framework in Ireland: The Government Supply Bill and Biennial Parliamentary Sessions, 1715–82', *Eighteenth-Century Ireland* 16 (2001): 9–34; idem, *Ireland and Empire, 1692–1770* (Abingdon: Routledge, 2012), chap. 7; Neil Johnston, 'State Formation in Seventeenth-Century Ireland: The Restoration Financial

Settlement, 1660–62', *Parliaments, Estates and Representation* 36, no. 2 (2016): 115–36.

24. D. A. Fleming, *Politics and Provincial People: Sligo and Limerick, 1691–1761* (Manchester: Manchester University Press, 2010), chap. 5; Patrick Walsh, 'The Fiscal State in Ireland, 1691–1769', *Historical Journal* 56, no. 3 (2013): 629–56; idem, 'Enforcing the Fiscal State: The Army, the Revenue and the Irish Experience of the Fiscal-Military State, 1690–1769', in *The British Fiscal-Military States, 1660–c. 1783*, ed. Aaron Graham and Patrick Walsh (Abingdon: Routledge, 2016), 131–58.
25. Timothy D. Watt, 'Taxation Riots and the Culture of Popular Protest in Ireland, 1714–1740', *English Historical Review* 130, no. 547 (2014): 1418–48.
26. Trevor McCavery, 'Politics, Public Finance and the British-Irish Act of Union of 1801', *Transactions of the Royal Historical Society*, 6th ser., 10 (2000): 353–75; A. P. W. Malcomson, *John Foster (1740–1829): The Politics of Improvement and Prosperity* (Dublin: Four Courts Press, 2011), chaps. 5–7.
27. Martin McElroy, 'The 1830 Budget and Repeal: Parliament and Public Opinion in Ireland', *Irish Historical Studies* 46, no. 141 (2008): 38–52; Douglas Kanter, 'The Politics of Irish Taxation, 1842–53', *English Historical Review* 127, no. 528 (2012): 1121–55; idem, 'The Galway Packet-Boat Contract and the Politics of Public Expenditure in Mid-Victorian Ireland', *Historical Journal* 59, no. 3 (2016): 747–74; Charles Read, 'The "Repeal Year" in Ireland: An Economic Reassessment', *Historical Journal* 58, no. 1 (2015): 111–35.
28. Sinéad Sturgeon, 'Maria Edgeworth, William Carleton and the Battle for the Spirit of Ireland', *Irish Studies Review* 14, no. 4 (2006): 431–45; Jim Herlihy, *The Irish Revenue Police: A Short History and Genealogical Guide to the 'Poteen Hussars'* (Dublin: Four Courts Press, 2018).
29. K. Theodore Hoppen, *Governing Hibernia: British Politicians and Ireland, 1800–1921* (Oxford: Oxford University Press, 2016).
30. Kieran Coleman and John Considine, 'The No Income Tax Campaign: Twenty-First-Century Tax Philosophy in 1920s Ireland', *Irish Economic and Social History* 33 (2006): 1–17; Ryan McCourt, 'Ernest Blythe as Minister for Finance in the Irish Free State, 1923–32', *Parliamentary History* 33, no. 3 (2014): 475–500; Dominic de Cogan, 'The Wartime Origins of the Irish Corporation Tax', *Irish Journal of Legal Studies* 3, no. 2 (2013): 15–32.
31. Niamh Hardiman, 'Taxing the Poor: The Politics of Income Taxation in Ireland', *Policy Studies Journal* 28, no. 4 (2000): 815–42; idem, 'The Development of the Irish Tax State', *Irish Political Studies* 17, no. 1 (2002): 29–58; idem, 'Paying for Government', in *Dissecting Irish Politics:*

Essays in Honour of Brian Farrell (Dublin: University College Dublin Press, 2004), 82–100; Hardiman and Regan, 'Politics of Austerity'; James Mitchell, 'Undignified and Inefficient: Financial Relations between London and Stormont', *Contemporary British History* 20, no. 1 (2006): 55–71.

32. Clarke, 'Historical Development'.
33. McGrath, *Irish Constitution*, 24–32.
34. D'Maris Coffman, *Excise Taxation and the Origins of Public Debt* (Basingstoke: Palgrave Macmillan, 2013).
35. See James Guilfoyle's chapter.
36. Charles Ivar McGrath, 'The Irish Experience of "Financial Revolution"', in *Money, Power, and Print: Interdisciplinary Studies on the Financial Revolution in the British Isles*, ed. Charles Ivar McGrath and Chris Fauske (Newark, NJ: University of Delaware Press, 2008), 157–88; Walsh, 'Irish Fiscal State', *passim*.
37. Watt, 'Taxation Riots'; Connell, 'Illicit Distillation'.
38. See also James Kelly, *Food Rioting in Ireland in the Eighteenth and Nineteenth Centuries: The 'Moral Economy' and the Irish Crowd* (Dublin: Four Courts Press, 2017), 62–92.
39. On turnpikes see David Broderick, *The First Toll-Roads: Ireland's Turnpike Roads, 1729–1858* (Cork: Collins Press, 2002); on tithes see Maurice Bric, 'The Tithe System in Eighteenth-Century Ireland', *Proceedings of the Royal Irish Academy*, section c, 86 (1987): 271–88.
40. On the Tithe War see David P. Reid, 'The Tithe War in Ireland, 1830–1838' (PhD diss., Trinity College Dublin, 2013).
41. Eoin Magennis, 'A "Presbyterian Insurrection"? Reconsidering the Hearts of Oak Disturbances of July 1763', *Irish Historical Studies* 31, no. 122 (1998): 165–87.
42. Vincent Morley, *The Popular Mind in Eighteenth-Century Ireland* (Cork: Cork University Press, 2017), 62–63; House of Commons, 'Report of the Select Committee Appointed to Consider of the Best Mode of Apportioning More Equally the Local Burthens Collected in Ireland', *Sessional Papers 1824* (445), vol. 8, p. 79, quoted in Jacinta Prunty *Maps and Map-Making in Local History* (Dublin: Four Courts Press, 2004), 22.
43. Virginia Crossman, 'The Growth of the State in Nineteenth-Century Ireland', in *The Cambridge History of Ireland*, vol. 3, ed. James Kelly (Cambridge: Cambridge University Press, 2018), 555.
44. Ibid.
45. See the chapter by Michelle D'Arcy and Marina Nistotskaya.
46. Dickson, 'Taxation and Disaffection'.

47. E. P. Thompson, 'The Moral Economy of the English Crowd in the Eighteenth Century', *Past and Present* 50 (1971): 115–18; Kelly, *Food Rioting*, 136–42.
48. Sarah H. Meacham, *Every Home a Distillery: Alcohol, Gender, and Technology in the Colonial Chesapeake* (Baltimore, MD: Johns Hopkins University Press, 2009).
49. Padhraig Higgins, 'Consumption, Gender, and the Politics of "Free Trade" in Eighteenth-Century Ireland', *Eighteenth-Century Studies* 41, no. 1 (2007): 87–105.
50. L. M. Cullen, *An Economic History of Ireland since 1660*, 2nd ed. (London: Batsford Press, 1987), 168.
51. Peter Leary, *Unapproved Routes: Histories of the Irish Border, 1922–1972* (Oxford: Oxford University Press, 2016), chap. 4.
52. For an earlier analysis, see Cullen, *Economic History of Ireland*, 55, 58–59, 131.
53. Green, *Devolution and Public Finance.*
54. Kevin Hjortshøj O'Rourke, 'Independent Ireland in Comparative Perspective', *Irish Economic and Social History* 44 (2017): 19–45.
55. Ibid., 36–37; idem, 'Ireland and the Bigger Picture', in *Refiguring Ireland: Essays in Honour of L. M. Cullen*, ed. David Dickson and Cormac Ó Gráda (Dublin: Lilliput Press, 2003), 354–55.
56. 'PIGS' was the shorthand employed by commentators during the Eurozone crisis to refer to Portugal, Ireland, Greece, and Spain.
57. Mary E. Daly, 'An Irish-Ireland for Business?: The Control of Manufactures Acts, 1932 and 1934', *Irish Historical Studies* 24, no. 94 (1984): 246–72; idem, *Industrial Development and Irish National Identity, 1922–1939* (Syracuse: Syracuse University Press, 1992); Frank Barry and Clare O'Mahony, *Costello, Lemass and the Politics of the New Foreign Investment Regime of the 1950s* (Trinity College Dublin: Mimeo, 2016).
58. Donovan and Murphy, *Fall of the Celtic Tiger*, 17.
59. For some consideration of these ideas see Seán Ó Riain, *The Rise and Fall of Ireland's Celtic Tiger: Liberalism, Boom and Bust* (Cambridge: Cambridge University Press, 2014).
60. Seán Ó Riain, 'The Road to Austerity', and Stephen Kinsella, 'Economic and Fiscal Policy', in *Austerity and Recovery*, ed. Roche, O'Connell, and Prothero, 23–39, 40–61.

CHAPTER 2

Ireland, Mercantilism, and the Navigation Acts, 1660–1686

James Guilfoyle

In a brief, path-breaking survey published in 1963, Francis G. James first challenged the myth that the discriminatory English Navigation Acts enacted during the Restoration period had prevented the development of virtually any trade between Ireland and the American colonies in the late seventeenth and eighteenth centuries.[1] Since that time, studies by R. C. Nash and Thomas M. Truxes have not only demonstrated that Ireland took an active role in Atlantic colonial trade but have established its changing volume and structure.[2] Works by L. M. Cullen and Denis O'Hearn, with those of Nash and Truxes, have also explored the impact of the acts on Ireland's economy and the organisation and financing of Irish-American trade.[3] None of these works, however, have investigated in detail the way in which the Navigation Acts took shape vis-à-vis Ireland in the late seventeenth century. This topic has remained clouded in relative obscurity and mired in supposition about the supposedly active role of English merchant interests in creating Ireland's second-class position within the 'mercantile system'. This chapter therefore presents a close study of the development of Ireland's place within the system of English law and regulation created by the major Restoration Navigation Acts.

J. Guilfoyle (✉)
University of Tennessee, Chattanooga, TN, USA
e-mail: james-guilfoyle@utc.edu

D. Kanter, P. Walsh (eds.), *Taxation, Politics, and Protest in Ireland, 1662–2016*, Palgrave Studies in the History of Finance,
https://doi.org/10.1007/978-3-030-04309-4_2

There are essentially two interpretations of the influences and objectives behind mercantilist economic regulations in the late seventeenth and eighteenth centuries. The first, associated with Adam Smith, is that the mercantile system was basically a contrivance of merchants for their own private profit.[4] The second, identified primarily with Gustav Schmoller and Eli Heckscher, is that colonial commercial regulations were substantially the work of state servants and bureaucrats pursuing the increase of state power in a competitive international setting.[5] The main thesis of this chapter is that the Schmoller/Heckscher position is the correct one with respect to Ireland and the Navigation Acts. The authors of Ireland's inferior and dependent commercial position in the early modern English/British Atlantic Empire were men with close ties to central government and the court under Charles II. Especially significant in the shaping of Ireland's position were the state servants at the reformed Treasury and its subordinate revenue boards—the 1671 English Customs Commission and the 1682 Irish Revenue Commission.

Ireland's shifting status under the late seventeenth-century Navigation Acts has usually been attributed, where an explanation has been offered by historians at all, to pressure exerted on the Westminster Parliament by jealous English merchant interests, who lobbied successfully for the exclusion of their rivals from full trading privileges with the plantations.[6] There is, however, no evidence for this view, and merchant pressure group involvement was really a factor only in passage of the Navigation Act of 1696, the last of the fundamental Laws of Trade, which was concerned principally with tightening enforcement in the colonies of already existing laws.[7] In actual fact, the movement towards excluding Ireland from full participation in the plantation commerce beginning in the early 1660s came overwhelmingly from the English central state authorities and needs to be viewed in light of the Irish government's surprisingly independent response to the mercantilist tariff legislation favouring England's commerce enacted by the Dublin Parliament in 1662.

The first of the great Restoration Navigation Acts, the Act of 1660, treated England and Ireland as a single commercial unit.[8] Under the terms of this law, which aimed both at the increase of native shipping and the creation of a national trading entrepôt to rival Amsterdam, the merchants of Ireland were granted the same trading privileges, and placed under the same regulations with respect to imports and the employment of domestic shipping, as their counterparts in England. It was explicitly acknowledged that Irish ships and seamen counted as English for the purposes of determining what constituted a legally built and manned vessel under the provisions of the act.[9] Crucially, the Act of 1660 also distinctly provided that the so-called enumerated colonial goods—chiefly tobacco, sugar, and dyestuffs for the cloth industry—could legally be carried direct from the plantations to either England or Ireland in properly qualified vessels. Violations of the law were punishable by seizure of ship and goods.

A new quasi-colonial policy towards Ireland's trade that ran counter to the kingdom's privileged status under the 1660 Navigation Act first emerged in 1662 with the enactment of the tariff in Dublin. In the early summer of that year, following extensive negotiations with the government, the leaders of the Irish House of Commons were induced to grant the Crown a permanent revenue from the customs of Tonnage and Poundage and also from a new excise levy, in exchange for government support for a favourable land settlement.[10] The significance of the 1662 Customs and Excise Acts in forming the basis of the Irish Restoration financial settlement and giving statutory form to an embryonic revenue bureaucracy is generally recognised by historians.[11] Less well known is that before the two major finance bills were returned from England and presented to the Commons for approval, the government at Whitehall had used the opportunity presented under Poynings' Law to modify extensively the Irish customs legislation to benefit general English trading interests and institute a mercantilist tariff arrangement that would endure with the Navigation Acts into the early nineteenth century. First, the commodity valuations in the previous Book of Rates were manipulated heavily to favour goods from England. Foreign woollens and tobacco of the Spanish plantations—to take just two outstanding examples—were virtually excluded from the Irish market through the assignment of exaggeratedly high official values. English cloth, by contrast, was to pay only nominal custom and no excise. Changes were also made to the export schedule. Existing duties on wool, woollen yarn, and other materials of the English cloth industry were slashed.[12] Finally, at the urging of the London Customs Commissioners, sweeping new clauses were added to the Tonnage and Poundage bill itself that granted blanket duty preference to English goods over foreign and that privileged the indirect plantation trade through England over direct exchange with the colonies.[13] With these alterations, which were made apparently without much regard to their fiscal consequences, Ireland was to become less a co-equal partner with England in the plantation trade than a sort of mercantilist colony, a supplier of raw materials for the cloth industry, and a reserved market for English exports, including re-exports of the enumerated plantation staples. A final new clause added to the customs legislation, doubtless inserted with the constitutional debates of the 1660 Dublin Convention in mind, which had maintained that English acts binding Ireland required the approval of the Irish Parliament, declared the 1660 Navigation Act to be in force in the kingdom.[14]

It was only after the revenue and land settlement bills had been enacted into law that the possible negative impact of the restrictive commercial clauses incorporated into the customs legislation in London was recognised in Ireland. Trade had been very slow to recover from the dislocations of the late 1650s and, by September 1662, the Irish government was facing an acute financial crisis.[15] A committee of trade of the Irish House of Commons had recently reported its opinion that the clauses in question, if enforced, would damage the kingdom's trade and revenue, and the whole House had requested the Chief Governor to intercede to protect Ireland's local interests.[16] In response, the Lord Lieutenant, James Butler, Duke of Ormond, who was then at the height of his independent power and influence during the Earl of Clarendon's ascendancy at court, took 'bold' independent action against English mercantilist restraint. He unilaterally suspended local enforcement of the Navigation Act for a time, 'wch would haue [otherwise] destroyed us', together with execution of the several clauses in the 1662 Irish Customs Act favouring English commerce.[17] After 12 September 1662, goods could be brought into Ireland in shipping belonging to any country, paying only the ordinary rate of customs and excise duty, and trade with the plantations through England would no longer be privileged. Subsequent proclamations extended the duration of the government's free trade dispensation until early 1669, when it was allowed to expire.[18] By that time, although prolonged by the economic disruptions brought about by the second Anglo-Dutch War of 1665–1667 and the English Cattle Act of 1667, the crisis that had prompted the Irish government to pursue a policy independent of English commercial priorities was over. Foreign trade was beginning to revive, receipts from the customs and import excise were beginning to climb under the revived system of revenue farming, and Ormond himself had been dismissed as Charles II moved in a post-Clarendonian political direction with the Cabal.[19] After Ormond's replacement in 1669, no Chief Governor would have either the freedom or the authority to pursue anything resembling a separate Irish trade policy. Indeed, Ormond's immediate successors, John, Lord Robartes and John, Lord Berkeley of Stratton, for example, were both instructed from Whitehall to avoid any action that might injure England's trade, 'most especially as to our forrein plantations ... which we mean shall not be wronged how much soever the benefit of that our other kingdom [of Ireland] might be concerned in it'.[20]

Ormond's local suspension of the 1660 Navigation Act after September 1662 forms the immediate background to the exclusion of Ireland from full participation in the plantation trade. In June 1663, the Westminster Parliament completed the basic framework of the closed colonial system by passing the Act for the Encouragement of Trade, or the Staple Act, which established the entrepôt function in the other direction by requiring the American colonists to receive their manufactured goods from England in English ships. Ireland's exports to the plantations were limited to horses, indentured servants, and salted and barrelled provisions.[21] Although the Staple Act treated Ireland at least partly as a foreign rival to exclusive English 'national monopolistic' control of the colonies, the clauses limiting Irish commerce do not appear to have been included in the statute so much to retaliate against Ormond's actions as to protect the integrity of the emerging English Atlantic Empire against foreign, particularly Dutch, penetration through the 'back door' of Ireland temporarily outside the shipping restrictions of the 1660 Navigation Act. This rationale was made explicit in early 1667, when the Irish government petitioned the English Council to restore the kingdom to full trading privileges with the colonies in exchange for the loss of the valuable export trade in livestock to England under the Westminster Parliament's recent Cattle Act.[22] To grant such a request, the Council declared in refusing the application, would 'haue brought all the Confusion, & Damadge yt can be Immagined to England by openinge ye Doore to such Lycense as would haue made ye Dutch & ye French masters of all the Traffique of our Plantacons'.[23]

The chief architect of the 1663 Staple Act was the fervently anti-Dutch Sir George Downing, a diplomat, Exchequer official, and government MP for Morpeth.[24] Together with Sir John Shaw of the London Customs Commissioners, Downing had also played a major role in framing the 1660 Navigation Act, and he is generally credited with the groundbreaking policy of enumeration. As a legislator and later as a Treasury reformer and a leading member of the Customs Commission in London, the Dublin-born Sir George, more than any other single individual, was responsible for shaping Ireland's second-class status in the English/British Atlantic Empire for the period of the next century.

Another clause in the Staple Act of 1663 could be interpreted to mean that the enumerated commodities could not legally be landed in Ireland without first passing through an English port. As was not altogether uncommon at the time, however, the clause in question was poorly worded and provided no clear legal guidance for enforcement. In addition, while the Act of 1663 had excluded Ireland from the list of places where the enumerated articles could be carried direct, Parliament had neglected to alter the provisions for giving bond with security to follow the law, which continued to contain the word 'Ireland'. As a result, customs officials in Ireland, unsure how to act, generally continued to accept the old bonds and to permit tobacco and occasionally other enumerated goods to be landed direct from the colonies upon payment of duty.[25] In response to this state of affairs, Downing introduced and guided through Parliament the Plantation Act of 1671, which is generally considered with the acts of 1660, 1663, and 1673 to be among the principal Acts of Trade and Navigation, along with the Williamite Act of 1696.[26] With this Law, which was made temporary by the legislature for a term of seven years, Ireland was explicitly excluded from the direct import trade with the colonies and the word 'Ireland' was ordered to be stricken from all bonds.[27]

Administration of the Act of 1671 rested ultimately with the authority of the King and Privy Council. From the time of Downing's administrative reforms while Secretary to the innovative Treasury Commission of 1667–1670, however, most matters pertaining to the Navigation Acts had been brought under the purview of the Treasury Lords at Whitehall, as part and parcel of the establishment of Treasury authority and autonomy from the Privy Council, the Secretaries of State, and other branches of English government during these years.[28] After 1671 and the end of customs farming in England, successive heads of the Treasury relied extensively on the expert opinion of their immediate subordinates, the six-man Customs Commission in London, which headed England's newly established national customs administration. The dominant voice on this important board throughout the 1670s and early 1680s was Downing. Another long-serving member was Sir Richard Temple, who had been active in the 'country' anti-Irish cattle agitation of the mid-1660s before going over to the court in 1671.[29] Although subordinate to the Treasury, the Customs Commissioners exercised considerable independence in their own right on policy matters, especially after the founding of the colonial customs service under their control in 1673, which granted them 'revolutionary' powers vis-à-vis the colonial governors in matters of external trade regulation and the collection of customs revenue.[30] The commissioners were clearly the main driving force behind the administrative shaping of Irish trade policy during the foundational Restoration era with its notable tendency towards centralisation. Not only were they responsible for the government's strict attitude towards upholding the Act of 1671 against occasional political pressure from Irish interests, but they originated virtually every one of the enforcement initiatives of the period.[31]

Despite vigorous efforts by the Treasury and Customs Commissioners, evasion of the Act of 1671, 'on pretences of Shipwrack and other fraudulent Devices' was widespread among Irish merchants prior to the mid-1680s.[32] Tobacco was in high demand among all classes of the population, as legally recorded imports rose from 1,817,775 pounds in 1665 to 2,834,926 pounds in 1683.[33] By virtually all accounts, 'large quantities' of that article continued after 1671 to be landed direct from Virginia and Maryland and from the English West Indies without having first been unloaded and 'put on shoare' in an English port, as required by the law.[34] According to both government officials and the merchant exporters of tobacco in England, one principal reason for this unwanted state of affairs was the encouragement given to illegal trading by the farmers of the customs and import excise revenue in Ireland and their own officers in the several trading ports, who had a financial incentive to maximise proceeds from colonial tobacco no matter how it was landed.[35] To watch over the ports, special teams of surveyors were deployed periodically from England.[36] Customs officers in Ireland were also exhorted to report any illegal trade with the plantations or evidence of collusion by the revenue farmers to the London Custom House and to prosecute violators to the fullest possible extent of the law.[37] While seizures of offending vessels were carried out from time to time—especially in 1678–1680 when, in a major enforcement sweep that netted some one hundred ships, Admiralty powers were employed from England to bypass the farmers' enforcement authority—local compliance certainly remained limited while the customs and import excise revenue continued under farm.[38]

Reliance on indirect revenue collection by tax farmers is usually seen as a sign of administrative and fiscal weakness in the early modern state.[39] As indicated by the passage of the Navigation Acts, the reform of the Treasury, the creation of a customs bureaucracy in England and the American colonies, and the increasing interference of the Customs Commissioners in Irish affairs, however, the English administrative state was becoming stronger and better organised during the Restoration, and tighter central controls were coming to the Irish periphery. In the long view, among the most significant actions ever taken by the state authorities to ensure conformity with the Navigation Acts in Ireland was the totally unplanned and ad hoc decision in August 1682 to abandon tax farming and place the Irish revenue under direct government collection. Although Ireland's revenue had been collected by government commissioners during the Commonwealth and the first years of the Restoration era, administrative confusion as well as disappointing yields led Charles II's government to resort to farming the customs and other major revenue branches after 1663. As Sean Egan has established, the dominant figure at the Treasury after the Earl of Danby's downfall, Laurence Hyde, was planning in 1682 to restructure the existing Irish tax farms following the winding down of the Earl of Ranelagh's privatisation scheme at the Irish Exchequer. When these plans collapsed abruptly in August of that year, however, the government had no better option than to put collection of the Irish revenue under a commission. A five-man board was hurriedly appointed in London, composed of Francis Aungier, Lord Longford from Ireland, together with two financiers and two experienced minor revenue officials from England. All had connections to the Treasury or the government.[40] This 'inauspicious arrangement', as David Dickson has called it, marked the birth of the Irish Revenue Commission.[41] Intended only as a temporary expedient, and expected by many in both London and Dublin not to be as successful as farming, the new board—very much like the English Customs Commission a decade earlier—nevertheless, ensured its permanence through its professionalism, its ruthlessly efficient management, and its aggressive campaign against corruption in the revenue service.[42]

The Revenue Commissioners have been portrayed as agents of centralisation.[43] Though nominally answerable to the Lord Lieutenant, they were, in reality, responsible to the Treasury Lords and took their instructions direct from Whitehall. Over the objections of Dublin Castle, the commissioners were granted sole power to appoint, dismiss, and discipline all the officers of the revenue.[44] The kingdom was divided into thirty-eight revenue districts, each overseen by a collector, with the commissioners responsible for what Patrick Walsh has described as a 'formidable' revenue bureaucracy numbering over 600 officers in 1684.[45] Independence from existing Irish political entanglements enabled the commissioners both to ignore local sensibilities in the operation of patronage and to enforce the increasingly complex Acts of Trade and Navigation to the letter against

Irish merchant communities.[46] Major frauds in the customs, including a ring at the Belfast Custom House that dealt in counterfeit trading documents, were moved against vigorously, as the commissioners travelled the kingdom on circuit rooting out abuses.[47] Tellingly, one of the commissioners, William Dickenson, earned the nickname 'Captain Snarl' from the merchants and traders.[48] By the mid-1680s, reports of large-scale frauds in the colonial commerce had virtually ceased.

The Revenue Commissioners were by no means merely compliant ciphers carrying out orders from England, however, as is sometimes suggested by Egan.[49] Indeed, within a year of their appointment, they were embroiled in an ongoing dispute with the English customs board over control and regulation of the tobacco trade. Among other things, this conflict was to illustrate the determination of the new Revenue Commissioners to protect and advance Ireland's local interests against what they viewed as administrative overreach by their counterparts in London. The background to the controversy lay in the unexpected lapse of the 1671 Plantation Act in the years between 1681 and 1685, while England was caught up in the political turmoil surrounding the Exclusion Crisis and the Tory Revenge. Considerable confusion resulted in the central government's administration of the tobacco commerce during this period. Direct imports to Ireland from the colonies were resumed at a very high level, as the law governing the giving of bond reverted to the more liberal Navigation Act of 1660, frustrating the strict mercantilist position developed by the English Customs Commissioners.[50]

The controversy can be said to have begun in August–September 1683, when the Treasury directed the Revenue Commissioners to reduce the duty on tobacco shipped from England by cocket from 2½d. in the pound to 2d., unless the latter had any objections.[51] Sir John Temple, the Irish Attorney General, opined to Ormond that the object seemed to be to increase the English customs revenue by lessening the Irish, but this was clearly not a revenue measure.[52] Proposed by the London commissioners, the policy was intended to equalise the duty with that payable on tobacco landed direct from the plantations and thereby channel more of the trade through the ports of England. Confused wording in a complicated clause in the 1662 Customs Act and the legal interpretation thereof, which had profited the then revenue farmers (James Shaen and partners) in the late 1670s, now had the wholly unintended result of favouring the direct Irish-American trade thrown open with the expiration of the Act of 1671.[53]

The Revenue Commissioners, however, delayed execution of their instructions for a time. Claiming their own views had been misunderstood or misrepresented in England, in October, they produced a lengthy report addressed to Lord Deputy Arran and Council.[54] In this document, the commissioners insisted that the question of abating any duties needed to be considered in light of a number of broader, controverted points pertaining to Ireland's current standing under the Acts of Trade and Navigation. These issues centred principally around the question of whether, since the Act of 1671 was no longer in force, Ireland was subject to the major Act of Trade passed at Westminster in 1673 imposing a 'Plantation Duty' of 1d. in the pound on tobacco, payable in the colonies, when bond had not been given beforehand to return the cargo to an English port.[55] This latter act, it was correctly pointed out, was aimed chiefly at New England, whose merchants had shipped the enumerated commodities direct to Europe on pretence of intercolonial trade. Ireland was not named in the statute, and so, the commissioners maintained, the law was never intended to regulate Irish-American trade. The interpretation of the statute by officials in England had been strained well beyond its original intent.[56] What was more, they asserted, if Irish ships were legally obliged to pay the plantation duty on tobacco—which the Irish commissioners vigorously denied—then the 'unavoidable effect' would be an even greater increase in illegal trading, to England's manifest disadvantage. For having not given bond to return to England, there was nothing to prevent qualified vessels trading in the colonies from carrying tobacco 'anywhere in the World' without incurring the penalty of seizure—a point which the English commissioners allegedly had admitted to be frequently the case in actual practice. The Irish board therefore proposed that the government might exercise its prerogative to absolve Irish ships from payment of the plantation duty in the colonies in exchange for the desired reduction of the duty on English tobacco in Ireland. This policy overture by the Revenue Commissioners, it should be pointed out, presumed the co-equal standing of England and Ireland that was contained in the original 1660 Navigation Act, and was pitched as an 'Equitable Expedient to both Nations' that would produce a 'moderate and friendly Ballance of the Trade' between the direct and indirect branches of the tobacco commerce.[57]

On the instructions of the Treasury, the English commissioners replied with a report of their own in April 1684. They rebutted many of the claims made by the Irish commissioners. The English board denied that their interpretation of the Act of 1673 was strained beyond its original meaning, pointing to an important Order in Council of 16 February 1681 that was designed to clarify the administrative confusion following the expiration of the Act of 1671. This stated that any qualified vessel lading the enumerated goods in the colonies without producing to customs officials' certification of bond to return to an English port had the option of either giving such bond in the colonies or paying the plantation duty.[58]

Although seemingly unequivocal, it should be noted that the Privy Council's ad hoc solution to the problem of the plantation duties had caused considerable controversy already in Maryland with the affair of Lord Baltimore, the proprietor of the colony. In May 1681, Nicholas Badcock, the Collector of the Customs in Maryland, had demanded payment of the plantation duty from the masters of four English ships loading tobacco with bond given under the 1660 Act to return their cargoes to Ireland. Citing the expiration of the Act of 1671 and the opening of the Irish-American trade, the masters all refused to pay. When Badcock requested Baltimore's assistance, he was turned down, allegedly threatened with violence, and told in no uncertain terms not to interfere with the Proprietor's prerogatives. In the end, the vessels in question were all allowed to depart for Ireland without paying the £2500 in plantation duties that customs officers insisted should have been due from them. Badcock complained to the Customs Commissioners as well as direct to the Privy Council.[59] For his part, Baltimore, after initially claiming ignorance of the Order in Council of 16 February 1681, became, as the controversy progressed, increasingly jealous of his supposed prerogatives and confrontational in his attitude towards the centralised authority represented by royal customs officials.[60] The Privy Council carefully investigated Badcock's claims. After hearing the testimony from George Downing and others, it was decided that Baltimore was very much in the wrong.[61] In a royal letter of 8 February 1682, therefore, the Proprietor of Maryland was harshly admonished by the Privy Council, ordered to pay back the £2500, and threatened with the revocation of his charter if he continued to obstruct customs officers in the performance of their duties.[62] In response to the Baltimore affair, an agent of the Customs Commissioners, Charles Horne, was sent to reside in Ireland and root out abuses in the plantation trade. Port collectors were instructed to open their books to him and to provide him with detailed descriptions of all ships engaging in the tobacco commerce.[63] Almost immediately, Horne was involved in arranging for vessels seized by Irish customs officers for non-payment of the plantation duty to be brought to England, where they could be dismantled and their cargoes, furniture, and tackle sold off to benefit the government following a successful trial and prosecution of the owners.[64]

In their April 1684 report, the English commissioners also took issue with some of the other claims made by the Irish board. While acknowledging that Ireland was not named in the Act of 1673, they pointed out that the wording of the statute had been made general enough certainly to apply to Irish ships that had not given bond for England, as with English or colonial vessels that had not done so. As to the allegation that customs officials in the plantations permitted ships to trade indiscriminately with foreign nations upon paying the plantation duty, this was, the commissioners averred, a 'totall Mistake' and was explicitly contradicted by their instructions.[65] It was furthermore pointed out that Ireland enjoyed the full privileges of the Navigation Act, which had been ratified by the Parliament there, and its merchants should be expected to trade according to the rules and regulations for giving bond and paying duties. Finally, in reply to the policy overture from their Dublin counterparts, the commissioners countered that they had no desire whatsoever to suspend an English law enacted for the regulation of the wider empire, the administration of which was in their own power, for a law made in Ireland, which was not. While they agreed the ½d. per pound custom on tobacco in Ireland should be abated, it would be 'a remedy much worse [than] the Disease' to suspend collection of the plantation duty in exchange. Indeed, they concluded, payment of that duty was the best way to encourage ships to carry the enumerated articles to England only now that the Act of 1671 had lapsed.[66] Meanwhile, the dispute between the two boards had intensified as the English commissioners intervened in local enforcement decisions.[67] Administrative confusion reigned, even though the English Attorney and Solicitor Generals had ruled in August 1683 that ships could be captured in Ireland and prosecuted for violating the Act of 1673.[68] The Irish lawyers' concurring opinion, though already given, was repeatedly asked for, as the number of seizures piled up and petitions from ship owners and merchants caught up in complex legal violations multiplied.[69] In June 1684, the Irish commissioners, clearly frustrated both at the interference from London and at the fact that their opinions were carrying little weight at the Treasury board, produced a short rather irritable reply to the Customs Commissioners' April report. They once again denied that the Act of 1673 had anything to do with Ireland and went on to accuse their English counterparts of attempting to 'usurp' enforcement powers that rightly belonged to them. What was more, they could now no longer support reducing the tobacco duties at all, as the Irish government would lose revenue and gain nothing in compensation.[70] All of these reports were read and considered by the Privy Council, which came down on the side of the English board. On 27 June 1684, the Lord Deputy was ordered to direct the Revenue Commissioners to take off the ½d. on tobacco from England until further notice.[71]

While these instructions were doubtless carried out, the Dublin commissioners continued to press their case for suspending collection of the plantation duty to the governments of both kingdoms. Second and then third rounds of back-and-forth replies to the London commissioners were made over the summer and autumn of 1684.[72] The legal and administrative issues involved, already confused and confusing, became perhaps even more so with these exchanges, as the issues at stake became overwhelmed in a mountain of words. A fair amount of this disarray can be laid at the feet of the Irish commissioners, who continued to insist that their own views had been misunderstood while seemingly demonstrating little willingness to give their opponents' generally cogent arguments a fair hearing. To cut through some of the confusion, the English Crown lawyers were instructed in December 1684 to restate their earlier opinion on a single point of interpretation—namely, were ships arriving in Ireland with tobacco but without certificates of having paid the plantation duty in the colonies liable to seizure? The answer was given in the affirmative, and the Revenue Commissioners were directed to focus their enforcement efforts accordingly.[73]

Shortly after this legal opinion was handed down, the government abruptly decided to attempt a different strategy for administering the Act of 1673. On 30 May 1685, the Customs Commissioners reported to Hyde, now Earl of Rochester and Lord Treasurer, their opinion that the policy of levying the plantation duty in the colonies on ships trading to Ireland had proved essentially unworkable. Numerous ships had been detained in both Ireland and the plantations for violating the law, and ongoing confusion over the bonds and certificates, many of which were discovered to be counterfeit, threatened to ruin even honest merchants and put a serious damper on trade. The commissioners therefore suggested that, in lieu of the export duty payable in the colonies, one-half of the plantation duty on tobacco should be collected on the arrival of the produce in Ireland and the sum remitted to the English Exchequer.[74] Rochester accepted this proposal in early July, and colonial customs officials were instructed to cease collecting the 1673 duties on tobacco shipped to Ireland. The Revenue Commissioners, on the other hand, were ordered to collect, in addition to the regular duties of customs and import excise on tobacco amounting to 2d. per pound, one-half the duty imposed by the Act of 1673 amounting to ½d. per pound, and to remit the revenue arising from the latter to London under separate account.[75] On around the same date, the Irish government was ordered to continue the abating of the ½d. taken on tobacco sent from England.[76]

This policy arrangement had been in effect for only a short time when, much to the dejection of the merchants of Ireland, the Westminster Parliament, convened by James II in the summer of 1685, revived the Act of 1671 prohibiting direct Irish-American trade.[77] The reasons why Parliament decided to renew the statute are not entirely clear. The most likely explanation, however, is that the legislature, sitting for the first time since being dissolved at Oxford at the height of the Exclusion Crisis in March 1681, simply took advantage of the first opportunity available to revive an act whose lapse had caused so much administrative confusion throughout the wider commercial empire.[78] Orders to enforce the renewed law were sent from the Treasury to the Irish Revenue Commissioners and the English Customs Commissioners in the late summer.[79]

The merchants of Ireland loudly protested the revival of the Act of 1671 to the Revenue Commissioners. These complaints were forwarded to the Lord Lieutenant, Henry Hyde, second Earl of Clarendon—who was the elder brother of the current Lord Treasurer—and Clarendon in turn charged the Irish commissioners with drawing up arguments on behalf of the merchants for not putting the revived act back into effect.[80] On 15 February 1686, therefore, the commissioners wrote a letter to Treasurer Rochester, in which they pointed out that the half-duty collected in Ireland on American tobacco had for the last six months of 1685 amounted to £5170. This sum, they claimed, was more than what had been collected in the colonies on account of the full plantation duty for the period of the last ten years. Consequently, they argued, the practice of collecting the half-duty in Ireland was far more advantageous to both England and Ireland than the total prohibition on transporting tobacco directly to Ireland, which had never been effectively enforced, despite all the 'Severity and Diligence' of the English government in seizing ships and goods and prosecuting violators.[81] The commissioners furthermore contended that the revival of the Act of 1671 would end up depriving Ireland's merchants of their established trade with the plantations, on account of the additional time, hazard, and expense of trading through England and the 'tedious Formalities of the Law' involved in giving security and processing claims for debentures. The merchants of Ireland would be obliged to maintain a 'Bank of Mony and Security at every Port', which would be impossibly ruinous for them and cause them to give up their trade altogether.[82]

This memorial was transmitted to Rochester on 16 March by Clarendon, and enclosed with it was a letter in support of the Revenue Commissioners' arguments. Clarendon told his brother that he had heard the debates in England on the subject, 'which were not as ingenious as I could have wished, or as such debates ought to be'.[83] He was particularly worried, as he informed the Lord Treasurer in private correspondence, about Dudley North's influence at the London Customs Board. North, a wealthy Tory merchant and later a celebrated writer on trade, had been the dominant power at the commission since Downing's death in June 1684. 'I never in my life, knew a man soe wedded to his own opinion, as well as Interest, as he was', Clarendon professed, and he hoped that the matter could be heard in front of the full Council board, where North's views would not hold as much sway.[84] The Lord Lieutenant believed with the Revenue Commissioners that a continuation of the expedient that had been put in place in June 1685, allowing tobacco to be shipped directly to Ireland, with payment of the half-duty at importation, was a highly workable policy in practice and would 'be to the Advantage of the Revenue of both Kingdoms'. He suggested that the government might dispense with the revived law for a year or two, as a trial, in order to see whether the revenue would suffer at all from the dispensation.[85]

Unsurprisingly, these views were vigorously opposed by the Customs Commissioners, to whom the Irish proposal was submitted by the Treasury for report. The English commissioners basically dismissed the issue of the revenue, pronouncing it trumped by commercial and colonial concerns. Paraphrasing more or less the text of the 1663 Staple Act, they insisted that it was 'the true interest of England, and the usage of all nations too [*sic*] keep the Plantation-Trades to themselves'.[86] The Irish merchants' complaints were in any case groundless, the commissioners maintained, in that prior to the expiration of the Act of 1671 in 1680, the kingdom had been plentifully supplied with plantation commodities through Bristol and the other English outports, and Ireland's merchants and traders, 'as far as we haue heard', were at that time perfectly 'well contented with enjoying the benefit of the Plantation Trade thro' England'.[87] While acknowledging that there might be some seeming disadvantages to the merchants of Ireland in reviving the Act of 1671, the commissioners charged that these were vastly overbalanced by the damage that would be incurred to both England's national interest and the English tobacco exporters by not putting the renewed law into execution. Indeed, if allowed to trade on equal terms with the merchants of England, the considerable advantages enjoyed by the Irish merchants, in terms of their favourable location and supply of cheap provisions, would enable them to 'in great measure robb' England of the flourishing trade with its own colonies. The board therefore advised that the revived Act of 1671 not be dispensed with.[88]

In response to this zero-sum rebuff, the Revenue Commissioners prepared a second representation, which they sent to Clarendon on 22 April 1686. Once again the Irish board focused mainly on the fiscal side of the problem. By way of a brief exercise in political arithmetic, they illustrated that what was desired by the merchants could not possibly damage the English revenue.[89] They also disputed the English commissioners' assertion that the proposed dispensation would allow Irish merchants to take over the plantation trade from England. For one, it was pointed out that the 1663 Staple Act already prohibited manufactured articles from being sent to the colonies from anywhere but England. For another, the lack of a drawback provision in the Irish Customs Act of 1662 virtually prohibited the Irish merchants from re-exporting any tobacco and thereby threatening England's jealously cherished position as the entrepôt between the plantations and Europe.[90] The Irish therefore had 'no Pretence' of trading upon equal terms with the English but asked only for the removal of the existing restraints on the direct import of colonial goods, which, although 'of absolutely no benefit ... to the True Interest of the Revenue and Customs of England and Ireland', placed an 'unnecessary Burthen' on the kingdom's merchants.[91] By way of conclusion, the Irish commissioners stated their opinion that the only real dispute seemed to be whether the revenue arising from the duties on tobacco and other colonial produce would be best collected in England or Ireland. This disagreement, they felt, 'cannot be of that Consequence as to put so great a Difficulty and Inconvenience on the Trade of a whole Nation'.[92]

In the Earl of Clarendon's view, the Revenue Commissioners' arguments were clear and persuasive, despite the 'specious glosses' put on them by the London Customs Board.[93] Whatever their objective merits, however, it seems beyond question that these arguments were not at all helped by the commissioners' 'tactless' inclusion of direct charges of corruption against English customs officials in Bristol.[94] Such accusations 'seem to Reflect upon our Managery in England', the Customs Commissioners retorted, clearly irritated. In their final report to the Treasury on the matter, dated 12 May 1686, they stated that although they had refrained earlier from bringing up the many customs frauds used by the Irish, they could easily produce a multitude of such examples, as could the merchants of England, whose trade had been much injured by these deceitful practices.[95] The English commissioners therefore upheld their original position, pointing out that the 'whole Body of the Plantation Laws' was under their own 'care and inspection', and that it was their business to correspond with officials in England and the colonies and to maintain a 'constant' and 'uniform' system of administration. This duty, they claimed, they could not perform, 'nor give due Account of their Managery, if so great and near a Kingdom as Ireland, be let into the Trade thereof, and suffered to Import the Enumerated Commodities without first coming to England as the Law directs'.[96]

These reports were all read and considered by the Committee of Trade and Plantations of the Privy Council, as the Earl of Clarendon had indeed hoped for. In the end, however, the government sided with the English board. In June 1686, orders were issued to officials in Ireland and the colonies to enforce the renewed Act of 1671.[97] Shortly after this, the London government ordered that the ½d. per pound duty on tobacco abated in Ireland in June 1684 be put back on.[98] Such temporary expedients to control the trade were no longer necessary. The Act of 1671 would not be allowed to lapse again. As a major component of the Navigation Code elaborated under the Restoration, it remained in force, helping to structure the main pattern of Ireland's commerce in the British Atlantic world, until the discriminatory statute was repealed in 1779 at the height of the Irish 'free trade' crisis. The decision made in 1686, therefore, was consequential economically and long-enduring politically.

The defeat of the Revenue Commissioners' proposal brought the dispute between the two boards to an end and signified the triumph of English imperial and colonial concerns over local Irish ones in the administration of the Navigation Acts. The revival of the Act of 1671 in 1686 greatly simplified the Navigation Code and decisively eliminated the problems of enforcement in Ireland that had plagued administrators since 1680. The end of revenue farming and the establishment of the Revenue Commissioners under Treasury control in 1682 had already contributed substantially to the goal of securing compliance with the English-made laws in Ireland. After 1686, under the watchful supervision of the Revenue Commissioners, complaints of large-scale violations of the Navigation Acts in Ireland, which had troubled English administrators throughout the 1670s and early 1680s, effectively ceased. In summing up, the constitutional implications of the events of 1660–1686 should be emphasised. With the notorious Irish Woollen Export Prohibition Act of 1699, the Navigation Acts are certainly among the foremost examples from the seventeenth and eighteenth centuries of English parliamentary acts purporting to bind Ireland, a power that was made explicit in 1720 with the Declaratory Act.[99]

Notes

1. Francis G. James, 'Irish Colonial Trade in the Eighteenth Century', *William and Mary Quarterly*, 3rd ser., 20, no. 4 (1963): 574–84.
2. R. C. Nash, 'Irish Atlantic Trade in the Seventeenth and Eighteenth Centuries', *William and Mary Quarterly*, 3rd ser., 42, no. 3 (1985): 329–56; Thomas M. Truxes, *Irish-American Trade, 1660–1783* (Cambridge: Cambridge University Press, 1988).
3. L. M. Cullen, 'Merchant Communities Overseas, the Navigation Acts and Irish and Scottish Responses', in *Comparative Aspects of Scottish and Irish Economic and Social History, 1600–1900*, ed. L. M. Cullen and T. C. Smout (Edinburgh: John Donald, 1977), 165–76; Denis O'Hearn, *The Atlantic Economy: Britain, Ireland and the US* (Manchester: Manchester University Press, 2001).
4. Adam Smith, *An Inquiry into the Nature and Causes of the Wealth of Nations*, 2 vols. (1776; repr., Indianapolis: Liberty Fund, 1981), bk. iv. The literature on mercantilism is vast, and will not be entered into here to any significant extent. Still the best short introduction to mercantilism as policy in early modern England and Europe is Charles Wilson, *Mercantilism* (London: Historical Association, 1958).
5. Gustav Schmoller, *The Mercantile System and its Historical Significance* (New York: Macmillan, 1897); Eli. F. Heckscher, *Mercantilism*, trans. Mendel Shapiro, 2 vols. (New York: Allen and Unwin, 1935).
6. Thomas Bartlett, '"This Famous Island Set in a Virginian Sea": Ireland in the British Empire', in *The Oxford History of the British Empire*, vol. 2: *The Eighteenth Century*, ed. P. J. Marshall (Oxford: Oxford University Press, 1998), 255; O' Hearn, *Atlantic Economy*, 46.
7. 7 & 8 Wm. III, c. 22.
8. 12 Car. II, c. 18.

9. Opinion of Solicitor General Sir William Jones on Irish shipping, c. 1672, British Library (hereafter, BL) Add. MS 30218, ff. 36–37.
10. Irish Lords Justices to Edward Nicholas, 16 Aug. 1661, The National Archives (hereafter, TNA): SP 63/307/185; Earl of Orrery to the Earl of Clarendon, 6 Sept. 1661, Bodleian Library (hereafter, Bodl. Lib.), Clarendon MS 75, ff. 172–73; Speaker of the Irish Commons [Audley Mervyn] to the Duke of Ormond, 4 June 1662, Bodl. Lib., Carte MS 31, f. 526.
11. T. J. Kiernan, *History of the Financial Administration of Ireland to 1817* (London: P. S. King and Son, 1930), 82–88, 259–61; Sean Réamonn, *History of the Revenue Commissioners* (Dublin: Institute of Public Administration, 1981), 12–17; Neil Johnston, 'State Formation in Seventeenth-Century Ireland: The Restoration Financial Settlement, 1660–62', *Parliaments, Estates and Representation* 36, no. 2 (2016): 115–36.
12. Based on a comparison of the 1662 rates with those given in the previous Irish Books of Rates of 1631 and the 1642 English Customs Book used in Ireland during the 1650s. The 1662 Custom and Excise Acts are 13 & 14 Car. II, c. 9 (Irish) and 14 & 15 Car. II, c. 7 (Irish). The 1631 rate schedules are published in *The Booke of Rates … [of] His Highnesse Kingdome of Ireland* (London: Robert Barker, 1631). A copy of the 1642 English book was published as *The Rates of Merchandizes* (London: Laurence Blaiklock, 1642).
13. Order concerning the Book of Rates for Ireland, 14 Jan. 1662, TNA: PC 2/55, f. 516.
14. 14 & 15 Car. II, c. 9 (Irish), clause xlix. On the constitutional debates during the Convention, see Patrick Kelly, ed., 'Sir William Domville, "A Disquisition Touching that Great Question Whether an Act of Parliament Made in England Shall Bind the Kingdom and People of Ireland"', *Analecta Hibernica* 40 (2007): 17–70; Aidan Clarke, 'Colonial Constitutional Attitudes in Ireland, 1640–60', *Proceedings of the Royal Irish Academy*, section c, 90 (1990): 363, 373–74.
15. Ormond to Clarendon, 10 Sept. 1662, Bodl. Lib., Carte MS 143, f. 11; Ormond to Sir Henry Bennet, 29 Nov. 1662, TNA: SP 63/310/135. See also [Earl of Anglesey], State of the Irish Debt, and Credit, 9 Aug. 1662, Bodl. Lib., Carte MS 52, f. 340.
16. *Journals of the Irish House of Commons*, 21 vols. (Dublin: House of Commons, 1796–1801), ii, 128–30.
17. Ormond to Clarendon, 29 Sept. 1662, Bodl. Lib., Clarendon MS 78, f. 15.
18. Proclamation by Lord Lieutenant and Council, 28 Jan. 1663, TNA: SP 63/314/134; Proclamation by Lord Lieutenant and Council, 27 Feb.

1664, TNA: SP 63/309, ff. 71–72; Proclamation by Lord Deputy and Council, 16 Aug. 1665, TNA: SP 63/309, ff. 86–87; *By the Lord Lieutenant and Council* (Dublin: Samuel Dancer, 23 Jan. 1667).

19. On the negative effects of the Dutch War and Cattle Acts, see Anglesey to the Earl of Arlington, 25 Sept. 1665, TNA: SP 63/319/163; Memorial of Anglesey, the Earl of Cork and Burlington, and Viscount Conway to the King, 17 Mar. 1667, Southwell Papers, BL Add. MS 21135, f. 37. For the revival of overseas trade, see George Warburton to Sir Joseph Williamson, 23 Apr.1667, TNA: SP 63/322/111; for the increase in customs and import excise receipts after 1668, see TNA: SP 63/323/152; Abstract of Anglesey's Accounts of the Revenue, 20 Mar. 1659 to 20 Mar. 1669, [1670s], BL Add. MS 18022, f. 48.
20. Instructions to Lord Robartes [late 1668] (misdated June 1660), TNA: SP 63/303/82; Instructions to Lord Berkeley of Stratton, Feb. 1670, TNA: SP 63/327/36.
21. 15 Car. II, c. 7.
22. Lord Lieutenant and Council to the King, 7 Feb. 1667, TNA: SP 63/322/45; Ormond to Anglesey, 11 Feb. 1667, Bodl. Lib., Carte MS 51, f. 28.
23. Orrery to Clarendon, 19 Mar. 1667, Orrery Correspondence, BL Add. MS 37207, f. 212.
24. 'Report of a Committee of the House of Commons concerning Lawes to prevent Incroachments in Trade by Jewes, ffrench and other fforreigners', 8 Apr. 1663, Downing Papers, BL Add. MS 22920, ff. 11–12; Sir George Downing to Secretary Morrice, 18/28 Sept. 1663, Bodl. Lib., Clarendon MS 80, ff. 209–10; Downing to Clarendon, 22 Apr./2 May 1664, Clarendon MS 107, ff. 210–11. The progress of the legislation can be followed in Leo Francis Stock, ed., *Proceedings and Debates of British Parliaments respecting North America, 1616–1753*, 4 vols. (Washington, DC: Carnegie Institution, 1924–1942) 1:294–98, 301–4, 306–8, 318–19.
25. Treasury Minutes, 24 June 1670, 27 June 1670, TNA: T 29/3, pp. 361, 363; Downing to Attorney and Solicitor General and Irish Customs Farmers, 20 June 1670, TNA: T 27/2, p. 318.
26. Downing to John Shaw, 31 Oct. 1670, Downing to James Hayes, 5 Dec. 1670, TNA: T 27/2, pp. 375, 398; Starkey's Newsletter for 1 Nov. 1670, Aston Papers, BL Add. MS 36916, f. 194. The progress of the legislation can once again be followed in Stock, ed., *Proceedings and Debates*, 1:370, 374–75, 376–77, 380, 391, 396–97.
27. 22 & 23 Car. II, c. 26.

28. Treasury to Plantation Governors, 11 Nov. 1667, TNA: T 11/1, p. 49; Henry Roseveare, *The Treasury, 1660–1870: The Foundations of Control* (London: Allen and Unwin, 1973), 17, 40–41.
29. Stuart Handley, 'Temple, Sir Richard, third baronet (1634–1697)', in *Oxford Dictionary of National Biography*, ed. H. C. G. Matthew et al., http://www.oxforddnb.com.ezproxy.fau.edu/view/10.1093/ref:odnb/9780198614128.001.0001/odnb-9780198614128-e-27118?rskey=6WqAfr&result=4 (accessed 31 Aug. 2018); Carolyn A. Edie, 'The Irish Cattle Bills: A Study in Restoration Politics', *Transactions of the American Philosophical Society*, n.s., 60, 2 (1970): 1–66.
30. Robert M. Bliss, *Revolution and Empire: English Politics and the American Colonies in the Seventeenth Century* (Manchester: Manchester University Press, 1993), 104.
31. Customs Commissioners' Report of Trading from Ireland to the Plantations, 10 Feb. 1673, National Library of Ireland MS 7334.
32. Committee of Trade and Plantations Minutes, 27 Jun. 1679, TNA: CO 391/3, p. 22. See also Lord Treasurer to the Earl of Essex, 8 Aug. 1673, TNA: PRO 30/32/48, pp. 482–83; Lord Treasurer to Essex, 26 Jan. 1677, TNA: PRO 30/32/52, p. 30; State of the Irish Plantation Trade, and Observation of the Navigation Acts [late 1670s], Papers on Irish Trade, BL Add. MS 21133, ff. 3–4.
33. Table showing the goods imported into Ireland for year ending 25 Dec. 1665, TNA: SP 63/319/261; Table of Imports and Exports of Ireland from 24 Dec. 1682 to 24 Dec. 1686, Milles Collection, BL Add. MS 4759, ff. 8, 10; Truxes, *Irish-American Trade*, 21, 28.
34. Warrant to Essex, 4 Jul. 1673, TNA: PRO 30/32/41, pp. 344–45.
35. Customs Commissioners' Report of Trading from Ireland to the Plantations, 10 Feb. 1673, National Library of Ireland MS 7334; Petition of English Merchants Trading to Europe, and also to America, to the King and Council, 19 Jan. 1676, TNA: CO 1/36/10: Tobacco Merchants' Petition to King and Council, [May 1676], TNA: SP 29/391/94; Treasury to Irish Customs Farmers, 19 May 1680, TNA: T 27/5 pp. 509–10.
36. Treasury to Customs Commissioners, 23 Jan. 1672, TNA: T 54/2, p. 157.
37. Essex to Lord Treasurer, 22 Mar. 1673, Essex Papers, BL Stowe MS 213, f. 161; Danby's Treasury Minutes, 24 Dec. 1675, TNA: PRO 30/32/33, pp. 88–89.
38. Appointment of Nicholas Bailey et al. to Prosecute for Violations of the Navigation Acts in Ireland, 10 July 1678, TNA: PRO 30/32/52, p. 220; Treasury to Customs Commissioners, 2 May 1678, 2 June 1678, 14 June 1678, TNA: T 11/5, pp. 24, 42, 47; Privy Council Register, 27 June 1678, TNA: PC 2/68, f. 149.

39. Michael J. Braddick, *The Nerves of State: Taxation and the Financing of the English State, 1558–1714* (Manchester: Manchester University Press, 1996), 60–65.
40. Sean Egan, 'Finance and the Government of Ireland, 1660–1685', 2 vols. (PhD diss., Trinity College Dublin, 1983), 2:150–60.
41. David Dickson, *New Foundations: Ireland, 1660–1800* (Dublin: Irish Academic Press, 2000), 21.
42. Egan, 'Finance and Government', 2:167–78.
43. Patrick A. Walsh, 'The Fiscal State in Ireland, 1691–1769', *Historical Journal* 56, no. 3 (2013): 639–42; Charles Ivar McGrath, 'The Irish Revenue System: Government and Administration, 1689–1702', (PhD diss., University of London, 1997), chap. 6.
44. Ormond to the Earl of Arran, 27 Aug. 1682, Bodl. Lib., Carte MS 50, f. 295; Warrant appointing Revenue Commissioners, 27 Aug. 1682, TNA: T 14/3, p. 20–30; Col. John Fitzpatrick to Arran, 8 Sept. 1682, Bodl. Lib., Carte MS 216, f. 161.
45. Walsh, 'Fiscal State', 641.
46. Observations on the Commission to Earl of Longford, etc. [1682?], Bodl. Lib., Carte MS 54, f. 138; Longford and Lemuel Kingdon to Arran, 24 Aug. 1683, *Calendar of the Manuscripts of the Marquess of Ormonde*, n.s., ed. Historical Manuscripts Commission, 7 vols. (London: H.M. Stationery Office, 1902–1911), 7:114; Revenue Commissioners' Observations, 4 Oct. 1683, Bodl. Lib., Carte MS 54, ff. 236–37.
47. Treasury to Customs Commissioners, 2 Dec. 1684, TNA: T 27/7, p. 456; Treasury to Revenue Commissioners, 9 Dec. 1684, 22 Jan. 1685, TNA: T 14/4, pp. 115, 129.
48. Egan, 'Finance and Government', 2:173.
49. Ibid., 2:14–15, 153–96.
50. Table of Imports and Exports of Ireland from 24 Dec. 1682 to 24 Dec. 1686, Milles Collection, BL Add. MS 4759, ff. 8, 10.
51. Treasury to Arran, 27 Aug. 1686, TNA: T 14/3, p. 189.
52. Sir John Temple to Ormond, 11 Sept. 1683, *Ormonde*, n.s., 7:127.
53. 'The Farmers of Ireland, their Case, in answer to a Petition exhibited to the King & Councill against them by the Merchants', [before 10 May 1676], Bodl. Lib., Carte MS 38, f. 436; Notes by Williamson of Proceedings at Privy Council, 12 May 1676, TNA: SP 29/336, f. 165.
54. Temple to Ormond, 27 Sept. 1683, *Ormonde*, n.s., 5:127.
55. 25 Car. II, c. 7.
56. Revenue Commissioners to Arran, 1 Oct. 1683, Bodl. Lib., Carte MS 54, f. 279.
57. Ibid., f. 280.

58. Customs Commissioners to Treasury, 22 Apr. 1684, ibid., f. 279. The original order may be found in the Privy Council Register, 16 Feb. 1681, TNA: PC 2/69, ff. 103–4; the instructions are in the Royal Letter to Governors, Mar. 1681, TNA: T 52/8, p. 134; Treasury to Customs Commissioners, 21 Feb. 1681, TNA: T 27/6, pp. 191–94.
59. Nicholas Badcock to King and Council, 26 May 1681, TNA: CO 1/46/150; Badcock to Customs Commissioners, 10 Jul. 1681, TNA: CO 5/723, pp. 61–65.
60. Lord Baltimore to Anglesey, [late 1681], TNA: CO 5/723, p. 49; Christopher Rousby, Maryland, to the Privy Council, 14 Dec. 1681, TNA: CO 1/47/107.
61. Committee of Trade and Plantations, 13 Dec. 1681, TNA: CO 391/3, pp. 317–18.
62. Privy Council Register, 8 Feb. 1682, TNA: PC 2/69, ff. 231–32.
63. Treasury to Ormond, 24 Jul. 1684, Bodl. Lib., Carte MS 53, f. 752.
64. Treasury to Revenue Commissioners, 8 Apr. 1684, TNA: T 14/4, p. 18.
65. Customs Commissioners to Treasury, 22 Apr. 1684, Bodl. Lib., Carte MS 54, f. 279.
66. Ibid., f. 280.
67. Treasury to Mr. Kennedy [an informer], 7 Apr. 1684, TNA: T 27/7, p. 316; Treasury to Revenue Commissioners, 14 May 1684, 7 Aug. 1684, TNA: T 14/4, pp. 34, 78; Privy Council Register, 11 July 1684, TNA: PC 2/70, f. 202.
68. Opinion of R. Sawyer, Attorney General, 30 Aug. 1683, Bodl. Lib., Carte MS 54, f. 281.
69. Revenue Commissioners to Treasury, 6 Jun. 1684, *Ormonde*, n.s., 7:242; Revenue Commissioners to Treasury, 7 Jul. 1684, Bodl. Lib., Carte MS 54, f. 271.
70. Reply of Revenue Commissioners, June 1684, Bodl. Lib., Carte MS 54, f. 280.
71. Privy Council Register, 27 Jun. 1684, TNA: PC 2/70, f. 196; Ormond to Arran, 3 Jul. 1684, *Ormonde*, n.s., 7:253–54.
72. Treasury to Revenue Commissioners, 10 Jul. 1684, TNA: T 14/4, p. 64; Revenue Commissioners to Treasury, 17 Jul. 1684, Bodl. Lib., Carte MS 54, f. 271; Extract of Report of Customs Commissioners, 19 Jul. 1684, Carte MS 54, f. 277; Treasury to Customs Commissioners, 27 Sept. 1684, 20 Nov. 1684, TNA: T 27/7, pp. 425, 448.
73. Treasury to Revenue Commissioners, 16 Dec. 1684, TNA: T 14/4, p. 125; Abstract of Law Cases under the 'Act of Navigation', [before 27 Jul. 1684], Bodl. Lib., Carte MS 54, f. 281; State of the Case of the Irish Plantation Trade, 23 Oct. 1686, TNA: CO 1/60/84.

74. Customs Commissioners to Lord Treasurer, [30 May 1685], TNA: SP 63/351, ff. 21–24.
75. Warrant to the Irish Lords Justices, 5 Jun. 1685, TNA: SO 1/11, ff. 223–25; Revenue Commissioners to Lord Treasurer, 15 Feb. 1686, TNA: CO 324/4, p. 184.
76. Warrant to the Irish Lords Justices, 12 May 1685, TNA: SO 1/11, ff. 208–9.
77. Memoranda by Sir John Percival, 14 Jul. 1685, Bodl. Lib., Carte MS 130, f. 301.
78. 1 James II, c. 17; Stock, ed., *Proceedings and Debates*, 1:423, 426, 428, 431–32.
79. Lord Treasurer to Revenue Commissioners, 25 Jul. 1685, TNA: SP 63/351, f. 61; Lord Treasurer to Customs Commissioners, 7 Aug. 1685, TNA: T 27/9, p. 121.
80. State of the Case of the Irish Plantation Trade, 23 Oct. 1686, TNA: CO 1/60/84.
81. Revenue Commissioners to Treasury, 15 Feb. 1686, TNA: CO 324/4, pp. 185–86.
82. Ibid., pp. 189, 190.
83. Clarendon to Rochester, 16 Mar. 1686, ibid., p. 182.
84. Clarendon to Rochester, 3 Apr. 1686, Hyde Papers, BL Add. MS 15893, f. 195.
85. Clarendon to Rochester, 16 Mar. 1686, TNA: CO 324/4, pp. 182–83.
86. Customs Commissioners' Report, 29 Mar. 1686, ibid., p. 208.
87. Ibid., p. 211.
88. Ibid., p. 213.
89. Revenue Commissioners' Reply, 22 Apr. 1686, ibid., pp. 191–93.
90. Ibid.
91. Ibid., pp. 195–202.
92. Ibid., p. 206.
93. Clarendon to Rochester, 27 Apr. 1686, Hyde Papers, BL Add. MS 15893, f. 257.
94. G. L. Beer, *The Old Colonial System, 1660–1754*, part 1: *The Establishment of the System, 1660–1688*, 2 vols. (New York: Macmillan, 1912), 1:103.
95. Customs Commissioners' Reply, 12 May 1686, TNA: CO 324/4, p. 217.
96. Ibid., pp. 214–15.
97. Privy Council Register, 10 Jun. 1686, TNA: PC 2/71, f. 290.
98. Warrant to Lord Lieutenant, 21 Jun. 1686, TNA: SO 1/12, ff. 31–32.
99. See the opinion of Attorney General Sir William Jones on the application of the Plantation Act of 1671 to Ireland in Petty-Fitzmaurice Papers, BL Add. MS 30218, ff. 40–41. The Woollen Act is 10 & 11 Wm. III, c. 10. The Declaratory Act is 6 Geo. I, c. 5.

CHAPTER 3

Politics, Parliament, Patriot Opinion, and the Irish National Debt in the Age of Jonathan Swift

Charles Ivar McGrath

This chapter examines the process by which the principal of the Irish national debt was increased fourfold in 1729–30 and the evolution in Irish taxation policy which accompanied that occurrence. It also assesses wider attitudes at the time towards parliamentary taxation and a national debt and the proposal for increasing it and offers a detailed analysis of the political and parliamentary activities relating to the increase in the debt, including the adoption of the concept of direct appropriation of taxation for debt repayment and the emergence of the idea for establishing a sinking fund. Such considerations also take into account the wider economic conditions of the time and their impact upon public and political opinion. Ultimately, the chapter highlights how the actions of the Irish Parliament in relation to taxation and the national debt in the late 1720s and early 1730s represented a key moment in the evolution of fiscal policy and structures in Ireland and the extent to which public or more specifically Patriot opinion and wider political and economic considerations impacted upon that process.

C. I. McGrath (✉)
University College Dublin, Dublin, Ireland
e-mail: ivar.mcgrath@ucd.ie

D. Kanter, P. Walsh (eds.), *Taxation, Politics, and Protest in Ireland, 1662–2016*, Palgrave Studies in the History of Finance,
https://doi.org/10.1007/978-3-030-04309-4_3

Patriot Opinion and the Emerging Focus upon the National Debt in the Later 1720s

There was little to no evident opposition to the introduction of a national debt in Ireland in 1715–16. The first Parliament-sanctioned loan to government of £50,000 in January 1716 was based upon a vote of credit in the House of Commons and an ensuing Supply Act and came about as a response to the threat of a Jacobite invasion. The money was used to raise 13 new regiments as replacements for those which had been dispatched from Ireland to Britain to assist with putting down a Jacobite rebellion in Scotland and northern England. The £50,000 principal debt continued to be serviced with interest payments legislated for by Parliament every two years thereafter through the later 1710s and into the 1720s. These biennial acts likewise did not appear to be contentious or form the focus for opposition either in Parliament or in wider society.[1]

It was not until the second half of the 1720s that any real sense of disquiet with the national debt and the taxation legislation enacted for servicing the interest payments on that debt began to become evident. It is therefore of note that Louis Cullen has argued that it was during this time that a genuine national debt, comparable to that of Britain in structure and nature, developed in Ireland. The most prominent source of disquiet with this debt was the printed output of a number of pamphlet writers, most notably Jonathan Swift, but also including Thomas Prior.[2] To what extent their utterances on the matter reflected the views of a larger group of people or were simply their own opinions was not wholly apparent, though their works clearly reflected in the broader sense the early eighteenth-century Irish Patriot perspective on matters to do with the socio-economic circumstances of Ireland.[3]

Swift was the best known of these writers and had previously taken issue in print with Britain's increased taxation legislation and national debt during his time as a political writer for the Tory ministry in London in the final years of Queen Anne's reign from 1710 to 1714.[4] However, he remained quiet on these matters following his return to Ireland after 1714 to take up his position as Dean of St Patrick's Cathedral in Dublin. Instead, he began to engage with matters relating to Ireland's socio-economic condition and its relationship with England, commencing with the publication in 1720 of *A Proposal for the Universal Use of Irish Manufacture*. Arguments about British subjugation of Ireland and the 1720 Declaratory Act aside, Swift used the pamphlet to lambaste the Irish Parliament, shopkeepers, traders and merchants, and the nobility and gentry—and their wives and daughters—for their failure to look after the good of the country, because of their excessive consumption of foreign goods such as 'silks, velvets, calicoes, and the whole lexicon of female fopperies', and their failure to promote domestic industry, trade, and manufacture. Irish landlords were also attacked for rack-renting their tenants, as were bankers and their schemes to get rich at the expense of others.[5] These themes would be developed further in other works during the 1720s, with other Patriot issues added. For example, an undate sermon on the 'Causes of the Wretched Condition of Ireland', composed at some point between 1725 and 1728, revisited the issue of English exploitation of Ireland, consumption of foreign goods, and rack-renting landlords but added in 'the folly ... vanity, and ingratitude' of the 'vast numbers' of Irish people spending their wealth in England to the detriment of their 'mother kingdom'.[6]

It was not until 1726 that Swift revisited the question of a national debt and the concomitant increased taxation with the publication of *Gulliver's Travels*. But once again his excursions into these matters were ostensibly concerned with Britain's national debt and taxes, as in the response of the King of Brobdingnag in Part II to Gulliver's description of British government finances, and in Gulliver's response in Part III to a projector's scheme in the Academy of Lagado for uncovering plots against the government by examining the excrement of suspects.[7]

It was not until 1728 that he started to reference Ireland's national debt and associated supply legislation in a negative manner. At first, the references were oblique and vague at best. The first sense of engagement with such matters occurred in *A Short View of the State of Ireland*, which was published in March 1728 in the last two months of the first Irish parliamentary session of the reign of George II. In refuting the view that Ireland was in a flourishing state, Swift presented reasons why a country might be considered thriving and then gave examples of how the opposite applied in Ireland. This brought forth reiterations of the previously raised concerns over rack-rented tenants, parasitical bankers, and the consumption of foreign goods and developed the argument regarding absentees by claiming that 'one-third of the rents of Ireland' were spent in England, which along with other remittances 'will amount to a full half of the income of the whole kingdom'. For good measure, the denial of a mint to Ireland was thrown in as well in order to raise the issue of the perennial shortage of ready specie. Swift's 12th reason for a thriving kingdom was 'the public revenues being all spent and employed at home; except on the occasions of foreign war'. In response, he argued that alongside the remitting of one-third of all rents to England, a large percentage of the public revenue left the country as part of the 'profits of employments, pensions ... the pay of all superior officers in the army; and other incidents'.[8] These various drains on Irish public revenue to England were not new sources of political discontent in Ireland, but would loom larger in 1729 during the debates in Parliament around supply and the increasing of the national debt, and would become regular tropes in Swift's writings during this period.

Not long afterwards, in *The Intelligencer* in mid-1728, Swift made reference to an occurrence in the Irish House of Lords on 18 December 1727, when James Barry, Earl of Barrymore, had proposed that an address be presented to the Lord Lieutenant calling for 'the public accounts of the nation' to be laid before the Upper House.[9] A debate ensued, which was postponed until 21 December, on which day the motion was defeated on a division by 'about 28 to 11'.[10] Seven Lords entered a protest, stating that it was 'the undoubted and inherent right of the Lords' to address the Lord Lieutenant for 'any accounts of papers, relating to the public'.[11]

Barrymore's purpose in proposing the address was unclear. Hugh Boulter, Archbishop of Armagh and a senior member of the Irish government, surmised that the intention was to create a rift between the two Houses by infringing upon the established procedure, which was part of a political compromise dating back to 1695, whereby the public accounts were presented to the Lower House at the beginning of each session in recognition of the rights of the Commons to assess the ways and means of raising taxation and of initiating such supply legislation.[12] In that respect, it was notable that the protest echoed the wording of the Commons' 1692 'sole right' claim.[13] And any break with established practice would readily be perceived by the Commons as an attempt to undermine that constitutional understanding.

Whatever Barrymore's purpose in proposing the motion, Swift presented it in comic fashion in the poem 'Mad Mullinix and Timothy' as part of the rantings of Timothy (the MP and Privy Councillor, Richard Tighe) about all Tories being Jacobites. In that guise, Barrymore (who was indeed later to become a Jacobite) called 'To bring in (I could Cut his Throat) / Our Whole Accounts of public Debts', which Swift ironically portrayed as a 'dangerous horrid motion', as 'Popish Craft', and as part of 'a Plot for the Pretender'.[14]

However, Barrymore's actions may have had a more immediate purpose, which would also explain Swift's replacing Barrymore's actual call for the public accounts with a request for an account of the 'public Debts'. Two years earlier, in the 1725–26 parliamentary session, the opposition in the Commons had successfully resisted government pressure for the introduction of new taxes to deal with increasing pay arrears for the army.[15] Following on from the first of a series of bad harvests in Ireland, the opposition had been able to mobilise significant support both within and outside Parliament for a campaign for no new parliamentary taxation (though this did not preclude renewing all of the existing parliamentary additional duties for another two years).[16] Yet renewed fears of war in early 1726 made the Commons look at the pay arrears once again. The opposition was led by St. John Brodrick, who had taken over from his father Alan, Viscount Midleton, as leader in the Commons of the powerful Munster faction, which now headed up the opposition as a result of Midleton's resignation earlier in 1725 from his position of Lord Chancellor and a more general falling-out with the government of Lord Lieutenant John, Baron Carteret.[17] Ably supported by Thomas Carter and Agmondisham Vesey,[18] Brodrick scuppered any chance at that point of a vote of credit that would have facilitated a new loan of about £10,000 to government to cover interest payments on a larger sum of about £50,000 to be advanced by bankers and others to clear some of the most pressing army pay arrears, by arguing that any such move would be 'involving the nation in a debt, which they did not owe ... [and] bringing the fatal inconvenience of taxes and loans upon us'. He threw in for good measure a vague claim to appeal to Irish Patriot sensibilities that the proposal was 'unparliamentary and destructive of the constitution of parliaments'.[19] As a compromise, the House eventually agreed instead to address the King requesting that £10,000 from the supplies already granted be set aside for payment of 7 per cent interest upon warrants for army pay that was in arrears, in order 'to make the warrants ... have a currency among the people, till money came in to pay them off'.[20] The theory was that 'bankers and other monied men' would advance money upon the security of the warrants, for which they would receive interest payments for two years, after which time Parliament would provide a fund to clear the principal.[21] The Commons thereby undertook in principle for a percentage of the Establishment pay arrears to be transformed into part of the national debt, by agreeing to take that percentage of the pay arrears upon themselves as a debt secured on the credit of the nation.

Despite attempts by the opposition to scare bankers and others away from the scheme,[22] it proved very successful and the warrants 'were immediately cleared by money advanced by several persons'. During the next two years, £8,395 was paid in interest upon the principal of £59,967, which was due to be repaid to the creditors at the end of 1727. However, such repayment 'being liable to many difficulties', in particular the absence of a parliamentary fund, on 22 December 1727 the Commons addressed the King once again that £10,000 be issued from the Treasury on warrants for army pay arrears.[23] The 1727 address had emerged out of the ongoing considerations of the Commons' Committee of Public Accounts (CPA), first convened on 5 December, and upon that committee's resolution reported to the House on 21 December that 'the debt of the nation' (a catch-all phrase for the £50,000 national debt plus unfunded pay arrears on the Establishment) was, 'at lady-day, 1727', £127,372.[24] Unlike in 1726, there was no opposition offered in the Commons at any stage in this process.[25] It may well be the case, therefore, that the real purpose of Barrymore's motion in the Lords was to try to disrupt the agreement on providing a fund for paying interest on the pay arrears. In that light, Swift's reference to 'public Debts' rather than public accounts makes more sense and places Timothy/Tighe, as a government supporter, in the position of attacking Barrymore for trying to destabilise proceedings aimed at the ongoing maintenance and expansion of the national debt.

It was also the case that the addresses of early 1726 and December 1727 demonstrated that there was a clear understanding in Parliament that the increasing level of army pay arrears and the associated 'debt of the nation' would have to be dealt with in a more forthright fashion at some point in the near future. The options were either to legislate for dramatically increased taxation or to facilitate a new Parliament-sanctioned and secured loan to government. Swift's oblique references to such issues suggested that there was a more general awareness of this reality as well. But the wider socio-economic situation in Ireland at the time would also have a role to play in the final decisions in this regard.

Around the same time as the 'Mad Mullinix' poem appeared in *The Intelligencer*, Swift had written to Alexander Pope: 'I do profess without affectation, that your kind opinion of me as a Patriot (since you call it so) is what I do not deserve; because what I do is owing to perfect rage and resentment, and the mortifying sight of slavery, folly, and baseness about me, among which I am forced to live.'[26] Such rage and resentment, as shown in the *Short View* and other works, was fuelled in the second half of the 1720s by the desperate socio-economic circumstances affecting the lives of the majority of the Irish population. Four poor harvests from 1725 onwards led to famine conditions in places and had contributed in part to significant emigration, especially from Ulster.[27] As Louis Cullen has argued, these circumstances, which Swift viewed first-hand on his regular journeying to different parts of the country during the later 1720s, made them 'real and immediate' concerns for him, which were reflected in his writings in 1728–1729. Cullen likewise views Swift's writings in those two years as part of an emerging 'literature … which was intended to influence public opinion, and especially opinion within the Irish parliament'.[28]

Negotiating the Fourfold Increase in the National Debt in Parliament, 1729

The climax for this new wave of political literary output was the convening of Parliament in late 1729 against a backdrop of extreme socio-economic crisis in the country, and an increased awareness of the pressure building upon government to find a viable solution to the extensive pay arrears on the Establishment, most probably by means of increasing the principal of the national debt. For the government, the pending parliamentary session was viewed with concern. The ill-health of Speaker William Conolly raised the prospect of possible instability in the government ranks in the Commons. The death of Archbishop William King raised similar concerns for the Lords.[29] But the dire socio-economic conditions in the country, even in light of a successful harvest in the summer of 1729, and public unrest in Dublin in particular loomed largest, alongside the year-on-year increases in the pay arrears to the military Establishment.

The session commenced on 23 September 1729 with Carteret's opening speech to both Houses of Parliament. The Lord Lieutenant commenced with the usual reminder of their good fortune to be reigned over by so gracious and mild a sovereign and then proceeded to the real heart of the matter. As had become standard practice since the Lord Deputyship of Henry Capel, Baron Tewksbury, in 1695, Carteret appealed directly to the 'Gentlemen of the House of Commons' for money:

> I have ordered the accounts and estimates to be laid before you, by which you will observe the revenue has fallen short of what is produced in the two former years, and thereby a considerable arrear is become due to the Establishment; and I have not the least reason to doubt, but that you will

> grant such supplies as will be necessary to answer the exigencies of the government in such manner as shall be most expedient, and may be least burdensome to the people.

The latter phrase had a particular resonance for MPs, given the evident suffering throughout the country in the preceding years. It was also aimed at facilitating the bigger issue of increasing the national debt, on the grounds that borrowed money allowed for a lesser tax burden upon people during a time of economic hardship.

Not surprisingly, therefore, Carteret immediately informed MPs that the King 'has been pleased, since your last meeting, to send three of those regiments to this kingdom, which the public service had required to be employed abroad; and I can assure you from His Majesty, that the rest shall be ordered back, as soon as the circumstances of affairs will permit'.[30] Carteret's intention was to try to prevent the discontent over money being sent abroad to pay for the army from disrupting the considerations of the Commons on supply. The exportation of Irish tax revenue and the concomitant removal of ready specie from circulation in Ireland were both easy pickings for those who wished to oppose increased taxation or Parliament-sanctioned government borrowing.

In response, the Commons resolved on the usual addresses of thanks to the Lord Lieutenant and to the King, though the finalising of the latter on 24 September provoked some unexpected debate. An amendment was proposed for adding in a reference to the socio-economic problems in Ireland at that time and was pursued with more 'warmth than was expected' by four MPs in particular: Eaton Stannard, who was deemed to be a protégé of Swift's, Charles Coote, Warden Flood, and Colonel Alexander Montgomery.[31] In order to avoid a division on the matter, the House agreed to add the words 'under our present circumstances' to the address, which promised the King that Parliament would 'give such supplies as shall be necessary to answer the exigencies of the government, and in such a manner as shall be most expedient and least burdensome to your people'. This echoing of Carteret's speech was also repeated in the address of thanks to the Lord Lieutenant.[32]

In reporting to London the events of the opening two days, Carteret felt he had 'good reason to hope, that this parliament will proceed in the best manner for His Majesty's service'.[33] However, the earlier concerns over Conolly's health, and the difficulties that might arise for the government's programme in Parliament if he had to vacate the Speakership, now came home to roost. On 26 September, he was 'seized of a sudden disorder' in the Commons, which rendered him 'some time insensible'.[34] All his friends were agreed he would not be able to return to the chair, and so Parliament was adjourned for ten days while plans were put in place for his replacement. The preferred candidate for the government was Sir Ralph Gore, the Chancellor of the Exchequer, but even though it was assumed his election would be uncontested, the government now feared that 'many other difficulties will arise in the conduct of the session'.[35]

Conolly, however, was still not ready to go and clung to the hope of returning to the Commons until mid-October. As a result, Parliament was adjourned once again on 6 October for a further week. But on its resumption on 13 October, even Conolly had come to see the writing on the wall and agreed to be replaced by Gore, who was thereupon unanimously elected Speaker.[36] However, the knock-on effects on government planning were seen immediately. It had originally been intended to put Gore forward for the chairmanship of the crucial Committee of the Whole House on Supply (CWHS), but now Marmaduke Coghill was to go forward as the government candidate. For his part, Coghill was already concerned as to what 'will be the issue of the session' in light of recent events: 'we have heard of no cabals, [but] nor are people settled under any head or person to quiet or direct'. By way of warning, he noted that 'we have a bitter book published against absentees, though it has some truths in it, it has many faults and [is] liable to many objections'.[37]

The book was Thomas Prior's *A List of the Absentees of Ireland*.[38] The timing of the pamphlet's publication early in the session was clearly with a view to influencing the opinions of MPs.[39] Most famously, Prior's primary target was the many absentee landlords who spent their incomes in England, while he also highlighted the large amounts of public revenue exported from the country to pay civil and military pensions, government officials, army officers, and the absent regiments in Gibraltar. But the work also focused on a further range of Patriot topics espoused by Swift and others, including English restrictions upon Irish trade and manufacture, the excessive consumption of foreign goods and commodities to the detriment of Irish commerce, manufacture, and employment, and rack-renting landlords.[40]

Prior also addressed three matters which were very clearly directed at the pending parliamentary considerations relating to supply and the national debt. First, he argued that one effect of 'our *Nobility* and *Gentry* deserting their own country, and spending all abroad' was that 'the public funds fall very short of the necessary Establishment, and must grow worse every day; so that, in time of peace, we shall be driven to the necessity, either of lessening our Establishment, or increasing our taxes, without any ability to pay them'.[41] Second, he advocated that the absentees should be made to contribute 'their quota towards the charge of the public', and that 'our legislature will take care' to make it so. To that end, he proposed the introduction of a tax of 4s. in the pound on the estates of all absentees.[42] And third, he warned that people should 'be very cautious, on all future elections of parliament men, or any other occasions, how we pay any regard to those, who do not live constantly among us. It must be of service, to take public notice of those actions, which tend both, to the good and hurt of one's country; in order to excite us to the practice of the first, and prevent our being guilty of the second.' With this final, more general warning to any MP who might be seen to do harm to Ireland (however that may be measured or assessed), Prior's three points clearly signposted for MPs exactly what Patriots believed would be good and bad for Ireland, including the perceived inability of Ireland to cope at that point with increased taxation—unless, of course, it was imposed upon the absentees.[43]

However, the formal supply process in the Commons had several stages to navigate before the impact of Prior's pamphlet might be readily perceived. On 14 October, the long-established first step in that process involved a resolution to take into consideration the Lord Lieutenant's opening speech, which was followed by a series of resolutions calling for the various government financial accounts to be laid before the Commons for assessment. At the same time, the House also resolved to sit in a week's time as a Committee of the Whole House on the State of the Nation (CWHSN).[44] If there was to be discontent in Parliament, the CWHSN was often the place to find it.

As the various government accounts began to be delivered to the Commons on 15 October, the House, as scheduled, took into consideration Carteret's opening speech. In keeping with the precedents established since the 1690s, a motion was then made that a supply be granted to the government, which was followed by the standard resolution for the CWHS to sit the following day.[45]

The CWHS sat as ordered for the first time on 16 October, when Coghill was elected to the chair and it was agreed that a supply be granted to the government. However, such accord was tempered the next day by the fact that the appointing of the all-important select Public Accounts

Committee (PAC) resulted in a division over a motion to allow the PAC to subdivide. The motion was lost by 50 to 51 in a victory for transparency and accountability but a defeat for the government.[46] Subdividing was intended to speed up the PAC's considerations, the conclusion of which was required before any further steps could be taken on voting taxes. But subdividing was also perceived as a means of glossing over or covering up any problematic issues from the full membership of the PAC and therefore from the Commons more generally.[47]

Accordingly, though the CWHS was due to sit again on 21 October, it had to be postponed until 24 October and then again to 28 October. In the interim, the CWHSN finally met.[48] Despite expectations to the contrary, no adverse resolutions emerged from this first sitting. However, the debate was long and arduous and touched upon all of the major economic and political concerns prevalent in Ireland at that time, including those highlighted by Prior in the *List of Absentees* and Swift in a *Short View* and other works.

At the outset of the debate, Robert Allen, 'from whom the warmest motions were expected', simply moved that 'some proper laws for the improvement of tillage' be considered. More telling, however, was the one-hour speech of Colonel Montgomery, which laid out

> all the grievances of the nation in great detail, our want of public spirit, the poverty of the kingdom, the ill consequences of our people going to America, occasioned he pretended by the oppression of landlords by setting their lands too high, and the hardships of collecting tithes, by the luxury of the better sort of people, by the extravagance of the ladies in their silks, laces and other vanities, by the irregular and uncertain state of our coin, by the tricks of bankers and merchants, by our excess in drinking French wines, by our gentlemen and ladies going abroad and living out of their native country ... [and] by the continual addition to our Establishments.

Yet he 'concluded without proposing anything'. Robert Cope also spoke, though 'short, and with temper and prudence, and said only in general that some things wanted to be redressed, and seemed to hint at a modest and decent representation' to the government. Coghill felt that 'if Cope and the Tories' could be prevented from making any such representation, 'we shall have no other disturbance, for the angry men find either that they can't get any persons of weight to join them, and can't cement with any party, or my Lord Lieutenant has found means to stop their mouths'.[49]

Reflecting on the debate in the CWHSN, Archbishop Boulter pointed out how central these itemised grievances had been to the Patriot arguments. Hence, he blamed Prior's pamphlet for having heightened an 'evil spirit', which had been 'artfully spread among all degrees of men amongst us'. However, although Boulter was the leading supporter of what he termed the 'English interest' in Ireland, he recognised that there were genuine economic issues that needed addressing: 'we are no doubt in a miserable condition here, by having had three or four bad harvests together, and if God had not blessed us with a plentiful crop last summer, we had been ruined for some years'. Yet he still believed that this 'evil spirit' among people distracted them from 'owning whence our calamities came for the most part' and instead were 'for throwing them on other causes that may be a subject of murmuring'.[50]

It was also the case, however, that Boulter at this point made clear in his correspondence exactly what the government was looking for from Parliament in terms of supply. Despite his concerns over the proceedings in the Commons, he still felt that 'most of the members seem [well] disposed and promise to provide some fund to answer the interest of about £200,000 of our debts, till we are able to pay the principal. And indeed without such a provision, the wheels of the government here will be so clogged, that in case of any accident, we shall hardly be able to send a regiment abroad, if called for.'[51] The latter point served to reiterate his belief that Ireland should make a contribution to imperial defence overseas, even if many Irish MPs felt otherwise.

The long-expected demise of Conolly finally occurred in the early morning of 30 October. Carteret was quick to remind London that Conolly's illness had caused a significant delay to the government's parliamentary business and to recommend that Coghill be granted Conolly's position as a Revenue Commissioner, as the government looked to consolidate the new group of parliamentary managers centred around Gore and Coghill.[52] The appointment was quickly agreed by London,[53] yet as Boulter reiterated when reflecting on Conolly's death, 'hitherto there has been very little agreement, nor any well concerted management in the House. There is no doubt, Mr. Conolly's illness has been one occasion of this disjointedness; and it will require some time to bring the several clans, which united in him, to centre in another.'[54]

Time was not a luxury the government had, however, not least because the proceedings of the PAC in late October had not gone as smoothly as might be wished. It had become the norm, given the quantity and detail of the accounts under consideration, for the PAC to meet every day. On several occasions during those sittings, conflict had broken out over attacks by some PAC members on the Privy Council for overspending on the Concordatum, which was an annual fund for covering numerous incidental or extraordinary costs, ranging from postage and repair of buildings to the care of widows and prisoners. It was a form of government petty cash and was regularly overdrawn, especially in times of crisis. However, it was also an easy means for stoking discontent and, as Boulter intimated, had arisen as an issue owing to the slackness of government supporters on the PAC: 'through non-attendance of some, and ill-concerted measures of those present, [it was] carried without dividing, that the overdrawings ... would be of ill consequence to the kingdom'.[55]

Following a failed attempt in the CWHSN on 3 November by Allen, Carter, and Montgomery to add fuel to the fire by referencing once again the socio-economic crisis and the importation of luxury goods,[56] the long-awaited PAC report was finally presented by Sir Thomas Taylor on 7 November. It first noted that the 'debt of the nation' had been agreed in 1727 as £127,372. Government expenses since that time had amounted to £982,710, resulting in total outgoings of £1,110,082. Government income in the same period was calculated at £889,351, thereby leaving a new 'debt of the nation' in 1729 of £220,731. This was very much in keeping with the government's own projected debt and the amount hoped for from Parliament. However, the PAC report also noted some contentious points, including the fact that only three of the six Irish Establishment regiments overseas in 1727 had as of yet been returned to Ireland. It was also reported that the allowance for military contingencies, of £6,000 for two years, had been exceeded by £5,175. Likewise, the overspend on the Concordatum was noted as being £6,802 in excess of the £10,000 two-year allowance. It was usual for both funds to be overdrawn, and for that overdrawing to be reported by the PAC to the Commons, but the difference on this occasion was the attempt to use it to attack the government and delay and undermine the supply process.[57]

However, the opposition's endeavours proved unsuccessful. As reported by Coghill, the 'resolution against the [privy] council [was] unanimously disagreed to [by the House], and ordered to be expunged [from the PAC report]'. He was still a bit mystified, however, as to why the attack had not been pursued in the House: 'How this came about I can't tell, but I believe it was imagined all this would have been done by a great majority', but when the opposition realised there was in fact little support for the resolution, they 'thought it better to give it up quickly, than to contest what they could not carry'.[58] For his part, Boulter was of the view that the 'great heats' over the overspends on both the Concordatum and military contingencies were defeated when it was made clear to MPs that the two funds were the only ones available to the government for dealing with any unforeseen expenses or emergencies.[59]

With the amended PAC report agreed to by the Commons, it was immediately referred to the CWHS, as the next phase of the supply process swung into action. The role of the CWHS now was to decide, on the basis of the PAC report and all the associated government accounts, how much money should be granted to the government. Coghill reported to the House on 8 November that the CWHS had resolved that, in order to cover the next two years of government expenditure and to address the 'debt of the nation' of £220,731, a supply be granted of a sum not exceeding £510,239.[60]

Some 'little dispute' arose over the CWHS resolutions owing to 'a false computation made by an unknown hand' which came into Allen's possession. However, 'the fallacy' of it 'soon appeared' and the House agreed unanimously to accept the CWHS resolutions.[61] The next major stage of the established supply process now got under way, with the CWHS resolutions being referred to the Committee of the Whole House on Ways and Means (CWHWM), which made the real decisions as to what would actually be taxed, for how long, and at what rates.[62] Such matters were expected to result in disagreement as to 'the new funds demanded to pay interest for the debt of the nation'. Evidently all of these matters had already been sketched out among MPs prior to the CWHWM convening. Carteret was understood to want the existing 4s. in the pound tax on absentee salaries and pensions to be dropped, which was highly unlikely given it was a favourite of the Commons. But the real difficulties were expected to arise when it came to the heads of the supply bills. Carteret wanted 'all the taxes in one bill', whereas 'the majority of the House seem to be of opinion to have two bills', one for renewing the existing additional duties and a second with 'the new duties to be appropriated to the payment of the interest of the national debt, and to apply the surplusage, if any, to the discharge of the principal'.[63] That such matters had already been discussed among MPs demonstrated the extent to which the groundwork had already been laid by government supporters in the preceding months regarding the proposed increase in the national debt and the associated need for new additional duties and their appropriation for interest repayments. It was evident also that MPs were in agreement on the plan for creating a sinking fund from any surplus arising from the appropriated duties for repayment of the principal of the debt. The sinking fund would offer further security against the appropriated duties being used by the government for any purpose other than servicing of the national debt.

For MPs, having two bills was crucial. The fear was that if everything was put into one bill, then the Privy Council in London could remove the appropriation of duties and the 4s. in the pound tax on absentee salaries and pensions, and the Irish Parliament would still feel obliged to pass such an amended bill, as to reject it would mean 'we must be undone by letting the funds run out, which the kingdom can't bear'. But if the new duties and appropriating clause were in a separate bill, then any alteration to it in London would allow the Commons to reject it 'without much detriment to the country' and without endangering the main supply in the 'grand money bill'. Carteret was apparently willing to agree to the appropriation but seemed very insistent on only one money bill. Coghill was at a loss as to know why, as he believed 'it is most certain the fund will be granted unanimously if the two bills were agreed to by my lord lieutenant'.[64] At the heart of the matter, stretching all the way back to 1692–1695, was the Commons' belief that supply bills in particular should only originate in the Commons and should not be altered in London, regardless of the Crown's prerogative rights or the continued application of Poynings' Law.[65] It was also the case that MPs feared that if there was no specific appropriation of the duties for debt repayment, then the income arising therefrom might be put to other nefarious uses.

As expected, matters did not go smoothly during the first two sittings of the CWHWM on 11–12 November.[66] It was agreed 'by all sides' that the supply be provided for in two bills, 'but a great debate arose' as to whether the taxes to be voted for repaying the national debt should be granted until such time as the interest and principal debt were fully repaid or whether they should only be granted for two years in accordance with existing supply policy in the Irish Parliament. The argument against an open-ended terminal date for the appropriated supplies was tied in with the fear that any move away from the established two-year duration of Supply Acts might open up an avenue for the government to avoid convening Parliament biennially. It was therefore not surprising that the matter occasioned 'a long debate', during which the CWHWM voted 93 to 90 in favour of retaining the 4s. in the pound tax on absentee salaries and pensions and 97 to 93 in favour of only a two-year duration for the proposed new debt repayment additional duties on wine, brandy, and manufactured silks. It was this latter division which in particular annoyed Carteret because he believed it was 'a breach of faith' by some MPs who had voted for the two-year duration despite having previously promised to support an open-ended terminal date. Coghill acknowledged that 'the opposition was a surprise to us, and we are a little mortified at the defeat'. Yet he pointed out that the key requirement of 'ascertaining the debt and getting an interest for it' had been achieved, despite many MPs having seemed opposed to it 'at the beginning of the session'. As for the 4s. in the pound tax on absentee salaries and pensions, despite the refusal to excuse those who sat as MPs in Westminster, a series of important exclusions had been agreed which it was believed would greatly lessen the impact of the tax.[67] Ultimately, however, the divisions in the CWHWM had demonstrated that even though the government was able to mobilise strong numbers in attempting to challenge the Commons' long-held key constitutional principle of only voting two-year durations on additional duties, not all MPs who were ostensibly government supporters were prepared to turn their backs on such strongly held beliefs.[68]

Coghill reported the CWHWM's resolutions to the House on 13 November. First, it was resolved that all of the existing additional parliamentary duties granted to the government on a biennial basis should be re-granted for a further two years. These comprised the key additional rates, duties, and impositions upon beer, ale, strong waters, wine, spirits, tobacco, and a range of lesser goods and merchandises, all of which were about to expire, but now were to be renewed to 25 December 1731 inclusive. Likewise, the long-standing appropriation of 6d. in the pound and all other fees payable to the Vice-Treasurer on the collection of parliamentary taxes was to be renewed for a further two years. The remaining resolutions covered the crucial introduction of new taxes. To that end, a further two-year additional duty of 13s. per ton was to be imposed on Portuguese wine and 40s. per ton on all other wines, and a further additional duty of 4d. per gallon on all strong waters, brandy, and spirits. The final new additional duty was to be 2s. 6d. per pound weight on all imported silk manufactures, excepting those of China, Persia, and the East Indies.[69]

There was some debate on the CWHWM resolutions. The key issue seems to have been the duration of the 4s. in the pound tax on absentee salaries and pensions, which was amended by the House to two years in line with all the other duties. This suggests it had come from the CWHWM with an open-ended terminal date, or that its duration had been overlooked or left unclear.[70] The Commons then ordered that the heads of the supply bills be drafted and appointed a select committee for the purpose, with Coghill in the chair. A second order was then agreed that the drafting committee be instructed to insert clauses for the 4s. tax and the several new additional duties to be applied to pay interest at 6 per cent on a principal debt of £200,000 and towards the discharge of that principal, thereby putting in place the facility for the creation of a sinking fund. Clauses were also to be inserted that the debentures to be drawn up for payment of the principal sum were to be made assignable, with registration of assignments being made in the Vice-Treasurer's office without paying any fees thereon.[71] This was the first explicit mention of the intention to increase the principal sum of the national debt from £50,000 to £200,000, which in practical terms meant a new Parliament-sanctioned and secured loan to the government of £150,000, representing a fourfold increase in the national debt. However, it was apparent that an understanding to that effect had been in place for quite some time, and Parliament was now putting in place the legal infrastructure to make it happen.

Coghill recounted the events of 13 November in a letter to Edward Southwell written later that same day. He signed off by noting he had 'enclosed ... a book of Swift's'.[72] It seems most likely that this was *A Modest Proposal for Preventing the Children of the Poor from Being a Burden to Their Parents or Country; and for Making Them Beneficial to the Publick* and suggests that it had just been published, given Coghill's tendency to send to England any such works as soon as they were produced. As Louis Cullen has argued, Swift's *Modest Proposal* was clearly printed with a view to influencing events in Parliament in the same manner as Prior's earlier pamphlet.[73] This was most particularly evident in respect of the crucial section, purposefully printed in italics towards the end of the pamphlet, where Swift reiterated all of the key Patriot concerns that he had itemised repeatedly through the 1720s, though ostensibly on this occasion dismissing them as pointless:

> Therefore let no Man talk to me of other Expedients: *Of taxing our Absentees at five Shillings a Pound: Of using neither Cloaths, nor Household Furniture; except what is of our own Growth and Manufacture: Of utterly rejecting the Materials and Instruments that promote foreign Luxury: Of curing the Expensiveness of Pride, Vanity, Idleness, and Gaming in our Women: Of introducing a Vein of Parsimony, Prudence and Temperance: Of learning to love our Country ... Of quitting our Animosities, and Factions ... Of being a little*

> *cautious not to sell our Country and Consciences for nothing: Of teaching Landlords to have, at least, one Degree of Mercy towards their Tenants. Lastly, Of putting a spirit of Honesty, Industry and Skill into our Shop-keepers.*

Swift then immediately re-emphasised the central importance of these concerns by stating: 'Therefore I repeat; let no Man talk to me of these and the like Expedients; till he hath, at least, a Glimpse of Hope, that there will ever be some hearty and sincere Attempt to put them in Practice.'[74]

There was no mention in *A Modest Proposal* of the plans for increasing the national debt or of imposing new taxes, though Sean Moore has suggested the pamphlet can be read as an allegory for Ireland being consumed by that debt.[75] Such arguments aside, the 'expedient' 'Of being a little cautious not to sell our Country and Consciences for nothing' certainly suggested that Swift was at least admonishing MPs for being too willing to vote for an increase in the national debt and to impose new taxation. He had previously taken issue with MPs for selling their votes by siding with the government in Parliament in return for patronage[76] and would do so again in the 1731 poem, 'Verses on the Death of Dr Swift', in which he accused MPs of selling their 'souls and votes' in order to strip the country of its wealth.[77]

There is no evidence of the immediate effect *A Modest Proposal* had, though both Moore and Cullen believe it impacted upon MPs who were cognisant of its political purpose.[78] But it certainly seemed the case that the continuing challenges the government faced in November and December over the supply process was in part a result of the endeavours of Swift, Prior, and others to keep such matters in the minds of MPs.

The next stage of the supply process awaited the presentation of the two heads of bills, which occurred on 15 November. The first, or 'grand money bill' as it was known, was for granting and continuing the additional duties on beer, ale, strong waters, wine, tobacco, and several other goods and merchandises. The second, or loan bill, was for granting the further additional duties on wine, strong waters, brandy, and spirits, and the tax of 4s. in the pound on absentee salaries and pensions, all of which were to be applied to pay the 6 per cent interest on the principal debt of £200,000 and towards the discharge of the principal. Both heads of bills were received, read, and referred to Committees of the Whole House (CWH).[79]

The CWH considered the grand money bill on 17 November and agreed to it without amendment. The bill was then read again and sent to the Lord Lieutenant for transmission to London. The loan bill went before the CWH on 18 November, when several amendments were made. The following day, the bill was sent to the Lord Lieutenant as well.[80] There is no record of what amendments were made, though the absence of discussion of them in any correspondence suggests they were minor.

On receipt of the two bills, Carteret set in motion the process of engrossing them for transmission to London in accordance with Poynings' Law. He informed the Duke of Newcastle that by 'the said bills the Establishment here will be put in a better condition than it has been for several years last past'.[81] For Carteret and other government officials, the point had now been reached where they felt that 'the king's business' in Parliament was completed.[82] Yet all reflected that it had not been easy, especially in light of Conolly's death. Carteret's Chief Secretary, Thomas Clutterbuck, acknowledged that they had been involved in a 'good deal of wrangling' to get the heads of the two supply bills agreed. However, his only remaining concern, though a prescient one, was that 'the manner in which it is done' might be 'disapproved of' in London.[83]

Boulter, likewise, hoped that Coghill and Gore 'will by degrees get together the friends of Mr Conolly, and others well-disposed to join heartily in his Majesty's service. But this is more than they will be able to effect this session.' The King's business, although now done, had 'met with great rubs and delays, and has been done with an ill grace'. However, in reflecting on the loan bill, Boulter was the first to highlight the important innovation introduced into the system for managing the national debt: '[It] is made up of several little taxes, by which it is proposed to pay the interest of 6 per cent. for £200,000 of our debts for two years; and if more is raised by it than £12,000 per ann. to sink part of the principal.' As already highlighted, the introduction of the concept of a sinking fund was a wholly new idea, and as Boulter pointed out, 'it was attempted to give this fund till the debt was sunk; but it was rejected by a majority of five voices. There was afterwards a motion made, that it should be inserted in the bill, that at the end of two years, either the principal should be repaid, or the interest continued. But this was opposed and dropped; though it was declared to be the sense of the House.'[84] This latter decision not to include some sort of general promise within the bill for the continued payment of interest to public creditors beyond the two-year duration of the additional duties was in fact out of sync with all previous loan legislation since 1716, which had always imposed an obligation upon Parliament to renew the legislation every two years for continued interest payments until such unknown date in the future when the principal would be fully repaid.[85] This omission in the heads of the bill would prove problematic when it was sent to London. As for the raising of the new loan of £150,000 on the basis of the bill, Carteret confidently reported that 'the money is all ready here, to be advanced upon the passing of them'.[86]

At around this point in time, Swift commenced writing *A Proposal that all the Ladies and Women of Ireland should Appear Constantly in Irish Manufactures*. Herbert Davis has suggested Swift started the piece after the publication on 29 November in the *Old Dublin Intelligence* of a report that the heads of the loan bill had recently been agreed in the Commons and left it unfinished and unpublished when the bill passed in Parliament on 22 December.[87] It is possible, however, that Swift started it a bit earlier in mid-November, given his reflections on the bill and the national debt. Swift noted that 'our national debt (and God knows how we wretches came by that fashionable thing a national debt) is about 250,000 l.', and that 'there are several schemes for raising a fund to pay the interest of this formidable sum, (not the principal, for this is allowed impossible)', one of which was the additional duty of 40s. per ton of wine.[88] These reflections suggest Swift was responding to the resolutions in the CWHWM on 13 November and the ensuing procedure on drafting the heads of the loan bill in the period 14–18 November, and that he was once again looking to stoke opposition.

To that end, he questioned the need 'to raise such a fund' in the first place, dismissing the arguments 'regularly and strongly pleaded' about existing deficiencies in customs and excise income: 'is it the fault of Ireland that these funds are deficient? If they depend on trade, can it possibly be otherwise, while we have neither liberty to trade, nor money to trade with; neither hands to work, nor business to employ them, if we had? Our diseases are visible enough, both in their causes and effects; and the cures are well known, but impossible to be applied.'[89] Swift then listed a hotchpotch of seemingly random and at times specious arguments against the proposed increased duty on wine, which prompted Irvin Ehrenpreis to argue that the primary reason for the pamphlet was Swift's love of cheap French wine.[90] However, Swift thereafter returned to more serious matters. Having dismissed the duty on wine as unviable, he claimed it was not his responsibility to come up with other solutions: 'I am not under the least concern about paying the interest on the national debt, but leave it, as in loyalty bound, wholly to the wisdom of the Honourable House of Commons.' He then immediately offered the core Patriot solutions to the issue: 'to lessen the importation of all unnecessary commodities ... to persuade our absentees to spend their money at home ... or tax them at five shillings in the pound during their absence ... or by permitting us a free trade'. He then rightly pointed out that 'the three last methods are treated by Mr. Prior, in his most useful treatise, added to his list of absentees'.[91]

While Swift was working on the pamphlet, the supply process continued apace in Parliament. The two supply bills were quickly dispatched to England on 20 November, as the clock was ticking in terms of the grand money bill being enacted in time to prevent any lapse in the additional duties voted two years earlier. Their importance was such that two separate messengers were sent, each with copies of both bills, one via Holyhead and the other via Chester.[92]

The National Debt Endangered and Secured, 1729–30

At least one set of the two supply bills had arrived in London by 25 November, when the English Privy Council referred the two bills to the Attorney and Solicitor General and the committee on Irish bills was appointed. On 28–29 November, the grand money bill was reported on, agreed to, and passed under the Great Seal without amendment, and a commission for granting of the royal assent was prepared.[93] However, on 1 December, the law officers recommended a series of amendments to the loan bill. In part, this was the result of a petition by English silk manufacturers against the additional duties on silk goods. While many of the amendments were owing primarily to minor errors arising from the haste with which the bill was originally drawn up, there were also three major changes. The first replaced the restricted provision for interest payments 'for two years commencing' from December 1729 and, instead, re-introduced wording that stated that the public creditors would continue to receive interest payments 'until such time as they be respectively paid their principal at one entire payment'. The second involved the inclusion of Britain among those countries excepted from the additional silk duties. The third was aimed at making the theoretical sinking fund more practicable by including a clarifying phrase which stated that any surplus would be applied 'in such order and manner, as by an act or acts of Parliament hereafter to be made shall be directed and provided, and to no other use, intent, or purpose whatever'. The bill was agreed with these amendments on 2 December, passed under the Great Seal, and dispatched back to Ireland with the grand money bill on 4 December.[94]

The amendments made to the loan bill were to create significant problems for the Irish government. Any amendments made in London to supply bills, however small, always provoked discontent on their return to Ireland over the issue of Poynings' Law, the Crown's prerogative powers, and the role of the Privy Councils in the legislative process. Ever since the 'sole right' crisis of 1692, the Irish Commons had made clear its view that the English and Irish Privy Councils had no role in the drafting of supply legislation and thereby that Poynings' Law and the Crown's prerogative powers did not extend to amending Irish supply legislation. On the few occasions when amendments had been made in London since the 1695 compromise on the question, government managers had had to go to great lengths to get the returned supply bills through the Commons.[95] It was therefore no surprise that Carteret and the government party more generally were very animated in their views as news of the amendments began to filter into Ireland.

It was evident that in expectation of the loan bill being passed, the £150,000 loan was already being subscribed to in Dublin in late November and early December. There were more than enough willing public creditors to hand, as Carteret pointed out when he first heard news of the amendments on 9 December. He wondered why the English Privy Council would jeopardise the loan, given that the bill sent over to London 'would have answered all the purposes of raising the money; the lenders of which here liked the security; and I have had more ready money offered here in the last fortnight, by fifty thousand pounds than can be taken, [supposing] the bill should pass'. He was particularly annoyed that all his hard work in 'inducing them to give, and to provide for more money, than ever was done at one time; and when the country by loss of trade, and bad harvests for the three preceding years, to the last, has been much exhausted … was not appreciated'. With regard to the exclusion of Britain from the additional silk duties, Carteret felt that the 'weavers in England are oftener tumultuous, than well-informed', a failing he also applied to the Dublin weavers. This ongoing economic competition between Irish and English manufacturers would ensure that the silk duties amendment would be seen as English interference once again in Irish concerns, much like the case of the woollen industry since the 1690s. With the Irish Parliament looking to promote the greatly improved native silk manufacture industry, few English imports came to Ireland anyway, and those that did were still outdone by the top-class French imports 'which the rich and extravagant people here affect [favour]'. As for the amendment regarding the public creditors, Carteret agreed it was 'doubtless highly just and reasonable', but he had already unsuccessfully tried to get that through the Commons, and despite the House declaring that it was 'their unanimous intention' that interest payments to public creditors would always be provided for until their whole principal sum was repaid, they 'insisted that it was sufficiently to be understood from the scope of the bill' as drafted. Carteret had therefore felt it imprudent 'to risk a question upon that matter, since my friends told me they were not sure of carrying it, and if we had lost it, the whole scheme had been defeated'. The key security for the future, Carteret argued, was the fact 'the debentures [are] ... entirely in their own hands' and were already valued at 'now near 2 per cent above par'.[96]

Following the arrival in Dublin of the amended loan bill, government concerns grew further. On 14 December, Carteret reported that people were 'so much out of humour' at the news. 'I have talked today with near fifty of the principal members. They seem to acquiesce as to the alteration with relation to the silk ... but as to the other alterations which tend to make the bill more accurate I can't as yet persuade them to be satisfied', especially with regard to the removal of the stipulated two-year duration for interest repayments: 'it is upon this, our difficulty here now turns'. Emphasising to London that their amendments had seriously endangered the required supply, Carteret once again bemoaned the changes, given that already 'above £50,000 has been subscribed to this loan, more than can be received', and that the Irish Treasury therefore would have been able 'to remit £40,000 to the pay office in England in the month of January' for the Irish regiments in Gibraltar. But if the bill was rejected, it would prove 'very difficult to find any way, by which the large arrear due to England upon account of the absent regiments, may be cleared'.[97]

The alterations to the second supply bill also had political connotations for government supporters in Ireland. Clutterbuck acknowledged that the changes were reasonable, and that the King had the prerogative power and right to make them, but he was still of the view that they would 'give us a great deal of trouble here. It is a difficulty laid upon the king's servants, who I can assure you had enough before.' There was no doubt they would all support the amended bill and the rights of the Crown in Parliament, 'but the bill as it went [to London], would have raised the money, for the subscription was full: I don't apprehend it will do more now'. He therefore wondered whether the true reason for the changes was 'a want of power in the [Irish] government and however well satisfied my Lord Lieutenant may be under that want, those who expect to be obliged by him will not be so'. From Clutterbuck's perspective, 'tis a very indifferent situation to serve under a governor that has neither power, nor party, to support it, but it is left at the mercy of a Parliament'. As had been the case in 1724 when Carteret was first sent to Ireland, the suspicion was that the infighting of English party-politics was the real cause of the changes, as once again Carteret's English enemies looked to undermine his reputation by causing him to fail in Ireland.[98]

The constitutional arguments were addressed by Boulter. Echoing others who had raised the fact that the alterations had put 'the Commons and several others without doors … in a great heat', he remarked how 'the point insisted upon is, that no alterations whatsoever shall be made either in the English or Irish Council to a money bill'. For Boulter, as the strongest supporter of the 'English interest' in Irish politics at that time, 'it is certain the law here is against these warm men, and so are the precedents'. He hoped that the majority of MPs would be 'sensible of the bad consequences of rejecting that bill, which will run this nation much deeper into debt, and may end in a dissolution'. Yet even if sense prevailed, he feared 'much heat and opposition' on the way.[99]

Reaction in London to the news of pending conflict in the Irish Parliament over the amendments was either disingenuous or naïve. Newcastle, one of the English Secretaries of State, informed Carteret that George II was surprised at the uneasiness of people in Ireland. Newcastle had not been at the Council when 'this matter was debated, but [I] have been assured by the lords who were present, that the only reason for altering the bill in the manner it was done was to make it consistent, and that all those who had advanced their money to supply the exigencies of his Majesty's government might have an equal security for their interest till the principal were repaid them'.[100]

Such an argument was of course acknowledged by all as a reasonable proposition. However, in light of the long-known history of the Irish Parliament's opposition to amendments being made in London to supply bills, and the many detailed accounts previously sent to Newcastle and others in London of the debates in the Commons on the supply process, what he next claimed rang very hollow. According to Newcastle, 'if the Privy Council, or his Majesty's servants, especially those employed in the management of his revenue, had been informed of the several steps taken in passing this bill' in Ireland, 'and that the substance of the most essential of these alterations had been proposed there, but they would not receive it', then the Council 'would have advised the sending it back as it came, how[ever] incorrect ... it might appear'. Such after-the-fact hypothesising served no value and seemed po-faced at best. Likewise, it was little solace to Carteret and others that George II and his English minsters were 'persuaded' that the Irish Parliament 'will not on account of these amendments reject a bill that appears to be so necessary, not only for supporting the honour of the government, but for the satisfaction and security of those who have already lent their money or are willing to advance further sums for the public service, upon parliamentary credit'.[101] The crux of the matter was of course, as Newcastle inadvertently admitted, that there were already more than enough people in Ireland who had subscribed to the new loan, demonstrating the existence of a viable community of public creditors willing and able to lend money to the government on the basis of the parliamentary security offered in the original draft of the bill.[102] And the reality was that, however much they might deny it, the British Privy Council had put it all at risk.

The views expressed by one of Newcastle's Under-Secretaries, Charles Delafaye, seemed even more disingenuous, given his background. Delafaye not only was a regular recipient of reports on Irish parliamentary affairs but had also served as joint Chief Secretary in Dublin from 1715 to 1717 and sat as an MP in the Irish Commons during that time. He knew first-hand the extreme lengths the government could be made to go to on supply bills in particular, and the very sensitive nature of the constitutional issues surrounding the 1692 'sole right' claim, the 1695 compromise, and the developed precedents and practices thereafter. He knew that to diverge from those practices and precedents was a dangerous undertaking.[103] Yet he was seemingly astonished that the amendments 'have raised such a ferment, for they make no alteration as to the intention of it, nor to the supplies or the term for which they are given'. He argued that Parliament would still have to meet every two years to enact legislation to pay the interest, so that all they were now doing was committing to doing so until such unknown point in the future when the principal sums would be fully repaid. Therefore, he saw no reason for the Commons to fear that 'future sessions of Parliament should become less necessary, which can be the only motive of all this bustle'.[104] As an ex-Chief Secretary, he surely knew that such apparent logic was not pertinent when such sensitive constitutional questions were raised in Ireland. Any perceived divergence from agreed principals was likely to provoke discord, no matter how logical the reason for divergence might appear in London.

However, it was also the case that Delafaye had a personal interest in the matter, as he was one of the 63 public creditors for the original £50,000 loan to government secured from Parliament in 1715–1716. Therefore, a personal desire for greater security for interest payments may have lain behind his berating of Clutterbuck with the view that 'the gentlemen of Ireland would not have it imagined that they should intend to draw people in to lend their money, pay two years interest and then drop the creditors without so much as a promise of the payment of any further interest or of the principal'.[105]

The various views and opinions put forward on both sides of the water were finally tested when the two returned bills came before the Commons in mid-December. The grand money bill was presented on 15 December and proceeded unhindered over the next three days through two readings, a CWH, the engrossment process, and then a third reading, before being dispatched to the Lords for their concurrence. However, at the outset of the process on 15 December, a select committee of inquiry was appointed for the purpose of examining what alterations had been made in the heads of bills sent from the House so far that session, 'and where the same have been so made'. It was significant that the first MPs named to this committee, Eaton Stannard and Richard Bettesworth, would turn out to be the main advocates for rejecting the amended loan bill, which was presented on 16 December. It proceeded unmolested through two readings before being referred to a CWH for 19 December. In advance of the CWH, Stannard reported from the committee of inquiry on the amendments made to the bill.[106] The scene was now set—the showdown would be in the CWH.

As reported by Coghill, the debate in the CWH on 19 December lasted 'near three hours'.[107] Boulter suggested it was more than four hours.[108] Either way, the opponents of the bill did not give up easily. Bettesworth opened proceedings by arguing about the 'ill consequences of passing any money bill that was altered, which might be drawn into a precedent, to prolong or increase our taxes as the crown is pleased'. As was to be expected, this 'brought on the debate of Poynings' Law, and the power and prerogative of the King and Council, the precedents of money bills altered, [and] the reasons of altering this bill'. It was evident the key focus of the opposition was the open-ended provision for interest payments, and the leverage this gave them for raising the associated underlying fear among many MPs that this was the British government's first stage in a policy ultimately aimed at the imposition of open-ended durations for all parliamentary taxes, which in turn would remove the need for regular parliamentary sessions. As a result, they showed little to no interest in debating the amendment relating to the silk duties, as it did not impact upon the duration of those taxes. Those who spoke in favour of the amended bill focused on the loss of revenue to the government (projected at about £17,000 a year) and the knock-on effect in terms of a further escalation in the government's very substantial pay arrears, a further increase in the existing national debt through unpaid interest and, for many, the greatest threat of all, the 'danger of a land tax' in the future to resolve these issues. It was also pointed out that rejection would do 'injury ... to those who had advanced the £50,000' principal of the national debt back in 1716, who were entitled to continued interest payments, and to those who had already subscribed to the new loan of £150,000, 'who could have no interest for two years, which was the highest injustice to those who had advanced their money on the public credit'.[109]

Bettesworth also took up the issue of the amendment to the sinking fund clause, arguing that

> the appropriating clause was ineffectual, for if the King should refuse an act of Parliament for the application of the surplusage it could not be disposed of as was intended by the transmitted bill. This was so absurd, that no other answer was given to it, but that it might as well be expected that the King would send a regiment of dragoons to take the money out of the Treasury as return such a bill, for as the bill was worded the vice treasurer could not pay it upon any warrant or order of the King's, so that it must lie in his hands till dispersed of by Parliament.

Infuriated at the lack of response to his argument, Bettesworth claimed that the bill was 'to be crammed down their throats by power'. Not surprisingly, Stannard also spoke against the bill, as did Patrick French, John Osborne, Vesey, and Carter. Those who spoke for the bill included Charles Coote, Robert Lindsay, Arthur Hill, Robert French, Robert Cope, and, much to the government's surprise, Robert Allen. It was notable that despite the length of the debate, the government felt the disposition of the House was so evidently for passing the bill that senior government MPs such as Henry Maxwell, Henry Singleton, and Thomas Trotter were not called upon to speak. Instead, it was 'thought ... better that the debate should be carried on by those who were not in the service of the crown'. The CWH ultimately divided in favour of the bill 'by a great majority [of] 124 to 62'. It was of great significance for the government that old Augustan Tories like Cope, as well as the likes of Coote and Allen who had both been deemed likely troublemakers earlier in the session, and unattached younger MPs, were all convinced to speak in favour of the bill. It was also pleasing to the government that Henry Boyle, the leader of the opposition grouping in the Commons, had put 'all his power against' the bill without success.[110]

Even after their defeat in the CWH, however, the opposition did not give up the fight, though only a small hard-core grouping continued to try to hinder the final progress of the bill. Following the report from the CWH, the House divided 99 to 27 in favour of the motion for engrossing the bill. The next day, they took the bill to two more divisions: the first on the motion for a third reading, which was carried 75 to 14; the second on the motion for the bill to pass the third reading, which was agreed 95 to 21. With all options for rejection exhausted, the government had secured their victory and the bill was dispatched to the Lords for concurrence.[111]

However, it was a hard-won victory despite the imbalance in the divisions. Carteret and his key government supporters had had to work extremely hard to win over the middle ground MPs. Boulter was convinced that 'if the debate had come on before there had been time to talk with the members, the bill had been lost, the warmth against the alterations at first was so great'.[112] The government's strategy in this respect was later explained by Coghill, who confirmed that the returned bill had been withheld from the Commons 'from Friday till Tuesday' in order to allow Carteret and his leading supporters the time to 'prepare against the attacks of his enemies ... to prevent the blow at first intended', and to explain to MPs 'the reason for it, and the ill consequences of rejecting it together with the utmost diligence to apprise young members of the nature and force of Poynings' Law'. Without such time to lobby MPs, Coghill felt sure the bill would have failed[113] and ascribed the government's success to the hard work and effort put in during those four or five days by 'everybody who is in the service of the crown', including Carteret, who 'has been indefatigable'.[114]

But there were also other, possibly more self-interested reasons why MPs voted for the bill. Boulter was of the view that their majority would not have been so large had MPs not genuinely feared a dissolution of Parliament if the bill was rejected, 'as the greatest part of our Commons are not willing to be at the expense of a new election'.[115] Coghill was in agreement with that view but also posited that other MPs voted for it because they 'had shares in the £50,000 and £150,000 loans', and so wanted 'their security ... made effectual both for principal and interest'. At the same time, he felt 'the sober considerate part of the House voted for the bill upon the true principle of the ill consequences the rejecting of it would be, and that the amendments were honest and just, and were so far from being prejudicial, that we should have done that ourselves, which was done for us'. Ultimately, the government's success, and Carteret's role in it, led Coghill to surmise that it might 'be a disappointment to some who don't wish him well', harking back once again to the belief that the amendments were at least in part motivated by party-political factionalism in London.[116]

For his part, Boulter now viewed 'the king's business' in Parliament to be finished, though he wished 'it had been done with a better grace'. Even still, he considered the final outcome to be a good result, 'considering that the greatest part of the debts of the nation is put in a method of payment, which will certainly be pursued the next session'.[117]

The Lords were not slow in confirming Boulter's views. On 22 December, the Upper House notified the Commons of their concurrence with both supply bills and Carteret attended Parliament immediately to give them the royal assent.[118] The passage of the bills in the Lords had as usual been smooth, despite surprise arising at Marcus Beresford, Viscount Tyrone, giving 'his single negative remarkably loud against' the loan bill.[119] For Carteret, the two bills meant that 'His Majesty's Establishment is put in a better condition, than it has been in for some years', and he believed the remainder of the session would be quiet from a government perspective.[120]

The granting of the royal assent always presented an opportunity for the Speaker of the Commons to hold forth on key issues. Gore obliged, pointing out that the Commons had recognised that 'the nation' was at that time 'in very difficult circumstances, the calamities of the times, which no human wisdom could prevent or remedy', having 'occasioned a great deficiency in the revenue, and thereby a considerable arrear on the Establishment; and these calamities which had been the principle cause of the great increase of the national debt, made it more difficult to find proper and effectual means to discharge it'. Yet as 'great as these difficulties were', the Commons, 'with cheerfulness and unanimity, resolved to use their utmost endeavours to surmount them', and, as previously desired by the King, 'in such manner as might be most expedient, and least burdensome to the people'. Here then was the official justification once again for increasing the principal of the national debt fourfold from £50,000 to £200,000. For Gore and the Commons, in so doing, they had 'given larger supplies than ever were granted in any former session'.[121]

The importance of the passing of the loan bill was seen within days. On 2 January 1730, Carteret reported that the deputy Vice-Treasurer had paid £40,000 to the bank of Henry and Burton for transmission to the pay office in London 'in part of the arrear due to England on account of the absent [Irish Establishment] regiments [in Gibraltar]'.[122]

The Ascendancy of the National Debt, 1730–32

During the series of adjournments in the early new year, when Parliament was in hiatus awaiting the return of bills from London, Swift once again looked to stoke the fires of discontent. On 3 February, Coghill recorded that the previous night a poem of Swift's had been 'publicly cried about the streets' of Dublin. Coghill felt it was worth reading, 'though I think very improper to be published'.[123] The poem, entitled *A Libel on D[octor] D[elany] and a Certain Great Lord*, was a satire on an earlier poem by Swift's friend and fellow clergyman, Patrick Delany, which had been addressed to Carteret and had pleaded for further preferment.[124] But Swift did not forgo the opportunity to take the government and Parliament to task once again, particularly in respect of Carteret's role as Lord Lieutenant:

> ... submitting still
> To W[alpole]'s more than R[oya]l Will.
> And what Condition can be worse?
> He comes to *drain a Beggar's Purse*:
> He comes to tie our Chains on faster,
> And show us E[ngland] is our Master:
> Caressing Knaves, and Dunces wooing,
> To make them work their own undoing.[125]

England's leading minister, Sir Robert Walpole, was thus abused for being overly powerful and dominating the King, while Carteret was admonished for continuing to serve his political enemies in Walpole's ministry. But it was the harsh reflections on the government's financial demands at a time of socio-economic crisis in Ireland and on the culpability of Irish MPS—

'Knaves and Dunces'—in that regard by agreeing to vote increased taxes and a fourfold increase in the national debt, coupled with yet another attack on England's economic policies towards Ireland, that were probably the most provocative elements of the poem.

The extent to which Swift genuinely believed these sentiments can be seen in his private correspondence shortly after the session concluded. On informing Edward Harley, Earl of Oxford, that Carteret had left Ireland, he echoed the language of the poem when he stated that the Viceroy had performed with great 'merit', at least in terms of what in Swift's opinion the London government desired, which was 'to put on more chains, [and] to get more money, wherein none of his predecessors ever equalled him, nor met with more stupid, slavish, complying beasts to manage'.[126]

Swift added further fuel to the fire later in the poem, again attacking the office of the Irish Chief Governor and English policy towards Ireland:

> So, to effect his *M*[onarc]*h*'s ends,
> From *Hell* a *V*[iceroy] Devil ascends,
> His *Budget*[127] with *Corruptions* crammed,
> The Contributions of the *damned*;
> Which, with unsparing Hand, he strows[128]
> Through *Courts*, and *Senates* as he goes;
> And then at *Beelzebub's Black-Hall*,
> Complains, his *Budget* was too small.[129]

Here, Swift portrayed Whitehall (Black-Hall) as Hell (and presumably Walpole as Beelzebub) from whence devil Viceroys were sent to Ireland to bribe, corrupt, and undermine both the law and Parliament. This was harsh indeed.

It was therefore unsurprising that the poem remained on the table in Parliament during February, with some members pressing for prosecution and others for a parliamentary censure. Joshua, Viscount Allen, was to the forefront of such endeavours. Having become infuriated by the concurrent machinations of Swift, Delany, and others to get Dublin Corporation to present Swift with the Freedom of the City in a gold box with a highly provocative inscription,[130] Allen had exclaimed at a meeting of the Privy Council with the members of Dublin Corporation on 13 February that Swift 'neither feared God nor honoured the King' and that, in what was evidently a reference to the poem, he had penned 'a libel on the King, Queen and the Government'. Allen's outburst put an end to the plans for the inscription and put the gold box itself on hold for several more months.[131]

With regard to *A Libel*, however, Allen's wish for a prosecution did not materialise. Coghill felt it wiser to let the issue 'fall without taking notice of it, and it will then die of itself, whereas a prosecution either in the courts, or by censure of Parliament will make it more public, and raise the curiosity of people to read and disperse it more than otherwise they would do'.[132] It seemed most others in Parliament were of the same view, as nothing more arose thereafter on the issue, and Swift remained quiet until the end of the session, though he did not forget Allen's spoiling of the plan for the gold box inscription.[133]

When Parliament finally reconvened for business in March, there was one final showdown over the Loan Act. The act included a clause to allow warrants for army pay and clothing arrears to be exchanged at the Treasury for interest-bearing debentures, thereby transforming the unpaid arrears into secured government debt. In reality, the officers, bankers, and others who held the warrants for such arrears had advanced their own money in payment to the soldiers or the clothiers, and so the government's unfunded debts owed to these individuals and groups were transformed into a parliament-funded and secured interest-bearing national debt without any money actually being paid into the Treasury by these new public creditors. Nor was it surprising that the warrants for such arrears had already gained a currency in Ireland in the same manner that various other paper credit instruments had in light of the shortages of ready specie.[134] The problem was the sheer number of these warrants that were in circulation, and the many owners who wished to exchange them for interest-bearing debentures, because, in reality, the government needed a large percentage of the loan to be subscribed in coin, including the £40,000 sent to London in January for the pay of the Gibraltar regiments. As a result, not all of the warrants could be taken into the Treasury. Politics also had a role to play, as MPs who had toed the government line in Parliament also needed to be pandered to.

These two different priorities came into conflict when one potential subscriber, a 'Mr Vesey' (probably the opposition MP Agmondisham Vesey[135]), a partner in James Swift's private bank,[136] tried to subscribe £2,000 in ready money but was refused on the grounds that warrants for arrears had to be prioritised. He then attempted to subscribe some clothing warrants but was refused on the grounds that his warrants were still 'in course of payment, and not due'. Vesey threatened to make an official complaint that the act was not being executed properly, as he knew others had already been allowed to subscribe ready money while there were still many warrants for arrears that had not been exchanged for debentures. Vesey was indeed correct in his accusation, though the government argued that the act could not be executed according to the letter of the law, in part because there were too many warrants 'in such small sums, to some ten pounds odd money, and other small sums with [fractions], that it was impossible to make out debentures to answer them all with their interest, without great difficulty and infinite number of such debentures'. At the same time, Carteret had, for political reasons, taken ready money subscriptions 'from about fifty Parliament men, and several others whom he had a mind to gratify'.[137]

The Lord Lieutenant also managed to prevail on Vesey to drop his complaint, but on 16 March the opposition revived the issue in the Commons. Hugh Dixon (aka Dickson), who had been a 'zealous Patriot' during the session, put forward a motion, which was seconded by Caesar Colclough, another noted MP of the Patriot ilk, for a full list of the subscribers to the loan to be laid before the House.[138] The list was laid before the Commons on 18 March, and showed that to that point in time £51,600 had been subscribed in warrants for pay and clothing arrears, while £90,000 had been subscribed in 'ready money'.[139] However, it was not until 13 April, as the session drew to a close, that Colclough tried to turn attention back to the list, though he was temporarily thwarted by a motion to adjourn for two days, which was passed by 65 to 31.[140]

When the Commons reconvened on what was the last day of the session—15 April—MPs were distracted by emerging disagreements with the Lords over proposals regarding the values of various gold and silver coins, which had been an ongoing discussion throughout the session. However, Colclough persisted in trying to use the debentures issue as a means of attacking the government. Other MPs—described tongue-in-cheek by Coghill as 'the great patriots for the good of the country'—including Dixon, Price Hartstonge, John Waller, Maurice Keating, and Sir Walter Dixon Borrowes, joined Colclough in trying to get a vote or an address passed in the House for 'punishing great men and officers for an illegal execution of the act in taking in the subscriptions'. It was of note that on this occasion the opposition 'were not supported by their friend Stannard', and their plans were ultimately undone when the Commons were called to the Lords later that day for the close of the session.[141]

As a leading light among the opposition and a protégé of Swift, Stannard's non-engagement with the debentures issue suggested that the battle was well and truly over, and the war had been lost a long time back. The government's victory was confirmed in Carteret's closing speech, when he made specific reference to the new government loan, and directed his thanks explicitly at the Lower House: 'Gentlemen of the House of Commons, I am commanded by His Majesty to return you thanks for the supplies you have granted for the support of the Establishment, and for making so effectual a provision for the national debt.' He also highlighted the fact that the interest rate on the whole principal debt had been reduced 'with a due regard to parliamentary credit, and [in order] to raise the money which the public service required at an easier rate than hath hitherto been known in this kingdom'.[142] The fact that the Loan Act had reduced the interest rate to 6 per cent, which was 1 per cent below the legal limit, further demonstrated how popular government debentures were.[143]

These final episodes in the story of the 1729 Loan Act are highly revealing. First and foremost, MPs and many others were extremely keen to loan money to the government, to the extent that agreeing to take subscriptions from people was used as a form of patronage and a means of ensuring MPs toed the line in Parliament. The obvious reason was because the interest payments were secured on parliamentary taxes, and repayment of the principal sum was likewise provided for. There could be no more certain investment and return for an individual's money, with very little chance of default. Indeed, the amendments made in London had actually increased that security in respect of interest repayments and provision of a sinking fund for the principal. It had been Irish constitutional sensibilities that had threatened to undermine such further security, though the extent to which British factional politics had threatened to plunge Irish finances into crisis should not be underestimated either. Likewise, the ability to reduce the interest rate on the debt without impacting negatively upon the number of willing public creditors was revealing.

Yet the support for expanding the government debt was not wholly unanimous. And not surprisingly, Swift looked to have the final word. As soon as Carteret left the Lords on the final day of the session, a new piece by Swift was 'cried about' the streets of Dublin. *A Vindication of His Excellency the Lord Carteret, from the Charge of Favouring None but Tories, High-Church-men, and Jacobites* purported to demonstrate that Irish Tories had not been preferred by Carteret during his term of office but also took the opportunity to make fun of both Richard Tighe and Lord Allen.[144] Yet oblique reference was once again made to events in Parliament regarding the process of supply and the increase of the national debt, as Swift argued that Carteret was surely entitled to some respite from 'Mornings spent in hearing and prescribing *Ways and Means* from and to his *most obedient* Politicians, for the Welfare of the Kingdom'. This probable reference to the debates of the CWHWM in mid-November, including Carteret's anger with a number of government supporters who reneged on their prior commitment to vote for the desired open-ended duration of the loan duties, was followed by what seemed an even more ironic reference to the Commons and their voting of an increase in taxes and the national debt at a time of socio-economic crisis in Ireland: 'Still submitting my Opinion to that *happy Majority*, which I am confident is *always in the Right*; by whom the *Liberty* of the Subject hath been so frequently, so strenuously, and so successfully asserted; who, by their wise Councils, have made the *Commerce* to flourish, Money to abound, Inhabitants to increase, the Value of lands and Rents to rise; and the whole Island put on a new Face of *Plenty and Prosperity*.'[145] Harking back to the purpose behind his 1728 *Short View*, Swift once again took issue with the idea that Ireland could in any way be described as a flourishing country.

Swift may have had the last word in April 1730, but in reality it was also an admission of failure. Despite the efforts of Prior and Swift, the national debt had been increased and additional new taxes voted without Parliament dealing with the kind of Patriot concerns that these writers had looked to highlight at key moments in the parliamentary process. In retrospect, even the Patriot MPs who espoused the views reflected in print by Swift and Prior were primarily concerned with the retention of control of the public purse-strings in the Commons by protecting their hard-won constitutional principles regarding the initiating of supply bills, access to the public accounts, the two-year duration of additional taxation, and the resisting of executive amendments to supply bills. The more idealistic opposition to the very idea of a national debt and the voting of taxes to fund it garnered little support. In truth, MPs seemed keener to benefit from being public creditors than to engage with the more esoteric arguments as to the dangers of an increasing national debt.

Thus, it was not surprising that when Parliament reconvened in late 1731, a new loan of £100,000 was legislated for, thereby increasing the principal of the funded debt to £300,000.[146] There was little difficulty in securing this new loan. At the end of 1730, Robert Clayton, Bishop of

Killala, had felt that if the government's affairs 'should require an additional loan of £50,000 it will be no difficult matter to obtain it next sessions'.[147] Closer to the convening of the session, the new Lord Lieutenant, Lionel Cranfield Sackville, Duke of Dorset, was of the opinion that 'if I could satisfy myself with proposing nothing more, than continuing the funds on the foot they now stand, and the providing an interest for an additional loan, I should not apprehend any great difficulty'.[148] Once the PAC had reported the debt of the nation as £335,466 at the end of October, the CWHWM was quick to resolve that a new loan of £100,000 be legislated for.[149] The whole process was perceived to have been 'carried on with great ease and quietness'. The government failed in an attempt to get the duration for the appropriated duties in the heads of the loan bill changed from 2 to 21 years, which had been attempted as a compromise on the desired open-ended duration in 1729.[150] Thereafter the 1731 loan bill encountered no further difficulties. In drafting the heads of the bill, the Commons had taken full account of all of the alterations made by the British Privy Council to the 1729 bill, thereby avoiding any issues arising once the 1731 bill was returned from London.[151] As in 1729, the loan served as both a means of avoiding overtaxation at a time of economic hardship and of transforming £100,000 of pay arrears into a funded debt.[152] The act also reasserted the general undertaking to continue interest payments until the principal was cleared and created a practical process for using the surplus in the sinking fund for paying down the principal debt. Whenever £5000 of surplus was held in the Treasury, the names of creditors would be drawn by lottery to decide which creditors were to be repaid their principal.[153] Therein, the theoretical sinking fund of 1729 became a reality.

So it was that once again, as had been the case since 1716, the Commons made certain that the national debt was tied into the politics of supply, by which Parliament ensured the continuation of biennial sessions and kept the government dependent upon Parliament. As Bishop Clayton noted in January 1732, 'as they now have experience that they can raise money on parliamentary security from two years to two years, I believe they will hardly be prevailed upon to grant it for a longer time'.[154] And, as before, there was little difficulty in finding people to subscribe to the new loan—indeed, the number of potential subscribers was such that 'many' MPs had their subscriptions refused.[155]

Such compliance did not escape Swift's gaze. In the footnotes to the 'Verses on the Death of Dr Swift', composed in November 1731 while the increase in the debt was being voted through Parliament, Swift claimed that in selling their souls and votes in return for financial incentives from government—including contracts for various public works such as building jails, army barracks, and roads in their localities—MPs had given 'five times more than [Ireland] ... can afford', thereby stripping the country of its wealth.[156] In that respect, it was of note that the national debt had increased sixfold since 1729, from £50,000 to £300,000.[157]

Swift revisited the topic of the Irish national debt in February 1732 in *A Proposal for an Act of Parliament to Pay Off the Debt of the Nation.* Although ultimately targeted at the Church of Ireland hierarchy, the opening lines communicated his continuing representation of the debt as unsustainable: 'The Debts contracted some Years past, for the Service and Safety of the Nation, are grown so great, that under our present distressed Condition, by the Want of Trade, the great Remittances to pay *Absentees*, Regiments serving abroad, and many other Drains on Money, well enough known and felt; the Kingdom seems altogether unable to discharge them by the common Methods of Payment.'[158] The key Patriot concerns were thus once again itemised, but with a greater emphasis on paying regiments stationed overseas, which was becoming even more of an issue for Irish MPs, especially in light of the indecent haste with which £40,000 of the 1729 loan had been sent to England for that purpose. When Parliament had reconvened in late 1731, the government had gone to great lengths to reassure MPs that all money raised from Irish taxes would be spent in Ireland, but yet again part of the 1731 loan was sent abroad to pay Irish Establishment regiments.[159]

Swift had not been alone in 1731–32 in taking issue with the increase in the national debt. Prior to the parliamentary session, an anonymous pamphlet had been published which argued against any new loans on the grounds that 'the nation is [already] run so much into debt' because a number of people were determined 'to serve a certain party': 'Pray what is all this, but laying the nation under the severest bonds, to do whatever the prime minister directs? The joke too is, that the money lent on the public faith, is all supplied by members of parliament, by which means they must be pensioners to the court, and obliged ... to comply with all future desires, on pain of forfeiting what is already advanced.'[160] There was a great deal of truth in that regard, given that many MPS were also public creditors and so had a vested interest in voting taxes to maintain the debt, and had clearly agreed to creating and increasing the debt out of self-interest.

But such views seemed to have little purchase for the self-same reasons the anonymous author had expressed. And the success of the legislative provision of a sinking fund in 1729 and 1731 would quickly reduce even further the potential for opponents of a national debt to gain any traction at all. The principal of the debt began to be paid down from 1733 onwards out of the sinking fund and was eventually reduced to just £5,000 in 1759, before the increasing financial pressures of the Seven Years' War upon the Irish government ensured that the logic of a national debt reasserted itself and the principal began to grow once more.[161] By then, Swift was long dead, and a new generation of politicians, writers, Patriots, and political thinkers had entered into the fray as the national debt and the taxes voted to maintain it increased with much greater rapidity and size.

Notes

1. Charles Ivar McGrath, '"The Public Wealth is the Sinew, the Life, of Every Public Measure": The Creation and Maintenance of a National Debt in Ireland, 1716–45', in *The Empire of Credit: The Financial Revolution in the British Atlantic World, 1688–1815*, ed. Daniel Carey and Christopher Finlay (Dublin: Irish Academic Press, 2011), 171–77; idem, 'Securing the Hanoverian Succession in Ireland: Jacobites, Money and Men, 1714–16', *Parliamentary History* 33, no. 1 (2014): 140–59.
2. L. M. Cullen, 'Swift's *Modest Proposal* (1729): Historical Context and Political Purpose', in *Ourselves Alone? Religion, Society and Politics in Eighteenth- and Nineteenth-Century Ireland: Essays Presented to S. J. Connolly*, ed. D. W. Hayton and A. R. Holmes (Dublin: Four Courts Press, 2016), 42–60.
3. For Patriot politics at the time, see Patrick McNally, *Parties, Patriots and Undertakers: Parliamentary Politics in Early Hanoverian Ireland* (Dublin: Four Courts Press, 1997), 174–95.
4. Alan Downie, '*Gulliver's Travels*, the Contemporary Debate on the Financial Revolution, and the Bourgeois Public Sphere', in *Money, Power and Print: Interdisciplinary Studies on the Financial Revolution in the British Isles*, ed. Charles Ivar McGrath and Chris Fauske (Newark, NJ: University of Delaware Press, 2008), 118–28.
5. Jonathan Swift, *A Proposal for the Universal Use of Irish Manufacture &c.*, in *Jonathan Swift: Major Works*, ed. Angus Ross and David Woolley (Oxford: Oxford University Press, 1984), 400–405.
6. Jonathan Swift, 'Causes of the Wretched Condition of Ireland', in *The Essential Writings of Jonathan Swift*, ed. Claude Rawson and Ian Higgins (New York: W.W. Norton, 2010), 242–43.

7. Jonathan Swift, *Gulliver's Travels*, in *Essential Writings*, 395–96, 434–35; Downie, 'Contemporary Debate', 115–18.
8. Jonathan Swift, *A Short View of the State of Ireland*, in *Essential Writings*, 289–93; *Jonathan Swift and Thomas Sheridan: The Intelligencer*, ed. James Woolley (Oxford: Oxford University Press, 1992), 170, 176, 178; Cullen, 'Swift's *Modest Proposal*', 53.
9. *Journals of the House of Lords of the Kingdom of Ireland* (hereafter, *LJI*), 8 vols. (Dublin: William Sleater, 1779–1800), iii, 18; *Intelligencer*, 104.
10. *The Boulter Letters*, ed. Kenneth Milne and Paddy McNally (Dublin: Four Courts Press, 2016), 223.
11. *LJI*, iii, 19.
12. *Boulter Letters*, 223. See also *Letters of Marmaduke Coghill, 1722–1738*, ed. David Hayton (Dublin: Irish Manuscripts Commission, 2005), 46.
13. For the 'sole right' claim of 1692 and the 1695 compromise, see Charles Ivar McGrath, *The Making of the Eighteenth-Century Irish Constitution: Government, Parliament and the Revenue, 1692–1714* (Dublin: Four Courts Press, 2000), 73–117; idem, 'English Ministers, Irish Politicians and the Making of a Parliamentary Settlement in Ireland, 1692–5', *English Historical Review* 119, no. 482 (2004): 585–613.
14. *Intelligencer*, 104, 111.
15. Robert E. Burns, *Irish Parliamentary Politics in the Eighteenth Century*, 2 vols. (Washington, DC: Catholic University of America Press, 1989–1990), 1:205–10.
16. James Kelly, 'Jonathan Swift and the Irish Economy in the 1720s', *Eighteenth-Century Ireland* 6 (1991): 16–17; Burns, *Parliamentary Politics*, 1:208.
17. D. W. Hayton, *Ruling Ireland, 1685–1742: Politics, Politicians and Parties* (Woodbridge: Boydell Press, 2004), 246–51.
18. For Brodrick, Carter, and Vesey, see E. M. Johnston-Liik, *History of the Irish Parliament, 1692–1800: Commons, Constituencies and Statutes*, 6 vols. (Belfast: Ulster Historical Foundation, 2002), 3:270–72, 377–84; 6:468–69.
19. *Coghill Letters*, 35. See also *Boulter Letters*, 142–44; Burns, *Parliamentary Politics*, 1:212–16.
20. Isaac Manley to [——], 25 Feb. 1726, The National Archives (hereafter, TNA): SP 63/387/73. See also TNA: SP 63/387/50–51, 55–56, 59–60, 75, 77, 79–82, 130; Coghill Letters, British Library (hereafter, BL) Add. MS 21122, f. 29; *Journals of the House of Commons of the Kingdom of Ireland* (hereafter, *CJI*), 21 vols. (Dublin: House of Commons, 1796–1800), iii, 444–45.
21. *Boulter Letters*, 145.
22. Ibid.

23. Baron Carteret to the Duke of Newcastle, 23 Dec. 1727, TNA: SP 63/389/123–24; *CJI*, iii, 490–91, 495.
24. *CJI*, iii, 477, 489, and app., cccxxxvi.
25. Burns, *Parliamentary Politics*, 1:230–33.
26. *The Correspondence of Jonathan Swift, D.D.*, ed. David Woolley, 4 vols. (Peter Lang: Frankfurt am Main, 2003): 3:184.
27. For the socio-economic circumstances in Ireland in the second half of the 1720s, see TNA: SP 63/390/113–14, 121, 173–77; SP 63/391/9, 33–34, 41, 73, 75, 77–79, 81–82; TNA: PC 2/90, pp. 401, 409, 418, 458–59; PC 2/91, p. 22; Coghill Letters, BL Add. MS 21122, ff. 61–65, 68; Cullen, 'Swift's *Modest Proposal*', 51; Hayton, *Ruling Ireland*, 251–52; Burns, *Parliamentary Politics*, 1:233–44; Kelly, 'Swift and the Irish Economy', 16–36.
28. Cullen, 'Swift's *Modest Proposal*', 46, 50–51, 53.
29. TNA: SP 63/391/43, 46, 53, 71–72. For Conolly see Patrick Walsh, *The Making of the Protestant Ascendancy: The Life of William Conolly, 1662–1729* (Woodbridge: Boydell Press, 2010).
30. *CJI*, iii, 579–80.
31. *Coghill Letters*, 73; Johnston-Liik, *Irish Parliament*, 3:494–95; 4:191–92; 5:274–75; 6:319–21.
32. *CJI*, iii, 581–82.
33. Carteret to Newcastle, 25 Sept. 1729, TNA: SP 63/391/124.
34. *Coghill Letters*, 73; Carteret to Newcastle, 27 Sept. 1729, TNA: SP 63/391/136.
35. *Coghill Letters*, 73. For Gore see Johnston-Liik, *Irish Parliament*, 4:284–86.
36. *CJI*, iii, 583; *Coghill Letters*, 74. See also TNA: SP 63/391/165–66.
37. *Coghill Letters*, 74.
38. [Thomas Prior], *A List of the Absentees of Ireland, and the Yearly Value of their Estates and Incomes Spent Abroad: With Observations on the Present State and Condition of that Kingdom* (Dublin: R. Gunne, 1729).
39. Cullen, 'Swift's *Modest Proposal*', 54.
40. [Prior,] *Absentees*, 11–12, 22–23, 27–29, 32.
41. Ibid., 23.
42. Ibid., 32–33.
43. Ibid., 36.
44. *CJI*, iii, 584.
45. Ibid., 585.
46. Ibid., 587; TNA: SP 63/391/168.
47. For a similar opposition victory in this respect in 1725, see Burns, *Parliamentary Politics*, 1:209.
48. *CJI*, iii, 588–90.

49. *Coghill Letters*, 74–75. For Cope, see Charles Ivar McGrath, '"The Grand Question debated": Jonathan Swift, Army Barracks, Parliament and Money', *Eighteenth-Century Ireland* 31 (2016): 128–29; Johnston-Liik, *Irish Parliament*, 3:505–06.
50. *Boulter Letters*, 291. For Boulter and the 'English interest' see Hayton, *Ruling Ireland*, 240–55; Patrick McNally, 'Irish and English Interests: National Conflict within the Church of Ireland Episcopate in the Reign of George I', *Irish Historical Studies* 29, no. 115 (1995): 310–13.
51. *Boulter Letters*, 291.
52. Carteret to Newcastle, 31 Oct. 1729, TNA: SP 63/391/190–91. See also *Coghill Letters*, 75–76; *Boulter Letters*, 293.
53. TNA: SP 63/391/200, 202.
54. *Boulter Letters*, 293.
55. Ibid.
56. *Coghill Letters*, 76.
57. *CJI*, iii, 594, and app., ccclxxvii–ccclxxxi.
58. *Coghill Letters*, 76.
59. *Boulter Letters*, 294.
60. *CJI*, iii, 594–95.
61. *Coghill Letters*, 77.
62. *CJI*, iii, 595.
63. *Coghill Letters*, 77.
64. Ibid.
65. See McGrath, *Irish Constitution*, chaps. 3–7.
66. *CJI*, iii, 596–97.
67. *Coghill Letters*, 78; *Boulter Letters*, 294–95.
68. For the evolution of these key constitutional principles, see McGrath, *Irish Constitution*, chaps. 3–7.
69. *CJI*, iii, 597–98.
70. *Coghill Letters*, 78.
71. *CJI*, iii, 597–98.
72. *Coghill Letters*, 78.
73. Cullen, 'Swift's *Modest Proposal*', 54, 59–60.
74. Jonathan Swift, *A Modest Proposal*, in *Essential Writings*, 300; Cullen, 'Swift's *Modest Proposal*', 58; Kelly, 'Swift and the Irish Economy', 33.
75. Sean Moore, *Swift, the Book and the Irish Financial Revolution: Satire and Sovereignty in Colonial Ireland* (Baltimore: John Hopkins Press, 2010), 173, 184–85; idem, 'Devouring Posterity: *A Modest Proposal*, Empire, and Ireland's "Debt of the Nation"', *PMLA: Publications of the Modern Language Association of America* 122, no. 3 (2007): 679–93. However, an implied caution in this regard seems to be suggested in Cullen, 'Swift's *Modest Proposal*', 43–44.

76. Jonathan Swift, 'The Grand Question Debated: Whether Hamilton's Bawn should be Turned into a Barracks or a Malt-House', in *Major Works*, 501; McGrath, 'Grand Question', 123.
77. Jonathan Swift, 'Verses on the Death of Dr. Swift, D.S.P.D., Occasioned by Reading a Maxim in Rochefoucault', in *Major Works*, 528–29; McGrath, 'Grand Question', 130–31.
78. Moore, *Swift*, 185–86; idem, 'Devouring Posterity', 690–91; Cullen, 'Swift's *Modest Proposal*', 54, 57.
79. *CJI*, iii, 598–99.
80. Ibid., 599–601.
81. Carteret to Newcastle, 18 Nov. 1729, TNA: SP 63/391/210–11.
82. *Boulter Letters*, 295.
83. Thomas Clutterbuck to Charles Delafaye, 20 Nov. 1729, TNA: SP 63/391/236–37.
84. *Boulter Letters*, 295.
85. Charles Ivar McGrath, *Ireland and Empire, 1692–1770* (London: Pickering and Chatto, 2012), 185–88.
86. Carteret to Edward Southwell, 30 Nov. 1729, Philips Manuscripts, BL Add. MS 38016, ff. 9–10.
87. *Jonathan Swift: Irish Tracts, 1728–1733,* ed. Herbert Davis (Oxford: Oxford University Press, 1971), xxi–xxii.
88. Jonathan Swift, *A Proposal that all the Ladies and Women of Ireland should Appear Constantly in Irish Manufactures*, in *Irish Tracts*, 123.
89. Ibid., 123–24.
90. Irvin Ehrenpreis, *Swift: The Man, His Works, and the Age*, 3 vols. (Cambridge, MA: Harvard University Press, 1983), 3:645–46.
91. Swift, *Proposal that all the Ladies*, 126.
92. TNA: SP 63/391/234, 238–39.
93. Privy Council Minutes, 25 Nov. 1729, 28–29 Nov. 1729, TNA: PC 2/91, pp. 86–87, 89–91.
94. Privy Council Minutes, 1–2 Dec. 1729, TNA: PC 2/91, pp. 92–95; TNA: SP 63/391/246; *The Statutes at Large Passed in the Parliaments held in Ireland* (hereafter *Stat. Ire.*), 20 vols. (Dublin: George Grierson, 1786–1801), 5:337–40.
95. McGrath, *Irish Constitution*, chaps. 3–7.
96. Carteret to Southwell, 9 Dec. 1729, Philips Manuscripts, BL Add. MS 38016, ff. 11–16.
97. Carteret to Charles, Viscount Townshend, 14 Dec. 1729, TNA: SP 63/391/254.
98. Clutterbuck to Delafaye, 14 Dec. 1729, TNA: SP 63/391/260–61.
99. *Boulter Letters*, 298–99.
100. Newcastle to Carteret, 25 Dec. 1729, TNA: SP 63/391/280.

101. Ibid.
102. McGrath, *Ireland and Empire*, 98–204.
103. McGrath, 'Securing the Hanoverian Succession', 154–55.
104. Delafaye to Clutterbuck, 27 Dec. 1729, TNA: SP 63/391/286–87.
105. Ibid.
106. *CJI*, iii, 619–22; Johnston-Liik, *Irish Parliament*, 3:179–80; 6:319–21.
107. *Coghill Letters*, 79.
108. *Boulter Letters*, 299.
109. *Coghill Letters*, 79–80.
110. Ibid. For the named MPs, see Johnston-Liik, *Irish Parliament*, 3:89, 241–46, 377–81, 494–95, 505–06; 4:243–44, 248, 417–18; 5:96–97, 222–23, 424; 6:276–77, 443–44, 468–69. For further on Boyle's party and the debate, see *Coghill Letters*, 81–2; Hayton, *Ruling Ireland*, 250–51, 254.
111. *CJI*, iii, 619–23.
112. *Boulter Letters*, 299.
113. *Coghill Letters*, 83.
114. Ibid., 79.
115. *Boulter Letters*, 299.
116. *Coghill Letters*, 80–81.
117. *Boulter Letters*, 299.
118. *CJI*, iii, 624–25.
119. *Coghill Letters*, 82.
120. Carteret to Newcastle, 22 Dec. 1729, TNA: SP 63/391/272; Carteret to Southwell, 26 Dec. 1729, Philips Manuscripts, BL Add. MS 38016, ff. 17–18.
121. *CJI*, iii, 624–25.
122. Carteret to Newcastle, 2 Jan. 1730, TNA: SP 63/392/3–4.
123. *Coghill Letters*, 89.
124. [Jonathan Swift,] *A Libel on D[octor] D[elany] and a Certain Great Lord* ([Dublin:] n.p., 1730). On Delany's poem and Swift's responses to it in general, see Ehrenpreis, *Swift*, 3:646–50, 660–65.
125. [Swift,] *Libel*, 9; *Jonathan Swift: The Complete Poems*, ed. Pat Rogers (Harmondsworth: Penguin Classics, 1983), 407; Ehrenpreis, *Swift*, 3:650.
126. *Correspondence of Jonathan Swift*, 3:306–7; *Complete Poems*, 807.
127. A wallet or pouch; *Complete Poems*, 810.
128. Strews.
129. [Swift,] *Libel*, 12; *Complete Poems*, 409; Ehrenpreis, *Swift*, 3:649.
130. The proposed inscription, probably composed by Delany but with significant input and approval from Swift himself, was: 'the lord Mayor, Sheriffs and Commons presented the freedom of this city in this box to Dr. Jon:

Swift, Dean of St. Patrick's, whom for his great zeal, unequalled abilities and distinguished munificence in asserting the rights and defending the liberties and encouraging the manufactures of the kingdom they justly esteemed the most eminent Patriot and greatest ornament of this his native city and country'; *Coghill Letters*, 92; Ehrenpreis, *Swift*, 3:651.

131. *Coghill Letters*, 91–92; Ehrenpreis, *Swift*, 3:652–55.
132. *Coghill Letters*, 91.
133. Ehrenpreis, *Swift*, 3:653, 656–60.
134. See Charles Ivar McGrath, 'Banks, Paper Currency and the Fiscal State: The Case of Ireland, Stated, 1660–1783', in *The British Fiscal-Military States, 1660–c.1783*, ed. Aaron Graham and Patrick Walsh (London: Routledge, 2016), 38–60.
135. Agmondisham Vesey had prior involvement in schemes for provision of credit facilities in Ireland, having been a subscriber to the two main national bank projects in 1720–1721, as well as being a close friend of one of Ireland's leading private bankers, Francis Harrison. See TNA: SP 63/375/152–53; National Library of Ireland MS 2256, pp. 39, 41, 67–69.
136. For James Swift see Patrick Walsh, *The South Sea Bubble and Ireland: Money, Banking and Investment, 1690–1721* (Woodbridge: Boydell Press, 2014), 50, 116, 133, 136.
137. *Coghill Letters*, 96–97.
138. Ibid; *CJI*, iii, 638; Johnston-Liik, *Irish Parliament*, 3:448–49; 4:63.
139. *CJI*, iii, 640, and app., cccxcvi–cccxcvii. The final total amount subscribed in ready money was £90,242 and in warrants £59,758; *CJI*, iv, app., v.
140. *Coghill Letters*, 97; *CJI*, iii, 649.
141. *Coghill Letters*, 97–98; *CJI*, iii, 649–52. For the named MPs, see Johnston-Liik, *Irish Parliament*, 3:224–25; 4:377; 5:8; 6:481–82.
142. *CJI*, iii, 651–52.
143. McGrath, *Ireland and Empire*, 185–89.
144. [Jonathan Swift,] *A Vindication of His Excellency the Lord Carteret, from the Charge of Favouring None but Tories, High-Church-men, and Jacobites*, in *Irish Tracts*, 155–69; *Coghill Letters*, 98.
145. [Swift,] *Vindication*, 162.
146. *Stat. Ire.*, 5:487–92.
147. Robert Clayton to Charlotte Clayton, 2 Dec. 1730, Sundon Papers, BL Add. MS 20102, ff. 138–39.
148. Duke of Dorset to Newcastle, 8 Oct. 1731, TNA: SP 63/394/93–94.
149. *CJI*, iv, 22–25 and app., iii–v, xi–xiii.
150. Robert Clayton to Charlotte Clayton, 9 Nov. 1731, Sundon Papers, BL Add. MS 20102, ff. 152–54.

151. TNA: SP 63/394/129, 145; TNA: PC 2/91, pp. 485–86; *CJI*, iv, 27–28, 38–41, 43.
152. *Stat. Ire.*, 5:487–92; David Dickson, *New Foundations: Ireland 1660–1800* (Dublin: Irish Academic Press, 1987), 102.
153. *Stat. Ire.*, 5:487–92.
154. Robert Clayton to Charlotte Clayton, 2 Jan. 1732, Sundon Papers, BL Add. MS 20102, ff. 158–60.
155. TNA: SP 63/394/141–42; *Stat. Ire.*, 5:508–10; Robert Clayton to Charlotte Clayton, 2 Jan. 1732, Sundon Papers, BL Add. MS 20102, ff. 158–60.
156. Swift, 'Verses', in *Major Works*, 528–29, 683.
157. McGrath, 'Public Wealth', 192.
158. Jonathan Swift, *A Proposal for an Act of Parliament to Pay Off the Debt of the Nation, without Taxing the Subject*, in *Irish Tracts*, 207; Moore, *Swift*, 195.
159. McGrath, *Ireland and Empire*, 157–58.
160. *Reflections on the National Debt: With Reasons for the Reducing the Legal Interest; And against a Public Loan. With some Advice to the Electors of Members of Parliament* ([Dublin:] n.p., 1731), 11–13.
161. McGrath, *Ireland and Empire*, 188–95.

CHAPTER 4

Patterns of Taxation in Eighteenth-Century Ireland

Patrick Walsh

Cíos rí, cíos tíre, cíos cléire,
cíos sróna, cíos tóna, cíos téite,
airgead ceann igceanngach féile,
airgead teallaigh is bealaigh do réiteach.
King's tax, land tax and clerical tax,
a nose tax, an arse tax and a heating tax,
a poll tax at the end of each gale,
hearth money and money for repairing roads.
Seán Ó'Gadhra, 'Staid nua na hÉireann, 1697 (Ireland's new state, 1697)', quoted in Vincent Morley, The Popular Mind in Eighteenth-Century Ireland *(Cork: Cork University Press, 2017), 62–63*

This verse composed as part of a poem written in Irish in 1697 offers a striking contemporary commentary on the impact of taxation in Ireland in the decade after the 1688–91 Williamite-Jacobite War. The poet, one Seán Ó'Gadhra, describes the variety of taxes imposed by national, local, and clerical authorities while adding in some further fantastical imposts to

P. Walsh (✉)
Trinity College Dublin, Dublin, Ireland
e-mail: walshp9@tcd.ie

D. Kanter, P. Walsh (eds.), *Taxation, Politics, and Protest in Ireland, 1662–2016*, Palgrave Studies in the History of Finance,
https://doi.org/10.1007/978-3-030-04309-4_4

convey his sense of the cumulative impact of these assessments. Obviously, there was no *cíos sróna*, let alone a *cíos tóna*, but the implication here is that the number and variety of taxes was increasing and merited commentary in a poem which more generally offered a damning indictment of the Williamite state in Ireland and the nascent Protestant Ascendancy which controlled it. Such commentaries on taxation in the Irish language sources are rare, making this an especially valuable source, revealing as it does some insight into popular attitudes to taxation, attitudes that were rarely verbalised in the surviving documentation. Instead historians have been largely obliged to infer popular attitudes to taxation from instances of illicit distillation, protest, riot, or smuggling.[1] More broadly, these lines raise a number of useful questions for the historian. What taxes were levied on the Irish population in this period and by whom? How was the burden of taxation spread across society and how did popular resistance shape the distribution and typologies of Irish taxation? This chapter seeks to address these subjects through an analysis of the patterns of Irish taxation in the period from the Williamite wars to the Act of Union. It is concerned with ascertaining what was the burden of taxation in eighteenth-century Ireland, how was it borne, by whom, and where. Finally this analysis of the political economy of Irish taxation and the geographies of fiscal extraction is situated, throughout the chapter, within a comparative context looking at both England and Scotland.[2]

The Components of Irish Taxation

Structurally, Irish taxation superficially resembled the contemporary English and Scottish models. All had their origins in the fiscal politics of the Cromwellian era and the subsequent adaptation and expansion of Commonwealth innovations by the Restoration regimes in Dublin, London, and Edinburgh in the early 1660s.[3] There were three main components of Irish taxation: customs duties, excise duties, and property taxes in the form of hearth money and quit rents—charges on estates formerly forfeited to the Crown during the turbulent sixteenth and seventeenth centuries. As Ó'Gadhra's poem reminds us, there were other elements within the Irish taxation landscape in this period, most notably tithes paid to the Anglican clergy and charges levied at county and parish level. Each of these categories of taxation caused significant friction at the local level. Tithes payable to the minority but established Church of Ireland were a grievance for Presbyterians and Catholics alike and they played a significant role in fuelling agrarian disorder from the 1760s through to the 1830s.[4] County cess—'money for repairing roads'—and the increasing demands of county grand juries in south Ulster in the 1760s, meanwhile, contributed to the Hearts of Oak and Steel Boy protests of the late 1760s and 1770s.[5] Like contemporary English turnpike riots, they are both part of the wider politics of taxation and also distinct phenomena and have thus been left out of the analysis that follows.[6]

Returning to the key components of national taxation—customs, excise, and property taxes—Fig. 4.1 presents their relative weighting across the period under discussion in visual form while Table 4.8 (see Appendix) provides figures for each category of taxation at decennial intervals from 1695 through to 1795. By 1795, the structure of Irish taxa-

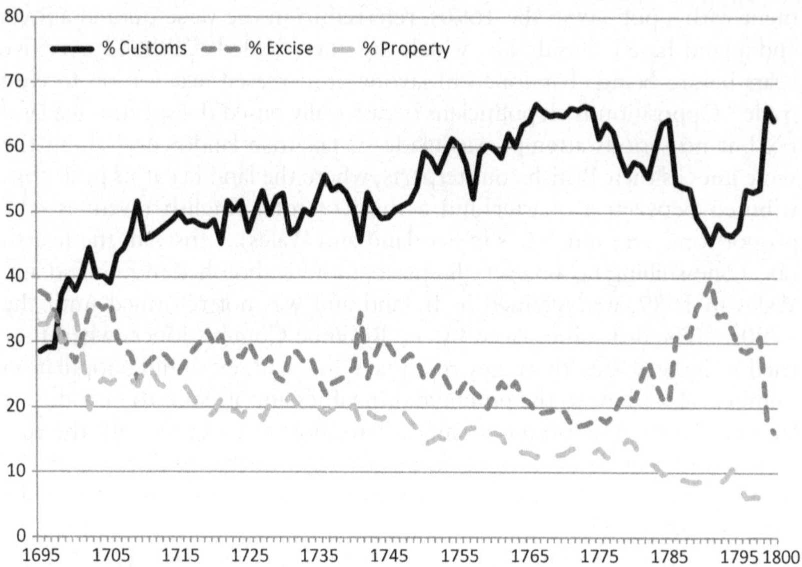

Fig. 4.1 The main components of taxation, 1695–1795 (%) (All figures in this chapter are in Irish pounds unless otherwise stated. These figures have been extracted from the appendices of the *Journals of the Irish House of Commons* (hereafter, *CJI*), 21 vols. (Dublin: House of Commons, 1796–1801), and are available online at http://www.duanaire.ie/dbases/public_finances_18_century. I am enormously grateful to Dr Aidan Kane for his help with this data. All national-level figures in this chapter are quoted from this source)

tion had changed significantly thanks to the passage of the 1793 Consolidated Fund Act, which heavily revised the Restoration legislation by ending the division between hereditary and additional duties, making comparisons with earlier periods trickier.[7]

Two immediate conclusions can be drawn from this data. Firstly, tax revenues grew significantly over the course of the eighteenth century even if total revenues still paled in comparison to those collected in Britain.[8] Secondly, as with contemporary England, customs and excise duties together comprised the greatest proportion of government income. In Ireland however their relative weightings were inverted, that is, customs revenues were much more important than their excise counterparts. This is a crucial point that we will come back to, but before doing so it is worth pointing out the other key difference between English and Irish taxation in this period. In Ireland there was no land tax. There was a brief experiment with a poll tax in the 1690s, referred to in the verse quoted above, and a land-based subsidy tax, which together yielded £290,844 over five years before being abandoned in favour of increased taxation on foreign trade.[9] Opposition Irish politicians occasionally raised the spectre of a land tax but no serious attempt was made to tax Irish landowners along the same lines as their British counterparts, where the land tax at its peak contributed between a quarter and a third of total English revenues (the proportions were much less in Scotland and Wales).[10] Instead, the hearth tax, a one-shilling tax on every fireplace, though abolished in England and Wales in 1689, was retained in Ireland and was not reformed until the 1790s.[11] The difficulties faced by the Revenue Commissioners when they tried to increase hearth money receipts in line with expanding population numbers also point to the potential difficulties any attempt to introduce a land tax on the English model might have posed. Together with the revenues from quit rents charged on properties formerly confiscated by the crown, the hearth tax provided a steady if unspectacular income stream for the Irish government.

Much more important, however, were receipts from customs and excise duties, and it is to them that we must turn to explain the patterns of growth in Irish revenue in this period. Indirect taxes in the form of customs and excise played a central role in the rise of the English fiscal state in the seventeenth and eighteenth centuries. Historians, such as John Brewer and Patrick O'Brien, amongst others, have identified how increased parliamentary control of taxation, combined with greater efficiencies in the bureaucratic framework that governed and collected new taxes, played an essential role in fostering the English 'financial revolution' and the creation of the eighteenth-century 'fiscal-military state'.[12] In particular, Brewer has demonstrated how the excise was the dynamo that drove the fiscal-military state. Recent work by Julian Hoppit has modified Brewer's view of the excise somewhat and suggested, inter alia, that the traditional view of the English customs system as the inferior bureaucracy needs to be revisited.[13] Nevertheless, the fiscal-military state model remains influential and has been effectively extended to Ireland, albeit in a modified format.[14]

Figure 4.1 shows how from the beginning of the eighteenth century, customs revenues charged on foreign trade (including the impost known as import excise) were the single most significant component of Irish government income. The gap between customs and excise revenues continued to widen apart from a brief blip in the 1740s (possibly a function of wartime conditions) even as excise revenues started to increase from the 1770s onwards.[15] Two questions arise. Why did the Irish excise not follow the English model, and what role did political decision making play in shaping the distinctive pattern of Irish taxation? Firstly, Ireland's economic and demographic structure mattered. The Irish economy did not experience structural change in the way that the early modern English economy made the precocious transition from one dominated by agrarian production to one increasingly dominated by manufacturing and commerce. The Irish economy continued to be dominated by agriculture right through the eighteenth and nineteenth centuries. Indeed, it is arguable that the increased industrialisation of the English/British economy and the consequent need for imported Irish foodstuffs to fuel this great transformation ensured Ireland did not experience structural change along the lines witnessed in its larger and much more powerful neighbour. There was consequently much less growth in Ireland in the numbers of excisable goods until the 1790s. This mattered in terms of taxation both because English real incomes rose, increasing consumer purchasing power there, and because the production of excisable goods rose to meet this consumer demand.[16] As Table 4.1 demonstrates, only in the 1790s following significant changes in the Irish tax code did excise per capita see any real gains.

Population growth can therefore be discounted as the key factor in explaining the late eighteenth-century rise in excise revenues. To be sure, it played a role, but other factors were more significant. Chief amongst these was the role of politics, what we might call the political economy of taxation.

Table 4.1 Excise revenues and per capita change, 1695–1795

Year	*Excise (£)*	*Excise per capita (£)*	*Population (millions)*
1695	97,380	N/A	N/A
1706	113,169	0.06	1.91
1712	115,541	0.05	2.15
1725	155,077	0.07	2.37
1732	149,340	0.06	2.35
1744	176,064	0.09	2.07
1749	177,683	0.08	2.12
1753	183,424	0.08	2.39
1791	635,555	0.14	4.42
1795	481,804	N/A	N/A

Note: Population figures are from Dickson, Ó Gráda, and Daultrey, 'Hearth Tax', *passim*. Mean population figures based on their upper and lower band estimates have been used for clarity

The basic structures of Irish taxation were codified in the Restoration customs and excise legislation of 1662 and 1663, which laid out what duties were paid on what goods.[17] The produce of these duties, together with hearth money, quit rents, and a succession of smaller charges, some of which were medieval in origin, made up what was known as the hereditary revenue. Following the 1688–91 Revolution and the increased spending demands placed on the Irish administration, new sources of revenue needed to be found and this in turn, as in England, revitalised the power of Parliament, helping it make the transition from being an event to becoming an institution.[18] The great bulk of this new expenditure came in the form of Ireland's contribution to the British fiscal-military state—the maintenance of a 12,000 strong standing army on the separate Irish establishment. This greatly increased expenditure needed new revenues which successive Irish Parliaments were happy to provide in return for the 'sole right' to introduce financial legislation into the Irish House of Commons.[19] MPs also of course benefitted from the security provided for the minority Protestant Ascendancy by the troops stationed in Ireland as well as from the ancillary economic advantages they brought with them in terms of contracts for building, maintaining, and supplying a countrywide network of barracks.[20] The hereditary revenues granted under the Restoration customs and excise legislation were insufficient to support this 'army for empire', leading to the rise of parliamentary sanctioned additional taxation from 1695 onwards.

Table 4.2 Parliamentary taxation, 1695–1795 (%)

Revenue type	*1695*	*1731*	*1755*	*1775*	*1785*	*1795*
Hereditary revenue	90.3	76.1	71.1	67.3	47.4	34.1
Additional duties	9.7	22.8	23.1	25.5	34.2	63.7
Loan duties	0	0.3	2.8	4.8	16.1	0
Other appropriated duties	0	0.7	3	2.4	2.2	2.2

Note: Compiled from the annual financial accounts presented to the Irish Parliament; for the raw data, see www.duanaire.ie

As Table 4.2 makes clear, by the beginning of the 1730s, these additional duties voted by Irish MPs made up almost a quarter of Irish revenues and, by the beginning of the American War, hereditary revenues made up only two-thirds of Irish government income, a proportion that would fall dramatically by the end of the century. Over time some of these additional revenues were appropriated for specific purposes, with the taxes on wine, silk, vinegar, hops, china, and japanned or lacquered earthenware from 1731 onwards allocated towards the maintenance of the Irish national debt, itself first established with an unsecured £50,000 loan from the Irish Protestant public in 1716.[21]

These additional revenues were made up exclusively from new or supplementary customs and excise duties. Unsurprisingly, given what we know about the structure of Irish taxation, nearly all of these additional duties, at least for the first three quarters of the eighteenth century, came from the customs side, with new levies introduced on a whole host of consumer goods and luxuries. Additional excise duties were placed on alcohol and on the sale of tobacco, but otherwise domestic producers were left untouched. The logic for imposing additional duties on the customs side was obvious enough. It was much easier, though far from straightforward, to collect duties at the port of entry than at the point of production. Also increased inland taxation was likely to lead to increased resistance and therefore increases in the cost of collection, costs that were already greater in Ireland because of the rural character of Irish society. The tax dividends produced by an increasingly urbanised society in England were not witnessed across the Irish Sea outside the larger port towns. Even without significant additional excise duties numbers of incidences of 'riot and rescue' directed at excise officers increased from the 1720s onwards.[22] By mid-century, it was acknowledged that it was impossible to counteract illegal distillers and brewers without military support.[23]

Eventually circumstances dictated a change in policy. It is clear from a variety of sources that politicians and senior revenue officials were by the 1760s increasingly frustrated with the lack of any sustained growth in excise revenues.[24] The expansion in the numbers employed in the revenue bureaucracy—which had seen total numbers double between the 1730s and the 1760s—had failed to yield significant gains in government income. At the same time, there was increased pressure on the Irish Exchequer to provide greater financial resources to meet the demands of the imperial fiscal-military state in the aftermath of the Seven Years War, most obviously through supporting greater numbers of troops on the Irish military establishment.[25] New solutions needed to be found.

Chief amongst them was legislation. As a result, the 1770s and especially the 1780s saw a shift in the political economy of Irish taxation. Lawmakers in Parliament turned to alcohol—long established as the key component in excise taxation—and sought new ways to raise taxes from its production. Firstly, new legislation was introduced in 1779 to regulate the minimum size of stills, the intended effect of which was to reduce the number of small producers. In reality, this led to increased instances of illicit distillation and therefore increased conflict between excise officers and the army on one side and illegal producers on the other.[26] In Strabane in west Ulster, for instance, it was noted that 'not near so much malt is distilled in this town as used to be, not the 5th part of it, owing to the strictness of the excise officers', while, at the same time, other evidence shows this area continued to be, and indeed increasingly became, known for its illicit producers.[27] Secondly, and more significantly in terms of its contribution to revenue, was the introduction of a malt tax in Ireland in 1785, almost ninety years after its institution in England and sixty years after its controversial introduction in Scotland. This immediately yielded revenues of about £120,000 per annum, mostly from the grain-producing districts in the eastern part of the country. The malt tax legislation offered incentives to larger producers in the form of tax rebates, increasing its acceptance amongst the propertied grain interests.[28]

Such legislative efforts were combined with the expansion of the scope of additional parliamentary excise duties and the growth of regulation, through the licensing of an increasing range of producers, of the production of excisable goods. Up until 1763, only alcohol and tobacco retailers were issued licences. In that year, cider licences were first issued with special sprits licences following in the same decade. By the mid-1780s, licences were issued to grocers, chandlers, and coffee house owners, while a decade later, over thirty industries were licensed, adding further revenue—some £12,000 per annum in the 1780s—to the state's coffers. All of this points to a shift in tax policy in this period and arguably a more interventionist regulatory state.[29] It also points to the increased 'torrent of legislation' passed by the Irish Parliament in the years after the granting of legislative independence in 1782. In the period 1781–1800, 1,125 acts were passed by the Irish Parliament, three more than had been passed in the period 1692–1781.[30] This increased parliamentary activity, which also included annual parliaments from 1782 onwards, is further illustrated in Fig. 4.2, which shows the growth in revenue raised by additional taxation in the period 1765–98.

What is striking here is the growth in additional revenue after 1782, suggesting that historiographical assessments of the economic impact of 'Grattan's Parliament' may need to need to be revisited.[31] Certainly, the increased regularity of Parliament, which now met every year rather than biennially, and the consequent increase in its legislative output, led to greater attention being paid to issues of taxation.[32] This was linked to the simultaneous increase in the ways in which Parliament sought to intervene

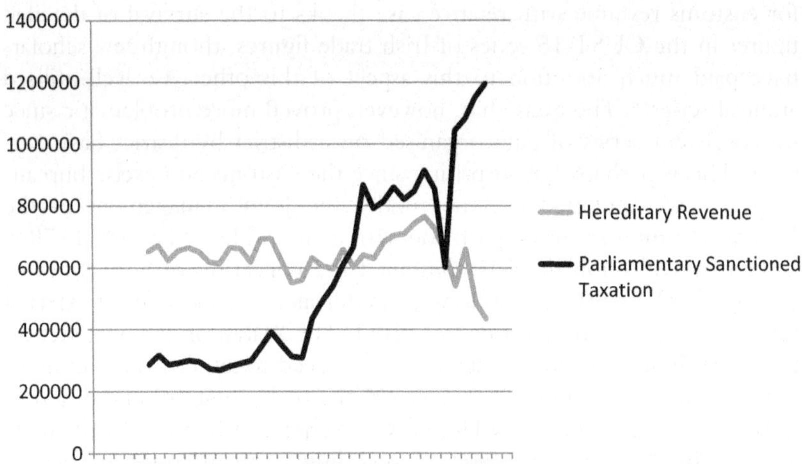

Fig. 4.2 1782 and all that: revenue raised by Acts of Parliament, 1765–98

in the management of the domestic economy through the use of bounties and other forms of parliamentary appropriation.[33] These forms of parliamentary intervention in the domestic economy have often been criticised as ineffective or as mere patronage but should instead be seen as evidence of an increasingly interventionist state and one which in a comparative British context stood out in terms of the volume and type of activity—the Irish state was exceptionally interventionist.[34] Such issues of expenditure, however, lie largely outside the scope of this chapter. Instead, what is important here is that at national level by the last quarter of the eighteenth century, excise revenues, while rising, were still firmly in second place compared to the contribution made by taxes on foreign trade, notably customs duties. To explore further the changing patterns of customs collection, we need to turn from the national to the regional to explore the shifting geographies of Irish taxation in this period.

The Geography of Irish Taxation

Existing analyses of Irish taxation have largely been concerned with national aggregate figures. Much of the accessible existing data were predominantly collected and presented on a national scale. Some regional disaggregation is possible as Dickson et al. demonstrated long ago with regards to the hearth tax.[35] It is possible to drill down to port-level data for customs revenue with relative ease thanks to the survival of detailed figures in the CUST 15 series of Irish trade figures, though few scholars have paid much attention to this aspect of this otherwise well-utilised archival series.[36] The excise has, however, proved more problematic since no consistent series of data organised on a district-by-district basis survives. This is perhaps not surprising since the customs and excise bureaucracies were combined together under the joint management of the Revenue Commissioners (apart from a brief interlude in the early 1770s), and many collection districts combined the collection of both types of taxation.[37] There was also no long-run equivalent of the series of external trade statistics capturing domestic output. The analysis in the next section therefore draws on a fragmentary record pieced together from a number of surviving observations. In this regard, the Irish situation is no different to the analysis conducted by Hoppit with respect to Britain and the findings, as shall become clear, are still revealing in terms of the burden of Irish taxation in this period.[38] More generally, a regional approach allows us to test further the impact of the Irish fiscal state both spatially and chronologically.

Having established that customs revenues made up the largest component of Irish income, it is imperative to outline where these revenues were collected and how, and if, their spatial footprint changed over time. The Irish Revenue Board made up of seven commissioners (officially five of whom were Excise Commissioners while all seven were Customs Commissioners) oversaw the collection of Irish taxation following the instigation of direct management in 1682 (see James Guilfoyle's chapter in this volume). The commissioners attending at daily meetings of the board at Dublin's Custom House (in practice usually only the Irish-born representatives on the board were in attendance) were responsible for a countrywide bureaucracy, which stretched across the kingdom. Stretched is the operative word; officials along the west coast whether employed in the customs or excise divisions often had unfeasibly large areas or 'walks' to patrol, while there were much greater concentrations of preventative officers employed in the major ports and urban areas.[39] For the purposes of tax collection, the country was divided into thirty-seven districts, each of which was managed by a collector. All twenty-five coastal districts combined the collection of excise and customs duties with all the inland districts responsible solely for collecting excise duties (there was a separate hearth money establishment). Finally, customs duties could only be collected at specific ports, which ranged in size from the tiny ports of Dingle and Newport on the west coast to the major transoceanic ports of Dublin, Cork, and Belfast. There were only very limited changes to the list of official ports of entry in the eighteenth century, with Newport, County Mayo, Clare, County Clare, Newry, Couty Down and Ballyraine in County Donegal the only additions. Of these, Newry, established as an official port in 1758, was the only one to alter significantly existing patterns of trade, taking as it did some of the existing trade from the neighbouring ports of Strangford and Dundalk.[40] By the end of the century, it was the sixth largest port on the island.

The majority of Irish trade was concentrated in a select number of ports and, by the middle of the century, over 90 per cent of legal trade passed through just six ports. Many of the remaining ports collected very little revenue, with ten ports never collecting more than £2,000 per annum and a further eight never reaching £10,000 per annum in the period surveyed. Indeed, John Beresford, the Chief Commissioner of the Revenue, claimed in 1783 that nineteen Irish ports did not cover their costs.[41] The propor-

Table 4.3 Gross revenues of seven largest ports, 1698–1798, rank order 1798 (% of total customs revenue)

Port	*1698*	*1724*	*1749*	*1774*	*1798*	*Total collected (£)*
Dublin	47.2	52.1	63.1	52.4	47.7	24,196,630
Cork	21.3	20.4	18.4	16.1	16.7	7,919,460
Belfast	5.3	4.6	4.2	9.3	9.1	3,458,154
Waterford	8.8	5.7	4.2	7.4	6.5	2,414,510
Londonderry	2.3	2.3	2.4	3.8	5.9	1,467,690
Newry	0	0	0	2	5.3	767,673
Limerick	3.7	3.1	1.7	3.8	3	1,271,259
Combined contribution of the national total	88.6	88.2	94	94.8	94.2	

Note: Gross customs revenue figures broken down by port and duty, annual figures in Irish Import and Export Ledgers, TNA: CUST 15/1, 27, 52, 77, 101

tion of national customs revenue collected in the remaining seven ports (each of which collected at least 3 per cent of the national total in 1798) is shown in Table 4.3.

A number of striking conclusions can be immediately drawn from this data. Unsurprisingly, Dublin emerges as the most significant port in the country. It was both the commercial and administrative capital, and the volume of trade entering it reflected this. In particular, Dublin was especially important in terms of Anglo-Irish trade, the trade in foreign luxuries (much of which came through London thanks to the Navigation Acts), and the wine trade with France.[42] However, when examined in a comparative context, Dublin's position at the top of this table looks less striking than at first sight. London, for instance, generated a greater proportion of British customs receipts, something partly of course explained by its status as the only legal port of entry for East India Company goods arriving from Asia; thus all tea arriving in Britain and Ireland, for example, had to be legally landed there first.[43] John Foster, the most commercially informed of the domestic Irish political leadership, grasped the value of this to national revenues and he actively, even obsessively, sought permission for even one East India Company ship to land first at Dublin in the early 1790s. Foster's pursuit of his 'hobby' came to nothing but it is revealing of the ways prominent members of the Irish 'cabinet' sought to subvert the limitations of the Navigation Acts to improve Irish trade and therefore revenues.[44]

What is revealing in an Irish context is the importance of the secondary ports, which together contributed on average almost half the total customs revenue raised in Ireland in this period. Cork, with its extensive provisions and victualing industries, was of course the most significant of these.[45] Nevertheless, in absolute terms, Cork's share of the national customs revenue declined over time. Its place was partly taken by the rising port of Belfast, which about mid-century overtook Waterford in the rank order of Irish ports. Belfast's rise owed much to the linen trade and increasing consumer demand in the American colonies. The long decline of Waterford meanwhile mirrored that of Galway, which had contributed 2.3 per cent of total customs revenue in 1724 but generated less than 1 per cent of the national total by the outbreak of the American War.[46] The growth of Belfast and the other northern ports of Londonderry and Newry, and the decline of Waterford and Galway over time, can be seen even more clearly in Table 4.4, which shows how little the relative revenues of Dublin rose throughout the century from 1698–1798.[47] These figures suggest that it enjoyed its greatest dominance in terms of revenues in the mid-century period before the north began to catch up during and after the American War.

The Connacht and Leinster figures appear especially striking here but the gross figures are smaller, meaning any change is more noticeable. Nevertheless, the decline of Galway, whereby its revenues fell by over a third from some £2,700 to £1,600 per annum in a century, is clearly revealed. In Leinster, the falling importance of Wexford and New Ross in the south and the effect of Newry's development (with its canal link to its inland hinterland and the Tyrone coalfields) on Dundalk and Drogheda are evident.[48]

While Table 4.4 offers a useful snapshot in time, it does not reveal the fluctuating nature of Irish trade and therefore customs revenues and with

Table 4.4 Gross customs receipts, by region, 1698–1798: percentage share at given dates, rank order 1798

Port	*1698*	*1724*	*1749*	*1774*	*1798*	*% change 1698–1798*
Dublin	47.2	52.1	63.1	52.4	47.7	1.1
Leinster	5.2	5.8	3.9	2.2	2.3	−55.8
Munster	36.7	30.8	24.8	27.7	27.2	−25.9
Ulster	8.6	8.6	7.5	16.3	21.8	153.5
Connacht	2.3	2.7	0.7	1.5	1	−56.5
Total	100	100	100	100	100	

them of course overall tax revenues. War and weather were the primary determinants of short-term periods of uncertainty. Bad harvests contributed to downturns in trade in 1727–29 and 1782–84, while the severe winter of 1740–1741 likewise saw a fall in customs revenues. War, however, had a greater impact. The beginning of each major international conflict in 1701, 1748, 1756, and 1775 saw embargos on trade and a decline in revenue, as official trade with the enemy was restricted. This could lead to short-term adjustments in trade patterns, with embargoes on the French wine trade, for instance, leading to increased trade with Spain and Portugal during the War of Spanish Succession and the War of Austrian Succession.[49] Alternatively, international war could lead to increasing levels of smuggling and other forms of subterfuge involving non-aligned shipping.[50] The impact of war, however, should not be overstated. While there was usually a short-term impact at the beginning of each conflict, trade levels, and therefore customs revenues, rose as hostilities continued. This is clear from Fig. 4.3, which shows the impact of the Seven Years War on Irish revenues.

After the fortunes of war turned in 1759–60, trade and revenues increased. This was important as in 1759 the Irish government faced a temporary funding crisis, which initially it found difficult to solve.

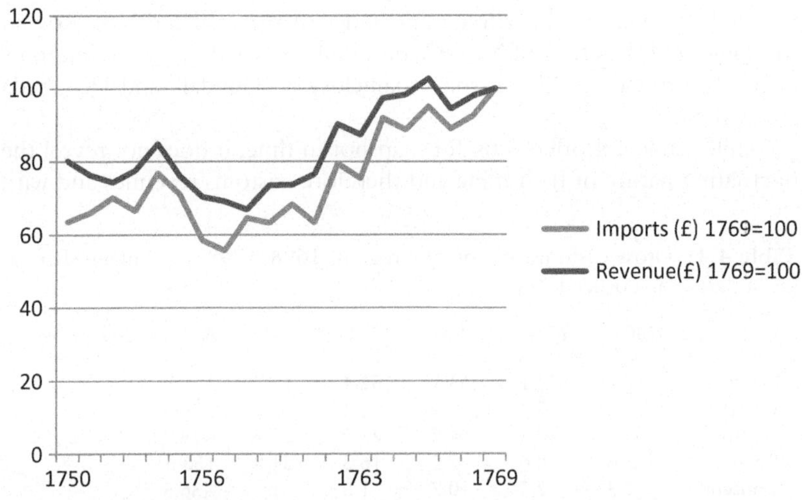

Fig. 4.3 Import and revenue data compared, 1750–69

Previously a shortfall in income could be supplemented by an appeal to the public and the raising of an additional loan. In 1759, however, for the first time since the establishment of the Irish national debt in 1716, there was initially little appetite from prospective lenders, something officials blamed on the reluctance of Catholics to lend to the state during wartime:

> The circumstances of the Kingdom were either not sufficient to enable government to borrow at so low an interest or else the Papists in whose hands a great quantity of the specie of the kingdom is generally lodged did not at that time when an invasion was apprehended choose to advance their money to the government. But the loan then opened was even if full considered by government as insufficient.[51]

Interest rates had to be raised, for the first time, to entice prospective lenders. There are of course two ways to read this episode. Were Irish Catholics hedging their bets at a time of war? Or was there a more general reluctance amongst prospective public creditors to advance money at a time when external military and diplomatic factors could influence the government's decision to credibly maintain their commitments? In the end 'The Year of Victories' improved the government's borrowing prospects, allowing for a reduction in the interest rate to its pre-war levels by 1763. When a similar problem arose in the 1790s, during the war with revolutionary France, the solution was to turn to the London money market for credit, an option not considered and probably not plausible in 1759.[52] The general pattern of a dip in revenues followed by a rise seen during the Seven Years War was also seen in earlier conflicts, notably the Wars of Spanish and Austrian Successions (1701–13 and 1739–48). The American War was different and it was not until after the conflict ended in 1783 that revenues rose again to their pre-war levels, demonstrating the greater impact of this conflict on the Irish economy in general. In this regard, the experience of the Irish ports echoed that of the British Atlantic ports of Liverpool, Bristol, and Glasgow.[53] The fall in customs revenues during both the Seven Years War and, especially, the American War influenced Irish policymakers' determination to increase the yield from domestic taxation evident from the reforms in the excise bureaucracy in the 1760s and the imposition of new excise taxes in the 1780s.[54] Similarly, the major reforms in both the excise and the hearth tax in the late 1790s cannot be divorced from their wartime context. War, as in Britain, stimulated financial innovation.

More generally, contemporaries, both officials and other interest groups, understood the importance of customs revenues. This is clear when one looks at the expansion of the physical and manpower infrastructure of the Irish fiscal state. Taking the built infrastructure first, the records of the Revenue Commissioners are replete with references to the building and expansion of custom houses and other port buildings throughout the country. Landmark buildings were erected in Cork, Kinsale, and Limerick, employing professional and fashionable architects long before James Gandon commenced building his Dublin masterpiece in the 1780s.[55] These imposing structures, built with a mix of the finest imported and native materials, demonstrated in stone and mortar the power and presence of the state as well as the wealth generated by commerce. They also reflect the increased office and storage space required to carry out the 'King's business' effectively. Even requests sent to Dublin for increased sentries and more secure 'strong boxes' indicate the increased importance of these revenues and the discontents they were inspiring in contemporary society.[56] More revealing perhaps were the repeated requests for 'swivel guns' and ammunition as officials struggled to deal with more sophisticated opponents determined to evade the increasing variety of customs duties. Customs officers at the small County Down port of Strangford in 1738, for instance, requested '2 swivel guns, 2 blunderbusses, 4 muskets, 4 pistols, 4 cutlasses, a small cask of powder and bullets' to deal with smuggling interests in their vicinity.[57]

The active and armed presence of smugglers off the Irish coast led to three key developments, which indicate the contemporary understanding of the importance of customs revenues to the Irish Exchequer. Firstly, the establishment in each port grew significantly, as more and more officials were employed to patrol the coasts and to oversee the landing of taxable goods.[58] Secondly, and linked to this, was the growth of the Revenue Commissioners' own fleet, with revenue cutters and wherries becoming an important part of the anti-smuggling arsenal from the 1730s onwards. New vessels were regularly deployed in the Irish Sea and off the southern coast, with each one vaingloriously named after a sitting Revenue Commissioner.[59] Eventually, this whole fleet was overseen by one official, Luke Mercer, who was appointed inspector of the boats with a salary commensurate to the rank of provincial Surveyor General (the rank just beneath the commissioners), having previously served as captain of one of the first revenue boats.[60] Finally, the maritime efforts of the Revenue Commissioners were supplemented by the deployment of Royal Navy vessels in Irish waters with specific instructions to support the Irish customs officers in their duties from the 1730s onwards. In reality they spent much of their time on impressment and other recruitment duties, but nevertheless contributed to the protection and growth of Irish revenues. Even better for the Irish Exchequer, unlike the troops deployed inland to help collect excise revenues, the cost of these naval vessels was borne by British rather than Irish taxpayers, a subject that would cause some controversy after the granting of legislative independence.[61] All of this expenditure laid out on protecting customs duties indicates their paramount importance to the Irish Exchequer. While producing cost-benefit analyses of each of these developments is tricky, it is clear that, while revenues did rise, unlike in England, there were not significant reductions in the costs of collection.[62]

The ready availability of customs data on a port-by-port basis makes it relatively easy to determine its geography. When it comes to the excise, the surviving data is more problematic. While customs data for individual ports was systematically isolated from the national aggregate gross revenue figures, excise data was only rarely collected and presented on a district-by-district basis. This means that the analysis that follows, like Hoppit's similar exercise for Britain, is based on a partial reconstruction of rather fragmentary evidence. Nevertheless, some interesting conclusions can be drawn from the available materials, which reveal much about the changing geographies of Irish taxation. Table 4.5 presents gross excise totals for each of the available sample years, calculated on a provincial basis.

Isolating Dublin City out from the data and grouping the remaining districts together by province allows us to assess the regional impact of excise taxation and the effectiveness of the infrastructure and bureaucracy of the Irish fiscal state. Division by province makes sense too since this was

Table 4.5 Gross excise revenue by region, 1692–1808 (£)

	1692	*1700*	*1730*	*1762*	*1768*	*1808*
Dublin City	24,134	42,340	59,044	73,146	60,557	541,304
Leinster	19,959	25,937	20,110	22,554	21,455	432,177
Munster	14,815	20,967	17,878	33,912	29,086	684,850
Ulster	11,455	20,816	14,888	15,706	11,808	188,811
Connacht	4,150	6,541	3,349	2,416	2,095	55,356

Source: Alan. J. Smyth, 'The Social and Economic Impact of the Williamite War on Ireland, 1688–91' (PhD diss., Trinity College Dublin, 2013), 208–9; *CJI*, iv, app., xcviii (1700 and 1730), viii, app., cclxxxvii (1762–1768)

how the bureaucracy was organised with a Surveyor General—the rank below commissioner—responsible for each province. Some immediate conclusions can be drawn from this table. Firstly, the impact of new taxes and the speed of the post-war economic recovery in the 1690s both emerge from a comparison of the figures for 1692 and 1700, though the former obviously was a low base from which to start. Secondly, it appears that outside Dublin excise revenues fell across all regions during the first three decades of the eighteenth century. Some caution should be exercised here as the late 1720s saw a succession of bad harvests, which were likely to have impacted negatively on tax revenues. Significantly, perhaps the greatest fall in revenues came in Ulster, the worst affected province.[63] Comparisons with national-level figures, however, suggest that 1730 was not an anomaly but rather that the early 1730s generally saw a dip in excise revenues (see Fig. 4.1). Thirdly, comparing the figures for 1730 and 1762 what stands out is the great increase in excise yields from Munster while those from Ulster and Leinster remained largely stagnant. It is important to note here that there were no major changes to the level or number of excise duties within this period, indeed one well-informed commentator noted in 1772 with only a slight exaggeration that there had been no new taxes introduced since 1727.[64] Fourthly, an examination of the figures for the 1760s (for which we have a run of figures from 1762 through to 1768) indicates that the great expansion in revenue personnel in this decade had little impact on improving revenues, something that is discussed in greater detail below. Change would only come in the early 1770s, when fragmentary evidence for some districts in Ulster indicates a doubling of revenue between 1768 and 1773. This increase can be partly attributed to improved harvests and the consequent removal of restrictions on distilling during a period of grain shortages, rather than other institutional developments.[65] Finally, it is clear that there was a significant, even dramatic, increase in excise revenues between the 1760s and the early 1800s. The available data does not allow for a detailed regional analysis of these changes, but some speculations are offered towards the end of this section.

The provincial breakdowns are useful, but they still obscure where precisely growth was taking place. Drilling down to district level, it becomes clear that the great bulk of excise revenues were collected in two categories of place, urban areas and the rich agricultural lands of the east, with the tillage farming districts of Naas (encompassing much of counties Kildare and Carlow), Trim (encompassing County Meath), and Armagh standing out.[66] This pattern, which holds good for the century, supports the snapshot drawing on 1770s data provided by K. H. Connell in his pioneering work on illicit distillation, which pointed towards a clear east-west divide.[67] The contemporary observations of John Monck Mason, the Revenue Commissioner who toured the northern half of the country in 1774, also give credence to an east-west divide, with his description of Foxford district (encompassing most of County Mayo), highlighting the impossibility of comparing conditions and practices in Connacht and Leinster:

> You cannot form any idea of the distillers in this part of the country from a comparison with those in Dublin, the people here having no money to lay in a stock of corn nor would the country afford them a sufficient quantity, if they had money to purchase it. They therefore work but seldom and but little at a time, and I have no doubt but four of the principal distillers in Naas or Trim district distill more spirits in the year than the 28 distillers in that of Foxford.[68]

Moving westward, a number of districts in Connacht and south and west Ulster barely yielded enough revenue to cover their own costs. In some cases, such as the revenue establishment in Dingle and Newport district, they did not even meet the salary costs of the gaugers employed to collect excise duties.[69] The role of excise officers in such areas was less about raising revenue than about providing a visible reminder of state power. Their existence could also be rather lonely and there is evidence to suggest that those who tried to be too assiduous in their pursuit of illicit stills and 'private' brewers quickly drew the opprobrium of local communities.[70]

Historians, myself included, have argued that the revenue service became the most 'pervasive agency of state' in the eighteenth century.[71] The expansion of numbers employed in the revenue has been documented, with the total numbers employed doubling between the 1690s and the late 1720s and then doubling again by the 1760s. There would be further increases in the 1780s, with the salary bill growing faster in the excise.[72] The relative roles of professionalisation and patronage in motivating this great expansion in personnel have been debated, and questions remain about whether more officials meant greater efficiencies or not.[73] The surviving regional excise data allows us to revisit this subject with specific reference to the 1760s, the period of greatest expansion in numbers employed. Before zooming in on that decade, Table 4.6 allows us to look at the relationship between the numbers employed and the revenue collected over the period 1700–68.

Table 4.6 Gross excise revenue by region per officer (£), 1700–68

	1700	*1730*	*1762*	*1768*
Dublin City	1628.46	1513.95	1590.13	1062.4
Leinster	305.14	153.51	159.96	110.03
Munster	349.45	205.49	335.76	209.25
Ulster	365.19	153.48	119.89	73.34
Connacht	225.55	95.69	75.5	39.53
National	453.7	296.32	327.57	206.61

Note: Figures calculated by using district totals cited above and the Establishment books for the same years in TNA: CUST 20

The first thing that stands out from this data is once again the exceptional nature of Dublin. Dublin, like London, provided the largest component of excise revenue, and the scale of production in key excisable industries like alcohol production and sugar baking, together with the more commercially and consumer-oriented methods of retailing wine and tobacco, made excise much easier to collect. This meant that while the excise establishment in the city expanded, each officer was still able to collect significant levels of duty. Leaving Dublin aside, it is less clear how much the increased number of gaugers contributed to improving revenues. In Connacht, for instance, in 1768, the average annual yield of each excise officer was £39.75, while the average annual salary was only £40. This indicates inefficiencies in the system but does of course hide differences across excise 'walks' and districts, with anomalies like Newport bringing down the average figures. More generally, it is far from clear that the great expansion in personnel yielded the desired results in terms of revenue collection. We should be careful not to generalise too much, however, because aside from intra-district differences, the intangible advantages of having greater numbers on the ground as population rose and as tensions increased between the populace and the agents of the state in just maintaining the status quo are unquantifiable. Of course the increasing presence of a greater numbers of gaugers may have contributed to rising tensions, something Timothy Watt's research on the 1720s and 1730s suggests. He argues that greater numbers of excise men emboldened officials to enforce the revenue laws more rigorously, thereby disrupting local customary practices and the established equilibrium built up over previous generations.[74] Local arrangements and accommodations made between excisemen and the brewers, distillers, and retailers they surveyed, while common across the British world, came under attack from the 1730s onwards as the Revenue Commissioners attempted to arrest the decline in revenues.[75]

Geographies of Resistance

Mapping the changing yields of customs and excise taxation reveals aspects of the political geography of Irish taxation in this period, not least in terms of showing where and by whom the majority of Irish taxes were paid. Further insight into the spatial limits of the Irish state's power and legitimacy can be garnered from examining the shifting geographies of resistance across the period covered by this chapter and by exploring how they map onto patterns identified for later periods by other contributors to this volume. There is an established literature on smuggling while historians are increasingly taking interest in other forms of protest against taxation, notably instances of 'riot and rescue' involving excisable goods and activities.[76] Louis Cullen's authoritative and extensive work on smuggling has highlighted the key commodities involved—wool, brandy, tobacco, and East India goods—and their respective geographies along the south and east coasts. The importance of the Isle of Man as a key entrepôt up until the mid-1760s is well known, as are the lucrative activities of leading smuggling interests, including the O'Connells and O'Sullivans in the southwest.[77] Admiralty records meanwhile reveal the extent of the Royal Navy's role in combatting, and also on occasion abetting, smuggling from the 1710s onwards.[78] The 1730s, amid concerns about increased wool smuggling, saw the previously ad hoc arrangements regarding the deployment of naval vessels to combat smuggling become more regularised with six ships stationed constantly off the Irish coast to assist the Revenue Commissioners. Twenty years later, their success was still being debated, with a 1755 Treasury report describing how Ireland's Atlantic coast remained populated by an 'uncivilised and unreduced people' despite the expenditure laid out on naval protection.[79] If some officials in London had misgivings about devoting precious naval resources to the Irish coast, they were overruled by their colleagues, not least because of their increased importance in defending Irish waters and in recruiting sailors.

Smuggling played an important role in coastal communities and was an important form of tax evasion, although precise figures regarding its scale are obviously impossible to calculate. Contemporary accounts were also likely to be exaggerated and need to be treated with caution. What is less clear are its political dimensions, with attempts to link smuggling activities to Jacobitism and other forms of political dissent often unconvincing.

Likewise, caution needs to be taken when examining the motivations of the crowds involved in protests against other forms of domestic taxation, whether those resisting quit rent drivers, hearth tax collectors, or excise men seeking out illegal stills or unlicensed breweries. Bearing in mind such caveats, it is still striking how the number of recorded instances of violent opposition to domestic taxation increased throughout the period under discussion. Watt's research on tax riots clearly shows that the once dominant idea that the Whiteboy-inspired agrarian unrest beginning in 1760 marked a watershed in the history of Irish violent protest is no longer tenable.[80] Nevertheless, the levels of lethal violence employed against revenue officers did increase from the 1760s onwards, reflecting trends elsewhere in Irish society, with reported fatal attacks on revenue officials more prevalent than during any previous decade.[81] Of particular interest to our present discussion are not just the increasing levels of resistance to taxes, which I have previously written about elsewhere, but also their spatial distribution and how this maps onto the political geography of Irish taxation outlined in this chapter.

Mapping geographical patterns of resistance is possible thanks to the reports submitted to the Revenue Commissioners of attacks on tax officials across the kingdom and to the submission of requests for military support to aid excise (and less often customs) officers in the exercise of their duties. This evidence was fairly systematically recorded up until the 1770s when, unfortunately for the historian, the Revenue Commissioners' minutes, though increasingly voluminous, stop recording such information on a consistent basis.[82] What follows draws on an in-depth analysis of the forty-six volumes covering the period 1761–69, though sampling of the data for previous decades taken together with Watt's in-depth research on the period 1720–40 suggests that many of the patterns identified hold true for the earlier period, even if the scale of activity significantly increased from the 1760s onwards.[83] The geography of resistance did however shift between these two periods, with Watt's findings stressing the importance of Munster, while my findings shift the centre of activity farther north into the midlands and south and west Ulster.[84] In particular, I focus on the deployment of the army as a proxy for violent opposition to the revenue officials, as this evidence is more robust and easier to chart spatially.

The army played a critical if reluctant role in collecting taxes in Ireland. This was perhaps appropriate; it was after all the main beneficiary of these taxes, with the great majority of Irish taxation devoted to supporting the Irish military establishment. From at least the 1720s, troops, stationed in the countrywide network of residential barracks, were regularly used to assist revenue officials in their duties. Assisting with seizures of illegal stills, challenging rioters, and protecting quit rent collectors, however, while increasingly part of their regular routine, were not popular activities for soldiers or indeed for their commanding officers, who frequently resisted orders to assist the civil power.[85] Theirs was, however, a losing battle. Soldiers were increasingly deemed necessary to 'keep people in awe' or more sinisterly to 'strike terror' into 'barbarous inhabitants'; or as one visitor to the country explained in 1773, 'every seizure in this kingdom is made at the most imminent peril of the officer's life'.[86]

New barracks were built specifically to assist the revenue officers, while the removal of soldiers to other parts of the country, or even empire, was greeted with disquiet by local officials. Where no barracks were available, troops were quartered in private residences; though unlike in contemporary England where this was standard practice, quartering was extremely unusual in Ireland and usually an option of last resort.[87] Purpose-built barracks or buildings that could be converted to provide adequate accommodation were preferred by the Irish military establishment, something that reflects both the lack of suitable private accommodation in Ireland and the different political and social conditions pertaining in that kingdom. By the early 1780s, the official lists of quarters produced by the army designated certain barracks as 'revenue barracks', anticipating the nineteenth-century establishment of a specifically designated revenue police force.[88]

Table 4.7 shows which districts had the most incidents of troops being deployed in support of the revenue in the period 1761–68. Over two-thirds of the 192 recorded incidences in these years took place in just six excise districts. Taken together with the less systematically recorded reports of attacks on revenue officials, a picture of the geography of tax

Table 4.7 Excise districts with > 10 instances of the army being deployed to support the revenue officers

District	*No. of deployments of the army, 1761–1768*
Cavan	42
Athlone	27
Sligo	19
Killybegs	16
Trim	15
Maryborough	11

resistance begins to emerge. The hinterlands of the major ports, especially the north Dublin coastline, the midlands, and the northwest, were the sites of greatest resistance to the state's revenue gathering apparatus. The southwest counties of Cork and Kerry, prominent in Watt's analysis, and the western coastal counties of Galway and Mayo, do not stand out here, but this may be less about lack of resistance and more about the continued inability of the institutions of the state to penetrate these regions fully, even by the late eighteenth century. Alongside the upland regions of Donegal, notorious for their resistance to the revenue officers well into the nineteenth century, limited infrastructural investment and linguistic barriers continued to restrict the state's impact in these regions for some time to come.[89] Also important was the increased concentration on pursuing illegal distillers rather than smugglers in the later period. As Connell pointed out, the latter were more common than illegal distillers in the Cork and Kerry mountains, something he explained by the opportunities provided by the butter trade.[90] The changing economics of the different varieties of illegal activity altered their geography.

Some Comparisons and Conclusions

This picture of the eighteenth-century Irish tax state with its uneven development and frayed edges should not surprise us. The same pattern after all was visible in Britain. Indeed, Ireland's revenue generating performance, like Wales's and Scotland's, can be seen as evidence of the weakening of centralised structures the farther they travelled westwards or northwards from the centre. Hoppit's research on England goes further and highlights the exceptional nature of London. In many ways, a similar argument might be made about Dublin. The Irish state, like its British counterpart, mutated and adapted to local circumstances the farther it travelled from the capital. This was understood and acknowledged by contemporaries and explains the greater use of force to overawe local populations and to collect taxes in Ireland and Scotland. Interestingly, and rather suggestively, the same pattern of taxation, a reliance on customs rather than excise revenues, pertained in eighteenth-century Scotland as in Ireland. Likewise, it was only after the American War that the excise saw significant growth, warning us perhaps against overestimating the role of Parliament in the Irish case but assuredly pointing to the significance of that conflict in reshaping fiscal policies throughout Britain and Ireland.[91]

Finally, it is worth considering how, and if, eighteenth-century patterns of taxation shaped later developments in Irish fiscal policy. This point is taken up in the final chapter in this book by Michelle D'Arcy and Marina Nistotskaya, but some preliminary remarks might be usefully made here. Firstly, the reliance on taxation of foreign trade rather than domestic production was crucial in establishing a pattern whereby consumers were more likely to be taxed indirectly, leading to greater resistance against forms of direct taxation. This, together with a sense that customary practices and traditions were being assaulted by outside forces—the moral economy argument adapted by Watt—explains the greater incidences of resistance to hearth and excise taxes. The *longue durée* impact on Irish mentalities can only be a matter of speculation, but opposition to direct taxation and infringements of perceived 'rights' continued, and indeed continue, to shape Irish attitudes to taxation. Secondly and finally, the geography of Irish fiscal extraction in the eighteenth century, like the related and to some degree intrinsically linked geography of Irish military deployment, shaped long-term patterns of state development in Ireland, both in terms of the expectation of different fiscal contributions to the state's coffers and in terms of the subsequent regional allocation of the state's resources. The patterns of taxation established in the face of the political, social, and economic upheavals of the late seventeenth century therefore cast a long shadow on Ireland's fiscal and economic history.

Appendix

Table 4.8 Customs, excise, and property revenues, 1695–1795

Year	*Customs (£)*	*Excise (£)*	*Property (£)*	*Other (£)*
1695	73,510	97,497	84,085	2,837
1705	149,078	137,605	89,577	3,812
1715	204,186	103,458	96,097	4,907
1725	244,069	155,176	105,353	5,190
1735	286,555	132,146	108,218	5,438
1745	278,813	167,906	106,643	6,240
1755	455,637	168,905	112,098	8,332
1765	602,037	194,329	121,104	11,265
1775	559,465	168,446	123,831	6,374
1785	826,139	266,958	127,062	7,701
1795	787,802	482,627	133,879	21,487

Note: 'Property' refers to hearth and quit rent revenues

Notes

1. K. H. Connell, 'Illicit Distillation', in K. H. Connell, *Irish Peasant Society: Four Historical Essays* (Oxford: Clarendon Press, 1968), 1–50; David Dickson, 'Taxation and Disaffection in Late Eighteenth-Century Ireland', in *Irish Peasants: Violence and Political Unrest, 1780–1914*, ed. Samuel Clark and James S. Donnelly Jr. (Madison: University of Wisconsin Press, 1983), 37–63; Louis Cullen, 'Smugglers in the Irish Sea in the Eighteenth Century', in L. M. Cullen, *Economy, Trade and Irish Merchants at Home and Abroad, 1600–1988* (Dublin: Four Courts Press, 2012), 118–36; Timothy D. Watt, 'Taxation Riots and the Culture of Popular Protest in Ireland, 1714–1740', *English Historical Review* 130, no. 547 (2016): 1418–48.
2. The analysis and methodology pursued in this chapter owes a significant debt to Julian Hoppit's path-breaking analysis in his *Britain's Political Economies: Parliament and Economic Life, 1660–1800* (Cambridge: Cambridge University Press, 2017), esp. chap. 9. Elsewhere I have sought to situate the phenomenon of the fiscal-military state within a 'four nations' comparative framework; see Patrick Walsh, 'The Eighteenth-Century Fiscal Military State: A Four Nations Perspective', in *Four Nations Approaches to Modern 'British' History: A Disunited Kingdom?*, ed. Naomi Lloyd Jones and Margaret Scull (Basingstoke: Palgrave Macmillan, 2017), 85–110.
3. M. J. Braddick, *The Nerves of State: Taxation and the Financing of the English State, 1558–1714* (Manchester; Manchester University Press, 1996); D'Maris Coffman, *Excise Taxation and the Origins of Public Debt* (Basingstoke: Palgrave Macmillan, 2013), esp. 157–81; Charles Ivar McGrath, *The Making of the Eighteenth-Century Irish Constitution: Government, Parliament and the Revenue, 1692–1714* (Dublin: Four Courts Press, 2000), 24–31.
4. Maurice J. Bric, 'Priests, Parsons and Politics: The Rightboy Protest in County Cork, 1785–88', in *Nationalism and Popular Protest in Ireland*, ed. C. H. E. Philpin (Cambridge: Cambridge University Press, 1987), 163–90.
5. For contemporary comment see Thomas Waite to Sir Robert Wilmot, 23 July 1763, Public Record Office of Northern Ireland (hereafter, PRONI), T3019/4655. See also Eoin Magennis, 'A "Presbyterian Insurrection"? Reconsidering the Hearts of Oak Disturbances of July 1763', *Irish Historical Studies* 31, no. 122 (1998): 165–87.
6. Hoppit, *Britain's Political Economies*, 58. For some discussion of increasing taxation at the county level see Dickson, 'Taxation and Disaffection', 50–52.

7. David Dickson, *New Foundations: Ireland, 1660–1800* (Dublin: Irish Academic Press, 2000), 191.
8. Dickson, 'Taxation and Disaffection', 39; Walsh, 'Towards a Four Nations History', 91–92.
9. McGrath, *Irish Constitution*, 42–43.
10. Patrick Walsh, 'The Fiscal State in Ireland, 1691–1769', *Historical Journal* 56, no. 3 (2013): 639.
11. David Dickson, Cormac Ó Gráda, and Stuart Daultrey, 'Hearth Tax, Household Size and Irish Population Change, 1672–1821', *Proceedings of the Royal Irish Academy*, section c, 82 (1982): 135–39.
12. Patrick K. O'Brien, 'The Political Economy of British Taxation, 1660–1815', *Economic History Review*, 2nd ser., 41, no. 1 (1988): 1–32; John Brewer, *The Sinews of Power: War, Money and the English State, 1688–1783* (London: Unwin, 1989).
13. Hoppit, *Britain's Political Economies*, 302.
14. Walsh, 'Fiscal State', *passim*.
15. David Dickson identified this trend in revenues for the period after 1780, but it holds true for the whole century; see Dickson, 'Taxation and Disaffection', 39.
16. For a vigorous argument about the role of tax policy in shaping the English industrial revolution see William Ashworth, *The Industrial Revolution: The State, Knowledge and Global Trade* (London: Bloomsbury, 2017).
17. See James Guilfoyle's chapter in this volume.
18. McGrath, *Irish Constitution*, 73–118; D. W. Hayton, 'Introduction: The Long Apprenticeship', *Parliamentary History* 20, no. 1 (2001): 1–22.
19. Charles Ivar McGrath, *Ireland and Empire, 1692–1770* (London: Pickering and Chatto, 2012), 44–45.
20. Ibid., 69–106.
21. McGrath, *Ireland and Empire*, 177.
22. Watt, 'Taxation Riots', 1429–30.
23. Patrick Walsh, 'Enforcing the Fiscal State: The Army, the Revenue and the Irish Experience of the Fiscal-Military State, 1690–1769', in *The British Fiscal-Military States, 1660–c. 1783*, ed. Patrick Walsh and Aaron Graham (London: Routledge, 2016), 131–58.
24. Minutes of the Irish Revenue Commissioners (hereafter, Rev. Commrs. Min. Bks.), 28 June 1759, 12 Sept. 1760, 6 Nov. 1769, The National Archives (hereafter, TNA): CUST 1/63, f. 7; CUST 1/65, ff. 25–27, CUST 1/110, f. 64; Waite to Wilmot, 16 Jan. 1772, PRONI, T3019/6267.
25. McGrath, *Ireland and Empire*, 140–42, 165–66.
26. Dickson, 'Taxation and Disaffection', 43; A. J. Fitzpatrick, 'The Economic Effects of the French Revolutionary and Napoleanic wars on Ireland' (PhD diss., Trinity College Dublin, 1973), 7–12; Patrick Given, 'Calico to Whiskey: A Case Study on the Development of the Distilling Industry in

the Naas Revenue Collection District, 1700–1921' (PhD diss., Maynooth University, 2011), 88–90, 215.
27. James Hamilton to Lord Abercorn, 23 June 1780, PRONI, D623/A/44/36.
28. Given, 'Calico to Whiskey', 222.
29. Data on licence yields comes from the Irish fiscal accounts. For the situation in 1785 see *CJI*, xi, app., dccx.
30. The phrase is Hoppit's, *Britain's Political Economies*, 39. For the growth in Irish legislation see Hayton, 'The Long Apprenticeship', 13.
31. The classic revisionist dismissal of the economic significance of the post-1782 Parliament is J. J. Lee, 'Grattan's Parliament', in *The Irish Parliamentary Tradition*, ed. Brian Farrell (Dublin, 1973), 149–59.
32. On the Irish Parliament's increasing regulatory role see Eoin Magennis, 'The Irish Parliament and the Regulatory Impulse: The Case of the Coal Trade', *Parliamentary History* 33, no. 1 (2014): 54–72.
33. Eoin Magennis, 'Coal, Corn and Canals: The Dispersal of Public Moneys, 1695–1772', *Parliamentary History* 20, no. 1 (2001): 71–86; Andrew Sneddon, 'Legislating for Economic Development: Irish Fisheries as a Case Study for the Limitations of Improvement', in *The Eighteenth-Century Composite State: Representative Institutions in Ireland and Europe, 1689–1800*, ed. D. W. Hayton, James Kelly, and John Bergin (Basingstoke: Palgrave Macmillan, 2010), 136–59.
34. Hoppit, *Britain's Political Economies*, 131.
35. Dickson, Ó Gráda, and Daultrey, 'Hearth Tax'.
36. Patrick Walsh, Aidan Kane, and Eoin Magennis, 'Ireland, 1698–1829' in *Revue de l'OFCE*, 140 (2015): 269–74.
37. The bureaucratic structure is laid out in T. J. Kiernan, *History of the Financial Administration of Ireland to 1817* (London: P. S. King and Son, 1930), 255–65.
38. Hoppit, *British Political Economies*, 281–88.
39. The geographical dispersal of revenue officials can be captured on a quarterly (i.e. three-monthly) basis for the period 1686–1769 in the Irish Establishment books, TNA: CUST 20/56–137. After 1769, inland excise officers are no longer listed, making it difficult to make direct comparisons with earlier periods, except for 1789 when an isolated excise establishment survives, National Library of Ireland (hereafter, NLI) MS 3877.
40. Trade flows for individual ports can be seen at www.duanaire.ie/trade.
41. Quoted in Given, 'Calico to Whiskey', 41.
42. David Dickson, 'Seven Sisters? The Seaport Cities of Mid-Eighteenth-Century Ireland', in *Ireland, France and the Atlantic in a Time of War: Reflections on the Bordeaux-Dublin Letters, 1757*, ed. Thomas M. Truxes (Abingdon: Routledge, 2017), 95.

43. Hoppit, *British Political Economies*, 284.
44. John Fitzgibbon to John Beresford, 14 May 1793, *Correspondence of the Rt. Hon. John Beresford*, ed. William Beresford, 2 vols. (London: Woodfall and Kinder, 1854), 2:13.
45. David Dickson, *Old World Colony: Cork and South Munster, 1630–1830* (Cork: Cork University Press, 2005), 148–59.
46. Irish Import and Export Ledgers, TNA: CUST 15/27, 101.
47. For an incisive analysis of the fluctuating fortunes of Ireland's port cities see Dickson, 'Seven Sisters?', 93–107.
48. On the Newry Canal see L. M. Cullen, *An Economic History of Ireland since 1660*, 2nd ed. (London: Batsford Press, 1987), 88–89.
49. See charts for imports of port and Spanish wine in the CUST 15 database of Irish trade at www.duanaire.ie/trade.
50. Stephen Conway, *War, State, and Society in Mid-Eighteenth-Century Britain and Ireland* (Oxford: Oxford University Press, 2006), 257.
51. George Macartney, 'A Sketch of the Revenue of Ireland' (1773), NLI MS 11,967, ff. 53–67.
52. Dickson, *New Foundations*, 215.
53. Hoppit, *Britain's Political Economies*, 286.
54. Rev. Commrs. Min. Bks., 12 Sept. 1760, TNA: Cust 1/65, ff. 25–27.
55. Rev. Commrs. Min. Bks., 18 Dec. 1738, 28 Mar. 1764, TNA: Cust 1/30, f. 69, Cust 1/81, f. 27; Edward McParland, *Public Architecture in Ireland, 1680–1760* (London: Yale University Press, 2001), 119, 130.
56. Rev. Commrs. Min. Bks., 16 Nov. 1739, 10 June 1760, 15 Sept. 1764, TNA: Cust 1/30, f. 244, Cust 1/64, f. 134, Cust 1/83, f. 102.
57. Rev. Commrs. Min. Bks., 16 May 1738, TNA: Cust 1/29, f. 184.
58. D. A. Fleming, *Politics and Provincial People: Sligo and Limerick, 1691–1761* (Manchester: Manchester University Press, 2010), 166–68.
59. See, for example, the *Boyle*, *Bessborough*, and *Boyne*, amongst others.
60. Rev. Commrs. Min. Bks., 19 Oct. 1759, TNA: Cust 1/63, 145. Mercer had previously commanded the *Thompson Galley* and the *Bessborough*; Customs Establishment books, 25 Mar. 1734, 15 Mar. 1744, TNA: Cust 20/102, 112.
61. Patrick Walsh, 'Ireland and the Royal Navy in the Eighteenth Century', in *The Royal Navy and the British Atlantic World, c. 1750–1820*, ed. John McAleer and Christer Petley (Basingstoke: Palgrave Macmillan, 2016), 51–76.
62. Walsh, 'Fiscal State', 643.
63. James Kelly, 'Harvests and Hardship: Famine and Scarcity in Ireland in the Late 1720s', *Studia Hibernica* 26 (1992): 65–106.
64. Waite to Wilmot, 16 Jan. 1772, PRONI, T3019/6267.

65. Given, 'Calico to Whiskey', 106–08. Similarly, the 1782–1784 subsistence crisis explains the dip in excise revenues at the beginning of the 1780s.
66. For a detailed analysis of Naas district see Given, 'Calico to Whiskey', 179–99, 211–18.
67. Connell, 'Illicit Distillation', 40.
68. Monck Mason, Report, NLI P4047 n.p.
69. Based on a comparison of the excise data and the Establishment books for these districts.
70. Timothy D. Watt, 'Order and Disorder in Ireland, 1692–1735' (PhD diss., Queen's University Belfast, 2013), 139.
71. Walsh, 'Fiscal State', 642.
72. Kiernan, *Financial Administration*, 266; for the excise establishment in 1789 see NLI MS 3877.
73. Walsh, 'Fiscal State', 644.
74. Watt, 'Order and Disorder', 5, 7, 156.
75. Walsh, 'Fiscal State', 654.
76. Watt, 'Taxation Riots', *passim.*
77. Cullen, 'Smugglers in the Irish Sea', *passim*; Gerard J. Lyne, *Murtaí Óg Ó Súilleabháin (c. 1710–54): A Life Contextualised* (Dublin: Geography Publications, 2017).
78. Walsh, 'Ireland and the Royal Navy', 58–59.
79. 'Report of the commissioners of revenue in Ireland on the running of wool from Ireland to France', 29 Jan. 1755, Treasury Papers, TNA: T 1/361/21; see also Walsh, 'Enforcing the Fiscal-Military State', 131.
80. Watt, 'Taxation Riots', 1418.
81. Walsh, 'Enforcing the Fiscal-Military State', 148.
82. Incidences of 'riot and rescue' can also be calculated from the same source; see Watt, 'Taxation Riots', 1431.
83. Rev. Commrs. Min. Bks., 1760–69, TNA: CUST 1/64–110; Watt, 'Taxation Riots', 1430–32.
84. Watt, 'Taxation Riots', 1432.
85. Walsh, 'Enforcing the Fiscal-Military State', 151–52.
86. Rev. Commrs. Min. Bks., 16 Mar. 1762, 25 June 1766, 27 Sept. 1767, TNA: Cust 1/71, f. 32, Cust 1/92, f. 100, Cust 1/99, f. 52; Diary of a journey through England and Wales to Ireland, made by Rev. J. Burrows, entry for 15 June [1773], PRONI, T3551/1.
87. Walsh, 'Enforcing the Fiscal-Military State', 144, 150.
88. Quarters of the Army in Ireland, 1784, Kilmainham Papers, NLI MS 1007. On the revenue police see Jim Herlihy, *The Irish Revenue Police: A Short History and Genealogical Guide to the 'Poteen Hussars'* (Dublin: Four Courts Press, 2018).

89. Connell, 'Illicit Distillation', *passim*; Cullen, *Economic History of Ireland*, 168; Nicholas M. Wolf, *An Irish-Speaking Island: State, Religion, Community, and the Linguistic Landscape in Ireland, 1770–1870* (Madison: University of Wisconsin Press, 2014).
90. Connell, 'Illicit Distillation', 34.
91. On Scotland see Hoppit, *British Political Economies*, 299–300; Philipp Robinson Rössner *Scottish Trade in the Wake of Union (1700–1760): The Rise of a Warehouse Economy* (Stuttgart: Franz Steiner Verlag, 2008), 38–40.

CHAPTER 5

Finance and Politics in Ireland, 1801–17

Trevor McCavery

This chapter explains how financial relations between Britain and Ireland were arranged by the British-Irish Act of Union, which passed in 1800 and came into effect in 1801. It presents some of the consequent financial and political difficulties. Before proceeding directly to these issues, some political context is provided.

The Political Context

The French Revolution, its violent aftermath in France, and the wars between Britain and France from 1793 cast long shadows over politics in Britain and Ireland. William Pitt had been Prime Minister of Great Britain since 1783. Because of his reforms across a range of policy areas, Pitt has been described as a 'new Tory' or even an 'independent Whig'. Fear of the contagion of revolution, however, pushed him into passing repressive legislation both in Britain and Ireland. In the latter, a reform movement called the United Irish Society was driven underground and transformed into an oath-bound secret society, pledged to sever the British connection with Ireland by violent means, with French help, in order to establish a more democratic, non-sectarian, independent republic. The 1798 Rebellion was the result.

T. McCavery (✉)
Independent Scholar, Newtownards, Northern Ireland

D. Kanter, P. Walsh (eds.), *Taxation, Politics, and Protest in Ireland, 1662–2016*, Palgrave Studies in the History of Finance,
https://doi.org/10.1007/978-3-030-04309-4_5

Pitt had long considered that if Ireland was to be stabilised and its sectarian divisions lessened, it would mean the removal of the Irish Parliament, a legislative assembly which exclusively represented Anglican landlord interests and which had shaken off its subordinate status to the British Parliament in 1782. The 1798 Rebellion, supported by an attempted invasion of Ireland by France, convinced Pitt of the necessity of a 'legislative Union' between Britain and Ireland. The Union was passed by a combination of large doses of compensation, corruption, and 'caressing'. It did not affect the executive in Ireland; although Ireland's legislature was abolished, its executive, in the form of a Viceroy (or Lord Lieutenant), his Chief Secretary, two Under-Secretaries, and a coterie of advisers, was retained. Therefore, two executives governed Ireland, even though Ireland was supposed to be assimilated into Great Britain to create one entity, the United Kingdom. Lord Cornwallis remained Viceroy in Ireland to manage this novel situation.

Pitt believed that the Union should be accompanied by measures to free Catholics from various restrictions and provide state provision for Catholic and Dissenting clergy. Such 'Emancipation' offended George III, who thought that the approval of such measures would violate his coronation oath to protect the Church of England. Pitt resigned in February 1801 and was succeeded by Henry Addington, who sent the Earl of Hardwicke to replace Cornwallis as Viceroy.

Between the extreme positions of Tory and Whig, there existed in the UK Parliament a spectrum on which several factions could be found, numbering between fifty and seventy MPs each; the rest of the MPs were mostly independent country gentlemen who would patriotically support whatever government was in power. At the extreme Tory end, stood Addington and his supporters. Then there were Pitt and his friends who sought Catholic Emancipation. A new group emerged led by Lord Grenville. A cousin of Pitt, Grenville had served under him in senior posts and resigned with him in 1801 over the issue of Catholic Emancipation. Grenville's more liberal approach, and being out of office, drew him closer to the opposition Whig leader, Charles James Fox. By April 1804, criticism of Addington's war policies culminated in a parliamentary attack by these factions and Pitt returned as Prime Minister—though without the support of the Grenvillites. Hardwicke remained as Lord Lieutenant. Pitt's health and his command of the House of Commons were weak, and he died in 1806.

Grenville became the head of a liberal coalition government called the 'Ministry of all the Talents'. This was supported by Fox and Henry Addington. Grenville and Fox were joint leaders, the former as First Lord of the Treasury and the latter as Foreign Secretary. These changes were reflected in the Irish executive when the enthusiastic Whig, the Duke of Bedford, was sent to Ireland as Viceroy and brought sweeping changes in the membership of the Irish executive. The 'Talents' ministry was short-lived, which was not a surprise given its mixed nature, and broke up over the decision to introduce a measure of Catholic relief. The elderly Duke of Portland was asked to head up a Pittite, but anti-Emancipationist, government in Britain. A period of 'No Popery', Tory rule ensued, led next by Spencer Perceval (until his assassination in 1812). From 1812 to 1827, the Earl of Liverpool led another Tory government, in which the issue of Catholic Emancipation was left as an open question, neither to be actively pushed nor opposed. In Ireland, the Duke of Bedford was recalled and was succeeded by, first, the Duke of Richmond (1807–13), and then Viscount Whitworth (1813–17).[1]

The Financial Arrangements

Having considered the political background, attention turns to the financial arrangements made in the British-Irish Act of Union. These were intended to be generous to Ireland. This view counters an Irish nationalist interpretation of the subject articulated in the early twentieth century.[2]

When the British Prime Minister, William Pitt, became convinced of the necessity of a legislative union between Britain and Ireland, he broached the subject seriously with his cabinet colleague, Grenville, on 2 June 1798. By 4 June, the joint Postmaster General, Lord Auckland, considered an expert on Irish financial affairs, had been brought into Pitt's confidence. Pitt told Auckland that he and Grenville had been able to 'see daylight in almost everything but what relates to trade and revenue. … We both agreed that we had the best chance of some useful suggestions on the difficult points … by bringing it under your view.'[3] Pitt and Grenville were concerned that the existing national debts of each country, and the cost of servicing them, were so disparate that it was a question of justice whether Ireland should be asked to take on the cost of sharing the British burden and a question of prudence whether she could bear British taxation levels to do so.

By 14 August, Edward Cooke, one of the two deputies to the Chief Secretary, had submitted a plan for union to Pitt. Earl Camden, a recent Lord Lieutenant, said, 'No-one understands Ireland better than Mr Cooke.'[4] Fortunately, Cooke's plan survives in the Auckland papers and Pitt's comments on it are also extant in the Sneyd papers, so we can examine the earliest thinking on the detail of the Act of Union.[5] Cooke suggested that Ireland should be responsible for her own government's expenditure and debts; only when Ireland's own debts were paid off, should she be asked to make a proportionate contribution to the British debt. Pitt agreed with the principle of proportionate contribution but thought that it should be applied immediately—but only to military expenditure, from which Ireland would receive benefit; the rest could go to her debts and local projects. He claimed that 'this will be still more advantageous to Ireland.' Cooke suggested that the current margin of difference between British and Irish levels of taxation be maintained. Pitt agreed again in principle that the levels ought not to be the same but thought that levels of indirect taxation in Ireland should reflect the differences in yield of an income tax were it to be levied. Regarding commercial relations between the two countries, Cooke suggested that the Anglo-French Commercial Treaty of 1787 serve as the model. This reduced all tariffs to a small amount to encourage trade without damaging domestic manufacturing. Pitt thought this was 'quite reasonable', but he was prepared to be more generous: 'It is desirable, gradually or immediately, to go further and make the intercourse duty-free, except so far as to countervail a difference in internal or import duties.'[6]

These ideas formed the basis of the commercial and financial articles of the Union and were modified over the next few months. For example, by November 1798, it was agreed that Ireland was to contribute to the civil as well as military expenses of the new unified state.[7] Viscount Castlereagh, the Chief Secretary, could write on 7 January 1799: 'The terms are considered as highly liberal, the proportional arrangement of the expenses having completely overset the argument on which the enemies of the measure had hitherto principally relied, namely, the extension of English debt and taxation to Ireland.'[8]

Castlereagh had responsibility for finalising the terms. By 17 January 1799 he envisaged that the system of proportionate contribution and separate Treasuries should not last forever because this was contrary to the spirit of union. He suggested that the arrangements last until 1821 and be reviewed every ten years. He was not satisfied that anyone had 'found a sufficiently accurate criterion … of the relative means of the two countries'. He objected to Pitt's suggestion of the yield of an Irish income tax. In Britain, the yield was the result of a patriotic response by landowners to wartime exigencies. This was not sustainable; in Ireland, the government could not be assured of a similar response, even in wartime. In the meantime, he suggested that it would be fairer to determine the proportion by comparing articles of consumption in the two countries.[9]

As late as 23 October 1799, Castlereagh assumed that there would be one quota for contributions in peace (one-seventh) and another for war (one-tenth). This idea was abandoned, and a letter from Robert Hobart, a former Chief Secretary, to the influential Auckland may contain the reasons: 'I … think that a similar proportion both for peace and war will be best understood and is … more reasonable … because … the ability of Ireland in time of war to bear her share of expenses is … as great, if not greater … than in peace. Her chief source of wealth, her linens, certainly do not fail her at that time and there can be no doubt of the increase of her provision trade. Such an arrangement would also … be more palatable here.'[10] Hobart's ideas were accepted by 13 November 1799.[11] It is not clear if optimism about Ireland's capacity in war, or a desire to make the idea 'more palatable' in Great Britain, explains why a common ratio was decided. The proportion decided was two-seventeenths, halfway between one-seventh and one-tenth. It was not until 18 December 1799, however, that Irish accounts were found that showed that the comparative consumption of beer, spirits, salt, tea, sugar, tobacco, and wine approximated to this ratio.[12]

Castlereagh was delighted. He accepted that 'any estimate of this nature must, however, be in a great degree vague and conjectural, both from the impossibility of forming any very precise computation of national wealth and from the uncertainty whether (even if such computations could be formed) it can be supposed that the two countries will advance in different degrees in their wealth, capital and industry and can afford to pay, with equal convenience, the same proportion to that wealth.'[13] When he read the accounts showing the relative consumption of certain articles, he wrote immediately to Auckland: 'You will be pleased at the coincidence in the proportional value of enumerated articles consumed in the two countries. This concordance in the criterion of relative wealth exceeds my most sanguine expectations. I think it places the system on a rock. The 7½ falling in with past expenditure is convenient, but supported by the tests of commerce and consumption, it is built on a foundation that cannot be shaken.'[14] The framers of the Act of Union were aware of the difficulties of calculating national wealth for the purposes of comparability: they could only draw satisfaction that their statistics *coincided* in the ratio of 7½:1.

Another important detail was settled in the period between October and December 1799—how long proportionate contribution should continue and what the conditions permitting financial amalgamation should be. Cooke introduced the novel idea that common taxation might ensue when the *debts* of each country were in the same proportion as their *contributions*. At present, the debt proportion stood at 12:1; when it became 7½:1, financial amalgamation could take place. He expected the British debt to be reduced from 12:1 to 7½:1, and the consequent level of British taxation would approach Irish levels.[15] Cooke's prognosis proved to be entirely wrong. The 7½:1 ratio in terms of debts was reached in a decade, but it was through a large *increase of Irish debt*, due to having to meet two-seventeenths of ever-increasing United Kingdom expenses from nearly fifteen years of costly war. The British debt did not increase as fast as the Irish because Britain discovered an unexpected capacity for sustaining extraordinarily high levels of taxation.

Castlereagh accepted Cooke's formula of debt ratio equalling contribution ratio; but he did not accept the accompanying prognosis. His own reading of the future was vindicated by later events and deserves full quotation:

> If war should continue, and Ireland finds her supplies [i.e., borrows] while England raises the greater part of hers within the year [i.e., by taxation] and mortgages her extraordinary funds to their rapid reduction in peace, Ireland must run proportionately in debt and her scale of taxes rise accordingly. It evidently depends, therefore, upon events—whether England shall descend, or Ireland be raised, to the level with England; but neither can be injured as the assimilation will be produced by natural causes and in no degree forced.[16]

Although Castlereagh foresaw the course of events, he did not see this as injurious to Ireland, because he believed that Ireland would gradually raise her levels of taxation to meet the increased debt charges 'by natural causes and in no degree forced'.

This was the final touch to the seventh article of the Act of Union. Castlereagh reported to Pitt, on the eve of the session of the Irish Parliament that was to pass the act:

> The articles of Union having now been gone through by our leading friends, I … assure you that the arrangement affords them all the fullest satisfaction. The question of expense they consider as most satisfactorily and liberally settled between the two countries and the only alteration they seemed to wish is the introduction of some words in the clause, which I have the honour to enclose, which may more distinctly explain, on the face of the resolution, the particular circumstances which would warrant the substitution of common taxes in lieu of proportionate contributions.[17]

English politicians were also willing to accept the financial terms. Auckland judged that 'Mr [Robert] Peel [MP for Tamworth and prominent industrialist] is very liberal and right minded, and I have reason to believe that he will make a speech to say that Ireland is much too well treated but that he and others cordially acquiesce under a conviction that the general arrangement is wise and most beneficial to all. I did not discourage this sort of speech. It will do no harm with us and good with you.'[18]

As the Treasuries, debts, and revenues of Ireland and Great Britain were to be managed separately, this Irish business would be conducted by a Chancellor of the Irish Exchequer. Financial amalgamation was to occur when

1. The separate debts of each country were paid off, or the debts of each country were in the same proportion to each other as Ireland's contribution to British expenditure, that is, two-seventeenths or 7½:1 and
2. Irish resources could bear British levels of taxation, subject to any exemptions as Parliament might see fit.

The Financial Consequences

Financial amalgamation finally occurred in January 1817, but the two conditions for this amalgamation were met much earlier. By about 1810, the debts of each country stood in the same proportion to one another as Ireland's contribution to UK expenses (7½:1). Because Irish Chancellors borrowed in London, they were able to borrow a lot more than they could have if they had borrowed only in Dublin. In 1801, the Irish government borrowed £16 million in Britain and £10 million in Ireland. By 1817, £92 million had been borrowed in Britain and £21 million in Ireland, a total of £113 million.[19] Debt interest payments spiralled. In 1800, Irish debt charges were only £1.6 million; in 1816, they were £6.8 million and exceeded the country's revenues of £5.56 million. In other words, the country was bankrupt.[20]

The second criterion—of Irish resources being broadly able to sustain current British rates of taxation—was reached by 1814. During the period of separate Exchequers, between 1801 and 1817, revenue from Irish taxation more than doubled, although direct taxation was never attempted. The first Chancellor of the Irish Exchequer after the Act of Union, Isaac Corry, promised a property tax for Ireland in his budget speech of 1803, 'but it would require some time to inform Ireland of the immensity of the danger with which she was threatened and some time to form the resolution to meet that danger'. The statement was made without consultation with the rest of the Irish government.[21] The Lord Lieutenant, the Earl of Hardwicke, objected to Corry's independent stance and to a property tax in principle. He believed that there was scope for pushing up the national debt of Ireland and a property tax should be avoided in the special circumstances of the country: 'the difference of its means, the inferiority of its capital and above all the great variety of its existing tenures'.[22]

Corry's successors as Chancellors of the Irish Exchequer never attempted direct taxation. Between 1811 and 1815, some British politicians, however, disagreed. They complained that Irish borrowing on the London money market was a burden on credit, and Irish landowners were accused of not paying their fair share of taxation. A full-scale debate in the United Kingdom Parliament occurred on 25 April 1815 when Henry Bankes, an English MP and economic reformer, tabled a motion on the merits of introducing a land tax for Ireland. The statement refuting Bankes from the current Chancellor of the Irish Exchequer, William Vesey FitzGerald, was hailed in and out of Parliament as the last word on the subject for this era. Bankes's motion was defeated by seventy-eight votes to five.[23]

When it came to indirect taxation, FitzGerald referred to 'the narrow limits to which taxation was reduced in Ireland'.[24] In 1800, 85 per cent of all exports were to Great Britain and 78 per cent of all imports were from Great Britain.[25] The Act of Union, however, stipulated that this Anglo-Irish trade was to be free from taxation with a few specified exceptions. Much of the trade of Ireland, therefore, escaped customs taxation. A second constraint, affecting the excise, also originated with the Union provisions: no duty could be laid in Ireland on any article not liable to one in

England, and a higher rate could not be levied in Ireland than the rate levied in England (though this was sometimes ignored by Irish Chancellors).

John Foster succeeded Isaac Corry in May 1804. He decided to tap the wealthy of Ireland through their expenditure rather than through their incomes. So, after Corry's rather mild budgets, in terms of indirect taxation, Foster's appeared draconian. He imposed 50 per cent increases in tobacco duties, 50 per cent on wine, and 40 to 70 per cent on tea. But the yield was disappointing. Irish revenue was expected to increase from £3 million to £4.25 million but the increase only went to less than £4 million. Such increases left little scope for subsequent Chancellors. This was recognised by Sir Henry Parnell when he said that 'it would be to no purpose to impose new taxes unless the collection of those at present was made effective.'[26]

When Foster returned to office in 1807, he explained that 'it was thought more prudent to go on raising our quota by a debt than to have it raised by additional taxes. The whole amount of the debt of Ireland is certainly stupendous, it being already no less than £76 millions of money—a sum which in former days many thought that Ireland could not exist under … and yet there is no reason to think it will injure her in her resources in any degree.'[27] By now it was accepted that Ireland's debt was going to increase to the point where the ratio of it to Britain's would equal the ratio of Ireland's contribution to UK expenses—that is, the conditions for financial amalgamation which might involve equality in taxation.[28] To hasten this, Foster began to bring rates of Irish taxation into line with current British rates. In 1810, the taxes on letters, tea, and the stamp on receipts were equalised. In 1811, the duties on tobacco, hemp, timber, and cotton wool were equalised, as were taxes on a wide range of goods and services. FitzGerald, Chancellor from August 1812, continued this policy by a near general 25 per cent increase in the customs duties, with tea and coffee bearing rates equal to the British. By 1814, all customs duties had been equalised.[29]

Both conditions for financial amalgamation had been met: by 1810 the ratio of the debts of each country was the same as the ratio of Ireland's contribution to UK expenses, and by 1814 the rates of taxation on several articles were the same in each country. FitzGerald's ambition was to have the honour of introducing the union of the Exchequers to the House of Commons. In November 1813, a conference of representatives from both governments agreed financial amalgamation in principle.[30]

Yet financial amalgamation did not come about until 1817. Lord Liverpool, the Prime Minister, insisted that the proper authority for taking this step must be a parliamentary committee on Irish finance, set up in March 1811. This committee worked very slowly. Sir John Newport, a member of the opposition, stated his intention of moving for a commission of enquiry into Irish expenditure and a select committee to consider the reports of the statutory commission of enquiry into the emoluments of civil officers in Ireland and abuses in the collection of the Irish revenue, which sat between 1804 and 1813. The government was spurred into action.[31] Ministers set up their own select committee in April 1815, and the committee recommended amalgamation at the end of June.

The principal reason, however, for delay in the period 1814–16 was the fact that the subject was, in Nicholas Vansittart's words, 'somewhat lost sight of in the pressure of foreign politics'.[32] It proved difficult to bring about complete military victory over Napoleon and then there was the subsequent involvement in peace negotiations. FitzGerald fretted at the task of producing budgets for a bankrupt country. In 1814, he explained to the Chancellor of the British Exchequer, 'I am sure that by no means other than a consolidation of our finances, or a change in the rate of contribution which Ireland is called to furnish, can she meet her share of the necessary charge this year. Our revenue has exceeded my estimate but we are still in a bankrupt state.'[33] The revenue was just about enough to pay the present interest charges on the Irish national debt, but £10 million was needed to be borrowed to meet Ireland's contribution. As for meeting the additional expenses, he confessed 'where to go, or how to obtain it, I profess I know not'. He had to admonish the Prime Minister 'that in a moment of such anxiety and interest as the present, when your minds must be occupied with all that involves the fate of the world, it should be hoped that the attention of the government could be turned to the financial state in Ireland'. As Liverpool explained, referring to the former Chief Secretary and current Foreign Secretary, 'the absence of Lord Castlereagh on the Continent, whose opinion on so important a branch of Irish politics is so very essential, has prevented our making any progress on the subject.'[34] Another year elapsed before FitzGerald recommended the consolidation of Irish and British finances to the House of Commons on 20 May 1816, to come into effect on 1 January 1817.[35]

Under the terms of the consolidation, Ireland was relieved of making the contribution of two-seventeenths to meet imperial expenses and instead was required to contribute one-seventeenth, though this was never actually carried through. Ireland's debt was written off. The office of Chancellor of the Irish Exchequer was suppressed because Ireland no longer needed budgets to raise taxes and borrow. Ireland was not expected to be taxed at the same rates as Britain. The British Treasury became responsible for the collection and management of the Irish revenue. Two of the Irish Lords of the Treasury would sit at the British Treasury Board to assist.[36]

Two vital areas remained untouched. The first was the right of the Viceroy to exercise discretionary powers in the remission of fines and penalties in matters relating to revenue and the second was the patronage of appointments. Regarding the first, it was accepted that, as the representative of the Crown, it was fitting that the Viceroy should hear and judge on appeals. Robert Peel, Chief Secretary from 1812 to 1818, claimed that to lose this power would have been 'a death blow to the vice-regal power in Ireland'. Regarding the second power, that of making appointments to posts in the revenue service, the current Viceroy declared that if he were to lose this power 'they had better do away with the office of lord lieutenant at once'.[37]

The Political Consequences

It is highly ironic that the Lord Lieutenant in 1816 should insist on controlling appointments in the revenue service so that viceregal political power could remain intact. In 1801, the first Viceroy after the Union, Hardwicke, had contrasting priorities. George III had famously remarked that the Act of Union would 'close the reign of Irish jobs'.[38] Hardwicke's private instructions were 'to inform yourself how far the collection of His Majesty's revenues may be rendered more simple, and less chargeable, without detriment to his services. And how far the expenditure thereof may be more effectually checked and controlled.'[39]

The thinking was that if the revenue service could be freed from exploitation as a resource for political patronage, a more efficient collection of the revenue must mean more money reaching the Exchequer. Abolishing sinecures would lessen the burden on the Exchequer. All this would make the acceptance of higher levels of taxation easier. The Irish taxpayer would be unwilling to see his money wasted on political appointments and sinecures. Oppositionists in Parliament were always quick to demand retrenchment before authorising fresh taxation. Also, it was pointless to place hopes in additional revenue if the revenue departments were not capable of collecting it. By 1816 thinking had changed. What had happened in the intervening period?[40]

The issue of administrative reform, and how this should be best carried out, became an important issue in post-Union politics. Hardwicke and his first Chief Secretary, Charles Abbot, began their administration by circulating, in August 1801, a questionnaire enquiring about the details of public offices, their expenses, and duties. It was not surprising that this met with uproar. Indeed, other members of the British cabinet who had served in Ireland were not enthusiastic about this inquisition. Officials completed the questionnaire but disclosed so little information that it was useless.[41] The Viceroy and Chief Secretary introduced some minor reforms.[42] The most radical moves in this direction during Abbott's period in office were to debar senior revenue officials from Parliament and to disenfranchise all revenue officials.[43]

The impetus for reform was slowed when William Wickham was appointed Chief Secretary in February 1802. Hardwicke and Wickham found it difficult to prevent Revenue Commissioners from enhancing their local interests.[44] Wickham was ineffective. Lady Londonderry described him as 'a very commonplace character without any presentable grace'; for the last six months of his period of office in Ireland he was confined to his room as an invalid. Another impediment to reform was the pressing problem of Robert Emmet's insurrection in Dublin in 1803, the suppression of which precipitated a dispute between the Home Secretary and the Viceroy over the powers of the Commander-in-Chief. [45] Compounding these problems was the fact that Isaac Corry, the Chancellor of the Irish Exchequer, was upstaging Wickham.

Hardwicke was concerned that Corry was building up a power base at Westminster. Wickham justified his low profile by referring to the fact that, because he had never sat in Parliament, he had 'made it an express condition with Mr Addington on my taking my seat that I should not be expected to take any share in debate this parliamentary session'.[46] Corry had been useful in steering the Act of Union through the Irish House of Commons in 1799, and Pitt and Addington were keen for him to continue in office after the Union. He was valued for his debating skills. Corry excelled himself on the larger stage in the British House of Commons. In 1802, he was able to see off the powerful anti-unionist and former speaker of the Irish House of Commons, John Foster, who, when 'he put himself within Corry's grip, has shrunk to nothing'.[47]

His pretensions to superiority over the Irish Chief Secretary seemed confirmed when, in the 1802–03 session, he demanded the secondment of the cream of the revenue service in Dublin to assist him with parliamentary business at Westminster. Wickham had disappointed Hardwicke: 'If he had taken a more active and forward part in the House of Commons, he would have kept things more in their proper course, and persons more in their proper places.'[48]

Corry's position would appear to have been in tune with British thinking. Addington revealed this to Lord Redesdale, the Lord Chancellor of Ireland, when he spoke of Wickham's duties: 'As the meeting of Parliament approaches, I … think that more would be lost on your side of the water by his residence in England than would be gained on ours. From the evidence … of the last session, I … believe that this would be my opinion even in time of peace and … apparent tranquillity.' This became cabinet policy on Sir Evan Nepean's appointment as Chief Secretary in January 1804. The statement of cabinet ran as follows:

> For this session at least, [he] will hardly be in a situation to leave Ireland at all, and … he should remain more upon the spot hereafter than Abbot or Wickham had been accustomed to do during the sitting of Parliament. And while the secretary of state for the home department is a member of the House of Commons and is assisted by an efficient chancellor of the Irish exchequer (who will of course take care of all details and points of trade, revenue and local interest) and has besides the advantage of Lord Castlereagh's presence and authority, there [is no] reason to expect that the attendance of the chief secretary … will be required otherwise than occasionally and for the purpose of holding confidential communication on points of great importance or circumstances not so well to be explained by correspondence.

Hardwicke lamented that his new Chief Secretary was 'too little a speaker in Parliament to answer the purpose, for Lord Redesdale tells me that he could never prevail upon himself to speak upon common Admiralty business. … We must not lose sight of parliamentary competence.'[49]

Because Corry spent so much time in London and not enough in consultation in Dublin, he made mistakes. These brought censure on the Irish government and Irish businesses. For example, he imposed a tax on the export of Irish linens and failed to inform his colleagues in the Irish government. His estimates fell short of expenditure in 1803 and Dublin's moneyed men refused to work with him in negotiating a loan. Corry had lost the confidence of Irish politicians and the business community. With a change of British ministers in 1804, the opportunity was taken to remove him from office.[50]

When William Pitt returned as Prime Minister in May 1804, he brought John Foster into office. The most interesting feature of this appointment was that Foster was to hold the post of Chancellor of the Irish Exchequer with that of First Lord of the Irish Treasury. Alexander Marsden, the Viceroy's Under-Secretary, was in no doubts about what this combination would mean for Hardwicke: 'The arrangements with Mr Foster will … leave you nothing substantially, although it may nominally, of the patronage of the revenue. I know Mr Foster too well … If he undertakes the Treasury and the management of the revenue, your Excellency will have to ask him for a gauger's place very soon. And why? Because his appointment takes place when you have no one at the other side representing your Excellency's interests.'[51]

As early as 1793, Pitt had entertained bold and enlarged views on Treasury powers at the expense of the Lord Lieutenant's powers of patronage. In an important conference in 1795 at Wimbledon, Pitt, Henry Dundas, and Cooke discussed, as part of a reform package, the notion of 'responsibility'. At the time, Cooke recorded his concerns that the 'object … was to take the patronage of the lord lieutenant as much as possible and to give the conduct of affairs to Irish parliamentary leaders. With this view of the subject, they did not see insuperable objections, as they were convinced that public opinion would sooner or later have a similar influence upon the administration of Ireland to that which it has in France.'[52] If Pitt, in 1795, was prepared to see the transfer of the patronage powers of the Irish Viceroy to the leaders of a colonial, constitutionally independent, assembly, it should be no surprise that, in 1804, he would be prepared to see them transferred to an officeholder of his own creation, who worked with him at Westminster.

Camden, with similar views, was used as a negotiator with Foster. In 1796, when Lord Lieutenant, Camden had sought to increase the powers of the Treasury over the revenue and had proposed that the lord lieutenancy should be abolished.[53] Vansittart, Chief Secretary between March and September 1805, made a very important comment regarding the new role for Foster: 'I know that he had accepted office under stipulations of a very considerable extension of authority. The limits of it were never explained to me, nor had I ever any intimation where I could interfere without the risk of being disavowed, besides the imputation which would certainly have been insinuated of some secret design to weaken the influence of the government here by breaking with so powerful and popular a man as he is generally in England supposed to be.'[54]

The most obvious reason for this combination of the Chancellorship of the Irish Exchequer with the First Lordship of the Treasury is that Hardwicke and his Chief Secretaries had failed decisively to confront the powerful political interests in the country. The blame for the miscarriage of reformist efforts was being shifted from Irish politicians to the Irish government. It is probable that the combining of the two finance posts was intended to invigorate the reform and retrenchment policy that had lapsed. Hardwicke could do little more than watch from the sidelines and 'trust that Foster's powers and authorities will be defined or else his interference with the chief secretary and lord lieutenant will be very unpleasant'. Sir Evan Nepean was more certain: 'Mr Foster will endeavour to possess himself of as much power and authority [as possible] and I see difficulties in keeping it down.'[55]

Foster's use of Treasury powers was deployed on several levels. For example, he implemented a real superintending power over the issue of money; he wrote 'approved' on Treasury issue of money, instead of the usual counter-signature accompanying the Lord Lieutenant's. Also, he was prepared to challenge the Lord Lieutenant's authority for expenditure. Foster exercised jurisdiction over the staff of the Revenue Board: he dismissed and transferred officers on his own authority.[56]

Foster overreached his authority, however, in his legislation of 1805. He pressed ahead with bills without proper consultation in Ireland. As well as insulting his colleagues, he left himself open to mistakes. When technical errors were discovered in several of his bills, they were detained in the Lords until Pitt's views were solicited. In June, Pitt agreed that three should be postponed and therefore lost for the session, while three others were so amended in the Lords as to be lost on their return to the Commons.[57] On 29 June 1805, Foster sent a letter of resignation to Hardwicke grounded 'not on the rejection of the bills, or on the political differences with your Excellency, but on Mr Pitt's inattention and want of civility'.[58] Foster expected that Pitt would have been more supportive in the project that had been agreed between them. Foster was persuaded to remain, however, and matters were clarified in arrangements made in the autumn.

The salient features of the restatement were as follows. Firstly, as Tom Grenville, brother to Lord Grenville (soon to be Prime Minister), curtly put it: '[Charles] Long is Irish secretary, Foster is to remain, and if Long cannot make peace between him and Lord Hardwicke, the lord lieutenant is to go to the wall.' Secondly, the two offices of Chief Secretary and Chancellor of the Irish Exchequer were to be kept separate, 'an Irishman being chancellor of the exchequer'. Although Hardwicke suggested a merger, 'it was not in [the Home Secretary] Lord Hawkesbury's contemplations'. Thirdly, the Chief Secretary must enjoy the confidence of the British ministers. This was not explicitly stated, but the nature of Long's appointment suggests it, as it did to contemporaries. In Wickham's opinion, 'Long's appointment is unquestionably, in my opinion, the best that has been made since the Union. I should rather say in my memory. I have always thought that Ireland never could be well governed without a [chief] secretary, the personal and really confidential friend of the [prime] minister and known to be such.' Hardwicke agreed that 'he will contribute materially to render the true state of Irish affairs better understood by his friends here and that the confidence which he enjoys here from his legitimate friendship with the [Prime] Minister will enable him to frame and carry into execution the means for adjusting the discordant powers which have been so inconveniently permitted to subsist'. A year before, Long had stated that he had no ambition for the Irish post, only to serve Pitt. Pitt therefore must have insisted on it.[59]

Although retaining the position of First Lord, Foster lost some powers at the Irish Treasury. First, 'the chief secretary's signature is required to every act of importance, as one of the three whose signature is necessary'. Secondly, 'the business is to be transacted through the commissioners of inferior boards, as in England'. On the other hand, it was decided to 'give the board of treasury such powers over the revenue as will make them responsible for it'; and on this point, Long asked for Foster's ideas on paper: 'I have offered in the meantime to adopt any salutary measures he may propose for better collecting the revenue.'[60]

Hardwicke did not quite 'go to the wall' nor, as his subsequent resignation suggests, was he totally vindicated. Pitt had been given the opportunity to disown Foster and uphold the Crown's representative in Dublin when his Irish Chancellor had submitted his own resignation. Foster was retained even though 'the lord lieutenant, the [lord] chancellor, the attorney and solicitor general and Marsden, etc., are so violent against Foster that it will be difficult to induce any of them to concur in any responsible manner respecting him'. This was an indication of the British government's intention to carry out a policy of retrenchment and economy.

Long's report to Redesdale of a conversation with Foster, in which Long attempted to justify Foster's retention, summarises the issue: 'He says that he was responsible for the revenue, and that he must have a sufficient degree of influence to manage that for which he was responsible. His principles in fact are not objectionable in themselves, but in the application of them, I fear I should not be able so perfectly to concur. He affects, however, great cordiality and a wish to co-operate in the measures of government.'[61]

Similar arrangements were made in 1806 by the newly formed 'Ministry of all the Talents'. The new government reverted to the *status quo* of 1805. The new Chief Secretary was a Scottish Whig—William Elliot, a former Military Under-Secretary to the Chief Secretary. He was expected to carry out reform, assisted by a native politician in charge of finance. Sir John Newport, a Grenvillite MP for Waterford and, controversially, a partner in the family bank, was appointed Chancellor of the Irish Exchequer because he would be 'completely subservient to [the Prime Minister] Lord Grenville'. To complete the picture, Grenville made himself First Lord of both Treasuries, and the Chancellor of the Irish Exchequer was an *ex-officio* Second Lord in Ireland. Grenville expected the superintendence of Ireland's finance to be conducted in a compact, well-informed, triangular relationship, consisting of Newport, Elliot, and himself. This government carried out several reforms in financial administration that would have been introduced by the previous ministry and, although commendable, they were arranged to serve the political interests of the government and its supporters.[62]

In 1807, Foster returned as Chancellor of the Irish Exchequer, but Pitt was dead and the British ministers he worked with were not prepared to allow him as much scope as Pitt had. The British Prime Minister, the Duke of Portland—not Foster—was made First Lord of the Irish Treasury, but lip service was paid to Foster's mission by his designation as Second Lord of the Irish Treasury and supernumerary Lord of the British Treasury. The new Lord Lieutenant, the Duke of Richmond, said, 'I am most anxious to retain [Sir Arthur] Wellesley as chief secretary … A firm man, as well as one of sense, is highly necessary. You know that Foster is rather difficult to deal with and in fact I find Wellesley extremely useful … otherwise Foster must lead in the House and would in fact be lord lieutenant which is always his wish.'[63] Wellesley, later the Duke of Wellington, was not going to be pushed around. On just Foster's second day in office, Wellesley reported: 'He began the battle respecting the treasury and made his first effort to supersede the authority of the lord lieutenant by that of the Irish treasury. I propose to adjourn the contest to London where it must be settled by the King's servants … to decide whether he or the Duke of Richmond is to govern this country.'[64]

If Foster was not given a free hand, however, in the period 1807–12, there was undoubtedly substantial progress in the direction of conducting Irish finances in a manner pleasing to him. There were appointments to the Treasury of 'men of business' so that they could be more involved in revenue superintendence. There were several laudable appointments and promotions at the highest levels of the revenue service. Most of the detailed recommendations of a commission of enquiry, which Foster had requested in 1804, were implemented, with its commission renewed until 1812. In 1810, the Chief Secretary, William Wellesley-Pole, was persuaded to make the Irish Revenue Boards completely subservient to the Irish Treasury. Foster and Pole agreed, to some extent, about the future direction of Irish government. Pole, like Foster, wanted the Irish Treasury to act as the supreme Revenue Board in Ireland, with its members meeting regularly to transact business. A significant difference was that he was concerned about how much such activity might be reconciled to the authority of the Lord Lieutenant.[65] In September 1810, Pole asked Foster and FitzGerald, at the time a newly appointed Lord of the Irish Treasury, about their views on what a reformed Treasury would look like. FitzGerald, writing on behalf of himself and Foster, said that it should meet regularly to conduct proper business by making it 'the channel of all communication between the government and all who in the collection and management of public revenue, are employed under them'; the Treasury should also have the sole power to remit fines, penalties, and forfeitures, and to investigate abuses.[66]

Despite all this, Foster still complained 'of a want of vigour and energy in the government' as far as financial administration was concerned. British officials wished to proceed more cautiously. Pole's predecessor, Robert Dundas, commented to Pole in 1809: 'I do not think Ireland is quite ripe for the same strictness and perhaps vigour with which the revenue is collected in England. Mr Foster, in this respect, is proceeding too violently and rapidly.'[67] It was this lack of adequate support from colleagues that caused Foster's resignation on 12 February 1811. He received warrants from the Viceroy for his counter-signature authorising the appointment of twenty-one additional customs officers. Ten were in Belfast, where trade was falling, and nine were clerks in the Dublin Stores even though Foster had pledged himself publicly to save £13,000 by freezing all appointments there. 'All without any previous communication or opportunity of advice,' he said, 'which made it impossible for me any longer to bear the appearance of responsibility.'[68]

At this point, Pole requested that he combine Foster's position with his own, arguing that without doing so, there was no hope of restoring the authority of government after the 'the jarring of interests, created by Foster between the Treasury and the Castle'.[69] Richmond pointed out that Foster could never have been trusted with such a merger: 'He may have formerly been a good chancellor of the exchequer, but he never could have held the two situations. With one he always wished to be lord lieutenant and with the two he would have succeeded.'[70] Pole held the two offices temporarily until a plan could be formulated which could give the Irish Treasury proper superintendence over the Revenue Board. But nothing came of this scheme and Pole was promoted to the British cabinet in March 1812.

In August 1812, William Vesey FitzGerald became the Chancellor of the Irish Exchequer. J. M. Barry, a supporter of John Foster, gave as his opinion:

> Depend on it, if the Castle does not give up the patronage of promotion in the revenue to the respective boards, and that each board is not rendered responsible for the due collection of its respective branch of the revenue, you will have as bad a tale to unfold as either Pole or Foster. However, I should speculate on a consolidation next session, after which … the Irish government will know nothing of what is going on in revenue matters, and all the springs will be moved by the imperial chancellor of the exchequer.[71]

As has been shown above, it was to be four years before consolidation occurred. In the meantime, FitzGerald complained of having insufficient control over the revenue departments, alleging that the Castle interfered too much with them and that some share of the patronage should be given to the Irish Treasury. By now, FitzGerald's colleagues in government were united in their determination that his demands could not be met. Lord Whitworth, recently appointed Lord Lieutenant, said of making concessions to FitzGerald: 'A divided authority is rarely efficient and in the present instance would be productive of the most pernicious effects.'[72] Liverpool, the Prime Minister, was most forthright:

> It is impracticable to draw that sort of line between the duties and powers of the chief secretary and chancellor of the exchequer as FitzGerald seems desirous should be marked out. The unity of the government in Ireland must be preserved. The chief secretary is the channel through which the power and patronage in Ireland must flow. … Judging from all I have known of Ireland itself I do not see anything but evil and inconvenience can arise from a supposed equality between the chief secretary and chancellor of the exchequer, which as the chief secretary is the organ of the lord lieutenant must put the chancellor of the exchequer upon an equality with the latter. This was the game of Foster. We know the consequences of it.[73]

The Chief Secretary from 1812, Peel, admitted that keeping revenue patronage out of the hands of the Lord Lieutenant and his Chief Secretary might indeed be of benefit to the revenue but he would not make efficient revenue administration a priority over the political initiative that command of patronage gave to the Lord Lieutenant: 'the power of the lord lieutenant must be paramount over everything in Ireland'. In a revealing passage, which shows how much had changed since 1801, Peel said:

> I shall be glad when the time comes when the government of this country can be conducted on different principles from what it at present is; when you can look for support (and I do not mean merely parliamentary support but that effectual support which active and loyal men can afford in this country) in an honest conviction of its necessity and a full sense of duty; but that time has not yet arrived and till it does, you must either try to carry on the government without such support or you must (and I fear there is no misapplication of the term) *purchase* it.[74]

Conclusions

K. T. Hoppen shows that in 1801, Lord Pelham, the Home Secretary, proposed the abolition of the lord lieutenancy after the Union.[75] Similar plans had been contemplated in 1793, when Pitt had proposed to remodel political authority in Ireland along British lines by giving 'responsibility' to an Irish Treasury, which was to have control and superintendence over all expenditure and other departments. The Treasury would be staffed by Irish politicians who could command the confidence of the legislature. This plan was never finalised. When Pitt returned to office in 1804, the plan was revived. We have seen that more authority was given to the Chancellor of the Irish Exchequer by combining his role with that of First

Lord of the Irish Treasury. Perhaps, in time, such a minister would have evolved into a secretary of state for Ireland and become part of the British executive, with the Viceroy relegated to the status of a ceremonial figure, like the Lord Lieutenant of a county. In the meantime, the viceregal exercise of patronage worked against the Chancellor of the Irish Exchequer in his attempts to manage Irish public finance through a programme of reform, retrenchment, and efficiency. During 1804 and 1805, Foster, who held both Irish offices, with the support of Pitt, was in effect making the Viceroy redundant. This progress in remodelling the Irish executive was checked even before the change of government in 1806. New arrangements in the autumn of 1805 modified the situation. Why was the project to replace the Viceroy abandoned?

First, Irish politicians had a reputation for 'jobbing' and it was assumed that Foster was no different. Foster was known for his energetic, talented leadership, and it was considered unwise to satisfy his supposed personal ambitions. When Pitt, the originator of the plan, died, the plan died with him. Perceval, and then Lord Liverpool, became the dominant figures in British politics, and each had jaundiced views of Foster. Perceval was the brother-in-law of Lord Redesdale, Lord Chancellor of Ireland between 1802 and 1806, and an arch-critic of Foster, while Lord Liverpool, when Home Secretary (as Lord Hawkesbury), had first-hand experience of the inconvenience and tensions which had been engendered when making these changes in government.

The main reason, perhaps, for ending the project was that Ireland was nowhere near the top of the British government's priorities. As Hardwicke conceded to Lord Hawkesbury, 'the circumstances of the times … have necessarily called the attention … of his majesty's ministers to points of more pressing importance'.[76] The main 'points of pressing importance' were the conduct of the war, security, and law and order. It was believed that there must be strong government, and this meant, in Lord Liverpool's words, 'the unity of the government in Ireland must be preserved'. This was not the time to bring structural change in government; the Lord Lieutenant must be strengthened not weakened.

The obsession with security is not surprising, given that the country was at war with France, and that the latter had tried to invade Ireland and continued to threaten invasion. Ireland had experienced insurrection in 1798 and 1803, and there was unrest in England as well.[77] William Wickham, Sir Evan Nepean, and Sir Arthur Wellesley were sent to Ireland as Chief Secretaries because of their respective expertise in espionage,

Admiralty business, and military affairs—but each was speedily recalled to service in Britain for the very reasons they were sent to Ireland.

Another issue which had priority in British ministerial thinking was concern for George III's health and what impact a regency would have on politics and policy. Related to this was the need to ensure support from enough factions in Parliament to enable ministers to govern with a majority. If Ireland came to the forefront of ministerial thinking—when it was not a matter of security and law and order—it usually featured on the question of Catholic Emancipation. Ireland's low status has already been seen in the six-year delay in accomplishing financial amalgamation (1810–16). It is also demonstrated by the 'revolving door' that characterised the appointment of the crucial post of Chief Secretary: five Chief Secretaries served Hardwicke in his five years as Viceroy, and four served the Duke of Richmond during his viceroyalty of 1807–13; in all, there were ten Chief Secretaries in the period 1801–17.

Another illustration of Ireland's place in Britain's priorities is seen in how often British governments prohibited the distillation of spirits from corn throughout the United Kingdom. Chancellors of the Irish Exchequer depended a great deal on the revenue obtained from excise duties on whiskey manufacture. These duties produced £1.2 million, which was one-third of the total Irish revenue and, with malt duties, constituted 96 per cent of the excise duties. Foster was confident that, provided more progress was made in the detection of distillers' fraud by excise officers and in the suppression of illicit distillation, the revenue from whiskey manufacture could produce £3 million per annum. Thus, a Chancellor of the Irish Exchequer could do his 'duty as a good finance minister, a good statesman and a good Christian'.[78] In addition, the distillation of spirits from corn was a great incentive to the encouragement of tillage in Ireland.

In five out of the sixteen years under review in this chapter, however, the British government prohibited the distillation of spirits from grain. British ministers such as Perceval had 'apprehension[s] of a possible [food] scarcity'.[79] Ministers chose to please the West Indian sugar interest who urged the distillation of spirits from sugar (which was not to Irish taste). Ministers also deferred to British distillers, who distilled from sugar, and did not want competition from Irish distillers. Also, if distillation was allowed, the increased demand for Irish grain would push up food prices for the British consumer. So the Irish finance minister had English manufacturing interests lined up against him too. A compromise—of allowing distillation from grain in Ireland while prohibiting the sale of Irish whiskey in Britain—was not possible because it would be a 'manifest breach of the articles of the Union'.[80]

For every year that prohibition was in force, revenue was greatly diminished and the grain in Ireland—where there was usually no shortage, but which British ministers wished to conserve ('just in case')—made its way to the illicit distillers, as was seen in the falling price of their untaxed product. John Foster 'believed this was the first time in English history … that the legislature attempted to tamper with the agricultural interests of the nation'.[81] Spencer Perceval summed up the matter when he wrote to Foster: 'You perhaps have a better estimate of the Irish feeling, but it is by the English one that our conduct will be judged.'[82] FitzGerald complained to Vansittart, the Chancellor of the British Exchequer, of 'the fair claim which Ireland may be supposed to have, in the present state of her finances, to dispose of the excess of grain produced by her in the way most profitable to herself'.[83] To Foster, he was more direct: 'Irish interests have not fair play.'[84]

The seventh article of the Act of Union had placed enormous pressure on Ireland's fiscal needs while at the same time limiting opportunities for meeting those needs. On the other hand, the Union did bring benefit. Before the Union, the Irish executive was never accountable, or 'responsible', to the Irish legislature. In the post-Union period, however, the Irish executive might be scrutinised henceforth by the UK legislature. The enquiry board, established by the UK Parliament in 1804 and working until 1813 in its name and by its authority, instigated many reforms in the administration of the revenue. This vehicle of reform succeeded, in contrast to the attempt by Abbott, who tried to instigate reform but acted only in the Viceroy's name. Although the enquiry board's reforms stopped short of removing the Lord Lieutenant's powers of patronage in the revenue service, successive Viceroys did try to have senior posts in the administration depoliticised and filled with 'men of business'.

Nationalist commentators have claimed that the proportionate contribution set at 7½:1 was unfair and unjust. Indeed, it proved to be so—but this was never intended. Even Henry Grattan, a consistent critic of the seventh Article of Union, identified the problem in the House of Commons in 1819: 'The truth is, the necessary and inevitable expenses of the war were beyond all possibility of calculation or foresight.'[85] The Earl of Dunraven, writing in 1912, argued that ministers should have intervened in these circumstances and hastened amalgamation. He accepted, however, that if the Union had not taken place, with no required proportionate contribution, Ireland would have still voluntarily raised additional taxation and increased borrowing to assist in paying for the war. He believed, however, that an Irish Parliament would never have taxed the country so heavily or borrowed so much as to bring the country to bankruptcy. He calculated that Ireland might have borrowed £62 million instead of the £112 million that she did borrow.[86]

T. J. Kiernan, writing in 1930, went further and claimed that there was a conspiracy to bring Ireland as quickly as possible to the point where equal taxation could be imposed through financial amalgamation. He alleged the conditions for amalgamation were arranged in the full knowledge that Ireland's debt would be rapidly forced up to the point where the contribution ratio equalled the debt ratio.[87] This conspiracy theory must be rejected. First, British and Irish ministers knew in 1799–1800 that it was possible Irish debt could increase to the point which triggered financial amalgamation and, potentially, equality of taxation—but they did not see this as unjust if it had been accompanied by a gradual increase in taxation ('produced by natural causes and in no degree forced'). This was said in public as well as private.[88] It is true that up until about 1806, in the annual debates in Parliament on the Irish budget, oppositionists did express fear that the seventh article would lead to spiralling Irish debt, which would bring on financial amalgamation and equal taxation far too prematurely. About 1806, however, the vocabulary of criticism changed. This was because Foster in 1804 and 1805 had tried to rely less on borrowing and more on additional taxation—and it was universally acknowledged that this had disappointing results. Thereafter, the discussion focused less on the need to avoid borrowing than on a realisation that borrowing was unavoidable and instead what needed to be changed was the quota itself. The Irish Chancellors and oppositionists alike wanted a review which would bring amalgamation, a revised quota, or no quota at all.

It should also be noted that if it was the case that British ministers sought financial amalgamation as soon as possible, then they were in no hurry to obtain financial amalgamation when they had the opportunity; they dragged their heels over the issue between 1811 and 1816. Financial amalgamation, when it came in 1817, did not usher in the equal taxation that Kiernan claimed was the goal. Even Dunraven admitted 'that at first no very rapid advance was made towards that "indiscriminate taxation"; which, as the Act of Union laid down, might be adopted on amalgamation of the exchequers, if parliament thought fit. … Between 1817 and 1853 only a few changes of any importance took place.'[89] Indeed, the arrangements were deemed generous. Ireland was never actually asked to make any further fixed contributions to imperial expenses; her revenue was placed to the common credit of the United Kingdom, and her contribution was calculated at the amount by which her true revenue exceeded her local expenditure.[90]

Dunraven and Kiernan could not accept that writing off Irish debt was of any benefit to Ireland because they claimed that in 1817 the country was left 'exhausted' through heavy taxation, which continued to be levied. It must be remembered, however, that 75 per cent of the revenues raised in the period 1801–16 came from duties levied on luxury goods. Over 40 per cent of total revenue came from the customs duties on sugar, tobacco, tea (consumed only by the upper classes at this time), and imported spirits. About 25 per cent came from excise—but 96 per cent of the excise came from whiskey and malt duties. A further 10 per cent came from stamp duties on legal documents, transactions, and newspapers.[91] It must be remembered, too, that there was no direct taxation on income or property. In 1811, after two relatively stiff budgets, the Chief Commissioner of Customs, Lord Castle Coote, no friend of Foster, could still write to him, 'it has been most happy and fortunate for Ireland that you have arranged [the taxes] to have them … light and little pressing on the country'.[92]

To summarise: the financial relationship arranged in 1800, and revised in 1816–17, was made with generous intentions towards Ireland. The outworking in the intervening period, however, brought headaches for the Chancellors of the Irish Exchequer, who found that their concerns about securing sources of revenue, Ireland's growing indebtedness, and lack of control of the revenue administration, took little priority with their colleagues. Pitt's bold plan to transfer additional powers to the Irish finance minister, in 1804–05, caused an uproar and was aborted. In 1800, it had been thought that the Union would enable the Viceroy to 'close the reign of Irish jobs', meaning that he would see to it that Irish politicians learned to live with less patronage. In fact, it was the Viceroy who found that he could not manage without retaining control of patronage in the revenue service.

Notes

1. Trevor Robert McCavery, 'Finance and Politics in Ireland, 1801–1817' (Ph.D. diss., Queen's University of Belfast, 1980), *passim*.

2. For this interpretation see Alice Effie Murray, *History of the Commercial and Financial Relations between England and Ireland since the Restoration* (London: P. S. King, 1903); Earl of Dunraven, *The Finances of Ireland before the Union and after: An Historical Study* (London: John Murray, 1912); George O'Brien, *The Economic History of Ireland from the Union to the Famine* (London: Longmans, Green and Co., 1921); T. J. Kiernan, *History of the Financial Administration of Ireland to 1817* (London: P. S. King and Son, 1930). For a more detailed study of this subject see McCavery, 'Finance', 13–45, 217–18.
3. William Pitt to Lord Auckland, 4 June 1798, *The Journals and Correspondence of William, Lord Auckland*, ed. Bishop of Bath and Wells, 4 vols. (London: Richard Bentley, 1861–62), 2:2.
4. Lord Camden to Pitt, 16 June 1798, quoted in H. M. Hyde, *The Rise of Castlereagh* (London: Macmillan, 1933), 219.
5. 'C.'s plan of Union', n.d., Auckland Papers, British Library (hereafter, BL) Add. MS 34455, f. 154; Pitt to Auckland, 14 Aug. 1798, Sneyd Papers, Keele University Library, photocopies in Public Record Office of Northern Ireland (hereafter, PRONI) T.3229/2/35.
6. Pitt to Auckland, 14 Aug. 1798, Sneyd Papers, PRONI T.3229/2/35.
7. Duke of Portland to Lord Cornwallis, 12 Nov. 1798, *Correspondence of Charles, 1st Marquis Cornwallis*, ed. Sir Charles Ross, 3 vols. (London: John Murray, 1859), 2:436.
8. Viscount Castlereagh to Portland, 7 Jan. 1799, *Memoirs and Correspondence of Viscount Castlereagh*, ed. Marquess of Londonderry, 4 vols. (London: Henry Colburn, 1848–49), 2:84.
9. Castlereagh, 'Plan of contribution', n.d. ('received 17 Jan 1799'), Chatham Papers, The National Archives (hereafter, TNA): 30/8/327, f. 21.
10. Robert Hobart to Auckland, Sneyd Papers, PRONI T.3229/12/43.
11. Cooke to Castlereagh, 13 Nov. 1799, Chatham Papers, TNA: 30/8/327, f. 169.
12. Edward Cooke to John Beresford, 18 Dec. 1799, *Correspondence of the Rt. Hon. John Beresford*, ed. William Beresford, 2 vols. (London: Woodfall and Kinder, 1854), 2:235.
13. 'Draft relative to proportional contributions and criterions [*sic*]', n.d., Castlereagh Papers, PRONI D.3030/1130; *Castlereagh Correspondence*, 3:191.
14. Castlereagh to Auckland, 20 [Dec. 1799], Sneyd Papers, PRONI T.3229/2/48.
15. Cooke to Castlereagh, 13 Nov. 1799, Chatham Papers, TNA: 30/8/327, f. 169.
16. Castlereagh Papers, PRONI D.3030/1127.
17. Castlereagh to Pitt, 18 Jan. 1800, *Cornwallis Correspondence*, 3:159.

18. Auckland to Castlereagh, Apr. 1800, Castlereagh Papers, PRONI D.3030/1271.
19. Dunraven, *Finances of Ireland*, 71; T. J. Kiernan's statistics are similar: he said that the total Irish debt rose from £27 million to £107 million in the period 1801–17: Kiernan, *Financial Administration*, 306.
20. For details on borrowing, see McCavery, 'Finance', 202–19.
21. Viscount Frankfort de Montmorency to Alexander Marsden, 27 May 1803, Chief Secretary's Office: Official Papers, National Archives of Ireland (hereafter, NAI) 522/145/6 (9); *Parliamentary Register*, vol. 3, p. 624 (20 June 1803); Earl of Hardwicke to Charles Yorke, 13 Apr. 1804, Hardwicke Papers, BL Add. MS 35705, f. 328.
22. Hardwicke to Lord Hawkesbury, 26 Feb. 1805, Hardwicke Papers, BL Add. MS 35710, f. 26.
23. For a more detailed study of the debates surrounding direct taxation in the period 1810–17 see McCavery, 'Finance', 219–24.
24. *Hansard Parliamentary Debates*, 1st ser., vol. 26, col. 257 (20 May 1813).
25. McCavery, 'Finance', 225.
26. *Hansard*, 1st ser., vol. 7, cols. 35–50 (7 May 1806).
27. Ibid., vol. 14, col. 679 (24 May 1809).
28. McCavery, 'Finance', 219.
29. For a detailed study of the fiscal policies pursued by successive Chancellors of the Irish Exchequer see McCavery, 'Finance', 202–307.
30. Earl of Liverpool to Robert Peel, 20 Oct. 1813, Peel Papers, BL Add. MS 40181, f. 48; Peel to Viscount Whitworth, 9 Nov. 1813, and reply, 12 Nov. 1813, Whitworth Papers, Centre for Kentish Studies, U.269/O.255 bundle 2, Peel Papers, BL Add. MS 40187, f. 104.
31. This commission of enquiry established in 1804 was set up at John Foster's request and chaired by his nephew, J. S. Rochfort, the son of his wife's sister. For its work see McCavery, 'Finance', 101, 134–37, 161–63.
32. Nicholas Vansittart to William Vesey FitzGerald, 28 Feb. 1814, Vesey FitzGerald Papers, National Library of Ireland (hereafter, NLI) MS 7828, p. 172.
33. FitzGerald to Vansittart, 23 Feb.1814, Vesey FitzGerald Papers, NLI MS 7828, p. 52.
34. Liverpool to FitzGerald, 28 Feb. 1814, Vesey FitzGerald papers, NLI MS 7828, p. 169.
35. McCavery, 'Finance', 173–79.
36. Dunraven, *Finances of Ireland*, 78, 86–89.
37. Whitworth to Peel, 14 June 1816, and reply, Peel Papers, BL Add. MSS, 40192, f. 154, 40291, f. 343.
38. George III to Henry Addington, [11] Feb. [1801], *The Viceroy's Post-Bag: Correspondence Hitherto Unpublished of the Earl of Hardwicke First Lord*

Lieutenant of Ireland after the Union, ed. Michael MacDonagh (London: John Murray, 1904), 3.

39. 'Heads of private instructions to be observed by the Earl of Hardwicke in the execution of his office of lord lieutenant of Ireland', n.d., Hardwicke Papers, BL Add. MS 35707, f. 33.
40. For a detailed study of this subject see McCavery, 'Finance', 46–201.
41. Yorke to Charles Abbot, 12 Oct. 1801, Colchester Papers, TNA: 30/9/16; Hardwicke to Addington, 26 Aug. 1801, Hardwicke Papers, BL Add. MS 35707, f. 100.
42. Beresford to Auckland, 11 Oct. 1801, Auckland Papers, Add. MS 34455, f. 438; St Leger to Viscount Doneraile, 4 Nov. 1801, Colchester Papers, TNA: 30/9/13; Fenwick to [Abbot], 9 Nov. 1801, Colchester Papers, TNA: 30/9/13; Abbot to Bishop of Meath, 22 Oct. 1801, Colchester Papers, TNA: 30/9/14; Abbot to Yorke, 21 Jan. 1802, Colchester Papers, TNA: 30/9/16; [?] to Abbot, n.d., Colchester Papers, TNA: 30/9/8, 30/9/20.
43. *Parliamentary Register*, vol. 15, pp. 403–5 (28 May 1801), 513–14 (10 June 1801); *Journals of the House of Commons of the United Kingdom*, vol. 56, pp. 352 (4 May 1801), 383 (8 May 1801), 476 (28 May 1801), 483 (1 June 1801), 535 (10 June I801).
44. For this conflict, see McCavery, 'Finance', 63–67.
45. Lady Londonderry to Maurice FitzGerald, FitzGerald Papers, PRONI MIC.639/8/24; Hardwicke to William Wickham, 11 July 1803, Hardwicke to Yorke, 2 Jan. 1804, Hardwicke Papers, BL Add. MSS 35772, f. 200, 35704, f. 254; Wickham to Addington, *passim*, Wickham Papers, Hampshire Record Office, photocopies in PRONI T.2627/5/D/63–65, 68, 72, 75–79, 82.
46. Wickham to Hardwicke, 8 Apr. 1802, Hardwicke Papers, BL Add. MS 35713, f. 254.
47. Abbot to Marsden, 27 June 1802, Chief Secretary's Office: Official Papers, NAI 5211/136/5 (2); Addington to Lord Redesdale, 29 June 1802, Redesdale Papers, Gloucestershire Record Office, photocopies in PRONI T.3030/3/8.
48. Hardwicke to Yorke, 10 Jan. 1804, Hardwicke Papers, BL Add. MS 35704, f. 254.
49. Addington to Redesdale, 23 Oct. 1803, Redesdale Papers, PRONI T.3030/3/J3; Yorke to Hardwicke, 14 Jan. 1804, Hardwicke to York, 14 Jan. 1804, Hardwicke Papers, BL Add. MS 35704, ff. 337, 254.
50. For details of Corry's errors see McCavery, 'Finance', 77–92.
51. Marsden to Hardwicke, 26 June 1804, Hardwicke Papers, BL Add. MS 35724, f. 163.

52. Memo of a conversation between Pitt, Henry Dundas, and Cooke, 21–22 Jan. 1793, Melville Papers, NLI MS 54A/74.
53. McCavery, 'Finance', 97.
54. Vansittart to Redesdale, 22 June 1805, Redesdale Papers, T.3030/10/J6.
55. Yorke to Hardwicke, 25 May 1804, and reply, Hardwicke Papers, BL Add. MS 35706, f. 46; Sir Evan Nepean to Hardwicke, 2 June 1804, 13 June 1804, Hardwicke Papers, BL Add. MS 35709, f. 71.
56. Foster's deployment of Treasury powers is more fully documented in McCavery, 'Finance', 102–7; for detailed treatment see A. P. W. Malcomson, *John Foster (1740–1828): The Politics of Improvement and Prosperity* (Dublin: Four Courts Press, 2011), 194–98.
57. McCavery, 'Finance', 107–13; Malcomson, *Foster*, 198–214.
58. John Foster to Pitt, 29 June 1805, Chatham Papers, TNA: 30/8/32B, f. 65; Vansittart to Hardwicke, 30 June 1805, Hardwicke Papers, BL Add. MS 35716, f. 113.
59. Thomas Grenville to Lord Grenville, 20 Sept. 1805, *The Manuscripts of J. B. Fortescue, Esq., Preserved at Dropmore*, ed. Historical Manuscripts Commission, 10 vols. (London: Eyre and Spottiswoode, 1892–1927), 7:304; Charles Long to Redesdale 25 Sept. 1805, Redesdale Papers, PRONI T.3030/8/13; Long to Pitt, 20 Oct. 1805, Chatham Papers, TNA: 30/8/238, f. 259; Hardwicke to Yorke, 4 Oct. 1805, Hardwicke Papers, BL Add. MS 35706, f. 296; Wickham to Redesdale, 13 Oct. 1805, Redesdale Papers, PRONI T.3030/4/7; Hardwicke to Abbot, 1 Jan. 1806, Hardwicke Papers, BL Add. MS 35764, f. 161; Long to Redesdale, 27 Sept. 1804, Redesdale Papers, PRONI T.3030/8/6.
60. Foster to Long, [20? Oct. 1805], 23 Oct. 1805, 27 Oct. 1805, TNA: HO 100/131, ff. 247, 249, 251, 259; Long to Pitt, [1?] Oct. 1805, 29 Oct. 1805, Chatham Papers, TNA: 30/8/328, ff. 261–63, 259.
61. Long to Pitt, 1 Oct. 1805, 29 Oct. 1805, Chatham Papers, TNA: 30/8/28, ff. 259, 261; Long to Redesdale, 25 Sept 1805, Redesdale Papers, PRONI T.3030/8/13.
62. For a detailed discussion of financial administration in Ireland by the 'Ministry of all the Talents', see McCavery, 'Finance', 129–45.
63. Duke of Richmond to the Earl of Bathurst, 20 June 1808, Whitworth Papers, V.269/O.214/2/71.
64. Sir Arthur Wellesley to Long, 6 June 1807, *The Supplementary Despatches, Letters and Memoranda of Arthur Wellesley, 1st Duke of Wellington*, ed. 2nd Duke of Wellington, 5 vols. (London: John Murray, 1860), 5:73.
65. For detailed discussion of financial administration in this period, see McCavery, 'Finance' 146–66.
66. FitzGerald to William Wellesley-Pole, 17 Sept. 1810, Wellesley Papers, BL Add. MS 40207, f. 2.

67. Long to Wellesley, 26 Oct 1807, Apsley House MS, photocopies in PRONI T.2627/3/2/208; Dundas to Pole, 22 Oct. 1809, Melville Papers, NLI MS 55A/34C.
68. Foster to Pole, 1 Feb. 1811, and reply, 13 Feb. 1811, Foster Papers, PRONI D.207/3B/42/44; Foster to James Crofton, 18 Feb. 1811; Spencer Perceval to Foster, Feb. 1811, Foster Papers, PRONI D.207/69/3.
69. Pole to Richmond, 15 June 1811, Richmond Papers, NLI MS 1730.
70. Richmond to Pole, 19 June 1811, Whitworth Papers, U.269/0.214/5.
71. J. M. Barry to FitzGerald, 30 Aug. 1812, Vesey FitzGerald Papers, NLI MS 7821, p. 6.
72. Whitworth to Lord Sidmouth, 4 Sept. 1813, Whitworth Papers, U.269/O.218/4/33.
73. Liverpool to Peel, 4 October 1813, Peel Papers, BL Add. MS 40183, f. 39.
74. Peel to Liverpool, 20 Oct. 1813, Liverpool Papers, BL Add. MS 38915, f. 14.
75. K. T. Hoppen, *Governing Hibernia: British Politicians and Ireland, 1800–1921* (Oxford: Oxford University Press, 2016), 18–20.
76. Hardwicke to Hawkesbury, 6 June 1805, TNA: HO 100/129, ff. 301–4.
77. For more detail on the British and Irish governments' obsession with security see Hoppen, *Governing Hibernia*, 46–59.
78. Foster to FitzGerald, 9 May 1813, Vesey FitzGerald Papers, NLI MS 7818, p. 275.
79. *Hansard*, 1st ser., vol. 11, col. 442 (19 May 1808).
80. Wellesley to James Trail, 9 May 1808, *Supplementary Despatches*, 5:412; Wellesley to Hawkesbury, 15 May 1808, idem, 422; Richmond to Wellesley, 12 May 1808, Apsley House MS, PRONI T.2627/3/3/272.
81. *Hansard*, 1st ser., vol. 11, cols. 428–51 (19 May 1808).
82. Perceval to Foster, 9 Apr. 1808, Foster Papers, PRONI D.562/2147; for a detailed study of the arguments for and against prohibition of distillation see McCavery, 'Finance', 240–57.
83. Quoted in McCavery, 'Finance', 253.
84. FitzGerald to Foster, 1 May 1813, FitzGerald, Papers, NLI MS 7818, pp. 37, 41.
85. Dunraven, *Finances of Ireland*, 67.
86. Ibid., 77–78.
87. Kiernan, *Financial Administration*, 300–6.
88. Privately, see Castlereagh Papers, PRONI D.3030/1127; publicly, Castlereagh spoke in the Irish House of Commons, 5 Feb. 1800, quoted in Dunraven, *Finances of Ireland*, 56–57.
89. Dunraven, *Finances of Ireland*, 86–87.
90. Ibid., 84.
91. McCavery, 'Finance', 236–41.
92. Castle Coote to Foster, 24 May 1811, Foster Papers, D.562/11864.

CHAPTER 6

That 'Absurd Phantom Called Free Trade': The Politics of Protection in Ireland, c. 1829–52

Andrew Shields

This chapter examines the evolution of protectionist ideas in Irish Conservative political circles between 1829 and 1852. In particular, it explores the attempts made by some Conservatives to, as Isaac Butt put it, use protectionism as a lever by which to reclaim 'from the priests and agitators the popular mind of this country'.[1] It also traces the tensions which emerged between the landed advocates of protectionism, who generally saw it as a necessary instrument to preserve the agricultural interest there, and those Protestant populists, active in the late 1820s and early 1830s, who supported it as a means of creating employment opportunities for their working-class co-religionists. The latter group saw protectionism as a key element in the promotion of Irish manufacturing. They also believed that it would strengthen the cross-class coalition of Irish Protestants on

From a speech by Colonel Chatterton, the Conservative MP for Cork, at a dinner held in his honour at the Imperial Hotel in Cork City; *Cork Examiner*, 23 Nov. 1849.

A. Shields (✉)
University of New South Wales, Sydney, NSW, Australia

D. Kanter, P. Walsh (eds.), *Taxation, Politics, and Protest in Ireland, 1662–2016*, Palgrave Studies in the History of Finance,
https://doi.org/10.1007/978-3-030-04309-4_6

which the party was based. This chapter also analyses the ways in which the other main force in Irish politics in this period, Daniel O'Connell's Repeal Association, responded to the issues raised in the debate over free trade. Finally, it explores the transformative effect which the Famine had on attitudes towards protection across the political spectrum in Ireland.

Generally speaking, this chapter is more concerned with the political uses to which protectionists and their opponents put such arguments rather than with their economic merits.[2] As Anna Gambles has pointed out in her study of protectionist economic discourse in England in this period, the arguments made both by its advocates and by free trade campaigners were essentially 'political' in character. In essence, the differences between them revolved around their conflicting ideas about how society should be structured. They also had opposing views in relation to the role which the state should play in regulating the relationships between the classes.[3] These conflicting views also need to be seen within the wider context of the political changes brought about by the reform agitation of the late 1820s and early 1830s and the subsequent introduction of the 'Great' Reform Act in 1832.

Reform created a new sense of urgency among Conservatives and convinced them of the necessity of defining their own distinctive political economy. They believed that this would be necessary in order to defend the supremacy of the landed class in Britain and Ireland. It would also enable them to combat the arguments against their continued predominance put forward by the advocates of the new urban manufacturing interest. The close connection between the Tory Party in Ireland and the landed class there meant that for most of the first half of the nineteenth century, it was deeply committed to the preservation of the Corn Laws. Given the nature of the Irish economy, Tory spokesmen there frequently stressed the necessity to retain protection for the agricultural sector in Ireland. They believed that it was a vital element in the defence of the landed interest there.[4]

From the 1820s onwards, however, the advance of free trade ideas on the British mainland and the emergence of a reform-minded Whig political elite there led to a defensive counter-reaction among Irish Tories. In consequence, a new generation of Tory political activists came to view free trade as part of a broader movement designed to undermine the traditional pillars on which British society rested. From this perspective, when coupled with the broader electoral and institutional reforms introduced by liberal Tory and Whig-Liberal governments from the late 1820s onwards, it seemed calculated to subvert the foundations of Protestant Ascendancy itself in Ireland. As a result, this period was a crucial one in the development of the Conservative Party in Ireland, which was fashioned to a large extent in response to this broader and seemingly existential threat.

Irish Conservatives and the Politics of Protection, 1829–32

In recent times, the effects of the Act of Union on the Irish economy have been the subject of a vigorous debate among historians.[5] Among contemporaries, however, there was little doubt that its principal effects had been deleterious ones. Many contemporaries saw the coincidence of the collapse in the textiles industry in the south of the country with the removal of the remaining protective duties on goods imported into Ireland from Britain in 1824 as conclusive proof of the economic devastation caused by the Union.[6] Although the Act of Union had left those duties in place in the short term, it had also provided for their gradual extinction. In consequence, the quarter century after 1800 had seen the gradual reduction of such protective duties. This left native Irish industries increasingly open to the threat of competition from more mechanised and more economically efficient British ones. The economic consequences of this created a very difficult situation for Irish Conservatives. As Jacqueline Hill has shown, a comparatively large percentage of the Dublin working class in this period were Protestants. In some industries, notably in silk weaving, their numbers were particularly high, amounting to up to a quarter of the total workforce.[7] At this time, many male artisans were actively involved in politics '[both] as voters and as members of political organisations', and this made it necessary for the leaders of both of the main Irish political parties to take their concerns seriously.[8]

The economic downturn (particularly in the manufacturing sector) which took place in the country from the mid-1820s onwards further exacerbated this already fraught political situation. The textiles industry was the one most severely affected by this depression. Up to that point, one of the chief centres of that industry had been in Dublin. The production of fine wools, linens, and more specialised silk products had long been a major source of employment in that city. In the 1790s, for example, the woollen trade there alone had employed up to 5,000 persons.[9]

Following his leadership of the campaign for Catholic Emancipation, finally achieved in 1829, Daniel O'Connell launched a new mass movement in 1830 with the ultimate objective of repealing the Act of Union of 1801. As such, it posed a direct challenge to the dominant position of the Anglo-Irish Ascendancy. Conservative activists were particularly fearful that economic pressures might lead some working-class voters in Ireland to look more favourably on the repeal agitation. They were also concerned that Daniel O'Connell might woo Protestant electors by suggesting that repeal would allow for the reintroduction of duties on imports into the country from Britain.[10] To counteract this threat, Conservative leaders were keen to stress that, in supporting protection, they were not simply prioritising the interests of landowners. Instead, they argued that they were concerned to see a sustainable and balanced economic development which would benefit all sections of British and Irish society equally.[11] A few Conservative commentators even went so far as to claim that while free trade would principally benefit the manufacturing element in British society, protectionism benefited all classes and reinforced the social ties which bound them together. It did so, its advocates claimed, by maintaining a stable equilibrium between the agricultural and the manufacturing interests. By preserving the livelihood of rural dwellers, it enabled them to remain on the land. This in turn ensured that they were not forced to compete with existing urban dwellers for employment in the new manufacturing industries.[12]

While such arguments could be seen as somewhat self-serving, contemporary Conservative commentators were nevertheless keenly aware that protectionism would not be a viable long-term proposition if it appealed solely to rural interests. As a result, they believed it necessary to create a cross-class alliance (however limited in numbers that might be) to support it. In Ireland, however, the necessity for such an alliance was even more critical than it was in the rest of the United Kingdom. Irish Conservatives were keenly aware of their minority position in Ireland. This fact was a key cause of the insecurity which they frequently displayed about the maintenance of their dominant position there.[13] In this context, class co-operation was not regarded as either an additional option or a disposable luxury but rather an imperative necessity.

Even the outside possibility of losing the support of the 'lower order' of Protestants was enough to induce a widespread sense of foreboding among leading Irish Conservatives. In December 1830, for example, Charles Boyton, a prominent Irish Conservative activist, warned Lord

Farnham, one of the largest landowners in the north of Ireland, that 'the lower classes (of the Protestants)' in some places there were 'in a very dubious state'.[14] He was particularly concerned at recent newspaper reports of a series of meetings held at Shane's Hill near Larne in County Antrim in the province of Ulster. According to those accounts, the speakers at the meetings had demanded the reduction of rents and an increase in labourers' wages. The meetings had also attracted large attendances, with one report claiming that not less 'than 4,000 persons' had attended one held on 5 December 1830.[15]

Even more worryingly, from an Irish Conservative perspective, reports indicated that Catholics and Protestants in that locality had achieved some form of rapprochement. As the *Londonderry Sentinel* noted, attendance at the meetings crossed sectarian lines. While Catholics and Protestants had arrived at one of the early meetings separately with their own 'green and orange flags', they subsequently joined together and 'agreed to burn [all of] their flags, fifes and drums'. They also agreed for the future 'to sink all party animosity and unite for a redress of common grievances'.[16] Such language was extremely concerning to leading members of the Irish Conservative Party. For most of them, cross-class Protestant solidarity was essential to the maintenance both of their privileged position in Ireland and of the Act of Union itself.

In these circumstances, some of the leaders of the party in Ireland feared that economic discontent might drive working-class Protestants in urban areas to back the demand for a repeal of the Union. To counter this prospect, Thomas Lefroy, the Conservative MP for Dublin University, suggested to Farnham that it was imperative for the party to find a new guiding 'principle' which would be as influential as 'the old Orange' one had been. A central feature of this new 'principle' ought to be, he suggested, that it should have some direct appeal to poorer Protestants in Ireland.[17] One possible avenue towards achieving this objective was for Irish Conservatives to extend their support of protectionism to encompass a defence of those Irish industries which had been in decline from the early nineteenth century onwards. In advancing this position, they could also claim to be part of a long-standing protectionist tradition within Irish Protestant political thought, one which went back as far as Bishop Berkeley and Jonathan Swift. Both of those thinkers had emphasised the necessity to defend fledgling Irish industries against the destructive effects of cheap goods imported from Britain. In this respect, their writings offered something of an alternative to the predominantly 'rural' focus of Irish protectionist thought.[18]

Charles Boyton and other urban Conservative spokesmen were keenly aware that the party needed to retain the support of working-class Protestants if it were to preserve its political potency in Ireland. As early as January 1830, Boyton had attended a meeting held at the Rotunda in Dublin to discuss the 'distressed' conditions among textile workers in the city. The meeting concentrated in particular on the need to alleviate the conditions among the remaining silk workers in the area of the city known as The Liberties.[19] Although Boyton did not speak at that meeting, he subsequently made clear his own concerns about the decline of Irish manufacturing. He did so primarily through the Protestant Conservative Association, which he played a central role in establishing in 1832. For Boyton, the Association's principal objective was to maintain Conservative unity by combining all classes of Protestants in a single unified organisation. He viewed this as being especially necessary to counteract O'Connell's success in mobilising Catholics behind the campaign for the repeal of the Union. While the society had several large landowners as patrons, its most active members were a group of Dublin lawyers, lesser gentry, and clergymen. For many of these men, membership in the society was their introduction to political life. A number of these individuals, including such notable figures as Lord Naas, George Alexander Hamilton, and Joseph Napier, were to be leading figures in the Conservative Party in the ensuing decades.[20]

The rhetoric used by the leaders of the society combined strident anti-Catholicism with Protestant populism. This combination was to be a consistent feature of a series of such organisations in Dublin from the time of the association, through the Irish Metropolitan Conservative Society, to the heyday of the Dublin Protestant Association in the 1850s and 1860s. These groups played a key role in the revitalisation of Irish conservatism in the period. Indeed, as K. T. Hoppen has pointed out, 'the first great centre of organised working class Protestantism' was 'Dublin, not Belfast'.[21] In this respect, the years between the late 1820s and mid-1830s saw Irish Conservatives develop a series of strategies designed to ensure Protestant unity in order to counteract O'Connell's success in mobilising Catholics from across all social classes in Ireland.

A strong focus on maintaining the privileged position of the Irish Protestant population was a key feature of Irish Conservative ideology in this period. However, as Joseph Spence has pointed out, the party's spokesmen were also keen to stress their broader 'national orientation'.[22] For example, Irish Conservatives frequently argued that foreign influences dominated Irish Catholics. With Roman Catholics there having surrendered their political independence to dictation by the papacy, Irish Conservatives could portray themselves as the only truly 'National' party in Ireland.[23] Irish Conservatives also viewed their Whig counterparts as being overly cosmopolitan and too inclined to base their arguments on ideas drawn from radical English thinkers. In their view, such ideas had only a limited application to Ireland. They frequently cited free trade as an example of such an idea. In their view, while free trade might have benefits for England with its comparatively developed manufacturing industries, it would be dangerously destructive for Ireland with its heavy reliance on agriculture. In 1851, for example, the *Irish Quarterly Review* defended protectionism on the grounds that it was essential in the Irish case as it 'was a country almost entirely agricultural, and destitute of manufactures'.[24]

In the early 1830s, leading Dublin Conservatives repeatedly pointed to the damaging effects which English competition was having on Irish industries. In January 1832, for example, Charles Boyton complained that the linen industry in the north of Ireland was being sacrificed solely in order 'to gratify the whims of the political economists' of the day. In Boyton's view, the economic policies pursued by the Whig-Liberal government had caused the annihilation of what had previously been 'the steady trade of that part of the province'. He was also concerned that the gradual lowering of the duties on agricultural imports would eventually lead to Russian and Polish corn swamping the English market. This would in turn, he believed, ultimately result in the collapse of the pastoral sector in Ireland itself.[25]

In a similar vein, in August of the same year, George Alexander Hamilton, another prominent Irish Conservative, warned of the imminent collapse of the Irish provision trade. He laid the blame for this on the Whig government's recent decision to remove the duties on imported salted beef and pork. While denying that he supported the repeal agitation, Hamilton also argued that the policies which the British administration was pursuing towards Ireland were leading to a rapid increase in popular enthusiasm for it. Indeed, he suggested that if the Irish people should come to believe 'that the interests of the foreigner ... [were] preferred to theirs—that our Irish trade and commerce, and national welfare ... [were] sacrificed on every occasion even to the advantage of subordinate

English interests ... that Ireland ... [was] regarded by England just so far as she may be thought conductive to the interests of England and no further ... [then] the time may come where they [that is, the British government] find the question of repeal more irresistible even than Emancipation itself'.[26]

For some other Conservatives, however, such attempts (however tenuous) to draw a link between Irish Protestant discontent with the British government and the repeal agitation were deeply concerning. Although Charles Boyton had once advocated the strategy of joining with the Catholics 'in pressing the expediency of a repeal, placing the contingency as depending on the measures & conduct of the Government', this approach was not one which commended itself to many of his colleagues.[27] As early as December 1830, for example, Thomas Lefroy had warned Lord Farnham that, if Boyton or any of his colleagues were to give any 'countenance' to the campaign for repeal, all 'Protestants of quality' would immediately desert them. He also observed that it was necessary to use very careful language and extreme discretion when seeking to appeal to 'lower class' Protestants.[28]

There was also the broader question of what precisely Irish Conservatives hoped to achieve through their advocacy of increased protection for Irish industries. Was this, as some contemporaries saw it, simply a short-term strategy designed to prevent working-class Protestants from supporting the repeal agitation? By focusing on an economic rather than a constitutional issue, however, Conservative activists could claim that they were attempting to surmount those sectarian divisions which were becoming steadily more entrenched in Irish society. In this respect, their support for protection could be seen as an early attempt to kill repeal 'by kindness' and to win over at least some sections of the Catholic community to support for the maintenance of the Union.

The problem with such a strategy, however, lay in the deep-rooted scepticism which both sides of the sectarian divide in Ireland felt about the motivations which drove the actions of their political and religious adversaries. In this context, the O'Connellite attempts to win Protestant support for repeal in the early 1830s often had unintended and counterproductive effects. O'Connell's opponents frequently characterised such approaches as a 'snare' designed to lure unsuspecting Protestants into a potentially disastrous course of action. If they were to support repeal, the eventual outcome would be, in Charles Boyton's view, 'the abolition' of the Church of Ireland and 'the creation of a Roman Catholic government in Ireland'.[29] In a similar vein, O'Connell warned Catholics in 1835 that they should avoid Boyton's blandishments as his ultimate aim was the restoration of the rule of 'Orangeists' in Ireland.[30] This kind of thinking meant that such attempts to reach across the sectarian divide even in the relatively fluid political situation from 1829 onwards were frequently doomed to failure.

From the late 1820s onwards, Charles Boyton had been the principal advocate of 'social radicalism' within the Irish Conservative Party. However, his appointment as rector of the Church of Ireland parish of Tullyaughnish in County Donegal in July 1836 brought to an end his most intense period of active political engagement. This shift was largely a result of Boyton's need for greater financial security. Given his central role in the revitalisation of Irish conservatism in the late 1820s and early 1830s, his departure 'as a public character' had the effect of dramatically changing the political dynamic within it.[31]

Although a few of Boyton's remaining colleagues within the party had similar populist leanings to his own, none of them (with the partial exception of Isaac Butt, Boyton's chief political protégé) had anything like his standing within the party.[32] Even during Boyton's time as a leading figure within the party, his brand of maverick and intermittently radical Toryism had come under direct challenge from more overtly sectarian organisation such as the Dublin Protestant Operatives Association (DPOA). The key figure in the DPOA was a charismatic clergyman, Tresham Dames Gregg, whose appeal to working-class Protestants owed a great deal to his combination of fervent anti-Catholicism and sectarian populism. Unlike Boyton and Butt, who were essentially reluctant populists, from the outset of his career, Gregg proved a natural in the role. His Protestant zeal led him into regular polemical encounters with Catholic clergymen in the mid-to-late 1830s. On Gregg's part, the primary aim of those meetings was to persuade Protestants of the disastrous effects of Catholic Emancipation.

He also stressed the necessity to avoid any further concessions to members of the Catholic church. Gregg's political vision was essentially an apocalyptic one. As a result of this fundamentally pessimistic world view, he believed that even the limited concessions made to Catholics had brought God's wrath down upon the country.[33] He was also adamant that any further extension of Catholic rights would lead to certain ruin both for Ireland itself and for the Protestant population of the country. His panacea for this state of affairs was to seek to overturn those concessions which had already been made to Irish Roman Catholics. In the long term, his solution to

Ireland's economic and political difficulties was the complete 'overthrow of Popery' in the country.[34]

For Gregg, the real issues at play in Ireland at this time were essentially religious rather than economic or social ones. In consequence, under his leadership, the Operatives Association devoted comparatively little attention to such topics. Indeed, a central plank of its platform was the contention that the revival of Protestant Ascendancy was the key to restoring Ireland's economic prosperity. In this view of things, protectionism, even if it were desirable, could only really be considered once that objective had been attained.[35] Gregg's hold over working-class Protestant opinion was such that it rendered it extremely difficult for more pragmatic Conservatives like Boyton and Butt to get their message across to its intended audience.

Isaac Butt, Irish Manufacturing, and the Intellectual Case for Conservative Protectionism

Along with the challenge posed by Gregg and the DPOA, Irish Conservative attempts to promote industrial protectionism were also affected by the continuing contraction in the textiles industry in Dublin in the later 1830s. By the end of that decade, there were only three spinning mills still in operation there.[36] In these circumstances, it became increasingly difficult for contemporaries to foresee an industrial revival in the city, in the short term at any rate. This period also saw the beginnings of the gradual decline of the Protestant population in Dublin, a trend which was particularly marked among the working class. One of the reasons for this phenomenon was that many Protestant artisans ultimately had little option but to leave the city and go elsewhere in search of work. This demographic decline can be gauged from the fact that while, in the eighteenth century, Protestants had been in a majority in the city as a whole, by 1834 they represented only 28 per cent of the metropolitan population. By 1861, this percentage had declined further to 23 per cent.[37] This sustained emigration posed an obvious threat to the interests of the Protestant Ascendancy. In May 1833, for example, the *Dublin University Magazine* drew attention to the phenomenon, claiming that up to 94,000 Protestants had left Ireland in the previous four years. If this outflow continued, the author suggested, the journal's promotion of the interests of Irish

Protestants would be entirely in vain. It was imperative, therefore, that those who were 'the bone and sinew of that body' should be persuaded to remain in the country.[38]

As Boyton's main successor as the voice of social radicalism within the Irish Conservative Party, Butt's public support for protectionism could be seen as part of a wider attempt to stem this flow of Protestant migrants from the country. His appointment as Whately Professor of Political Economy at Trinity College Dublin in 1836 was critical in terms of giving him a public platform from which to express his support for protectionist ideas. A key element in Butt's advocacy of protection was his desire to maintain the cross-class alliance on which Irish conservatism ultimately rested. Although hardly an egalitarian, Butt was keen to see Irish landlords adopt a more socially responsible role than they had done in the past. In consequence, he was extremely critical of absentee landowners. In his view, their wasteful expenditure abroad was of no practical economic benefit to Ireland. Instead, they spent 'their superfluous wealth' outside the country 'without sharing it, in the shape of wages, with one single Irish workingman'.[39]

Butt also argued that if home-produced goods turned out to be slightly inferior in quality to those which had previously been imported into the country, this would be a relatively small price to pay in order to ensure 'a certain amount of comforts' for the Irish 'labouring class'. In essence, then, Butt's proposals envisaged a type of 'import-substitution' policy which was not that far removed from the economic policies pursued by the independent Irish state in the 1930s.[40] Finally, Butt recommended that protective duties should be accompanied by a tax on absentee landlords. Such a combination of measures would, he believed, ensure that the skilled craftsmen and general labourers in Dublin and other Irish cities would have sufficient employment to ensure them a reasonable standard of living. In later years, Butt also argued for the introduction of a wealth tax in Ireland in order to create a fund for the employment of the poor there. In Irish circumstances, this proposal implied some form of property tax to be applied presumably to prosperous landowners.[41] In that regard, Butt's vision of a future 'protectionist' Ireland was much broader than that envisaged by many of his Conservative Party colleagues. Most of them, despite their occasional protestations to the contrary, were principally concerned with the interests of the landed class. Unlike Butt, they also tended to conflate the interests of landlords with those of their tenants and those of the shopkeepers and merchants who operated in rural areas in Ireland.

The Repeal Movement and Protectionism, 1832–45

The development of Irish Conservative attitudes towards free trade must also be understood in the wider context of Irish politics at this time. If the issue of protection posed considerable difficulties for them, it was almost equally challenging for Whigs, moderate O'Connellites, and radicals in Ireland. While O'Connell's biographers have often presented him as, in Oliver MacDonagh's words, 'a doctrinaire free trader',[42] recent research has shown his position on that issue to be far more equivocal in Ireland than it was in England.[43] His ambiguousness on the subject owed a good deal to the fact that protectionism had a strong appeal to large sections of his domestic support base. Like their Protestant counterparts, many of O'Connell's Catholic supporters worked in industries which were in decline due to competition from cheaper English imports. In consequence, many of them were attracted to the idea that a post-repeal Irish government would protect existing native industries and foster the growth of new ones.

In the early 1830s, the formation of a number of Irish Manufacture Associations, most notably in Waterford and Cork City, clearly displayed the appeal which such ideas had among a section of O'Connell's supporters. The subsequent emergence of more explicitly working-class organisations designed to revive Irish industries followed on from this initiative. Among the more important of these was the establishment of the Cork Trades Association for the Encouragement of Irish Manufactures in June 1832.[44] The creation of such bodies presented both opportunities and difficulties for O'Connell. On the one hand, such institutions clearly energised particular sections of his political base. On the other hand, however, they posed a potential threat to O'Connell's alliance with prominent English radicals. Their shared enthusiasm for free trade principles had previously been the cement that held together those alliances.

Despite this risk, throughout the 1830s and the early 1840s, O'Connell regularly encouraged Irish people to 'wear and prefer the manufactures of their own country'.[45] By 1841, indeed, he was prepared to go further and pledge himself never to 'consume, for the rest of his life, anything but Irish manufactures'.[46] He defended this divergence from strict free trade doctrines by arguing that while their rigid application might be suitable under English conditions, Ireland's backward state meant that the normal rules of political economy did not apply there. O'Connell also repeatedly stressed his belief that Irish economic difficulties were a direct result of the

Act of Union. In consequence, a post-repeal Ireland could only combat economic underdevelopment though direct intervention to foster native industries there.[47]

Such beliefs served, in part at least, to shape O'Connell's eventual decision in 1841 that it would be necessary to 'bind up' the manufacture movement with the repeal agitation.[48] The decision also had more directly partisan objectives. The movement gave him an opportunity to rebuild his relationship with the Dublin working class. His standing with many Dublin artisans had been severely damaged by his outspoken (and for some contemporary observers, intemperate) attacks on the trade union movement there in 1837. In consequence, his association with the Trades Associations (as the working-class manufacture organisations were known) gave him an opportunity to restore his reputation as a protector of the interests of the Catholic 'lower orders'.[49] In capturing the campaign, he was able to link it directly with the agitation for repeal. In many respects, this was at odds with the wishes of the founders of the manufacture movement, who had intended that it should be non-partisan. Towards that end, they had made overtures to a number of leading Conservatives including Butt and George Alexander Hamilton.[50] Indeed, O'Connell's takeover of the movement was designed, in part at least, to prevent its being co-opted by his political opponents.

For many Irish radicals, however, protectionism was associated almost exclusively with the maintenance of the dominant position of the landed class. Many of them saw it as an instrument to keep food prices high. In consequence, in the early 1840s, 'cheap bread' became *the* slogan for many of those radicals who supported the repeal of the Corn Laws. For example, a placard posted around the town of Loughrea in County Galway before a protectionist meeting there in early 1841 called on local activists to be at their 'posts[s] ... to convince the grinding aristocracy of this country ... that you shall have no Corn Laws'. It also encouraged them to make 'cheap bread ... [their] motto'. In response to the implied message contained in that placard, a large crowd made up of many of the poorer working-class inhabitants of the town attended the meeting. Several of the anti-Corn Law speakers there continued in the same anti-landlord vein which the placard had begun. For example, one of them, Andrew Browne, a local landowner, claimed that protective duties were necessary only in order to enable Irish landlords to pay off the mortgage debts they owed to the 'fundholder[s]'. Rather than continuing these duties, he demanded the British government invest in improving Irish agriculture to 'enable her to successfully compete with—aye, and distance any foreign competitions'. Another speaker at the same meeting, Michael Winter, furiously denounced the protectionists for seeking to preserve 'the already bursting purses of … a grinding, oppressive, monopolising and iron-hearted aristocracy'.[51]

Like many of his contemporaries, Winter also stressed the wealth of Ireland's natural resources, referring to 'her noble harbours, her capacious bays … her majestic lakes … [and] her navigable rivers'. If properly developed, he argued, these natural advantages would have enabled the country to become 'the linking point … [and] the bond of connection' between the United Kingdom and the United States. In this scenario, the removal of the Corn Laws would allow a new focus to be placed on other previously neglected parts of the Irish economy.[52] To combat such arguments, Irish Conservative spokesmen frequently claimed that the interests of tenants and landlords should be regarded not as opposed but as complementary. As Lord Glengall, a leading protectionist put it in January 1850, they should be seen 'merely as two parties who row in the same boat'.[53] The Irish economy's overwhelming reliance on agriculture also meant that they viewed the preservation of the position of the landed interest as being essential to the country's long-term prosperity. In 1849, for example, the Cork landowner, Sir Henry Longfield, suggested that as Ireland 'altogether depended on agriculture', when 'that interest was injured, all others, from the highest to the lowest … [suffered] with it'.[54]

The Famine and the Free Trade/Protectionist Debate in Ireland, 1845–52

In the long term, however, the Famine caused many people in both Britain and Ireland to lose faith in the governing capacity of the existing Irish elite. As a result, in its aftermath, the widespread identification of protectionism with the maintenance of the interests of Irish landlords ensured that it proved very difficult for its advocates to broaden its appeal beyond a relatively narrow section of the population. In consequence, the attempt by a number of leading Irish landowners to launch an agitation for the reintroduction of protective duties in late 1849 had relatively little success. With the reputation of Irish landlords now at a low ebb,[55] the advocates of free trade had a great deal of ammunition to attack the proponents of the movement to reinstate protection. Such critics frequently pointed to the fact that the landowners' campaign had been launched only after the repeal of the Corn Laws in July 1846. This showed, the argument ran, that they were concerned only to maintain their own sectional interests rather than to advance the 'national' interests of Ireland. Having stood aside while Irish manufacturing industry had effectively been 'destroyed', landlords had only gone into action when it was their own interests which were under threat.[56] Indeed, John O'Connell, Daniel O'Connell's son and his successor as leader of the Repeal Association, characterised their agitation as 'the rackrent ... and bread-taxing movement'.[57] Despite the landowners' attempts to counter such attacks by claiming that the campaign for protection was not 'a landlord's, a manufacturer's or a merchant's question, but a great national question', it became clear over time that such O'Connellite attacks were having a significant effect on popular opinion.[58] By focusing their criticism on the issue of rents and food prices, Irish free traders could also hope to avoid the more complex issue surrounding protectionism, which had rendered it such a divisive issue in the past. In early 1850, for example, William Sharman Crawford, the leading northern Liberal, linked free trade with 'cheap corn' and 'low rents'. Crawford believed that the real questions concerning Irish agriculture were unrelated to protection. Rather, they were whether rents would be 'properly accommodate[d]' to prices and when tenants would be given 'ample security' for the expenditure of their 'labour and capital' on their holdings. The resolution of those questions would, he claimed, give a stimulus to agriculture in the country such 'as had never existed before'. Crawford optimistically claimed that a comprehensive land reform measure would result in such an increase in the produce of the country that it would no longer 'need any foreign corn'.[59]

Although the repeal of the Corn Laws had united Irish landlords behind the campaign for the restoration of protective duties on agricultural imports in both Britain and Ireland, it had made the position of those Tories in favour of greater protection for Irish industries more isolated than they had been in the past. In January 1850, however, Butt stressed his own long-term interest in the subject and expressed his conviction that the Irish gentry had 'forgot their own interest' when they failed to 'stand by the artisans'. He also suggested that there was an implicit contradiction in the stance of those popular politicians who claimed to be against protection for agriculture while, at the same time, they professed themselves favourable to the maintenance of Irish industries. According to Butt, it was now in 'the true interests of all classes in Ireland to demand the immediate restoration of protection to all branches of industry in Ireland, agricultural, commercial and manufacturing'.[60]

As this suggested, the protectionist movement in Ireland had become deeply enmeshed in the wider debates on that issue which followed on from the repeal of the Corn Laws in 1846. Indeed, a number of Irish landowners had played a prominent role in the organisation of the Protectionist Party from its inception in July 1846.[61] In both England and Ireland, the protectionist movement was heavily dependent on the social prestige and financial muscle of the landed class. Their domination of the movement in Ireland, however, made it extremely difficult for it to make much headway there. The problems it faced in securing popular support were clearly demonstrated by the fact that many of the meetings which were held under Protectionist auspices in 1849–50 actually concluded by passing resolutions in support of free trade. A number of other proposed meetings were simply abandoned when their organisers realised that they had little prospect of achieving their initial objectives.[62] By the time of the 1852 general election, it had become clear that, while protection had united Irish Conservative landowners, it did not, except in a relatively small number of constituencies, have a great deal of purchase among the wider Irish electorate.[63]

Conclusion

This chapter has explored the political character of the protectionist movement in Ireland between 1829 and 1852. It has concentrated in particular on the early 1830s, when a number of leading Irish Conservatives strongly advocated the protection of native Irish industries. Given the exceptionally fluid nature of Irish politics in this period, their strategy was intended to shore up the Conservative support base among the Irish Protestant working class, to demonstrate the party's 'national' credentials, and to win at least some Catholics away from O'Connell's repeal agitation. It was also significant that two of the major figures in this movement, Charles Boyton and Isaac Butt, were strongly committed to the idea of Irish exceptionalism. This belief led both on occasion to display an ambivalence towards the Union settlement itself. In Butt's case, indeed, this ambivalence ultimately led him to support home rule. For both Boyton and Butt, protection was necessary precisely because Irish conditions differed so markedly from those on the British mainland. As a result, while free trade might be suitable for conditions there, it was totally inappropriate in a country as economically underdeveloped as was Ireland.[64]

Such attitudes were also tied in with broader questions about the Union, which were an integral part of Irish political debate both at this time and subsequently. Should it be an 'incorporating' settlement—under which Ireland would be governed as an integral part of the United Kingdom—becoming, in Joseph Hume's words, 'the same' as any other 'county of England'?[65] Against this view stood the arguments of those who maintained that Irish economic circumstances were so different from those of England that the creation of such an integrated system was not a realistic possibility. According to this view, the exceptional nature of Ireland meant that it would be necessary to maintain special governmental structures and legislative measures there to take these differences into account.

Along with such tensions, the debate over free trade also brought out other underlying divisions within the Irish Conservative Party. These included the strains which existed between maverick Tories such as Butt and Boyton and the landed element which formed the backbone of the party's strength in Ireland. Some of the latter group were concerned that the comparative radicalism of the former might undermine the existing social structures in Ireland on which their own power and prestige depended.[66] In the long term, the ongoing decline in manufacturing in Ireland and the shrinking of the Protestant working class meant that industrial protectionism lost a good deal of its salience as an issue, especially for Irish Conservatives. The growing sectarian divisions in Irish politics also made it increasingly difficult for politicians there to advocate policies designed to cross the religious divide. Irish Conservatives faced other difficulties in promoting the protection of Irish industries as a 'nationally' minded policy. The most important of these was their close association with the Irish landed class, which meant that it proved difficult for them to spread their message beyond a relatively small audience. Outside of Ulster, moreover, the Irish Protestant working class provided too shallow a base on which to build a movement which would have the reach necessary to affect policymaking at Westminster.

Finally, protection in general was of little interest to many Irish Catholic small farmers in this period. Generally speaking, they were far more concerned with retaining their precarious foothold on the land than they were with an issue which seemed to have little real relevance to their lives. For the larger farmers, especially in the province of Leinster, their close integration into the British cattle market, especially from the mid-nineteenth century onwards, ushered in a period of relative prosperity.

Furthermore, despite Daniel O'Connell's flirtation with the manufacture movement in the 1830s and 1840s, by the mid-1840s, most Irish Liberals had moved towards an acceptance of the contemporary orthodoxy in favour of free trade. This was, to a large extent, driven by the growing centrality of the land question in Irish politics and the increasing identification of protectionism with the interests of the landed class. In the short term, then, the industrial protectionist movement had little concrete success. Its longer-term significance, however, came through the appeal which some of its ideas had for more advanced nationalist politicians such as John Mitchel. Through Mitchel, some of its key ideas were later to re-emerge in the political thought of Arthur Griffith.[67] Their later flourishing was, however, to be in a very different context and in very different circumstances to those in which they were first conceived.

Notes

1. Isaac Butt to Benjamin Disraeli, 22 Oct. 1849, Hughenden Papers, Bodleian Library B/111/35; see also Robert Stewart, *The Foundation of the Conservative Party, 1830–1867* (London: Longman, 1978), 236.
2. The classic study of the economic debates on the 'Irish Question' in this period is R. D. Collison Black, *Economic Thought and the Irish Question, 1817–1870* (London: Cambridge University Press, 1960); see also Thomas Boylan, Renee Prendergast, and John D. Turner, eds., *A History of Irish Economic Thought* (London: Routledge, 2011).
3. Anna Gambles, *Protection and Politics: Conservative Economic Discourse, 1815–1852* (Woodbridge: Boydell and Brewer, 1999), 1–10.
4. See, for example, the reports of the speeches of Richard Pennefather, Colonel William Stopford, and Lord Doneraile at protectionist meetings in Clonmel, Gorey, and Mallow; *Dublin Evening Post*, 16 Mar. 1839; *Wexford Independent*, 20 Feb. 1839; *Freeman's Journal*, 26 Feb. 1839. See also the editorial on the Corn Law question in the *Dublin Evening Mail*, 5 May 1841.
5. For a discussion of this debate, see David S. Johnson and Liam Kennedy, 'Nationalist Historiography and the Decline of the Irish Economy: George O'Brien Revisited', in *Ireland's Histories: Aspects of State, Society and Ideology*, ed. Seán Hutton and Paul Stewart (London: Routledge, 1991), 19; Liam Kennedy and David S. Johnson, 'The Union of Ireland and Britain, 1801–1921', in *The Making of Modern Irish History: Revisionism and the Revisionist Controversy*, ed. D. George Boyce and Alan O'Day (London: Routledge, 1996), 44, 46–48.

6. Jacqueline Hill, 'Artisans, Sectarianism and Politics in Dublin, 1829–48', *Saothar* 7 (1981): 20; Helen Mulvey, *Thomas Davis and Ireland: A Biographical Study* (Washington, DC: Catholic University of America Press, 2003), 87.
7. Hill 'Artisans, Sectarianism and Politics', 12–16, 20–22; Charles Boyton to Baron Farnham, 30 Dec. 1830, Farnham Papers, National Library of Ireland (hereafter NLI) MS 18,609/1.
8. K. Theodore Hoppen, *Elections, Politics, and Society in Ireland, 1832–1885* (Oxford: Clarendon Press, 1984), 47.
9. David Dickson, *Dublin: The Making of a Capital City* (London: Profile Books, 2014), 282.
10. Jacqueline Hill, 'The Protestant Response to Repeal: The Case of the Dublin Working Class', in *Ireland under the Union: Varieties of Tension*, ed. F. S. L. Lyons and R. A. J. Hawkins (Oxford: Clarendon Press, 1980), 35.
11. Gambles, *Protection*, 205–10, 232–34.
12. Ibid., 32–33, 48–50.
13. For a fuller discussion of this topic, see Andrew Shields, *The Irish Conservative Party, 1852–68: Land, Politics and Religion* (Dublin: Irish Academic Press, 2007), 209–13.
14. Boyton to Farnham, 30 Dec. 1830, Farnham Papers, NLI MS 18,609/1.
15. *Londonderry Sentinel*, 11 Dec. 1830.
16. Ibid.
17. Thomas Lefroy to Farnham, 3 Dec. 1830, Farnham Papers, NLI MS 18,611/1.
18. Thomas Duddy, *A History of Irish Political Thought* (London: Routledge, 2002),125–28, 143–46.
19. *Freeman's Journal*, 15 Jan. 1830.
20. Shields, *Irish Conservative Party*, xiv–xv.
21. Hoppen, *Elections, Politics, and Society*, 312.
22. Joseph Spence, 'The Philosophy of Irish Toryism 1833–52: A Study of Reactions to Liberal Reformism in Ireland in the Generation between the First Reform Act and the Famine, with Especial Reference to Expressions of National Feeling among the Protestant Ascendancy' (PhD diss., Birkbeck College, University of London, 1990), 10.
23. *Dublin Evening Mail*, 14 July 1852.
24. 'Notices of New Works', *Irish Quarterly Review* 1, no. 1 (1851): 342.
25. *Londonderry Sentinel*, 21 Jan. 1852.
26. *The Warder*, 29 Aug. 1832.
27. Boyton to Farnham, n.d. (Dec. 1830?), Farnham Papers, NLI MS 18,609/2.
28. Lefroy to Farnham, 2 and 25 Dec. 1830, Farnham Papers, NLI MS 18,611/1.

29. Boyton to Farnham, n.d. (Dec. 1830?), Farnham Papers, NLI MS 18,609/2.
30. *Morning Chronicle*, 4 May 1835.
31. *Londonderry Sentinel*, 28 Nov. 1838.
32. Joseph Spence, 'Isaac Butt, Irish Nationality and the Conditional Defence of the Union, 1833–70', in *Defenders of the Union: A Survey of British and Irish Unionism since 1801*, ed. D. G. Boyce and Alan O'Day (London: Routledge, 2001), 68–69.
33. Hill, 'Protestant Response to Repeal', 35–68; John Crawford, '"An overriding providence": The Life and Ministry of Tresham Dames Gregg (1800–81)', in *The Clergy of the Church of Ireland, 1000–2000*, ed. T. G. Barnard and W. G. Neely (Dublin: Four Courts Press, 2005), 157–68.
34. Tresham Dames Gregg, *Free Thoughts on Protestant Matters* (Dublin: Curry and Oldham, 1847), 5.
35. Tresham Dames Gregg, *Protestant Ascendancy Vindicated and National Regeneration through the Instrumentality of National Religion Urged* (Dublin: D. R. Bleakly, 1840); Hill, 'Protestant Response to Repeal', 55.
36. Andy Bielenberg, 'Industrial Growth in Ireland, c. 1790–1910', (PhD diss., London School of Economics and Political Science, 1994), 130.
37. Martin Maguire, 'A Socio-Economic Analysis of the Dublin Protestant Working Class, 1870–1926', *Irish Economic and Social History* 20 (1993): 35–61; Dickson, *Dublin*, 310; Hill, 'Artisans, Sectarianism and Politics', 20–23; idem, *From Patriots to Unionists: Dublin Civic Politics and Irish Protestant Patriotism, 1660–1840* (Oxford: Clarendon Press, 1993), 313–14.
38. 'On the Emigration of Protestants', *Dublin University Magazine* 1, no. 5 (1833), 470–83.
39. Alan O'Day, 'Nationalism and Political Economy in Ireland: Isaac Butt's Analysis', in *Politics and Power in Victorian Ireland*, ed. Roger Swift and Christine Kinealy (Dublin: Four Courts Press, 2006), 122–27; Isaac Butt, *Protection to Home Industry: Some Cases of its Advantages Considered* (Dublin: Hodges and Smith, 1846), 40.
40. Butt, *Protection to Home Industry*, 15.
41. Isaac Butt, *Home Government for Ireland: Irish Federalism! Its Meaning, Its Objects, and Its Hopes*, 3rd ed. (Dublin: John Falconer, 1871), 32.
42. Oliver MacDonagh, *O'Connell: The Life of Daniel O'Connell* (London: Weidenfeld and Nicolson, 1991), 309; see also Joseph Lee, 'The Social and Economic Ideas of O'Connell', in *Daniel O'Connell: Portrait of a Radical*, ed. K. B. Nowlan and M. R. O'Connell (Belfast: Appletree Press, 1984), 70–86. For a recent discussion of this topic, see Paul Pickering, 'Irish First: Daniel O'Connell, the Native Manufacture Campaign and Economic Nationalism, 1840–44', *Albion* 32, no. 4 (2000), 598–616.

43. Douglas Kanter, 'The Politics of Irish Taxation, 1842–53', *English Historical Review* 127, no. 528 (2012): 1127; Charles Read, 'The Repeal Year in Ireland: An Economic Reassessment', *Historical Journal* 58, no. 1 (2015): 115–17.
44. Fintan Lane, *In Search of Thomas Sheahan: Radical Politics in Cork, 1824–1836* (Dublin: Irish Academic Press, 2001), 38; Maura Cronin, *Country, Class or Craft? The Politicisation of Skilled Artisans in Nineteenth Century Cork* (Cork: Cork University Press, 1994), 99–101.
45. At one point, O'Connell even expressed a wish to be 'buried in Irish manufacture'; William Fagan, *The Life and Times of Daniel O'Connell*, 2 vols. (Cork: John O'Brien, 1847), 1:265; see also Pickering, 'Irish First', 605.
46. *Dublin Morning Register*, 29 July 1841.
47. Pickering, 'Irish First', 610–11; see also Read, 'Repeal Year', 116.
48. Pickering, 'Irish First', 604.
49. For O'Connell's conflicts with the trade union movement in Dublin, see MacDonagh, *O'Connell*, 445–50; see also Feargus D'Arcy, 'The Artisans of Dublin and Daniel O'Connell, 1830–1847', *Irish Historical Studies* 17, no. 66 (1970), 221–43.
50. Pickering, 'Irish First', 602, 604.
51. *Tuam Herald*, 29 May 1841
52. Ibid.
53. *Dublin Evening Mail*, 18 Jan. 1850.
54. Ibid., 31 Dec. 1849.
55. K. T. Hoppen, *Governing Hibernia: British Politicians and Ireland, 1800–1921* (Oxford: Oxford University Press, 2016), 139.
56. See, for example, the anti-protectionist speech made by Father Peter Daly at a meeting in Galway in Dec. 1849, *Freeman's Journal*, 31 Dec. 1849; see also Cormac Ó Grada, *Ireland: A New Economic History, 1780–1939* (Oxford: Oxford University Press), 407–11.
57. *Freeman's Journal*, 10 Dec. 1849; *Limerick and Clare Examiner*, 15 Dec. 1849.
58. *Northern Whig*, 10 Jan. 1850.
59. *Evening Standard*, 15 Jan. 1850.
60. *Dublin Evening Mail*, 30 Jan. 1850.
61. For example, the first Protectionist whip in the House of Commons was William Beresford, a member of a prominent landed family in County Waterford. Among the other prominent Irish Protectionists were Sir Arthur Brooke, Viscount Bernard, George Alexander Hamilton, Anthony Lefroy, Augustus Stafford O'Brien, and Evelyn Shirley. By contrast, there were very few Irish Peelites. The most notable of this small group, perhaps, was Henry Herbert, who served as Chief Secretary of Ireland under Lord Palmerston from 1857 to 1858; see Shields, *Irish Conservative Party*, 16,

121–22; Angus Hawkins, *The Forgotten Prime Minister: The 14th Earl of Derby*, vol. 1: *Ascent, 1799–1851* (Oxford: Oxford University Press, 2007), 316.

62. See, for example, *Morning Chronicle*, 7 Jan. 1850; *Cork Examiner*, 11 Jan. 1850; *Dublin Mercantile Advertiser*, 11 Jan. 1850; *Newry Examiner*, 26 Jan. 1850.
63. One of the major exceptions to this rule was the Cork City by-election of Nov. 1849, when the Protectionist candidate, Colonel Chatterton, won an impressive victory over his Liberal opponent, Alexander McCarthy. By the time of the 1852 election, however, Hoppen claims that most Irish Conservatives were more interested in Protestantism than they were in protection; see Hoppen, *Elections, Politics, and Society*, 284. See also Robert Stewart, The *Politics of Protection: Lord Derby and the Protectionist Party, 1841–1852* (London: Cambridge University Press, 1971), 143.
64. See Spence, 'Philosophy', 240–47.
65. For an excellent discussion of this topic, which concentrates, in particular, on the way in which it was addressed in the aftermath of the passing of the Act of Union, see K. T. Hoppen, 'An Incorporating Union? British Politicians and Ireland, 1800–1830', *English Historical Review* 123, no. 501 (2008): 328–50.
66. Lefroy to Farnham, 25 Dec. 1830, Farnham Papers, NLI MS 18,611/1; see also Hoppen, *Elections, Politics, and Society*, 311–13, although Hoppen goes on to argue that such tensions ultimately operated as a 'safety valve', and that they 'paradoxically strengthened the sense of overall religious identity' across the class divide.
67. David Thornley, *Isaac Butt and Home Rule* (London: MacGibbon and Kee, 1964), 17; Patrick Maume, *The Long Gestation: Irish Nationalist Life, 1891–1918* (Dublin: Gill and Macmillan, 1999), 49; James Quinn, 'John Mitchel and the Rejection of the Nineteenth Century', *Éire-Ireland* 38, nos. 3–4 (2003): 92–94.

CHAPTER 7

Resistance to the Collection of Rates Under the Poor Law, 1842–44

Mel Cousins

The Irish Poor Law was introduced in 1838.[1] There was initially little opposition to the implementation of the legislation in practice. However, as the financial implications of the act, in particular the collection of poor rates, became more apparent, opposition grew. This chapter examines the resistance to the collection of poor rates, which peaked around 1843, from a geographical and political perspective. It reconstructs the political context for the opposition to rates, with O'Connell encouraging hostility to the Poor Law in late 1842 and 1843 and some Conservative landowners also showing a reluctance to support rates. We study three Unions where there was a long-term resistance in detail (Waterford, Galway, and Tuam), in order to identify the different local and national factors at play, and analyse both the immediate response of the state and the poor rates reforms introduced by the Conservative government in 1843. We then consider why the opposition ultimately had only a limited impact.

M. Cousins (✉)
Trinity College Dublin, Dublin, Ireland
e-mail: cousinsm@tcd.ie

D. Kanter, P. Walsh (eds.), *Taxation, Politics, and Protest in Ireland, 1662–2016*, Palgrave Studies in the History of Finance,
https://doi.org/10.1007/978-3-030-04309-4_7

The Introduction of the Poor Law in Ireland

A national Poor Law was enacted for Ireland in 1838, based largely on the English model of 1834. By the terms of the act, Ireland was to be divided into 130 Poor Law Unions, and the law was to be administered by local boards of guardians which were partially elected and partially appointed. The English Poor Law Commissioners were put in charge of the implementation of the Poor Law and the local boards were placed under the supervision of the commission. The commission was responsible for issuing detailed orders for the operation of the law and for the 'guidance and control' of guardians.[2] In extreme cases, the commission had the power to dissolve a board and to appoint paid guardians in its stead.[3]

The adoption of the legislation was only the first stage in putting in place an Irish Poor Law. The major task of implementing the law still remained. The Home Secretary, Lord John Russell, dispatched George Nicholls, one of the existing English Poor Law Commissioners (and also one of the authors of the Irish law) to Ireland in September 1838. This meant that Nicholls reported directly to the Home Office rather than being subordinate to the Irish government. Although Nicholls was nominally part of a board of commissioners, it would appear that he acted largely on his own authority in Ireland. His first task was to oversee the implementation of the new law. This involved the establishment of the Unions, the election of local boards, the building of workhouses, and the assessment and collection of the local rates which were to be the source of funding.

The boards of guardians consisted of both elected and ex officio members, with the latter initially limited to one-third of each board. Elections were held annually in March. All ratepayers were entitled to vote, leading to an electorate of about one million persons. This was a very high level of enfranchisement by the standards of the time. However, to balance the rights of property, the number of votes to which each person was entitled increased in accordance with the valuation of their property. After the annual election, the boards elected a chairman, and vice and deputy chairmen.

In order to assess a rate, the Unions first had to value the assessable property (principally land and buildings) in the Union. Although the Poor Law gave them the possibility of relying on existing valuations (Griffith's valuation was then ongoing), it appears that boards overwhelmingly rejected this option (where it was relevant) and decided to carry out their own valuations. This process was quite controversial in itself although this story must remain for another day.[4] Having completed this process, the boards were then required to set a rate 'for the purpose of defraying the expenses incurred in the execution of [the] Act'.[5] This process took some time and was implemented, generally, in the larger towns and cities first and in the western counties last. By March 1841, 127 Unions had been declared and ninety-nine boards elected. However, only about fifty Unions had struck rates by the end of 1841, and by May 1843, only 110 workhouses had been declared ready to receive paupers.[6] Thus, it was not until 1842–43 in many Unions that rates were set and collection was underway. By August 1843, rates of £605,864 had been assessed by ninety-eight Unions, of which over 90 per cent had been collected.[7] This was a significant amount in the context of Irish local government and compares to the £1,269,900 in county cess raised by the grand juries in 1840.[8]

The law provided that the boards were to levy rates on the occupiers of land based on the value of the rent which could be expected.[9] The rates were to be paid by the occupier which meant that, where land was rented, rates were to be paid by the tenant, though half the rate could be deducted from any rent due.[10] It had originally been proposed that smallholders (occupying land worth under £5 valuation) should be excluded from liability (with rates being paid by the landlord), but the House of Lords had removed this provision.[11] The effect of this was that in such cases many landlords were indifferent to whether or not the smallholders could or did pay the rates.[12] Given the division of property in pre-Famine Ireland, this affected very many tenants, and the commission reported that over half of those rated (53 per cent) had a valuation of £5 or less.[13]

While there have been a number of studies of the Poor Law in post-Famine Ireland, there has to date been limited study of the Poor Law before the Famine.[14] Gray's essential study of the making of the Poor Law focuses primarily on the debates leading up to, and the adoption of, the Poor Law in 1838.[15] Gray does indeed devote a chapter to the implementation of the Poor Law up to 1843. However, the number of issues which arose in the implementation of the Poor Law means that his discussion of the 1843 resistance to the law is necessarily limited.[16] This chapter explores in more detail this important aspect of the Poor Law. One of the most interesting studies of the Poor Law has been Feingold's excellent study of the 'social transformation of power' in Ireland as nationalist tenants took over control of the Poor Law boards of guardians from the landlords in the 1870s and 1880s. Indeed, Cousins has argued that the boards played an important role in the broader politicisation of their communities.[17] The current study also throws light on the extent to which the local boards were politicised (in a broad sense) before the Famine.

Opposition to the Act

Although the Poor Law was generally seen as unpopular in Ireland, there was surprisingly little early opposition to its implementation. Indeed, in some areas, local opinion pressed for the act to be brought into effect quickly in order to deal with distress.[18] However, as the financial implications of the act, in particular the collection of poor rates, became more apparent, opposition grew. Doubtless, the general raising of the political temperature, as the campaign to repeal the Act of Union commenced in earnest, contributed to tensions.[19] There is also evidence of an economic downturn in the early 1840s, which may also have contributed to resistance to payment of rates.[20] In particular, Charles Read has shown that there was a significant fall in pig and cattle prices in 1842.[21] While comprehensive data are lacking, Read also identifies evidence of rising rent arrears, falling real wages, falling land values, and rising interest rates in the period.[22] However, as we will also see, local influences played an important part and resistance was by no means universal. The first resistance appears to have arisen in the Tipperary, Skibbereen (County Cork), and Waterford Unions in 1842, but by 1843, resistance was more widespread.[23]

There were particular difficulties in collecting the rates from poorer occupiers—many of whom were in poverty if not distress themselves. By 1843, forces of up to one hundred soldiers and constables were commonly in use in an effort to collect the rates and, along the west coast, even the Royal Navy had been called in to assist in collection.[24] In Waterford, men carrying sticks marched into the city in a show of resistance.[25] Violence was used against rate collectors in a number of cases.[26] A number of boards of guardians also resisted implementation of the act and, in some cases, although workhouses were built, they were not opened (or opened only to very small numbers of poor). The repeal campaign appears to have contributed to some of the opposition to the act with, for example, the Tuam board being one of the leading opponents.

Drawing on the 1843 return as to the use of the military and constabulary to collect the rates, we can identify eighteen Unions in which force was used to assist in collection (see Table 7.1).

Table 7.1 Use of police and military in collection of poor rates, 1843[27]

Union	*Dates*	*Max no. of constables deployed*	*Max no. of military deployed*	*Amount collected*
Ballinasloe	Mar.–Nov.	100	12	£2 8s.
Baltinglass	Oct.–Dec.	11	0	£30 18s.
Boyle	June–Dec.	62	78	£82 19s.
Carrickmacross	Nov.	53	91	£22 1s.
Carrick-on-Shannon	Feb.–Oct.	60	0	£68 14s.
Cashel	Feb.–Oct.	8	0	£4 12s.
Clogheen	Nov.–Dec.	4	0	£1 5s.
Donegal	Aug.–Dec.	42	50	£343 5s.
Dunmanway	Mar.–Sept.	86	0	£14 13s.
Fermoy	June–Dec.	48	49	£281 9s.
Galway	Sept.–Dec.	50	72	£116 12s.
Kilmallock	June–Oct.	30	0	£5 12s.
Limerick	Feb.–Dec.	41	120	£99 14s.
Longford	June–July	102	28	£1 19s.
Naas	Nov–Dec.	5	0	£6 12s.
Tipperary	Feb.–Sept.	100	40	£177 6s.
Tralee	June–Oct.	30	0	£19 5s.
Waterford	Mar.–May	100	167	£383 14s.
Westport	Dec.	36	50	£8 12s.

Table 7.2 Unions with 10 per cent or more of rates outstanding on 1 January 1844[28]

10–20% Outstanding	*21–30% Outstanding*	*31% or More*
Athlone	Armagh	Athy
Bandon	Balrothery	Ballinalsoe
Boyle	Callan	Ballinrobe
Cashel	Carrickmacross	Banbridge
Dublin South	Castlerea	Carrick-on-Shannon
Fermoy	Cavan	Castlebar
Inishowen	Gort	Donegal
Lisburn	Kells	Dungarvan
Lismore	Kilmallock	Galway
Magherafelt	Limerick	Granard
Naas	Mohill	Longford
New Ross	Navan	Loughrea
Oldcastle	Roscommon	Newry
Skibbereen	Tralee	Scarrif
Thurles		Tuam
Tipperary		Westport
Wexford		

However, Unions such as Tuam, where the board opposed the collection of rates, do not appear. An alternative source of information is from returns as to the level of rates outstanding in Unions. Unions with significant levels of arrears are set out in Table 7.2.

As can be seen, arrears of at least 10 per cent of the last rate set could be found in at least forty-six Unions (or 35 per cent of all Unions, including those which had not yet set a rate).[29] However, serious arrears (21 per cent or more) were confined to thirty Unions (23 per cent). Unions with the highest levels of arrears included Tuam (100 per cent), Loughrea (80 per cent), Ballinrobe (76 per cent), Longford (67 per cent),[30] Galway (56 per cent), and Dungarvan (51 per cent). Of the three large cities (Belfast, Cork, and Dublin), arrears were recorded only in Dublin South, and this was attributed by the Poor Law Commission (henceforth, PLC) to technical issues concerning incorrect recording of who was actually liable for rates.[31]

Combining the information as to Unions in which at least 10 per cent of rates were outstanding and those where police and military were used in the collection of rates, we can identify the geography of resistance in the Map 7.1 set out below.[32]

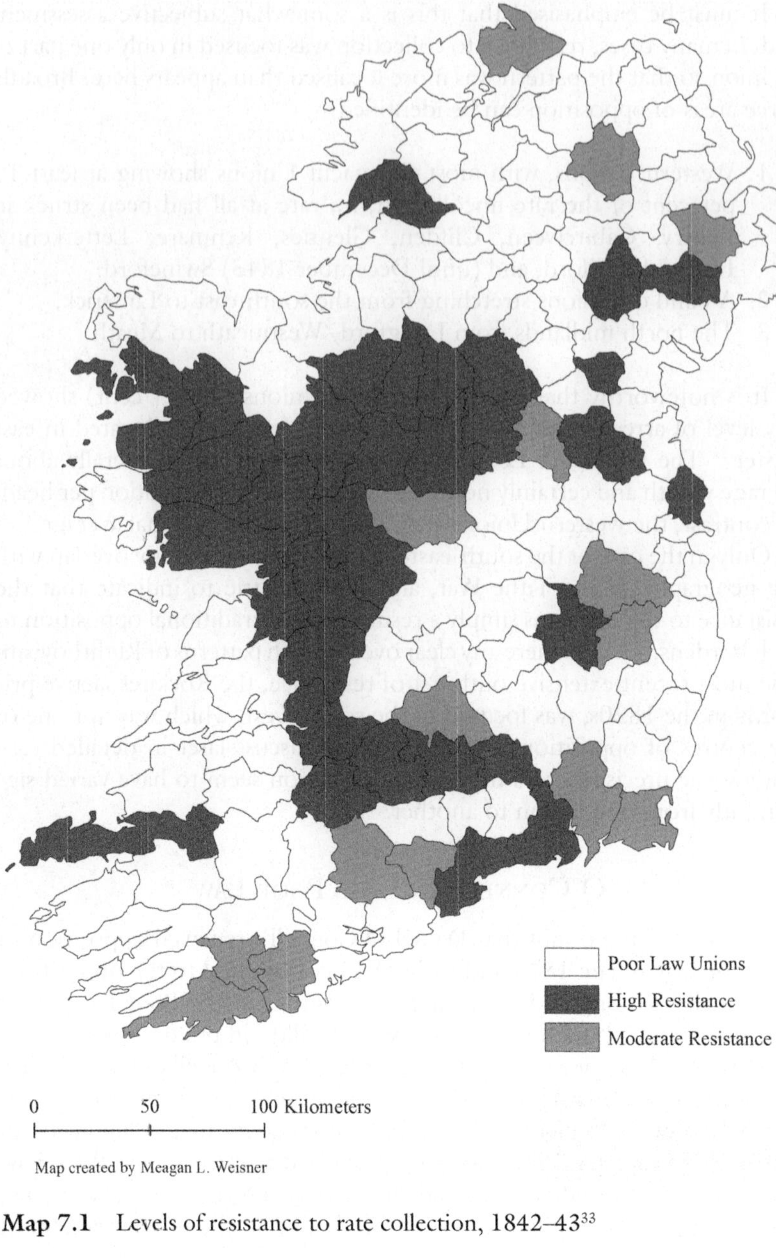

Map 7.1 Levels of resistance to rate collection, 1842–43[33]

It must be emphasised that this is a somewhat subjective assessment and, in many cases, resistance to collection was focused in only one part of a Union so that the pattern was more localised than appears here. Broadly three areas of opposition can be identified:

1. Western Unions, with most Connacht Unions showing at least 10 per cent of the rate uncollected; no rate at all had been struck in Bantry, Cahirciveen, Clifden, Glenties, Kenmare, Letterkenny, Listowel, Milford, and (until December 1843) Swineford.
2. A band of Unions stretching from the south-east to Limerick.
3. The north midlands from Longford/Westmeath to Meath.

It is noteworthy that only eight Ulster Unions (22 per cent) showed any level of arrears, and only three of these Unions were located in east Ulster.[34] The Unions in Leinster and east Munster were generally about average wealth and certainly not those with the highest valuation per head. In contrast, the western Unions were well below the national average.

Only in the case of the south-eastern Unions was there any overlap with the geography of the Tithe War, and there is little to indicate that the resistance to the rates was simply a resumption of traditional opposition to such burdens.[35] Nor is there any clear overlap with patterns of Rightboyism. The most recent extensive outburst of resistance, the Rockites, active primarily in the 1820s, was focused in the south-west, which was not one of the centres of opposition to rates.[36] As we discuss later in detailed case studies, the precise factors triggering opposition seem to have varied significantly from one Union to another.

O'Connell and the Poor Law

There can be little doubt that Daniel O'Connell's renewed opposition to the Poor Law in late 1842 and early 1843 contributed to the opposition. O'Connell had long had an intuitive opposition to the Poor Law (or at least poor rates) though he had occasionally allowed political pragmatism to outweigh these views.[37] In December 1842, O'Connell published a letter to the Cork guardians setting out his opposition to the Poor Law, which he saw as 'replete with the utmost dangers' to the landlords of Ireland.[38] In January 1843, he again published a letter on the Poor Law which, he announced, constituted his 'second exertion to arouse [his] constituents to a combined exertion for abolishing the present system of poor laws'.[39] He repeated his claim, first made in 1838, that Ireland was too poor for a Poor Law, and favoured the encouragement of charities, with the state donating pro rata to the voluntary contributions collected. He also proposed an income tax for those earning over £500 per annum to support relief. He concluded by claiming that he did not oppose the Poor Law with a view to advancing repeal and warning that there was nothing more likely to promote repeal than a failure to reform the law.

However, a subsequent report of the committee of the Repeal Association 'about the evils and remedies of the existing poor law in Ireland' was rather equivocal.[40] Although the report agreed on the 'evils' of the Poor Law, complaining of the arbitrary conduct of the PLC and its disregard of the views of guardians, the enormous expense of the system, and the limited relief afforded to the poverty of the country, it was less clear on the remedies. Here, it set out a number of options but came to no clear conclusions.[41] By February, O'Connell had tempered his opposition. During a somewhat rambling discussion of the Poor Law at the Repeal Association, O'Connell stated that 'He did not wish for any great movement against the poor law until there was a thorough conviction of the horrors of it, and when it did come he trusted he would be able to assist in regulating it in such a way as to protect the interests of suffering humanity.'[42] In order to look at the factors giving rise to the resistance (and its ultimate failure), we focus on three Unions: Waterford, Galway, and Tuam.[43] As we have seen, Waterford and Galway were amongst the earliest Unions to show resistance to rates. Tuam was probably the Union that continued its resistance for the longest period; the board of guardians there was taken to court by the Poor Law Commissioners, and ultimately dissolved, before resistance ceased.

Resistance in Waterford

Waterford was a relatively wealthy Union with a Poor Law valuation above the national average (£2 8s. 2d. per head of population compared to a national average of about £1 12s.). The board was chaired by Sir Benjamin Morris. Resistance to collection of rates in Waterford appears to have commenced in 1842. However, unlike Tuam, the board always attempted (with a greater or lesser degree of conviction) to enforce the law, and resistance seems to have been confined largely to one barony, Gaultier.[44] Waterford Union was one of two Unions (the other being Galway) in which the commissioners described collection of rates as 'attended with the greatest difficulty'.[45]

In January 1843, with over £5,000 in rates outstanding, the Waterford board wrote to the Assistant Poor Law Commissioner, Richard Muggeridge, informing him that the rate collector had resigned. The guardians were of the view that it would be impossible to collect rates without the assistance of the police.[46] By this stage, the board was in financial difficulties, and its bank would advance no more money.[47] The PLC encouraged the board to take action, assuring it that the constabulary would provide the necessary support.[48] In February the neighbouring Dungarvan board—which was also encountering resistance—instructed its collectors to suspend proceedings against defaulting ratepayers until the Poor Law was repealed or amended.[49] Meanwhile, the new Waterford Poor Law collector attempted to get support for his efforts to collect the rates, requesting Dr Fitzgerald, the stipendiary magistrate, to accompany him to collect the rates and calling a meeting of magistrates as advised by Edward Lucas, Under-Secretary in Dublin Castle.[50] The magistrates met privately in March 1843 but appear to have decided not to call in the military (presumably to avoid conflict). Tensions were clearly mounting and the *Waterford Chronicle* referred to a 'deadly hate' for the Poor Law, reporting that notices had been posted calling for people to assemble. In view of the tensions, the *Chronicle* called on the Waterford board to suspend collection, as in Dungarvan.[51]

On 13 March 1843, a large crowd marched into Waterford City protesting against the collection of rates. The size of the crowd was put at anything from 1,000 by the Chief Secretary to between 5,000 and 6,000 by the local newspapers. The crowd, allegedly armed with bludgeons, proceeded down the quay and to the mall where the Riot Act was read by a Captain Newport, after which the crowd dispersed.[52] The *Chronicle* referred to the 'extraordinary display of physical force and popular excitement' caused by the angry multitude. The paper, reflecting local opposition, now opposed the Poor Law but called for reforms to avoid bloodshed. It warned against seeking redress by illegal means and proposed meetings and petitions for a repeal of the law. It attributed resistance to the Conservative Party and pointed out that in Lismore, where the Whig Duke of Devonshire owned land, there was no opposition.[53] The *Waterford Mail* described the crowd as peasantry from Gaultier and surrounding districts.[54]

The protest was noticed in Parliament, and the Chief Secretary, Lord Eliot, presumably based on local police reports, told the Commons that 1,000 men carrying sticks had marched into the city in a show of resistance.[55] However, no attempt at riot or disturbance had taken place, and he believed that the reports had been much exaggerated. Given the low estimate of the numbers involved and the fact that the Riot Act had apparently been read by the authorities, Lord Eliot might perhaps be accused of downplaying the event.

However, the opposition to the Poor Law, rather than weakening the resolve of the authorities, appears to have strengthened it. In the aftermath of the demonstration in Waterford, the local magistrates again met to plan rate collection, and a troop of hussars arrived to assist. Meanwhile, both the local Catholic clergy and Conservative landowners moved to calm the situation. The *Chronicle* reported that the agents of both Lord Waterford and Lord Carew had called on their tenants to pay the rates.[56] A week after the protest, a mission to collect rates went into Gaultier, including the 'strongholds' of Lord Waterford and Lord Carew, supported by troops. The incursion appears to have collected relatively little but indicated the determination of the authorities to enforce the rates.[57] By the end of March, the *Chronicle* was reporting that the landlords had decided to pay the rates.[58] However, in April, there was continued resistance to collection, with the rate collector resigning and discussions at the board that tenants were unable to pay rates.[59] The new rate collector was threatened by a 'crowd of country people' in Gaultier until he promised to desist. The new collector subsequently (and understandably) resigned.[60] The board formed a committee to oversee collection, a new rate collector was sent down from Dublin, and there was a further expedition to Gaultier in April, with some claimed success in collection.[61] By the end of the month, Mr Pickering, the new collector, was able to hand in almost £50, and there were some additional cattle and property still distrained. Some resistance continued in May, with threatening notices continuing to appear warning against payment of rates, but Pickering was able to collect significant sums.[62] The police and military were used extensively in the period from March to June 1843 to assist in the collection of rates, with considerable success.[63]

By April 1843, the Poor Law amendment bill (discussed later) had been published. The *Chronicle* responded negatively, with criticism of the increase in ex officio guardians and the augmented powers of the PLC.[64] With the adoption of the legislation later in 1843, resistance appears to have largely died, and by 1844, the PLC was able to report that 'the cases in which resistance to the collection of the rate has occurred within the last 12 months are comparatively few.'[65] The PLC noted that of a total rate of £12,012 only £772 was outstanding on 1 January 1844 (of which over £200 was considered to be legally uncollectable at this stage).[66]

Resistance in Galway

Galway Union was not a wealthy Union (the valuation per head was £1 2s. 10d.), although it was more prosperous than the generally poor western Unions. The board was chaired by T. N. Redington (Liberal MP for Dundalk and a future Under-Secretary for Ireland), with Anthony O'Flaherty (a landowner and future Repeal/Liberal MP for Galway) as vice-chair. Galway was one of the Unions most strongly opposed to the collection of rates.[67] This formed part of a broader pattern of resistance, and by the end of 1842 and early 1843, resistance was taking place in a number of western Unions including Ballinasloe, Ballinrobe, and Castlebar.[68]

The resistance in Galway appears to have been related to dissatisfaction amongst the urban guardians concerning the proportion of the cost of relief borne by the urban electoral districts. This issue had already been raised in a number of urban Unions, including Cork and Limerick. George Nicholls had originally envisaged that all costs would be borne by the Union-at-large, but the House of Lords has insisted on making each electoral district responsible for the costs of its 'own' poor, defined as persons who were resident in the district.[69] However, residence was not defined in the act, which led to lengthy disputes in some districts.

The Cork board—obviously reflecting the views of the urban guardians—had established a very tenuous understanding of residence, which led to persons originally from rural areas being charged to rural districts even when they had lived in the city for many years. This interpretation of residence was objected to by the PLC, which eventually obtained the opinion of the law officers that this approach was unlawful.[70] A similar dispute arose in Limerick when property owners in the rural districts (including the chairman of the board) complained that, despite the low level of pauperism in the rural districts, they were burdened with heavy rates, largely because over 40 per cent of the inmates were charged to the Union-at-large.[71] As in Cork, it appears that the urban guardians interpreted the residence test in a flexible manner in order to throw as much of the cost as possible on the rural divisions.

In Galway, a rate had been set in February 1842, and the workhouse was opened shortly afterwards due to the exhaustion of the funds of the mendicity institution.[72] Initially, the Assistant Poor Law Commissioner for the area, Joseph Burke, reported that difficulty in collecting rates was due to problems in recruiting competent collectors. In the autumn of 1842, Burke argued that there was a need to make a further rate, but the guardians for the Galway City district were opposed to this as the rates from the rural districts had not yet been collected.

There appears to have been widespread dissatisfaction with the Poor Law in Galway by early 1843.[73] Following a notice by some guardians to rescind the rate, it was agreed to limit the rate to the amount necessary to discharge the debts of the board and to keep open the workhouse until 25 March (and no later).[74] A public meeting of ratepayers was held in Galway in January, which passed a resolution critical of the Poor Law.[75] In March, the Galway Grand Jury called for an inquiry into the Poor Law.[76]

Burke attributed local opposition to the system of charging paupers to the electoral district in which they were resident and claimed that the approach was inapplicable in Ireland. He pointed out that although the valuation of the Galway rural districts was higher than the urban districts, the cost of six months' maintenance was £696 in the urban district and only £141 in the combined rural districts. Finally, in April 1843, the Galway board agreed to Burke's proposal to set an adequate rate.[77]

However, resistance to the collection of the rates continued and ultimately—as in Waterford—a collector was sent down by the PLC.[78] Military and police were used extensively, to assist both in the serving of notices and summons and in the actual collection of rates in late 1843.[79] By mid-1844, the PLC was able to report that the greater part of the rates had been collected, and that all violent resistance had ceased.[80]

Resistance in Tuam

The Tuam Union was of similar average wealth to Galway (£1 3s. valuation per head). There was no apparent opposition to the law in Tuam until 1842, and the workhouse for 800 persons had been declared fit for use in August. However, opposition was emerging by later in that year, and the decision to strike a rate in October was carried only by the casting vote of the acting chair, Michael Joseph Browne.[81] The guardians took little or no action to enforce the collection of that rate despite being directed by the PLC to do so in November. By January 1843, opposition to the law was widespread.[82] The nationalist *Tuam Herald* argued that amendment of the law was 'indispensably necessary'. While supporting a Poor Law, the *Herald* desired one radically different to the existing legislation, funded by an absentee tax, landlord tax, and tithes.[83] That same month, a meeting to petition for the repeal of the law was called by the nationalist Archbishop of Tuam, John MacHale, with the support of J. J. Bodkin (MP for County Galway) and several Poor Law guardians.[84] Later that month, in preparation for the meeting, MacHale addressed a public letter to the Prime Minister, Sir Robert Peel, critical of the Poor Law.[85] The subsequent meeting, chaired by MacHale, adopted resolutions critical of the existing law and calling for its repeal. With the annual elections upcoming, the *Herald* called for the election of guardians opposed to the collection of rates.[86]

In April, the board (then meeting only monthly) reconvened after the elections, and Browne was re-elected chair.[87] It is clear that there were tensions between guardians as to the approach which they should take. On the one hand, there was strong opposition to the collection of rates. On the other, however, they had already incurred expenses in building and fitting out the workhouse, which could not be repaid without an income. A resolution was proposed to adjourn for a month as the government intended to amend the law, and an amendment to this motion was offered to borrow to pay off the debts due to contractors. Burke, the Assistant Poor Law Commissioner, argued that it would be illegal to borrow as a rate had been struck and should be collected. Despite his intervention, the board overwhelmingly agreed to the amended resolution. However, in late April, a special meeting was called to discuss how to discharge the debts and to comply with the law requiring weekly meetings.[88] It appeared that legal proceedings had been threatened or commenced by one of the contractors. The board agreed to adjourn for three weeks while its application for a loan was being considered. A proposal to start collecting the rates was heavily defeated, but an amendment to review tenders for collection was carried.[89] When the Poor Law amendment bill was published, it was not welcomed by the *Herald* which—like the *Waterford Chronicle*—criticised the proposals to increase the powers of the PLC and the number of ex officio guardians.[90]

When the board reconvened, internal tensions re-emerged. A resolution was proposed to continue to advertise for rate collectors, but an amendment was moved to take no further action. The board split, and the chair cast his vote for the resolution. Subsequently, however, the board considered that the tenders received were too expensive and did not consider them.[91] By July 1843, an instalment of the loan to the Union had fallen due, and the board was being pursued by one of the contractors.[92] By September, the board had finally agreed to appoint rate collectors, but only a small number of guardians attended, and a final decision was deferred to October.[93] By this stage, the PLC had threatened legal proceedings against the board to force them to implement the Poor Law. A special meeting was called in October, at which the board finally agreed to increase compensation for the collectors, but again rejected all tenders.[94] By the end of October, one rate collector had finally been appointed.[95]

As the year drew to a close, the board's effective resistance seemed to be starting to weaken. Further rate collectors were accepted, although the board decided not to appoint them formally until all districts were covered and still refused to open the workhouse, despite the calls of the PLC.[96] Nonetheless, significant opposition continued and, without much active debate, the board simply refused (or failed) to implement the law. In January and February 1844, the board agreed a proposal to invite the military to occupy the workhouse and to submit a resolution to the Lord Lieutenant. However, further opposition to the appointment of rate collectors by guardian Charles Blake Sr was narrowly defeated (twelve votes to eleven).[97] In March, the board rather optimistically agreed to circulate landed proprietors to seek assistance in paying the contractors.[98] Unsurprisingly, there was no response and the *Tuam Herald* conceded that the board must now collect the rate, although it argued that no further debts should be incurred by opening the house.[99] By June, the board had been served with a notice of ejectment for non-payment of rent.[100] A motion to appoint the rate collectors formally was defeated eleven votes to thirteen despite the support of Caesar Otway, the new Assistant Poor Law Commissioner.[101] In view of the slow progress, the PLC wrote to all of the Tuam guardians threatening legal proceedings to enforce the law.[102] In August, with further loan instalments due, Otway advised the board to collect rates and to ask the PLC to send down collectors from Dublin (following the approach successfully adopted in Waterford and Galway). But when such a proposal was put to the board in September, there was no seconder, and in October, a tender for a collector for a vacant district was rejected by the board.[103] In November, after the PLC had finally taken legal proceedings, an extraordinary meeting of the board was held. Despite the legal threat, the board still refused to commence rate collection.[104]

Only in December, after goods in the workhouse were seized by suppliers, did the board finally agree to appoint rate collectors.[105]

The PLC had obtained a court order requiring the guardians to implement the law but agreed not to enforce it if the collectors were sent out to collect, and the board finally agreed to do so in February 1845.[106] However, it appears that rate collection did not begin until October.[107] Opposition to the collection of rates continued, including assaults on rate collectors, and many guardians remained reluctant to implement the law.[108] Ultimately, the PLC dissolved the board in February 1846, just before the annual elections which took place in March.[109] While the guardians continued to object to the Poor Law, with Famine approaching, paupers were finally admitted to the Tuam workhouse in May 1846. In his evidence to the 1846 House of Lords select committee, Denis Kirwan—son of the first chair of the board and himself a guardian—attributed the resistance to the combined opposition of Archbishop MacHale (who was, of course, based in Tuam) and local land owners.[110]

Amending the Law

The government responded to the opposition by making limited changes to the Poor Law in 1843.[111] In particular, it restored the original exclusion of smaller occupiers (which had been struck out by the House of Lords when the bill was being debated in 1838).[112] Occupiers of property of under £4 (or in some boroughs £8) were no longer liable for rates, which were to be collected from the lessor.[113] The act also modified the residency rules by providing that, in order to be chargeable to a particular electoral district, a person had to be resident there for eighteen months, for at least twelve of which the person must have occupied a tenement or at least slept in the district. This change was intended to reduce the extent to which paupers were charged to one district and, conversely, to increase the proportion charged to the Union-at-large.

Meanwhile, the PLC took legal proceedings against recalcitrant boards. However, in response to the act, the PLC also adopted a pragmatic approach and called on the boards of guardians to consider discharging any arrears due by occupiers below £4 without enforcing their collection. While noting that there was no 'express provision' in the act to this effect, the commissioners felt that they were 'only acting in the same spirit' in which the law had been adopted by Parliament.[114] By 1844—notwithstanding the existence of a few refractory Unions, such as Tuam—the PLC was able to report that resistance to the collection of rates had in great measure been overcome.

Only 8 per cent of the rate struck before August 1843 was outstanding by January 1844. By May 1845, there were only twelve Unions, including Tuam, in which the workhouse was not in operation. In four western Unions (Cahirciveen, Clifden, Glenties, and Milford) no rate had been made.[115] As in Tuam, the PLC used its powers to dissolve Castlerea board and to order new elections. The commission threatened that failure by the new boards to operate the law would lead to their dissolution and the appointment of vice-guardians to exercise their powers.[116] By May 1846, the PLC was able to report that all workhouses were open except for the two small Unions of Cahirciveen and Clifden, in which steps were being taken to bring the law into operation.[117]

Discussion

The Poor Law was a major reform and imposed significant new taxes on Irish landowners and occupiers. As Alexander C. Lambert, a landowner and land agent who served as chair of Ballinrobe Union, later told a select committee of the House of Lords, 'I think there was a very general call for Poor Laws; but when they came, every one began to find Fault with them.'[118] While one might debate how universal the initial support really was, there is no doubt that implementation of the Poor Law led to significant opposition. Opposition to the imposition of new taxes from at least some of those involved was only to be expected. In part, the opposition appears to have arisen from the fact that the introduction of the law coincided with a short-lived agricultural downturn. Unluckily for the PLC, the initial implementation also overlapped with a call for the repeal of the Act of Union, and O'Connell cynically used the opposition to the Poor Law to fan the flames of the repeal movement. As can be seen, in the Waterford, Galway, and Tuam Unions, there was opposition to poor rates from both nationalists and Conservatives, landlords and tenants. However, while the breadth of this opposition was a potential strength, in the conjuncture of the 1840s, it acted as a weakness to any consistent policy of resistance.

First, given O'Connell's repeal commitment, he was unwilling to form any temporary alliance with Conservative forces on the Poor Law. While O'Connell undoubtedly contributed to the initial resistance to collection, he seems to have had little fundamental commitment to any public position on the Poor Law (notwithstanding that he himself was obviously strongly opposed). As the repeal campaign developed in 1843, his focus lay on this larger cause, and outbreaks of violence on a 'minor' issue such as the Poor Law would call the credibility of this campaign into question. Likewise, Conservative forces also opposed the Poor Law and rates. However, the memory of the Tithe War must still have been fresh in the minds of landowners, and encouraging resistance to the payment of rates by their tenants must have appeared a double-edged sword, which could easily develop into resistance to payment of rents. The local Catholic clergy appear to have generally discouraged resistance, either from support for the Poor Law or from a realisation that resistance was ultimately futile.

In Unions such as Waterford and Galway, there must have been broad class opposition to the payment of rates. However, it would appear that this opposition was led by landowners in Waterford and Galway. In Tuam, the opposition was led by the guardians, who never tried to collect the rates. Here, opposition was more political, but while large farmers such as Blake and attorneys such as Jeremiah Tully may not have had the wealth or social cachet of men such as Lord Carew, leadership of O'Connellite opposition to the 'odious and degrading' Poor Law came from a rising Catholic middle class and not from those who might benefit from poor relief (as indeed was to be the case later in the century).[119] Indeed, this study illustrates the extent to which the implementation of the Poor Law and the role of the boards of guardians were implicated in the broader politicisation of communities well before the Land War.

The failure of repeal and the decline of O'Connell as a political force after October 1843, combined with improvements in the agricultural economy,[120] removed two of the factors tending to support resistance to the collection of rates. In addition, the authorities used a combination of law reform and careful enforcement (both through the use of the police and military and, where necessary, the courts) to overcome resistance.

While, as we have seen, there was a significant failure to implement the Poor Law in the west of Ireland, it would probably not be appropriate to ascribe this primarily to political motives.[121] It is clear that some western Unions, such as Tuam, were inspired, at least in part, by O'Connellite opposition to the Poor Law. However, it seems likely that slow progress in implementing the law in many western Unions was due as much (and arguably more) to the poverty of those Unions and to the limited administrative capacity of the local bourgeoisie. The theory that local property should pay for local poverty was to experience an ongoing clash with local realities in many Unions in the west of Ireland throughout the history of the Poor Law.

The changes to the law in 1843 removed about half the potential ratepayers from the immediate burden of rates, targeting those most likely to have difficulty paying and involving significant collection costs for limited return. In addition, the PLC was determined to enforce the law and did so in a reasonably efficient manner—with the support of the local magistrates and the police and military where necessary. In this way, the commission 'encouraged' boards—such as Waterford—which were broadly supportive of the act, and wore down opposition in boards hostile to the law such as Tuam. The amendments to the law also addressed the concerns of Unions such as Galway, where opposition appears to have arisen largely from a feeling by the urban guardians that they were being burdened with a disproportionate share of the cost.

This study demonstrates, first, that the implementation of the Poor Law was not merely a technical matter, but it was also closely bound up in the political and socio-economic issues of the period. Second it shows—as have other studies of the English and Irish Poor Laws—the extent to which the Poor Law was locally implemented and the significant variations which took place from area to area. Third, while Nicholls and the Poor Law administrators were often portrayed as bureaucratic and inflexible, in this case they adopted a nuanced approach, recommending changes to the law, on the one hand, and applying force on the other, where there was a degree of local support. Where local support was largely lacking, the commission was prepared to play a long game, perhaps recognising that precipitate action in Tuam might have provoked broader opposition. Finally, it shows that the governance of the Poor Law at local level had been politicised (in the broad sense of the term) from the very outset, and that Feingold's famous 'revolt of the tenantry' was in fact a second wave of politicisation rather than an entirely new phenomenon.[122]

Notes

1. See Peter Gray, *The Making of the Irish Poor Law, 1815–43* (Manchester: Manchester University Press, 2009).
2. Sec. 3 of the Poor Relief (Ireland) Act, 1 & 2 Vict., c. 56.
3. Sec. 26.
4. *Reports Relative to the Valuations for Poor Rates, and to the Registered Elective Franchise, in Ireland*, No. 292–93 (1841–1); *Third General*

Report Relative to the Valuations for Poor Rates, and to the Registered Elective Franchise, in Ireland, No. 329 (1841–1).
5. Sec. 61 of the Poor Law (Ireland) Act, 1838.
6. 'Return of the Dates on which and the Places where the Military and Police have been Employed in Enforcing the Collection of Poor Rates in Ireland', in *Appendices A to C. to the Tenth Annual Report of the Poor Law Commissioners*, No. 589 (1844), vol. 19, pp. 340–44.
7. *Tenth Annual Report of the Poor Law Commissioners*, No. 560 (1844), vol. 19, p. 41.
8. *Report of the Commissioners Appointed to Revise the Several Laws under or by Virtue of which Moneys are now Raised by Grand Jury Presentment in Ireland*, No. 386 (1842), vol. 24, p. 16.
9. Sec. 61 of the Poor Law (Ireland) Act, 1838.
10. Secs. 71 and 74.
11. Gray, *Making of the Irish Poor Law*, 213.
12. Ibid., 214.
13. *Ninth Annual Report of the Poor Law Commissioners*, No. 468 (1843), vol. 21, p. 47.
14. Mel Cousins, *Poor Relief in Ireland, 1851–1914* (Oxford: Peter Lang, 2011); Virginia Crossman, *Politics, Pauperism and Power in Late Nineteenth-Century Ireland* (Manchester: Manchester University Press, 2006); idem, *Poverty and the Poor Law in Ireland, 1850–1914* (Liverpool: Liverpool University Press, 2013).
15. Gray, *Making of the Irish Poor Law*.
16. See, in particular, ibid., 310–15.
17. Cousins, *Poor Relief*, Chap. 9. The term 'politicisation' is used in the sense that the politicisation of a group or a society is the socio-historic action by which political issues penetrate the daily lives of the members of that group or society.
18. Gerard O'Brien 'The New Poor Law in Pre-Famine Ireland: A Case History', *Irish Economic and Social History* 12 (1985): 34.
19. On this, see generally, Kevin Nowlan, *The Politics of Repeal: A Study in the Relations between Great Britain and Ireland, 1841–50* (London: Routledge and Kegan Paul, 1965).
20. Cormac Ó Gráda, *Ireland: A New Economic History, 1790–1939* (Oxford: Clarendon Press, 1994), 166.
21. Charles Read, 'The "Repeal Year" in Ireland: An Economic Assessment', *Historical Journal* 58, no. 1 (2015): 124–29. Read attributes this fall to trade policy changes in the 1842 budget.
22. Ibid., 129–31.

23. *Eighth Annual Report of the Poor Law Commissioners*, No. 389 (1842), vol. 19, p. 69; *Ninth Annual Report*, 35–38; 41–43; *Tenth Annual Report*, 43–49.
24. George Nicholls, *A History of the Irish Poor Law* (1856; repr., New York: A. M. Kelley, 1967), 294–98. In twenty-one Unions, the military or constabulary were called in to assist the collection in 1843; see *Appendices A to C. to the Tenth Annual Report*, 340–44. This return covers events up to 1 Jan. 1844. It would appear that there was some further resistance in 1844 and further use of police and/or military force, in particular, in Ballinasloe, Ballinrobe, Loughrea, and Westport Unions: see *Tenth Annual Report*, 29–30; *Eleventh Annual Report of the Poor Law Commissioners*, No. 624 (1845), vol. 27, pp. 21–22.
25. *Hansard Parliamentary Debates*, 3rd ser., vol. 67, col. 1126 (20 Mar. 1843). However, no attempt at riot or disturbance had taken placed, and Lord Eliot, the Chief Secretary, believed that the reports had been much exaggerated.
26. However, there is no sign that this resistance ever took on a more organised national or regional approach, nor that it became particularly violent. For example, Beams' study of Whiteboy killings in Tipperary in the period 1837–47 does not show any Poor Law-related deaths; M. R. Beames, 'Rural Conflict in Pre-Famine Ireland: *Peasant Assassinations in Tipperary, 1837–1847*', *Past & Present* 81 (1978): 75–91.
27. House of Commons, 'Return of Dates on which Military and Police Were Employed in Collection of Poor Rates in Ireland', *Sessional Papers, 1844* (186) (218). In total, twenty-one Unions are listed in the return. However, the return indicates that in Nenagh Union, the Royal Irish Constabulary was involved in collecting county cess (not poor rates); the return for Castleblaney appears to relate to activity in Carrickmacross; and we have excluded Clogheen Union where the constabulary was used only twice (with a maximum of four men) to collect £1 5s. 5d. Arrears in Clogheen were very low (as shown in the same return).
28. *Appendices A to C. to the Tenth Annual Report*, 340–44. Rates were set at different times in different Unions and, obviously, even in Unions with no problems it took some time to collect rates. Therefore, the figures in this table are calculated in relation to rates set at least six months prior to the cut-off date, that is, by 30 June 1843. These data should be interpreted with some caution. As discussed below, the Poor Law Commission (henceforth, PLC) encouraged Unions to write off arrears but no information appears to be available as to the extent to which this occurred. Waterford had less than 10 per cent of arrears outstanding by 1 Jan. 1844, which would suggest that the Union wrote off considerable rates. The *Tenth Annual Report*, 40, states that the Waterford guardians had

'cleared their books' of 'legally uncollectable' arrears. For Dublin South, see below. The rate in Newry was set in late June 1843 on two divisions only (with more in late 1843) so it has not been included in the map below.

29. No rate had yet been struck in twelve Unions: Bantry, Cahirciveen, Clifden, Enniskillen, Glenties, Kanturk, Kenmare, Killarney, Letterkenny, Listowel, Lowtherstown, and Milford.
30. Though here, this must, in part, have been due to the fact that the rate was set on 17 June 1843, only just creeping into the analysis, only about 15 per cent of the previous (Aug. 1842) rate was outstanding.
31. For this reason, Dublin South is also excluded from Map 7.1.
32. In general, there is a strong overlap between the two sources with almost all the Unions where force was used also showing arrears. The only exceptions are Baltinglass, Dunmanaway (both with low arrears), and Waterford, where arrears appear to have been written off. We show those Unions with 10–20 per cent of rates outstanding and/or with limited use of police and military as showing moderate resistance and Unions with 21 per cent or more of arrears outstanding and/or more extensive use of police and military as areas of higher resistance.
33. Adapted from I. Gregory and P. Ell, *Irish Poor Law Union and Barony Boundaries, 1841–1871*, https://doi.org/10.5255/UKDA-SN-4999-1 (accessed 5 Jan. 2018).
34. Though no rate had been struck in some Unions including the Enniskillen Union under the incompetent (if not corrupt) leadership of the Earl of Enniskillen; see Desmond McCabe and Cormac Ó Gráda, '"Better off thrown behind a ditch": Enniskillen Workhouse during the Great Famine', in *Power and Popular Culture in Modern Ireland: Essays in Honour of James S. Donnelly, Jr.*, ed. Michael de Nie and Sean Farrell (Dublin: Irish Academic Press, 2010).
35. This group also overlaps, to a certain extent, with the pattern identified in Kanter's study of opposition to tax in the 1860s; see Chap. 9.
36. James S. Donnelly Jr., *Captain Rock: The Irish Agrarian Rebellion of 1821–1824* (Cork: Collins Press, 2009).
37. Gray, *Making of the Irish Poor Law,* 87–91, 151–52, 184–88, 197–206, 232–44, 255–58.
38. *Nation,* 31 Dec. 1842. O'Connell had been elected as MP for County Cork in the 1841 election. His letter to the Cork guardians was covered extensively in the press. However, the nationalist *Waterford Chronicle* (hereafter, *WC*), despite its general support for O'Connell, did not agree on this issue and supported the Poor Law, 7 Jan. 1843. Interestingly, the Tory *Waterford Mail* (hereafter, *WM*) gave a guarded welcome to O'Connell's opposition to the Poor Law, 4 Jan. 1843. See also

O'Connell's letter (read in his absence by his son John to the Repeal Association) calling for a range of measures including the extinction of tithes, fixity of tenure, protection of native manufacturers, the extension of the franchise, ballot voting, and the abolition of the Poor Law and its replacement by a great increase of public charities, *WC*, 10 Jan. 1843.

39. *WM*, 25 Jan. 1843.
40. The committee was chaired by John O'Connell; *WC*, 24 Jan. 1842. This appears to have been because of the different views taken by the Young Ireland faction who were much more supportive of the Poor Law; see Gray, *Making of the Irish Poor Law*, 313, and, for example, the editorial in the *Nation*, 31 Dec. 1842. For a contemporary criticism of the report, see Anon., *The South of Ireland and Her Poor* (London: Saunders and Otley, 1843), 118 et seq.
41. The options included: 1. broader reforms, such as repeal of the Act of Union; 2. modification or abolition of the Poor Law; 3. giving outdoor relief; 4. suppression of mendicancy and an increase in workhouses; 5. fixing the rate on the richer classes; 6. settlement; 7. limiting relief to the aged, infirm, and orphans; 8. public works; and 9. total abolition of the law.
42. *WM*, 23 Feb. 1843. This statement, greeted with 'loud cheers', presumably had more resonance for its intended audience than it does today.
43. These Unions have been selected as they are the Unions identified in contemporary reports (including the annual reports of the PLC) as being amongst those where resistance to the rates was most apparent; see, for example, *Tenth Annual Report*, 40–41.
44. The barony of Gaultier (Gáll Tír—Danes' or foreigners' land in Irish) lies to the south of Waterford City between the west side of Waterford harbour and the coast.
45. *Tenth Annual Report*, 40.
46. *WC* 14 Jan. 1843, 21 Jan. 1843.
47. Ibid., 28 Jan. 1843.
48. Ibid., 21 Jan. 1843, 28 Jan. 1843.
49. Ibid., 25 Feb. 1843. Indeed, the later return of rates (see below) showed that 50 per cent of the rate set in Nov. 1842 was still outstanding in Jan. 1844.
50. Ibid., 11 Mar. 1843. For reasons which are unclear, Fitzgerald, who was later to be active in assisting the collection, refused to accompany the collector.
51. Ibid., 14 Mar. 1843.
52. *WM*, 15 Mar. 1843. Probably Capt. Simon Newport JP, who was, in fact, a land agent for Lord Carew.

53. *WC*, 16 Mar. 1843. It attributed opposition in Dungarvan to 'a Conservative Gentleman of high respectability and considerable influence'.
54. *WM*, 15 Mar. 1843.
55. *Hansard*, 3rd ser., vol. 67, col. 1126 (20 Mar. 1843).
56. *WC*, 16 Mar. 1843, 21 Mar. 1843.
57. *WC*, 1 Apr. 1843, claimed that £70 had been collected at a cost of £100; see also *WM*, 22 Mar. 1843.
58. *WC*, 25 Mar. 1843.
59. Ibid., 6 Apr. 1843.
60. *WC*, 11 Apr. 1843, 22 Apr. 1843; *WM*, 15 Apr. 1843. The city rate collector, however, reported that occupiers were now 'paying more willingly'; *WC*, 15 Apr. 1843.
61. *WM*, 15, 24 and 27 Apr. 1843.
62. Ibid., 6 May (£50) and 13 May (£174 12s.).
63. In total, over £380 in rates were collected with the direct support of the police and military; *Appendices A to C. to the Tenth Annual Report*, 340–44.
64. *WC*, 18 Apr. 1843.
65. *Eleventh Annual Report*, 21. By 1 May 1845 only £772 was outstanding; idem, 40.
66. Ibid., 28.
67. See *Tenth Annual Report*, 40. On the opposition in Galway, see the Tory *Galway Standard* (hereafter, *GS*), 30 Dec. 1842, 6 Jan. 1843, 13 Jan. 1843, 27 Jan. 1843.
68. *Tenth Annual Report*, 41–42.
69. Persons whose residence could not be established were charged to the Union-at-large.
70. *Seventh Annual Report of the Poor Law Commissioners*, No. 327 (1841–1), vol. 11, pp. 344–45, 488–93.
71. *Eighth Annual Report*, 45. Half of the forty elected guardians represented the urban division, and six of the thirteen ex officios lived in the urban area. The urban guardians attended more assiduously than did their rural colleagues; see *Appendices B. to F. to the Eighth Annual Report of the Poor Law Commissioners*, No. 399 (1842), vol. 19, pp. 190–91. The rural proprietors explained that some residing between seven and twelve miles were 'frequently prevented from attending the Board'.
72. See the report by Joseph Burke to the PLC, 20 Mar. 1843, Joseph Burke Papers, National Archives of Ireland 2/440/44, vol. 3.
73. The Conservative *Standard* argued that the people of Galway were not able to pay; see *GS*, 6 Jan. 1843.
74. See Joseph Burke to the PLC, 20 Mar. 1843, Burke Papers, National Archives of Ireland 2/440/44, vol. 3; *Galway Observer*, 13 Jan. 1843.

75. *GS*, 20 Jan. 1843, 27 Jan. 1843.
76. Ibid., 25 Feb. 1843.
77. Burke to the PLC, 12 Apr. 1843, Burke Papers, 2/440/44, vol. 3.
78. *Tenth Annual Report*, 28–29.
79. *Appendices A to C. to the Tenth Annual Report*, 340–44. For the local resistance to such incursions, and a violent response, see the *Freeman's Journal*, 6 Oct. 1843 (quoting the *Galway Vindicator*).
80. The *Tenth Annual Report*, 29, states that of the £5211 in rates struck by Aug. 1843, the amounts uncollected had been reduced from £2064 on 1 Jan. 1844 to £1005 by 20 Apr. 1844.
81. *GS*, 4 Nov. 1842.
82. See generally, the *Tuam Herald* (henceforth, *TH*), which reported anti-Poor Law meetings in Galway (28 Jan. 1843); 'on the plains of Mayo' attended by the archbishop's nephew Rev. John MacHale, and Mark Blake MP (idem); Ballinasloe (28 Feb. 1843); Ballinrobe attended by many guardians, including Valentine O'Connor (the chair of the board) and many Catholic priests (11 Feb. 1843); Roscommon (18 Feb. 1843); Ballyhaunis (25 Feb. 1843); Connemara (1 Apr. 1843).
83. Ibid., 7 Jan. 1843.
84. Ibid.
85. Ibid., 18 Feb. 1843.
86. Ibid.
87. Ibid., 15 Apr. 1843. There had been a contest in the Tuam electoral district which Charles Blake had won with 1273 votes, followed by Patrick Egan with 955. The size of the vote is striking in this (pre-1843 act) election, especially when we recall that in some parliamentary constituencies in the 1840s, votes of less than 200 were sufficient to elect an MP. Browne was again elected as chair in 1844; see idem, 6 Apr. 1844.
88. Ibid., 29 Apr. 1843.
89. Ibid., 6 May 1843.
90. Ibid., 29 Apr. 1843.
91. Ibid., 24 June 1843, 19 Aug. 1843.
92. Ibid., 22 July 1843.
93. Ibid., 2 Sept. 1843, 9 Sept. 1843, 19 Sept. 1843.
94. Ibid., 14 Oct. 1843.
95. Ibid., 28 Oct. 1843.
96. Ibid., 23 Dec. 1843.
97. Ibid., 20 Jan. 1844, 17 Feb. 1844.
98. Ibid., 9 Mar. 1844.
99. Ibid., 11 May 1844.
100. Ibid., 8 June 1844. Despite the conflict with the PLC, a motion of thanks was adopted to Joseph Burke, who was leaving.

101. Ibid., 6 July 1844.
102. Ibid., 13 July 1844.
103. Ibid., 31 Aug. 1844, 30 Sept. 1844, 2 Nov. 1844.
104. Ibid., 23 Nov. 1844.
105. Ibid., 28 Dec. 1844.
106. Ibid., 22 Feb. 1845; see 'The Queen (Poor Law Commissioners) v The Guardians of the Poor of the Tuam Union', *Irish Law Reports*, vol. 9 (Dublin: Hodges and Smith, 1847), 320–27.
107. *TH*, 25 Oct. 1845.
108. Ibid., 7 Feb. 1846, 14 Feb. 1846.
109. *Twelfth Annual Report of the Poor Law Commissioners*, No. 704 (1846), vol. 19, p. 25; *TH*, 7 Feb. 1846. The timing of the action meant that it had little practical impact and was more in the nature of a warning. The new board commenced meeting on 6 Apr. and Browne was re-elected chair; idem, 11 Apr. 1846.
110. He named two of the main opponents on the board as Charles Blake and Jeremiah Tully, an attorney.
111. Gray, *Making of the Irish Poor Law*, 324–28.
112. It appears that this option had been considered as early as late 1841; see Lord Eliot to George Nicholls, 29 Nov. 1841, seeking details of the number of persons valued under £5, £5–£10, and so on; *Seventh Annual Report*, 54. The PLC showed that of the almost one million ratepayers, nearly half (46 per cent) were rated below £4; *Ninth Annual Report*, 43.
113. The act also made a number of other, generally minor, changes, including defining 'residence' for the purposes of charge.
114. *Tenth Annual Report*, 43.
115. Nicholls, *History of the Irish Poor* Law, 301.
116. Ibid., 305.
117. Ibid., 303.
118. House of Commons, 'Report from the Select Committee of the House of Lords on the Laws Relating to the Relief of the Destitute Poor, and into the Operation of the Medical Charities in Ireland', *Sessional Papers, 1846* (694) (694–II) (694–III), vol. 11 pts. 1–2, p. 173.
119. William L. Feingold, *The Revolt of the Tenantry: The Transformation of Local Government in Ireland, 1872–1886* (Boston: Northeastern University Press, 1984), Chap. 6.
120. Read, 'Repeal Year', 135.
121. For example, Lambert, chair of the Ballinrobe Union, stated in 1846 the unpopularity of the Poor Law in that Union was 'quite different' to that in Tuam, and that there was 'scarcely any political Feeling' in Ballinrobe; Commons, 'Report from the Select Committee of the House of Lords', 173.
122. Feingold, *Revolt of the Tenantry*.

CHAPTER 8

Taxation and the Economics of Nationalism in 1840s Ireland

Charles Read

Recent work by Douglas Kanter has uncovered how much the issue of Irish taxation was debated at Westminster in the 1840s.[1] But there has been little study of the popular reaction to changes in taxation in Ireland during the Famine decade, even though the consequences of those changes were arguably more dramatic than anything experienced in the rest of the United Kingdom during this era. Sir Robert Peel's budget of 1842 introduced sweeping reductions in import tariffs on agricultural goods that caused a severe downturn in Ireland.[2] The years 1844 and 1845 saw further revision to tariffs that affected the Irish economy, though this time more positively. The Corn Laws were partly repealed by Peel, citing the Famine in Ireland as the best reason to do it, in 1846, with consequences for food markets in Ireland as well as the national budget in London. A growing deficit contributed to a series of financial crises in Britain in 1847, which persuaded politicians in London of the need to shift the burden of taxation to fund Famine relief onto local ratepayers.[3] That burden reached 5 per cent of GDP by 1848, an extraordinary sum of money to raise from property taxes in the period.[4] In 1853, these taxes, and the loans given by

C. Read (✉)
University of Cambridge, Cambridge, UK
e-mail: cpr34@cam.ac.uk

D. Kanter, P. Walsh (eds.), *Taxation, Politics, and Protest in Ireland, 1662–2016*, Palgrave Studies in the History of Finance,
https://doi.org/10.1007/978-3-030-04309-4_8

the Treasury in London on security of them, were cancelled when the British income tax was extended to Ireland.

The lack of focus on taxation in narratives of the Famine decade, and Irish history more generally, is surprising. Taxation invites conflict between the state and its citizens. 'Grievances about taxation and tribute', David Dickson has pointed out, 'have formed the basis of tactical class and regional alliances against imperial and central authorities probably as long as coins have been minted.'[5] Taxation is a central theme of nineteenth-century British history, with Philip Harling writing about the waning of Old Corruption at the start of the century, Norman Gash on why Peel's repeal of the Corn Laws made him the 'chief architect' of the mid-Victorian age of stability, and Colin Matthew on how, in the ensuing two decades, the budgets of Benjamin Disraeli and William Gladstone formed a political consensus around fiscal policy that lasted until the 1930s.[6] And, as Martin Daunton has more recently shown, arguments over government taxation and spending dominated political discourse in Victorian Britain.[7] It was an important factor in the development of the relationship between the population and the state, as seen by commentators at the time and in more recent scholarship.

Although Martin McElroy has suggested that the budget of 1830 helped to spark Daniel O'Connell's first campaign to repeal the Act of Union, the surge of popular support for it in the 1840s has traditionally been seen as a protest with political and religious roots rather than as a protest driven by grievances induced by tax changes.[8] This approach arose from Peel's response to the movement in the 1840s. The nineteenth-century perspective of Charles Parker was echoed in the work of Gash and Donal Kerr at the end of the twentieth.[9] It stated that Peel's reaction to the rise of the repeal movement was a liberal policy of religious conciliation towards Roman Catholics, and it has been used by historians, such as Gash, to support Peel's reputation as a founder of modern conservatism and by those, such as Parker, who characterised Peel as a proto-Liberal.[10] Peel's introduction of a pro-Catholic patronage policy in 1843, the passage of the Charitable Bequests Act in 1844, the foundation of the Queen's Colleges, and the increase in the size of the Maynooth Grant in 1845 have all been cited as central to his Irish policy, which was designed to counter any further rise in the popularity of the repeal movement.[11] The suggestion here is that these policies were necessary to counter the reaction against his tax reforms.

Later that decade, the Irish Famine has a good claim to be the worst economic and humanitarian disaster in the modern history of the British

Isles. Yet taxation issues have generally been ignored. The crisis began in 1845 with the arrival of two potato diseases, *Phytophthora infestans* and dry rot, from the Americas.[12] These blights reduced potato yields in Ireland by between a third and a quarter in 1845 and between 75 per cent and 97 per cent the following year.[13] Although fiscal transfers from the rest of the United Kingdom initially blunted the impact of the harvest failures on the Irish economy, a set of severe financial crises in Great Britain in 1847 resulted in this support being withdrawn by the British government.[14] This combination of events soon turned what started out as a manageable harvest crisis into one characterised by mass mortality. The crop failure caused mass unemployment and a shortage of cheap foodstuffs in the Irish countryside. As a result, the Irish population fell by a quarter during the decade of the crisis, due to death and emigration. The Famine cast a long-term demographic shadow. High levels of outward migration from Ireland persisted until the 1990s. And today Ireland is the only part of Europe to have a lower population than it did in 1845.

Scholars have long downplayed the extent of protest during the Famine. Kevin Nowlan suggested in 1956 that the Famine years were 'conspicuous for their tranquillity rather than their turbulence'.[15] But as more recent work has shown, this is more a Famine legend than part of reality.[16] As Cormac Ó Gráda and others have pointed out, agrarian crime surged and the activities of secret agrarian societies increased.[17] The number of committals to trial for crimes against property (which included crimes associated with food rioting) rose, comparing the period immediately before 1846 to that of the Famine.[18]

In 2015, Enda Delaney and Breandán Mac Suibhne edited and published a collection of essays on this subject.[19] They show that the poor did resist authority figures during the Famine, defying landlords, merchants, and agents of the state. They rioted for food, opposed rent and rate collection, and challenged the decisions of those controlling relief works, as well as local clergy. More recent work by James Kelly, published in 2017, suggests that instances of food rioting were numerous in the century up to the Famine.[20] But their thrust is substantially on the poor and issues such as eviction that have long preoccupied historians. Taxation, when it comes into their story, is a local matter and generally a marginal one.

This chapter presents two case studies of how dramatic changes in taxation affected popular opinion and protest in the 1840s, fundamentally changing the course of Irish history. Firstly, the consequences of the tariff reductions in Peel's budget of 1842 are examined. In Ireland these remissions caused a sharp drop in the price of pig meat, the cash crop of the small peasant farmer, and an agricultural recession, which resulted in a rise in popular support for Daniel O'Connell's campaign to repeal the Act of Union and mass attendance at the 'monster meetings' held by the Repeal Association. Secondly, the decision to place the tax burden for relief on local ratepayers in Ireland from 1847 onwards is considered. Although politicians in London did this in the belief that it would help prevent bullion flows out of the United Kingdom and enable the pound sterling to stay on the gold standard, the consequences for Ireland were mass emigration and capital flight. An analysis of local tax rates and the amounts actually collected suggests that there was a strong Laffer effect (diminishing returns of higher rates) occurring in Ireland during this period. The development of viciously anti-British sentiment among the resulting taxpaying emigrants, many of whom went to America, can be seen as a result of this British tax policy. In these two ways, British tax policy can be seen as a contributor to the ongoing redefinition of the relationship of the Irish people and the British state in the nineteenth century—one which placed southern Ireland on the path to independence in the 1920s.

The Budget of 1842 and the Repeal Movement

Peel's 1842 budget was aimed at improving the lot of the working classes in the whole of the United Kingdom using macroeconomics as his tool. This method contrasted with previous practice in Ireland and the expectations of the Irish Lord Lieutenant, the second Earl de Grey. De Grey had sent over to England draft bills with a number of specific policies to help Ireland. But the Home Secretary, Sir James Graham, told him that national trade policy was 'the cardinal point on which our Fortunes turn'.[21] Peel's budget removed import and export duties and prohibitions on more than 700 items, including meat imports which had previously been banned. To replace government income from the duties, income tax was reintroduced at 7d. in the pound on the British mainland, theoretically transferring the tax burden from the poor when they bought high-priced meat to those wealthy enough to pay income tax. The poor were intended to benefit from cheaper food and the wealthy from a stable political situation. A balance between expenditure and income was also expected to help the government service Britain's enormous national debt.[22]

But Peel's knowledge of the labouring classes was mainly confined to the industrial workers of Northern England and the Midlands, similar to those in his constituency of Tamworth. He had considered whether a fall in prices would cause a fall in wages, but discounted the effects of this, relying on increased consumption and demand to keep up farmers' incomes. In Ireland, a different situation existed. Still a mostly agricultural society, the principal monetary income of the poor came from the sale of pigs. As Austin Bourke has noted from Poor Law records, bacon pigs tended to be the family pigs kept by 'the small man', or poor labourer, and were sold to obtain cash to pay the rent.[23] To quote Mr and Mrs S. C. Hall's contemporary description of the situation, poor Irish farmers regarded a pig as 'the gentleman who pays the rent'.[24] A sharp fall in the price of pigs might cut off the small farmers' supply of cash and reduce their income and their ability to pay the rent. As many Irish estates were encumbered by loans, this situation seemed to have the potential to leave the whole of Irish society in distress.

Historians' perception of whether this outcome was likely to have occurred has varied. Alice Murray, an Edwardian economic historian, linked reductions in food prices resulting from Peel's lower tariffs in the 1840s to falling real incomes in Ireland: 'The mass of the Irish people are dependent on agriculture, and have been dependent upon it all through the century. As consumers they may have slightly gained by the abolition of the duties on food stuffs, but as producers, nearly altogether dependent upon agriculture, they have lost in a far greater degree.'[25] More recently, Louis Cullen has argued that there is a link between periods of low food prices and increased distress and unrest in 1820s and 1830s Ireland.[26] By contrast, Cormac Ó Gráda has presented a commonly held view that a neo-classical growth model suggests that in the long run, Irish agricultural protection in the nineteenth century damaged the living standards of agricultural labourers.[27] The reasoning is that the benefits from the higher food prices fed more into higher rents for absentee landlords than farmers' wages or profits. Farmers and labourers gained little from high food prices as producers and lost out more as consumers. However, this neo-classical model overestimates the price elasticity of rents and underestimates the available underemployed labour supplies in a harvest situation, as in autumn 1842. Chronic underemployment in Ireland during this period meant that the elasticity of change in labour supply would have been high, even in the short run. However, as rents were set before the size of the harvest was known, changes in rents would have been slow and therefore less than the conventional model requires, and any 'sticky' (slow-to-change) rents during the agricultural year would have had the same effect.[28] With 'sticky' rents, variations in prices would disproportionately impact farmers' incomes and employment levels.[29] Adjusting for an inelastic change in land rents curve and elastic change in labour curve in the short run, the model would in fact show that employment would disproportionately gain from tariff (and price) increases, and lose from falling tariffs.

The actual effect of the 1842 tariff reductions on Irish food prices and the Irish economy can be investigated by examining the market prices which were commonly published in the Irish local newspapers of the time. Liam Kennedy and Peter Solar have made an extensive study of local newspaper market reports in order to produce a reliable set of food prices for Ireland.[30] However, data for this study was resampled from the original sources on a high-frequency, monthly, basis, from January 1837 to December 1850, and weekly from January 1842 to December 1843. An initial investigation of five food types in nine locations found that meat markets exhibited the greatest price changes. Using this information, a decision was made to sample systematically, by focusing on bacon pigs and beef as main income-producing products for small and larger farmers, respectively, in three major ports of export: Cork, Dublin, and Waterford. Prices were taken from the *Constitution; or Cork Advertiser*, the *Freeman's Journal*, and the *Waterford Mail.* Bacon prices were substituted for pigs in Dublin in the longer time period, as bacon pig prices were not available for some of the period.

Comparing the timing of the budget with variations in prices in the data collected from these newspapers, a dramatic fall in the price of bacon pigs (or bacon for Dublin) can be seen coinciding exactly with the period between the budget of 11 March 1842, when proposals were announced, and October 1842, when import restrictions were lifted. It is clear that the range within which seasonal prices fluctuated fell dramatically: from 28–39 s/cwt in the year before 1842 in Cork to 18–26 s/cwt in the year after the changes. The corresponding change for Dublin bacon was from 40–61 s/cwt to 28–46 s/cwt and for Waterford bacon pigs from 39–51 s/cwt to 25–41 s/cwt. These figures suggest that the tariff probably contributed to reducing bacon pig prices by about a third between 1841 and 1843—by 30 per cent in Waterford, 38 per cent in Dublin, and 44 per cent in Cork for the year before and after the changes.

An examination of the price/quantity of pigs sold in Cork shows that the quantity sold did not increase greatly in 1842 and fell in 1843.[31] This suggests the price fall associated with the tariff changes of 1842 was an initiating factor and not due to increased availability. Neither was this fall in the price of pigs linked to the cost of feed, as Bourke notes that these types of pigs were only fed on the potato 'peelings and waste of those used by the family', and that 'it would not be worth keeping pigs if one had to buy the food for them'.[32]

Overall, the sales would have produced less money for farmers because the quantity sold had not increased to compensate for the fall in price, contributing to falling household incomes. In confirmation of this, Lord Eliot, the Chief Secretary, noted in a letter to Graham after a tour of Ireland that labourers were seeking more employment to 'compensate them for the loss they have sustained in the diminished value of their pigs'.[33]

Falling beef prices would have also contributed to this fall in real incomes. Although beef prices display a less rapid decline, the general downward trend is still clear. Local market reports show the price of beef in the Cork (d/lb), Dublin (s/cwt), and Waterford (d/lb) markets.[34] The change occurred about the time of an outbreak of cattle distemper, in which beef prices should have risen, but instead they fell as the effect of the tariff reductions outweighed this supply shock. As the *Freeman's Journal* noted: 'from the epidemic which … has been very destructive among cattle and milch cows … we were led to expect high prices, as the quantity of fresh meat used at present in Ireland is large, arising from the consumption of the great military force. As it is, beef is about 35s per cwt. over the last year [1843], but would have been 50s to 60s were it not for the operation of the tariff.'[35]

That there was a fall in price in 1842, rather than an increase, during a supply shock in domestic production is therefore significant. It is most obvious for prices in Dublin, which are wholesale and fell from a range of 50–54 s/cwt in April 1842 to a low of 34–35 s/cwt in June 1843. A similar downward trend can be seen in the Waterford markets, although in Cork it was momentary and prices rose again almost immediately. There is a smaller price movement in Cork and Waterford low-grade beef, which can be linked to the increased numbers of soldiers who were brought into the area to boost security during the 'repeal year' agitation and had to be supplied with meat. The demand for beef for the military was so great that the government reopened a depot in Haulbowline in Cork harbour to import beef from Deptford, near London.[36] But this boost in military demand did not penetrate much inland. For example, only 37 km away in Fermoy, a meeting was held to protest the falling price of beef and pork.[37] Rural locations sampled such as Nenagh and Ennis also show price movement patterns similar to Dublin.[38]

Alongside the downward price movement for beef, the quantities sold fell dramatically as farmers became unwilling to sell at reduced prices, producing an overall negative effect on real incomes. As several newspapers, including the *Freeman's Journal* and the *Tuam Herald*, noted in October 1842, the impact of the tariff reforms meant that beef and cattle prices fell 'so low that very few sales were made'.[39] The quantitative effect of this can be seen in the Ballinasloe Fair records of cattle sold.[40] Whereas less than 10 per cent of cattle remained unsold in 1840, over 40 per cent were unsold in 1842.

It is unlikely that the general drop in prices at the time of the 1842 budget was due to a sudden increase in the quantity available that year. Quantity information on pigs is available for the Cork markets.[41] It is clear that 1842 was not a year in which the quantities available rose suddenly, for instance after a good harvest. This conclusion is supported by observations made in the market reports of the *Freeman's Journal*, which suggest that the harvest of 1842 was similar in size to those of 1840 and 1841.[42] Lower food prices, which are clearly seen in food price data, were therefore sharper and greater than Peel's intended effect.

However, the negative impact on the economic welfare of the poor may have been more psychological than to do with any great influx of imported goods. As Colin Matthew has noted, although 'nineteenth-century budgets could not affect aggregate demand on any significant scale', businessmen still paid 'the closest and most anxious attention' to them and particularly to their impact on 'the state of psychological expectation' in the economy.[43] As the chairman of the National Bank of Ireland noted in his annual statement: 'the effect of the tariff has been to strike down the price of every article in which Ireland dealt', and the outcome of the tariff 'changes preceded their actual announcement'.[44] In an 1842 market report in the *Cork Advertiser*, it was noted that the tariff reductions on pigs 'were expected and the very expectation produced the effect'; in other words, the negative impact on business confidence produced the price change in anticipation of the change in market fundamentals.[45] The beef market, in particular, was damaged by an expectation of lower prices rather than the number of actual imports of foreign cattle, which were low in 1842, a fact noted in contemporary newspapers and official government records.[46]

The expected economic downturn, however, became a real one. There are numerous references to it, in terms of rising rent arrears, falling real wages, falling land values, and rising interest rates, to be found in estate records, local newspapers, and government statistics. Elizabeth Smith recorded in her diaries that her tenants were unable to pay rent in 1843 because of falling food prices and incomes, whereas they had been able to do so up until late 1842.[47] Other landlords' experiences were similar and sometimes worse. The *Tuam Herald* noted in September 1842 that some landlords in County Wicklow had 'not yet received 5s. in the pound of the March rent'.[48] Estate records from County Kildare include a letter from W. Bookey, dated 27 April 1842, which said that he had been 'very badly paid the rents owing to the panick caused by Sir R. Peel's Tariff', and another letter from Richard Doyle in January 1843 claiming that 'was it not for the deplorable change that has taken place in the price of cattle, corn &c., I would now be able to pay the May rents.'[49]

Other features of the downturn were rising unemployment and falling real wages. Most notably, in an open letter to Peel, the Archbishop of Tuam reported that 'during the last week … I was besieged by men looking for work at any wages' due to 'the change of the tariff' and 'the doubts and fears and panic to which it gave rise'.[50] There is little reliable data available on real wages, but the *Freeman's Journal* does contain some statistics indicating day wage levels in the agricultural sector.[51] These suggest a decrease in real wages in both sectors between 1841 and 1842, with a fall in the agricultural sector of nearly 50 per cent in a year. The persistence of the 1842 shock caused by the tariff reduction is shown by the subsequent recovery in real wages levels in the building sector being considerably more rapid than that of the agricultural sector.

The falling price of agricultural produce was felt all the way through the economic system to reduced land values. When the Navan Poor Law Union announced an 'Alteration in the Valuation' of agricultural land, the decision was attributed by many to the 'reduction in agricultural produce arising from legislative enactments with regard to the tariff on cattle and corn'.[52] The falling price of land increased business risk, and the *Freeman's Journal* reported rising interest rates through the summer of 1842, which made the slump in agriculture and commerce worse.[53] 'The scarcity of money, and the depression of business of every kind, was never more felt. We believe that provisions would be higher before now but for the apprehension that the new tariff would cause a considerable fall in prices.'[54] The records of bankruptcies also indicate a slump in 1842 in the agricultural sector.[55] The *Freeman's Journal* noted that 'applications to the Insolvent Debtor's Court in the NW district' had 'quadrupled' because of impoverished farmers, and official statistics show that bankruptcies per year increased by over 50 per cent outside commercial Dublin between 1841 and 1842.[56]

Government records from Dublin Castle suggest that the economic downturn was accompanied by unrest and violence which were specifically related to economic issues. In his diary entry of 24 May 1842, de Grey noted that in Tipperary 'the system of intimidation is fearful ... fortunately neither religion [n]or politics is yet mixed up in it.'[57] Dublin Castle certainly thought that civil unrest and the repeal agitation were more driven by economic factors than religious or political ones.

A comparison of economic and political indicators shows the link between the 1842 downturn and the rise in support for the repeal movement in 1842–43. This culminated in the biggest manifestation of popular protest hitherto seen in Irish history: the series of 'monster meetings' held in 1843, with over a million reputed to have attended one at the hill of Tara in August that year. As a proxy for economic conditions, agricultural prices have been used. As a political proxy for the popularity of repeal, the amounts of repeal 'rent' donations collected between January 1842 and April 1844 have been extracted from the *Nation* newspaper. This was chosen over 'monster meeting' attendance as estimates of the numbers attending these varied significantly depending on the political affiliation of the observer, and attendees did not always support O'Connell's movement. The repeal 'rent' figures, in contrast, indicate the level of financial support Irish people were willing to give to the movement, particularly as, according to Michael Keyes, 'much of the rent was subscribed in modest amounts' by the poor, rather than in large donations from the wealthy.[58] The data set is a continuous set of data, unlike the isolated examples used by earlier historians, including Lawrence McCaffrey and Nowlan.[59]

Figure 8.1 compares repeal 'rent', as the political proxy, with bacon pig prices in Cork, Dublin, and Waterford, main export ports for Ireland. Figure 8.2 does the same for beef prices. Bacon pigs and beef were chosen because they are the food items most obviously influenced by the 1842 tariff reforms, without too much 'noise' in the data caused by other factors. There is a gentle fall in bacon pig and beef prices after the budget was announced on 11 March 1842, with a more severe fall in prices after 10

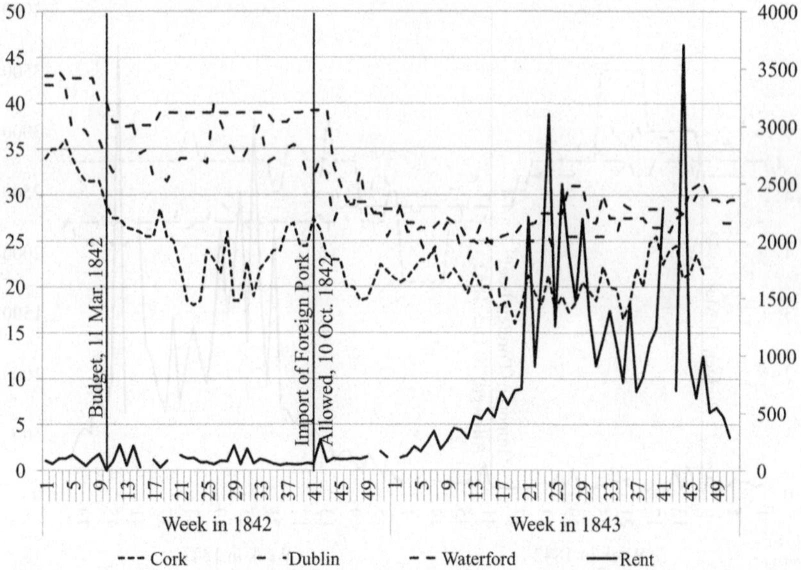

Fig. 8.1 A comparison of the amount of repeal 'rent' (£, *right-hand scale*) and prices of Cork, Dublin, and Waterford bacon pigs (s/cwt, *left-hand scale*) between January 1842 and December 1843. Weeks are numbered 1–52 during each year[60]

October 1842, which is reflected by a gradual increase in repeal 'rent' contributions after this same month, with large spikes in donations coinciding with the summer months of high economic distress as savings from the last harvest proved inadequate to reach the next.

The visual analysis can be checked by analysing the relationship between bacon pig and beef prices and the repeal-'rent' data using a time-series linear regression, utilising the ordinary least squares model.

The resulting p-values suggest a statistically significant correlation between bacon pig and beef prices for 1842–43 and increased donations towards the repeal-'rent' fund. A very strong correlation, where $p < 0.01$, and there is a more than 99 per cent confidence level, can be found for bacon pigs in all three ports and for beef in Dublin and Waterford, when set individually against the repeal-'rent' data set. The exception is beef in Cork, which does not correlate, probably because military consumption temporarily propped up prices in mid-1843. The R-squared values for the correlations, which are a measure of the variation of the data from the line

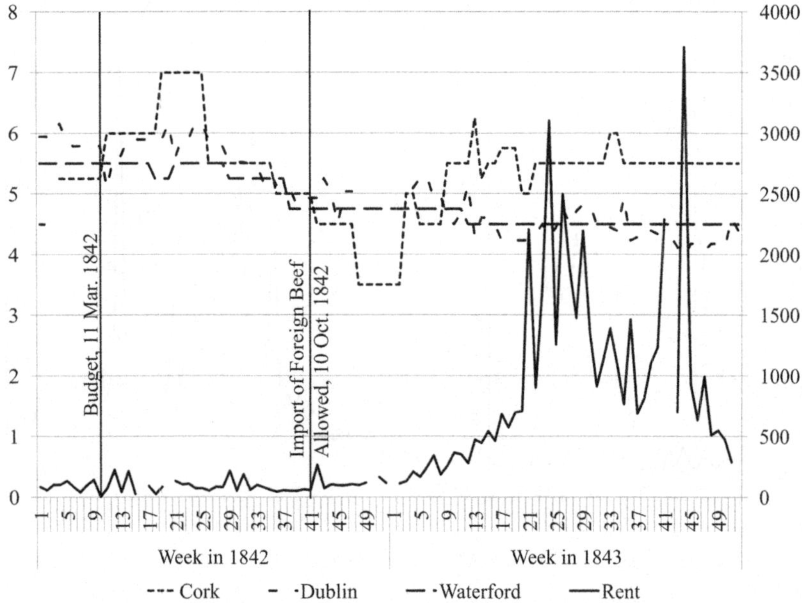

Fig. 8.2 A comparison of the amount of repeal 'rent' (£, *right-hand scale*) and prices of Cork, Dublin, and Waterford beef (d/lb, *left-hand scale*) between January 1842 and December 1843. Weeks are numbered 1–52 during each year[61]

of correlation, are within a reasonable range in view of the different types and sources of data under analysis. Although the result of this test should be approached with caution due to the age and nature of the data, it suggests that there is a statistically significant negative correlation, visible in Figs. 8.1 and 8.2, between bacon pig and beef prices, representing agricultural incomes, and the rise in repeal-'rent' contributions, representing the political support for repeal expressed in fiscal terms.

The mechanism behind this conclusion can be explained by the realisation that Daniel O'Connell put economic issues at the heart of his campaign to repeal the Act of Union. Contrary to Joseph Lee's emphasis on O'Connell's free trade rhetoric in Britain, the evidence from contemporary Irish newspaper reports suggests that O'Connell and the Repeal Association appealed to the peasantry's protectionist instincts.[62] From its early days, O'Connell sought to unite Protestants and Catholics behind repeal using promises of economic benefit as an incentive. At a repeal meeting of 1841, he asked, 'How do I propose to obtain Repeal? I answer—first by conciliating men of all persuasions and opinions.'[63] He went on to describe the way that Protestant landowners would benefit through abolition of the cess, a tax assessment, and increasing property values, and how poor Catholic voters would be given support from the repeal 'rent'. The Irish share of national debt was argued to be unfair, and reducing this burden would benefit both Protestant and Catholic taxpayers.

In the 1842–43 period, O'Connell focused more on 'native manufactures', which he claimed had been disadvantaged by British trade policy since the Union. When promoting the repeal 'rent' fund for donations to the movement in October 1842, the *Nation* reported the Repeal Association's economic case for Irish people to donate to the repeal 'rent': 'Recollect that you are not working for yourselves and your own best interests. In sustaining O'Connell, you assist in reviving Irish trade and manufactures.'[64]

O'Connell himself, at 'monster meetings' and in the press, argued that repeal would undo Irish economic decline under the Union through a repeal parliament's 'protection'. In November 1842, he complained of 'the want of protection, or rather ... the disadvantagement of Irish manufactures', which he blamed on 'political economy'.[65] In launching the 'repeal year', O'Connell explicitly cited 'the encouragement and perfecting of Irish manufactures' and 'agriculture' as a key reason behind pressing forth with 'our Repeal agitation for 1843'.[66] This formed a key theme of his 'monster meeting' speeches throughout 1843, which often focused on economic issues for about two-thirds to three-quarters of their total length. He often attempted to relate the poverty of individuals he met on the repeal agitation campaign to free trade policies conducted under the Union.[67]

O'Connell also stressed how an Irish legislature could reverse post-Union economic distress in each area he visited. In Wicklow, on 6 August 1843, O'Connell argued that the Repeal Association was the only group campaigning to reverse the economic decline of Irish agriculture and industry: 'Is there any person endeavouring to do good to the people but the Repealers? Is there anybody labouring for the improvement of her manufactures, or her commerce, or for her agricultural prosperity, but the Repealers?'[68] O'Connell particularly gave the appearance of supporting some forms of protectionism at a repeal banquet in July 1843:

> We want the protection of a domestic legislature ... thus you will observe that the export trade of Ireland in that time [before free trade with Britain] amounted to two millions of pounds sterling more than we imported. What is the case now? We export scarcely anything of Irish manufacture—we import more than five million pounds worth. And what is the remedy for that? Nothing but the existence of an Irish parliament.[69]

As O'Connell was supporting free trade in England at this time, newspapers in Britain started to attack him for appearing to abandon his previous free trade stance in favour of protectionism. The *Times* alleged that the object of O'Connell's protectionism was to 'keep alive the slumbering embers of sedition' and to gain popular support for the repeal campaign.[70] Newspapers supporting the Whigs were equally critical. The *Morning Chronicle* labelled O'Connell's protectionism as 'ignorant', a 'folly', and a cynical bid for public support.[71] The *Era* satirised O'Connell as saying that 'everything coming from England should be burnt, except coals'.[72] O'Connell's actual stance on the Corn Laws from early 1842 had been that it was an English matter and related to the conflict between 'aristocracy' and 'serfs'; as such, the poor should be supported because relieving poverty was 'a cause of all—a holy—a religious cause'.[73] 'The question', he claimed, 'between you [the English] and the sordid aristocracy—for sordid they are—is whether or not they have a right to tax your bread ... it is a question of the loaf. It is a question of whether one class of Englishmen shall say to another "you shan't eat your breakfast until you have paid me for leave with some of the loaf."' Whilst Peel might dance the 'Jim Crow'—in O'Connell's words—for the English working classes, the nationalist leader could thus support the lowering of wheat tariffs for England but 'protection' for Ireland.[74]

The economic rhetoric being produced by O'Connell was noted by *Punch* and the *Times*. *Punch* magazine represented repeal as an economic issue in the early 1840s, by suggesting the agitation shared economic characteristics with the Rebecca riots of the previous year in Wales. 'Rebecca and her Daughters', published in July 1843, shows O'Connell, dressed as a woman, leading a crowd to destroy the gate of British government, represented by the Duke of Wellington on the gatepost and Peel at the tollhouse. On the gate were written some of repeal's economic grievances, including free trade under the 'Union', the introduction of 'Poor Law' rates, and increases in the 'Church Rate' and 'Tithes'.[75] The *Times* criticised 'the late selfish attempt to merge the cause of the Irish poor in that of factious Radicalism and Repeal' which, it suggested, intended to create support based on economic nationalism for repeal. It came to the conclusion from letters by repealers that the movement was not religious, to the extent of seeking 'the banishment from the country of *all* religion, whether Protestant, Roman Catholic, or any other whatsoever'.[76]

It is therefore reasonable to conclude that there was a relationship between the rise in the popularity of the repeal movement and falling prices of the main export meats as a result of the tax changes of the 1842 budget. The mechanism behind this correlation was that economic and trade issues were at the heart of the repeal campaign during this period, and that O'Connell, nominally a free trade Benthamite, was willing to take advantage of the tariff-induced 1842–43 slump in order to boost popular support for his movement.[77] The fact that support for the repeal movement collapsed in October 1843, the same period that Ireland experienced an unexpectedly good harvest and a recovery in international food prices driven by an upward swing in the British business cycle, is further testament to the strong relationship between economic factors and the sudden rise, and subsequent fall, in support for the repeal agitation. Even in Dublin Castle, de Grey and Eliot noted at the time that the good harvest of October 1843 contributed to the collapse in support for the repeal movement and less civil unrest, in spite of the decision to take legal action against the repeal movement in that same month.[78]

In contrast, Peel thought nationalist grievances could be smoothed over with targeted religious conciliation until the economic situation improved. However, the immediate impact on Ireland of the economic reforms of 1842 was a surprise to Peel. In 1849, he admitted that in 1842 'there was great and needless alarm, and considerable loss was the consequence'.[79] But Peel's preoccupations in 1842 were with the 'reduction in the price of food' his electorate in Tamworth had demanded, and with eliminating the UK-wide budget deficit, leaving him no time to consider specific Irish policy.[80] This combination of circumstances created a situation that was highly conducive to the budget having the unintended consequence of damaging the Irish economy and, in its immediate aftermath, boosting the popularity of the repeal movement, as well as the huge 'monster meetings' held in its support.

Local Taxation and Emigration During the Famine

Move forwards five years, and there was another change in British tax policy that hit Ireland harder still than Peel's tariff reductions in 1842. Much had changed by then. The repeal movement lost popular support due to economic recovery in 1844 and 1845, a split within its ranks, and the death of O'Connell in 1847. Potato diseases and famine arrived in Ireland from 1845. The Peel government initially paid for relief efforts in Ireland with a fiscal expansion. But the ministry collapsed in 1846 due to splits in the governing Conservative Party over the issue of repealing the Corn Laws.

By the middle of 1847, due to a series of severe financial crises, it appeared to the new Whig government that it was impossible to fund Peel's generous relief policies at the required level by raising government loans.[81] A lack of a majority in Parliament meant that income taxes could not be raised either.[82] Charles Wood, the new Chancellor of the Exchequer, therefore decided to move the burden of relief spending onto local Irish taxes. In particular, he targeted landlords and the middle-class farmers. He wanted them to employ as labourers those who used to live a subsistence lifestyle, which would have entailed a transfer from farmers to the poorest in society. By charging local taxes to fund the relief required for those not employed, he hoped to encourage those being taxed to offer employment instead of being forced to pay tax. Early on in his time as the Chancellor, he regarded local taxation as a fall-back solution if the poor could not be employed through public or private funding.[83] As the government soon found that it could not borrow without panicking markets, and the hoped-for employment did not materialise, local taxation to redistribute wealth became the main plank of Wood's policies. The Russell government amended the Poor Law in 1847, which was only paid by those occupying rateable land of £4 or above, to shift the burden of Famine relief costs wholly onto the Irish ratepayer. This resulted in local taxes collected in Ireland doubling, from around £1,500,000 in 1845 to about £3,000,000 in 1848, accounting for around 5 per cent of the GDP.[84] In effect, this transferred wealth from upper- and middle-class taxpayers to those with little monetary income.

However, the British government encountered problems with redistribution which are still controversial issues with the policy today. The system began to break down as some Poor Law Unions went bankrupt or failed to act through lack of funds. In proposing the transfer of entitlements as a remedy for famine, Amartya Sen claimed to counter Thomas Malthus, who had held out that transfer of wealth from rich to poor would mean 'all would have the same quantity of money. All the provisions of the country would be consumed and all the people would starve together.'[85] Sen proposed that the transfer should be increased as long as the income of the poor is insufficient to purchase an adequate ration of food and the income of the poor is less than the rich.[86] The transfer was to stop only when the income of the poor would buy an adequate ration. Arthur Laffer, the economist, pointed out a problem with the economic effect of higher taxes because they can lead to diminishing returns. He quoted John Maynard Keynes explaining that 'taxation may be so high as to defeat its object, and ... given sufficient time to gather the fruits, a reduction of taxation will run a better chance than an increase of balancing the budget.'[87] The loss of revenue as tax rates become very high can be caused by tax avoidance or a refusal or inability to pay. The theoretical curve can be represented as shown in Fig. 8.3 (top). The first section of rising revenue approximates to a straight line (shown dotted), the arithmetical effect of rising revenue with rising tax rate. However, as the economic effect of resistance to payment becomes stronger, a maximum revenue point is reached and the revenue collected declines. Zolt Becsi has demonstrated that the second part of the Laffer curve can shift about, causing a wide spread of points seen in reality, although the first section tends to shift far less.[88]

Data for tax receipts in Ireland have been collected from parliamentary papers.[89] Figures for total local tax rate poundage, including Poor Law, cess, and annuity charges for government loans, is only available for Unions with annuities and the amount of rates collected is only available for the period when Unions had paid guardians. Therefore, the data cover the eighteen Unions most in distress, having government loan annuities and paid guardians, for the period just before the rate-in-aid legislation which introduced transfers from poor to wealthier Unions to try and solve the problems.

It can be seen from Fig. 8.3 (bottom) that whatever the rate charged, the maximum revenue extracted was about 50 per cent of the valuation in 1849. Even the theoretical poundage producing a maximum income was unlikely to have gone beyond 70 per cent. However, the total rates for local taxation in 1849 went up to a height of 34s. 3½d. in the pound for Ballinarobe Union, the highest in the country, and there were altogether

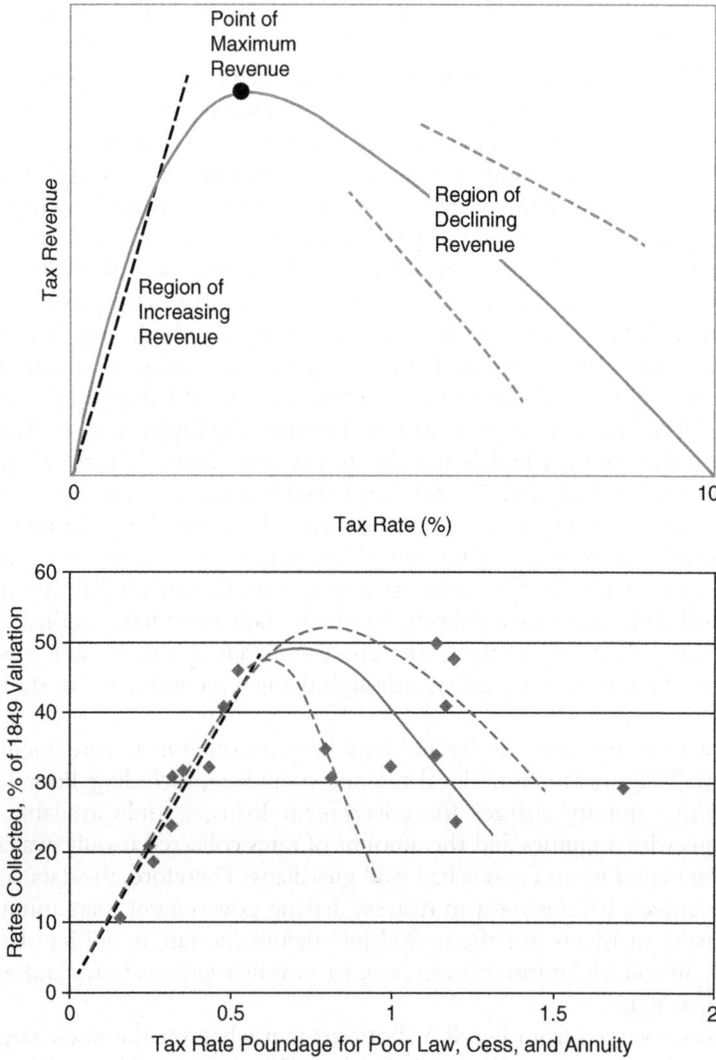

Fig. 8.3 *Top*: Theoretical Laffer curve diagram. *Bottom*: Scatter diagram of rates collected for each union whilst paid guardians were in place as a percentage of 1849 valuation against the tax rate poundage for Poor Law, cess, and annuity in the same year (1 = 100 per cent tax rate)

sixty-two Unions in which local taxation was over the 10s. in the pound rate.

This effect was recognised at the time. In August and September 1848, Wood was pressing for the imposition of high rates of taxation. Edward Twisleton on behalf of the Poor Law Commissioners defended the then current 3s. rate by anticipating by a century Laffer's observations about maximising tax collection rates: 'I have not the slightest doubt that more money will really be collected throughout Ireland from a 3/- Rate than would have been collected from a 5/- Rate with the general opposition against it.'[90] Many wealthier farmers escaped the high tax rates through emigration to the United States. As over 95 per cent of Irish emigrants were forced to pay for their emigration themselves (just 50,000 were given assistance to emigrate out of Ireland), only the wealthier could afford to travel to the United States.[91] The destitute ended up in Britain or parts of its empire. Contemporary accounts typically describe emigrants to America as 'comfortable in appearance, young and healthy'.[92] Witnesses at the 1849 select committee on Irish Poor Laws included Alfred Power, Twisleton's successor, who gave his impression 'that those who have emigrated have been of the farming [i.e. middle] class', and John Hamilton, who confirmed that 'the better class of farmers are much more anxious to emigrate than they were.'[93] The higher socio-economic status of emigrants to America is confirmed by an analysis of savings accounts of emigrants in the United States, which indicates that Irish emigrants in the 1840s and 1850s were disproportionately richer and better educated than the Irish-American population already living in New York City.[94] Landlords, even the absentee ones, found escape more difficult and could be reduced from lavish lifestyles to bankruptcy and involvement in crime.[95]

A comparison between local tax rates and emigration levels to America shows a link between the two due to the stress caused by local taxation, which underlies the Laffer curve analysis results and which was suggested by Archbishop Richard Whately at the time.[96] The Irish data for the emigration to the United States and local taxes comprising poor rates and grand jury presentments are plotted on the same graph, and it is evident that that they follow a similar pattern with about a three-year lag (Fig. 8.4).

The co-movement of local taxation and emigration data suggests that it was not nativism, as historians such as Raymond Cohn have suggested, but the cutting of local taxation which helped curb the flood of middle classes leaving the country.[98] The cut in taxation was due to Gladstone's budget

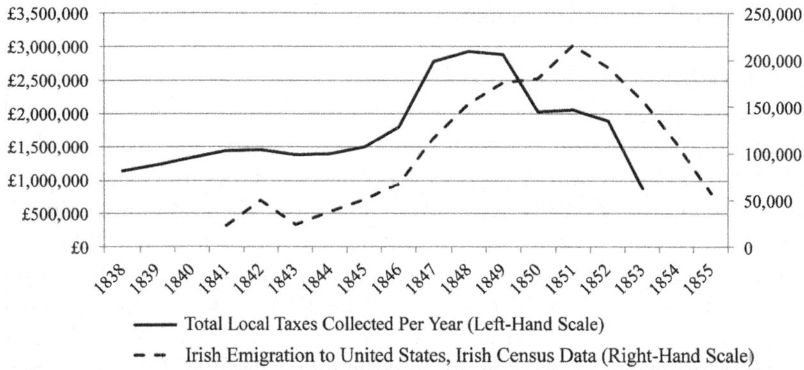

Fig. 8.4 A comparison of emigration to the United States and local taxation in Ireland (*£* s.), 1837–53[97]

of 1853, which wiped out the debts from Famine relief they were servicing. As he explained in his budget speech:

> The Government have determined to make a large proposition. The 4,500,000l. of Consolidated Annuities include 1,500,000l. of debt that strictly belongs to the establishment of the Poor Law in Ireland. That was a great social and national good—a great and permanent good to Ireland. But every good to Ireland is also a good to England. The other 3,000,000l. consists of debts entirely connected with the Famine. A Committee of the other House of Parliament have sat on this subject, and they have recommended a remission of 2,000,000l. of this taxation. Sir, the plan of the Government, after maturely considering the whole question, is, to propose to Parliament that, from and after the 29th of last September, the Consolidated Annuities shall be wholly wiped away. They propose that the whole sum due from Ireland to England shall be remitted.[99]

The conclusion that a high proportion of emigrants to the United States, in comparison with other destinations, was drawn from the politicised middle classes who were anxious to improve themselves provides an explanation for the observation made by David Doyle that ‘the major scholars of Irish migrations to Britain, Australia and Canada have by now demonstrated that, while their Irish populations increased after [the Famine], that event neither reshaped nor originated Irish subcultures and communities therein to anything like the degree that was the case of the United

States.'[100] That subculture retained an animosity to Irish landlords and Britain, carried with it from the period of the Famine. Its resentment arose to a great extent from the inability for economic advancement due to the tax system, as the ballad proclaimed:

> Now that the Corn Laws are gone
> Our Grain's so mighty cheap
> I'll hardly find it worth my while
> My Plot of Oats to reap …
> I'm now going to a country, where
> From Poor rate I'll be free,
> Poor Ireland's going to the dogs
> As fast as fast can be.
>
> *Your Honor won't you cry?*[101]

Conclusion

Since the Irish Famine, both nationalist and revisionist writers have downplayed the level of popular protest during the Famine. Recent work has emphasised that there was a big rise in agrarian crime and food rioting during the Famine. But the histories of taxation and of popular protest against it during the decade of the Famine have remained a notable blind spot for historians and economists interested in the period. The two case studies in this chapter show that this is an area worthy of more investigation. Changes in tax policy by British politicians did provoke strong reactions in Ireland. The tariff reductions of 1842, by damaging Ireland's economy, enabled O'Connell to turn economic discontent into attendance at 'monster meetings' and financial support for the movement to repeal the Act of Union. The decision to move relief funding away from central government and onto local ratepayers fuelled emigration to the United States and hardened the attitudes of the emigrant community there against the British state. The same conclusion from both episodes is that adverse changes in British tax policy played a role in fuelling anti-British sentiment and Irish nationalism. It is a narrative that historians should consider more seriously when writing about the rise of Irish nationalism throughout the nineteenth and early twentieth centuries.

Notes

1. Douglas Kanter, 'The Politics of Irish Taxation, 1842–53', *English Historical Review* 127, no. 528 (2012): 1121–55.
2. Charles Read, 'The "Repeal Year" in Ireland: An Economic Reassessment', *Historical Journal* 58, no. 1 (2015): 111–35.
3. Idem, 'Laissez-Faire, the Irish Famine and British Financial Crisis', *Economic History Review* 69, no. 2 (2016): 419–30.
4. Using the consensus estimate that GDP fell by 25 per cent during this period; Poor Relief (Ireland) (No. 2) Act, 10 & 11 Vict., c. 90.
5. David Dickson, 'Taxation and Disaffection in Late Eighteenth-Century Ireland', in *Irish Peasants: Violence and Political Unrest, 1780–1914*, ed. Samuel Clark and James S. Donnelly Jr. (Madison: University of Wisconsin Press, 1983), 37.
6. Philip Harling, *The Waning of 'Old Corruption': The Politics of Economical Reform in Britain, 1779–1846* (Oxford: Oxford University Press, 1996); Norman Gash, *Sir Robert Peel: The Life of Sir Robert Peel after 1830* (London: Longman, 1972), 714; H. C. G. Matthew, 'Disraeli, Gladstone, and the Politics of Mid-Victorian Budgets', *Historical Journal* 22, no. 3 (1979): 615–43.
7. Martin Daunton, *Trusting Leviathan: The Politics of Taxation in Britain, 1799–1914* (Cambridge: Cambridge University Press, 2007).
8. Martin McElroy, 'The 1830 Budget and Repeal: Parliament and Public Opinion in Ireland', *Irish Historical Studies* 36, no. 141 (2008): 50–52.
9. Charles Stuart Parker, *Sir Robert Peel from his Private Papers*, vol. 3 (London: John Murray, 1899), 34, 101; Gash, *Peel*, 394–96; Donal A. Kerr, *Peel, Priests and Politics: Sir Robert Peel's Administration and the Roman Catholic Church in Ireland, 1841–1846* (Oxford: Oxford University Press, 1982), 2.
10. A summary of the use of Peel's policy to support these viewpoints can be found in Richard A. Gaunt, *Sir Robert Peel: The Life and Legacy* (London: I. B. Tauris, 2010), 2, 149–55.
11. John Prest, 'Peel, Sir Robert, second baronet (1788–1850)', in *Oxford Dictionary of National Biography*, ed. H. C. G. Matthew et al., http://www.oxforddnb.com/view/article/21764 (accessed 15 Apr. 2013); Kerr, *Peel, Priests and Politics*, 110–22, 276.
12. Report of Royal Dublin Society, British Library (hereafter, BL) Add. MS 40577, ff. 21–24; Report of Agricultural Chemistry Association, Edinburgh, BL Add. MS 40577, f. 141.
13. *Correspondence Explanatory of the Measures Adopted by Her Majesty's Government for the Relief of Distress*, No. 735 (1846), vol. 37, pp. 56–57; for the low estimate of loss in 1846 see P. M. A. Bourke, 'The Extent of

the Potato Crop in Ireland at the Time of the Famine', *Journal of the Statistical and Social Inquiry Society of Ireland* 20, pt. 3 (1959–60): 11; for the high estimate of loss in 1846, see *Correspondence from July, 1846, to January, 1847, Relating to the Measures Adopted for the Relief of Distress in Ireland*, No. 761 (1847), vol. 51, p. 79.
14. Read, 'Laissez-Faire'.
15. Kevin B. Nowlan, 'The Political Background', in *The Great Famine: Studies in Irish History, 1845–52*, ed. R. D. Edwards and T. D. Williams (Dublin: Browne and Nolan, 1956), 136.
16. Enda Delaney and Brendán Mac Suibhne, 'Editor's Introduction', in *Ireland's Great Famine and Popular Politics*, ed. Enda Delaney and Brendán Mac Suibhne (New York: Routledge, 2015), 3.
17. Cormac Ó Gráda, *The Great Irish Famine* (Cambridge: Cambridge University Press, 1995), 36.
18. Ibid.
19. See Delaney and Mac Suibhne, eds., *Ireland's Great Famine.*
20. James Kelly, *Food Rioting in Ireland in the Eighteenth and Nineteenth Centuries: The 'Moral Economy' and the Irish Crowd* (Dublin: Four Courts Press, 2017).
21. Sir James Graham to Earl de Grey, 8 Mar. 1842, Graham Papers, BL Add. MS 79620, f. 34.
22. Daunton, *Trusting Leviathan*, 73.
23. P. M. A. Bourke, 'The Use of the Potato Crop in Pre-Famine Ireland', *Journal of the Statistical and Social Inquiry Society of Ireland* 21, pt. 6 (1967–68): 84.
24. Mr and Mrs S. C. Hall, *Ireland: Its Scenery, Character, etc.*, vol. 3 (London: Hall, 1843), 451.
25. Alice Effie Murray, *A History of the Commercial and Financial Relations between England and Ireland from the Period of the Restoration* (London: Macmillan, 1903), 391–92.
26. L. M. Cullen, *An Economic History of Ireland since 1660* (London: B. T. Batsford, 1987), 113.
27. Cormac Ó Gráda, *Ireland Before and After the Famine: Explorations in Economic History, 1800–1925* (Manchester: Manchester University Press, 1993), 38.
28. Ó Gráda, *Ireland Before and After the Famine*, 38–39; for the basic concept of stickiness in economics, see J. M. Keynes, *The General Theory of Employment, Interest and Money* (London: Macmillan, 1936), 257–71.
29. Read, 'Repeal Year', 121–23.
30. Liam Kennedy and Peter M. Solar, *Irish Agriculture: A Price History; From the Mid-Eighteenth Century to the Eve of the First World War* (Dublin: Royal Irish Academy, 2007).

31. *Constitution; or Cork Advertiser.*
32. Bourke, 'The Use of the Potato Crop in Pre-Famine Ireland', 84–85.
33. Lord Eliot to Graham, 9 Nov. 1842, Graham Papers, BL Add. MS 79636, f. 70.
34. Waterford from the *Waterford Mail*, Dublin the *Freeman's Journal*, and Cork the *Constitution*.
35. *Freeman's Journal*, 7 Feb. 1844.
36. *Cork Examiner*, 7 July 1843.
37. *Cork Examiner*, evening 16 Jan. 1843.
38. *Nenagh Guardian* and *Enniskillen Chronicle and Erne Packet*, market reports, 1842–43.
39. *Tuam Herald*, 8 Oct. 1842; *Freeman's Journal*, 8 Oct. 1842.
40. *Farmers' Gazette*, 11 Oct. 1845; *Freeman's Journal* and *Tuam Herald* (various).
41. *Constitution; or Cork Advertiser.*
42. *Freeman's Journal*, market reports, July to Dec. 1842.
43. Matthew, 'Mid-Victorian Budgets', 615; Keynes, *General Theory*, 202, 148.
44. *Freeman's Journal*, 28 May 1842.
45. *Constitution; or Cork Advertiser*, 17 Jan. 1843, 18 Jan. 1843.
46. Ibid., 7 Jan. 1843.
47. *The Irish Journals of Elizabeth Smith, 1840–1850*, ed. David Thomson and Moyra McGusty (Oxford: Oxford University Press, 1980), 56, 63.
48. *Tuam Herald*, 17 Sept. 1842.
49. From auction sale catalogue by Adam's, Dublin, 18 May 2010, item 18, item 27.
50. *Freeman's Journal*, 7 July 1842.
51. Ibid., 24 Jan. 1837, 18 Sept. 1839, 7 Feb. 1840, 18 July 1842, 8 Jan. 1846, 7 Feb. 1840, 20 May 1846, 26 June 1846, 6 May 1847, 16 June 1847, 5 Jan. 1850, 2 May 1850.
52. Ibid., 27 Dec. 1842.
53. Ibid., 5 July 1842.
54. Ibid., 2 June 1842.
55. House of Commons, 'Bankruptcy (Ireland)', *Sessional Papers, 1852–53* (433), vol. 94, p. 15.
56. *Freeman's Journal*, 27 Sept. 1843.
57. Earl de Grey, Irish Diary, 1842 vol., Bedfordshire and Luton Archives and Record Service, L31/114/18, 40–41.
58. Michael J. Keyes, 'Money and Nationalist Politics in Nineteenth Century Ireland: From O'Connell to Parnell' (PhD diss., National University of Ireland Maynooth, 2009), 142.

59. Lawrence J. McCaffrey, *Daniel O'Connell and the Repeal Year* (Lexington: University of Kentucky Press, 1966), 80; Kevin B. Nowlan, *The Politics of Repeal: A Study in the Relations between Great Britain and Ireland, 1841–50* (London: Routledge and Kegan Paul, 1965), 40.
60. Repeal 'rent' from the *Nation*; price data from the *Constitution, Freeman's Journal,* and *Waterford Mail.*
61. Sources as in Fig. 8.1.
62. Joseph Lee, 'The Social and Economic Ideas of O'Connell', in *Daniel O'Connell: Portrait of a Radical,* ed. Kevin B. Nowlan and Maurice R. O'Connell (Belfast: Appletree Press, 1994), 70–86.
63. *Freeman's Journal*, 16 Apr. 1841.
64. *Nation*, 22 Oct. 1842.
65. Ibid., 5 Nov. 1842.
66. Ibid., 7 Jan. 1843.
67. *Weekly Freeman's Journal*, 7 Jan. 1843.
68. *Nation*, 12 Aug. 1843.
69. Ibid., 22 July 1843.
70. *Times*, 29 Dec. 1841.
71. *Morning Chronicle*, 24 Nov. 1840.
72. *Era*, 3 Oct. 1841; see also the *Tablet*, 25 Sept. 1841.
73. *Freeman's Journal*, 12 Feb. 1842.
74. Ibid. To dance 'Jim Crow' in this context means constantly to change one's mind in a ridiculous manner, like the popular dance of the same name. O'Connell was accusing Peel of doing this in order to please the English working classes.
75. *Punch*, 1 July 1843.
76. *Times*, 2 Jan. 1843, 6 Jan. 1843.
77. *Morning Chronicle*, 24 Nov. 1840; *Times*, 2 Jan. 1843; de Grey to Sir Robert Peel, 17 June 1843, Peel Papers, BL Add. MS 40478, f. 88.
78. *Belfast Newsletter*, 3 Oct. 1843; de Grey, Irish Diary, 1844 vol., Bedfordshire and Luton Archives and Record Service, L31/114/21, 21, 28.
79. *Hansard Parliamentary Debates*, 3rd ser., vol. 106, cols. 1454–62 (6 July 1849).
80. Sir Robert Peel, *Tamworth Election: Speech of Sir Robert Peel* (London: John Ollivier, 1841), 12.
81. Read, 'Laissez-Faire', 419–30.
82. Ibid., 429.
83. John Young to Peel, 16 Jan. 1847, Peel Papers, BL Add. MS 40598, ff. 38–42.
84. Using the consensus estimate that GDP fell by 25 per cent during this period; Poor Relief (Ireland) (No. 2) Act, 10 & 11 Vict., c. 90. For tax data sources see note to Fig. 8.3.

85. T. R. Malthus, *An Investigation of the Cause of the Present High Price of Provisions* (London: Johnson, 1800), 17–18.
86. Amartya Sen, *Poverty and Famines: An Essay on Entitlements and Deprivation* (Oxford: Oxford University Press, 1981), 177–78.
87. Arthur Laffer, 'The Laffer Curve: Past, Present and Future', *Backgrounder*, no. 1765 (June 2004), 2. For recent exploration and verification of the Laffer Curve effect in a modern context, see Mathias Trabant and Harald Uhlig, 'How Far Are We from the Slippery Slope? The Laffer Curve Revisited', *NBER Working Paper No. 15434* (2009; rev. 2011); idem., 'How do Laffer Curves Differ Across Countries?', in *Fiscal Policy after the Financial Crisis*, ed. Alberto Alesina and Francesco Giavazzi (Cambridge, MA: NBER Books, 2013), 211–49.
88. Zsolt Becsi, 'The Shifty Laffer Curve', *Federal Reserve Bank of Atlanta Economic Review* 85, no. 3 (2000): 53–64.
89. For the combined poundage for Poor Law, cess, and annuity charges for government loans to Poor Law Unions, see House of Commons, 'Consolidated Annuities (Ireland)', *Sessional Papers, 1852* (19), vol. 47, pp. 125–27; for rates collected and not collected, see idem, 'Poor Law Unions (Ireland)', *Sessional Papers, 1850* (251), vol. 50, pp. 112–13; for valuation, see idem, 'Rate in Aid (Ireland)', *Sessional Papers, 1851* (554), vol. 49.
90. Edward Twisleton to Charles Trevelyan, 17 Sept. 1848, Trevelyan Papers, The National Archives: T 64/366A.
91. Oliver MacDonagh, 'Irish Emigration to the United States of America and the British Colonies during the Famine', *The Great Famine*; David Fitzpatrick, *Irish Emigration, 1801–1921* (Dundalk: Dundalgan Press, 1984), 19–20.
92. *Constitution; or Cork Advertiser*, quoted in *Reynold's Newspaper*, 16 Mar. 1851.
93. House of Commons, 'First Report from the Select Committee of the House of Lords Appointed to Inquire into the Operation of the Irish Poor Law', *Sessional Papers, 1849* (192), vol. 16, p. 70; idem, 'Second Report from the Select Committee of the House of Lords Appointed to Inquire into the Operation of the Irish Poor Law', *Sessional Papers, 1849* (228), vol. 16, p. 454.
94. Tyler Anbinder, 'Moving beyond "Rags to Riches": New York's Irish Famine Immigrants and their Surprising Savings Accounts', *Journal of American History* 99, no. 3 (2012): 741–70; R. J. Ernst, *Immigrant Life in New York City, 1825–63* (New York: Columbia University Press, 1949), 214–18.

95. For example, Lord Mountcashel (a.k.a. Lord Kilworth); *Freeman's Journal*, 23 Aug. 1847; *Nenagh Guardian*, 4 May 1850; *Lloyd's Weekly Newspaper*, 26 Sept. 1852, 3 Oct. 1852.
96. *Hansard*, 3rd ser., vol. 105, col. 277 (11 May 1849).
97. House of Commons, 'Grand Jury Presentments', *Sessional Papers, 1837–38* (207), vol. 46, *Sessional Papers, 1839* (104), vol. 47, *Sessional Papers, 1840* (41), vol. 48, *Sessional Papers, 1841–1* (143), vol. 27, *Sessional Papers, 1852* (20), vol. 47, *Sessional Papers, 1852* (152), vol. 47, *Sessional Papers, 1852–53* (366), vol. 94, *Sessional Papers, 1854* (207), vol. 58; idem, 'Poor Rate', *Sessional Papers, 1852* (319), vol. 45; idem, 'County Rates, &c. Charges', *Sessional Papers, 1864* (538), vol. 50; idem, 'General Report of the Colonial Land and Emigration Commissioners', *Sessional Papers, 1842* (567), vol. 25; *Census of Ireland 1851 General Report*, part 6: *General Report* (Dublin: Alexander Thom, 1856), lv.
98. Raymond L. Cohn, 'Nativism and the End of the Mass Migration of the 1840s and 1850s', *Journal of Economic History* 60, no. 2 (2000): 361–83.
99. *Hansard*, 3rd ser., vol. 125, cols. 1402–3 (18 Apr. 1853).
100. David Noel Doyle, 'Review Article: Cohesion and Diversity in the Irish Diaspora', *Irish Historical Studies* 31, no. 123 (1999): 414.
101. 'The Irish Emigrant's Address', Treasury note, 2 Apr. 1850, Trevelyan Papers, The National Archives: T 64/370C/1.

CHAPTER 9

The Campaign Against Over-Taxation, 1863–65: A Reappraisal

Douglas Kanter

On 21 April 1863, John Blake Dillon addressed Dublin Corporation on the subject of 'the public accounts between Great Britain and Ireland'. After being 'received with loud applause', the former Young Ireland rebel, who had returned to public life two months earlier in the more sedate role of town councillor for Dublin's Wood Quay Ward, moved for the establishment of a committee of inquiry into the Anglo-Irish financial relationship. The country, he insisted, had a 'just and grievous cause of complaint' where fiscal policy was concerned. Ireland, he maintained, suffered from 'excessive taxation on the one hand, and the expenditure of the national revenue in a foreign country', by which he meant Britain, 'on the other'. 'By this drain of her wealth', Dillon contended, Ireland was 'starved and paralysed'. 'The wail of distress', he lamented, 'which week after week reaches this building from every quarter of the island—the untilled field, the crowded immigrant ship—all tell the sad tale of ruin.' Though city hall was increasingly riven by sectarian and partisan tensions in the early 1860s, councillors found themselves to be in agreement on the motion, which they unanimously approved.[1] In the aftermath of the proceedings, moreover, it became apparent that Dillon enjoyed the support of a broad

D. Kanter (✉)
Florida Atlantic University, Boca Raton, FL, USA
e-mail: dkanter1@fau.edu

D. Kanter, P. Walsh (eds.), *Taxation, Politics, and Protest in Ireland, 1662–2016*, Palgrave Studies in the History of Finance,
https://doi.org/10.1007/978-3-030-04309-4_9

spectrum of Irish opinion.[2] Indeed, Dublin Corporation's endorsement of his proposal represented only the most visible manifestation of widespread Irish discontent with the Anglo-Irish financial relationship. Between 1863 and 1865, Conservative activists and popular politicians united in a campaign against what they alleged to be Ireland's over-taxation, orchestrating a substantial petitioning drive to air their fiscal grievances, launching a single-issue pressure group for Irish tax relief, and helping to secure a parliamentary committee of inquiry into Irish public finance.

Despite the prominence of the tax protest in the early 1860s, it scarcely features in historiographic treatments of the post-Famine period. Thomas Kennedy offered the most detailed examination of the agitation more than a century ago, but his partisan account uncritically accepted that Ireland was overtaxed.[3] In recent decades, economic historians have greeted such claims sceptically. W. E. Vaughan has calculated that Ireland's contribution to UK revenue circa 1870 was roughly proportionate to the Irish share of national income, and has concluded that there was nothing 'intrinsically unfair' about post-Famine taxation.[4] David Johnson and Liam Kennedy have supported Vaughan's findings, estimating that the tax transfers from Ireland were less significant than Dillon and other contemporary commentators believed, both in terms of the amount of capital removed to Britain and in terms of their impact on Ireland's economic performance.[5] If economic historians have found allegations that post-Famine Ireland was overtaxed to be unconvincing, political historians have scarcely noticed the campaign for tax relief at all.[6] The tax protest of 1863–65, therefore, has not been subjected to close investigation since the appearance of Kennedy's work at the end of the nineteenth century.

The present essay uses the ephemeral movement against over-taxation as a window onto the politics of Irish public finance in the mid-nineteenth century. While accepting that Irish activists exaggerated the economic impact of post-Famine tax increases, it recognises that notions of fiscal fairness are politically and socially constructed.[7] Rather than attempting to revive the moribund debate on Irish tax policy, consequently, it identifies the influences that encouraged the tax protest, analyses the organisation and geography of the agitation, and reappraises the case against post-Famine public finance in order to recover an alternative Irish fiscal policy. By demonstrating that grievances concerning taxation were incorporated into the nascent home rule movement, it concludes that a long-forgotten campaign for tax reform had significant political ramifications.

Contexts, 1800–64

Irish attitudes to taxation in the early 1860s were shaped by a number of factors, including the fiscal framework provided by the Act of Union (1800), recent developments in public finance, and the severe depression that beset Irish agriculture as the decade began. The seventh article of the Union established the parameters for Anglo-Irish financial relations throughout the nineteenth century, but it was flexible enough to accommodate widely divergent approaches to Irish taxation. Although the architects of the Union had been constrained by the different levels of British and Irish debt to maintain a separate fiscal system in Ireland, they had also stipulated that UK revenue could, under certain conditions, be raised 'indiscriminately, by equal taxes imposed on the same articles in each country'. This proviso, however, was itself qualified by the allowance of 'such particular exemptions or abatements in Ireland … as circumstances may appear from time to time to demand'.[8] Without departing from the terms of article seven, therefore, Ireland could be treated as a separate fiscal unit paying a fixed proportion of the United Kingdom's total revenue; as a favoured region within a fiscal union; or as a fully assimilated district within a unitary state.

Necessity had obliged policymakers to choose the first option between 1801 and 1816, while fiscal and political considerations alike had encouraged them to embrace the second alternative from 1817 to 1851.[9] Ireland's distinctive financial departments all survived the Union, only to be merged with their British equivalents after 1816.[10] Under the new dispensation, Ireland ceased to be responsible for a predetermined ratio of UK expenditure, set by the Union at two-seventeenths of the total, and instead 'simply paid over her whole revenue to the united exchequer, and Great Britain became liable for the remainder of the expenditure of the United Kingdom'.[11] Despite these moves in the direction of institutional assimilation, no systematic attempt was made to equalise Irish and British taxation. As late as 1852, resident Irish taxpayers enjoyed exemptions from the income tax, the land tax, and the assessed taxes, as well as various excise and stamp duties, which collectively yielded over £11.7 million in Britain.[12] Irish consumers also paid the spirit duty—a major source of UK revenue—at a lower rate than their English and Scottish counterparts.[13]

By the early 1850s, however, British politicians had come to regard Ireland's financial treatment as excessively favourable.[14] Mounting central government expenditure during the Great Famine had drawn adverse attention to the Irish income tax exemption, while the collapse of Daniel O'Connell's agitation for the repeal of the Union had removed a brake on Irish tax increases. Accordingly, between 1852 and 1860, successive Chancellors of the Exchequer pursued a policy of fiscal assimilation. The central figure in the recalibration of Irish public finance was William Gladstone, Chancellor in the Aberdeen and second Palmerston administrations (1852–55, 1859–65). Gladstone's 1853 budget, celebrated in Britain for its promotion of free trade through tariff reform, was a watershed in Irish finance. The budget extended the income tax to Ireland, raised the Irish spirit duty by 25 per cent, and introduced a new succession duty, levied on the inheritance of real estate, in Ireland as well as in Britain. Although Gladstone's financial plan provided for the gradual reduction and eventual expiration of the income tax over a period of seven years, British involvement in the Crimean War (1854–56), and heightened defence expenditure in its aftermath, upset his calculations. Not only did the income tax remain a prominent—and permanent—feature of the fiscal system, but the rate was increased from 2.9 per cent in 1853 to 6.7 per cent in 1855, before settling at 4.2 per cent in 1860.[15] Gladstone and subsequent Chancellors also had recourse to repeated augmentations of the Irish spirit duty in order to help balance the budget, raising the rate on five occasions between 1854 and 1860. In the process, the Irish and British spirit duties were equalised and the Irish rate was set at 275 per cent of its 1852 level.[16]

Though these changes to the tax code did not complete the fiscal assimilation of Ireland to Britain, they profoundly altered the Anglo-Irish financial relationship. The partial equalisation of British and Irish taxation, in conjunction with the elimination of some duties levied exclusively in Britain, curtailed the fiscal privileges that Ireland had enjoyed until 1852. Resident Irish taxpayers remained exempt from the land and assessed taxes, as well as a handful of excise and stamp duties, but by 1860 these imposts yielded only about £4.5 million in Britain.[17] Between 1852 and 1860, meanwhile, the gross receipt from Irish taxation grew by almost 50 per cent, according to the returns of revenue provided in the annual finance accounts. The official statistics, which did not register tax transfers from Ireland to Britain resulting from Anglo-Irish trade, must be treated as rough approximations rather than precise measurements, but they provide some sense of the scale of the Irish tax increases. The actual amount that Ireland paid was the subject of dispute in the 1860s, and the exact figure is unascertainable, but the finance accounts indicated that the Irish tax burden had risen by upwards of £2 million in less than a decade, from over £4.4 million to more than £6.6 million per annum.[18] Irish expenditure failed to climb in tandem with taxation, as contemporaries recognised.[19]

Irish MPs, who lacked either the necessary votes or the political will to prevent the tax increases of 1853–60, posed little obstacle to fiscal integration. For much of the 1850s, moreover, criticism of public finance was muted in Ireland, as rising prosperity enabled taxpayers to bear their additional burdens without undue difficulty.[20] Yet Ireland's venerable tradition of tax protest, outlined in the earlier chapters of this volume, ensured that fiscal assimilation remained a politically hazardous policy. The mobilising capacity of grievances relating to taxation became apparent during the Irish agricultural depression of 1859–64. In these years, a succession of bad seasons lowered crop, livestock, and dairy yields, bringing severe hardship to the smallholders who endured in the west and forcing retrenchment upon prosperous southern graziers. By 1862, landlords were also beginning to feel the pinch.[21] For those who were less fortunately circumstanced, economic adversity often entailed social dislocation. After more than a half-decade of post-Famine decline, evictions, emigration, and the number of people resorting to the workhouse all began ticking upwards in 1859–60, before peaking in 1863–64.[22] In this context, recent changes to the structure of taxation provided a familiar political focus for economically induced discontent.

Disaffection, Agitation, Disintegration: The Course of the Campaign, 1860–65

Irish politicians and opinion makers intermittently expressed grievances relating to public finance in the late 1850s, but criticism mounted from 1860 as the agricultural depression worsened.[23] The initial target of reproach was the budget of 1860, introduced by Gladstone in February after his return to the Exchequer in Palmerston's second Liberal government. Irish Conservatives, joined by the remnants of the Independent Irish Party (IIP), attacked the free trade provisions of the budget as insufficiently sensitive to Ireland's agricultural and commercial interests, singling out the remission of import duties on butter, eggs, and cork.[24] An article in the short-lived *Irish Quarterly Review* raised broader concerns about the accuracy of the United Kingdom's public accounts at this time, observing (correctly) that official records underestimated Irish revenue, while claiming (inaccurately) that they exaggerated Irish expenditure, encouraging an erroneous belief that Ireland did not pay its fair share of taxation.[25] These arguments were brought together in March by Colonel Francis Plunket Dunne, MP for Queen's County.[26] An independently minded Irish Conservative with a long-standing interest in fiscal policy, Dunne had opposed the extension of the income tax to Ireland in 1853, unsuccessfully seeking to delay its imposition by moving for a committee of inquiry into the Anglo-Irish financial relationship during the budget debates of that year.[27] Better informed about Irish public finance than many of his contemporaries, and inclined to favour subjects on which bipartisan collaboration might be possible, Dunne recurred to the issue in 1860, giving notice of a motion to differentiate the income tax geographically and proposing to set the rate 1d. lower in Ireland than in Britain.[28]

Though nothing came of Dunne's motion, Irish allegations of overtaxation revived in July, when Gladstone introduced a supplemental budget that raised spirit duties throughout the United Kingdom.[29] Not only did Irish retailers and distillers mobilise against what they rightly regarded as a deterrent to domestic spirit consumption but the nationalist press also began to comment adversely on Irish public finance.[30] In December, prominent members of the National Petition Committee, which was seeking to resuscitate the agitation for the repeal of the Union, took the matter up at an aggregate meeting in Dublin. William J. O'Neill Daunt, a veteran of the earlier O'Connellite campaigns, dwelt upon Irish financial exploitation at some length on the occasion, with other speakers also alluding to Ireland's fiscal grievances.[31] The following year Daunt briefly withheld payment of the income tax, penning 'a strong remonstrance to Gladstone' that publicised his action.[32]

If Daunt hoped to inspire a tax protest, he was to be disappointed, as none materialised. But the nationalist press continued to run strident editorials on Irish public finance, and Irish Conservatives returned to the attack in Parliament when Gladstone's 1861 budget failed to make concessions to Irish interests.[33] Irish support for Gladstonian finance reached its nadir in that year, when only fifteen Irish MPs voted in favour of the Chancellor's controversial plan to repeal the paper duties.[34] Though the alterations proposed in the 1862 budget were too modest to provoke Irish Conservative opposition, nationalist criticism showed little sign of abating, with William Smith O'Brien enumerating Irish fiscal grievances in a set of 'Resolutions' published in May.[35]

The persistence of Irish complaints about taxation between 1860 and 1862 revealed a reservoir of discontent that transcended traditional political affiliations. Yet disaffected elites lacked a clearly articulated agenda and an organisational vehicle that might focus opinion, mobilise the public, and harmonise the efforts of Irish Conservatives with those of popular politicians. Crucial leadership in these matters was provided from the middle of 1862 by the Conservative proprietor of the *Waterford Mail*, Joseph Fisher.[36] A paternalistic Protestant who regarded prosperity as an antidote to nationalism, Fisher's preoccupation with economic development situated him within a Patriot political tradition that dated back to the eighteenth century.[37] It also provided him with an ideological connection to Dunne, which was reinforced by their shared conception of the Union as a contract between two equal kingdoms, whose terms could not be altered without Irish consent.[38]

Despite an avowed interest in Irish finance, Fisher devoted little attention to tax reform in the early 1860s. This changed in 1862, when he authored a series of eight public letters to the Lord Lieutenant of Ireland, originally issued in instalments and subsequently collected in *How Ireland may be Saved*. Fisher's concern in these letters was broadly economic rather than specifically fiscal. But his final letter offered a slashing partisan attack on Gladstonian financial policy, pointing out that Irish taxation had risen more rapidly than British taxation over two decades, and maintaining that recent tax increases had siphoned capital from Ireland which would otherwise have been available for investment and employment. This observation led Fisher to the damaging though simplistic conclusion that Liberal finance had helped to precipitate the agricultural depression. Claiming, inaccurately, that the Act of Union protected Ireland against indiscriminate taxation, he demanded the repeal of the income tax and a reduction of the spirit duty 'to the scale levied in 1852'. Ireland should also be compensated for its excess tax burden, he insisted, through increased expenditure on 'local improvements'.[39] Though the letter had the merit of being clearly argued, it said little that was entirely new. What distinguished Fisher from other aspirant tax reformers was the energy with which he promoted his views during the autumn and winter of 1862–63.[40] His efforts attracted the favourable attention of the nationalist press, and Daunt endorsed his endeavours in the new year, signalling the possibility of cooperation between popular politicians and Irish Conservatives at grassroots level.[41]

By this time, Fisher was pivoting from a press campaign to a political agitation. In November 1862 he seized upon a suggestion, initially made in the *Dublin Morning News*, that Ireland's 'representative' bodies ought to 'rouse public opinion against' over-taxation.[42] Early in 1863 Fisher sought to interest the Waterford Town Council and Chamber of Commerce in the subject, with little success.[43] He found a more receptive audience when he took his case to the Waterford Poor Law Union in the company of one of Waterford City's MPs, John Blake, a member of the IIP who had proven amenable to Conservative approaches since 1859.[44] Appealing to the board of guardians at their 'usual weekly meeting' on 4 February, Fisher revealed that Colonel Dunne had recently 'urged' him to 'induce the boards of guardians to express, by petitions, their opinions on' Irish taxation.[45] He came prepared with a petition for the consideration of the guardians, which called attention to Ireland's 'very oppressive' taxation, complained 'that, in the expenditure of the income of the empire, Ireland does not participate to an extent at all equal to the proportion which she contributes', and asked the Commons to 'afford ... such relief as your honourable House may in its wisdom consider just and reasonable'.[46] Not only did the Waterford guardians adopt the petition but they also agreed to circularise Ireland's other Poor Law Unions, encouraging guardians throughout the country to join the nascent campaign for tax relief.[47]

By May, no less than thirty-eight of Ireland's 163 Poor Law Unions had endorsed the prayer of the Waterford petition.[48] The Unions were the only local government bodies in rural Ireland to include an elective element at mid-century, with half of the guardians chosen on a ratepayer franchise and the remainder appointed ex officio from amongst the resident justices of the peace.[49] Because even the elected guardians had to meet a property qualification in order to serve, the boards were composed of a local elite and reflected the upper echelons of the provincial social hierarchy, including landowners, professionals, businessmen, and large farmers.[50] The petitions, then, expressed the opinion of an important stratum of Irish society and emanated from bodies that could claim a representative character by contemporary standards.

The receptivity of the boards of guardians to Fisher's appeal is partially explicable in material terms. The amount of poor rate collected in Ireland, which fell steadily from 1852 to 1860, rose by some 42 per cent between 1860 and 1863, driven primarily by mounting relief costs during the agricultural depression.[51] The anxieties of the rural and provincial middle class, squeezed by a combination of falling income and rising local taxation, seem to have provided the impetus for the petitioning drive. Fisher's attempt to engage the support of the grand juries, which were appointive bodies dominated by landowners, enjoyed less success, with only five of Ireland's forty-one grand juries approving petitions.[52] When the effective rate of local taxation paid by the petitioning Unions is examined, however, it becomes clear that geography and politicisation were also important elements in the decision to petition. Of the thirty-nine Unions that adopted a petition for tax relief, twenty-two paid rates higher than the national average, two paid rates at the national average, and fifteen paid comparatively low rates.[53] The correlation between the level of local taxation and the decision to petition was, therefore, relatively weak. The connection between geography and participation in the petitioning movement, by contrast, was strong (see Map 9.1). The majority of petitions originated in a band stretching from south Leinster through north Munster, where twenty-three contiguous Unions between Gorey, Enniscorthy, and Wexford in the east and Ennistymon and Kilrush in the west approved petitions. Their efforts were supplemented by a cluster of seven Unions in western Connacht, extending north from Galway to West Dromore. The heart of the campaign roughly corresponded to an area that had been reluctant to levy poor rate in the early 1840s and had experienced increased politicisation since the Famine, beginning with the tenant right movement of the early 1850s.[54]

What began as a provincial agitation also secured metropolitan support. From its earliest stages Fisher's campaign attracted the attention of John Blake Dillon, who was planning a return to public life after some fifteen years in the political wilderness.[56] When a seat in the Dublin Town Council for Wood Quay Ward opened in February, Dillon emerged as the popular candidate, highlighting Ireland's fiscal grievances and alluding sympathetically to Fisher's activities in a speech accepting the nomination.[57] Some two months after his election, as noted above, Dillon secured unanimous support for a municipal committee of inquiry into the Anglo-Irish financial relationship. Though Dublin Corporation's circumstances were different from those of the provincial Poor Law Unions, the town council had pressing financial concerns of its own. These related less to the agricultural depression than to the city's chronically straitened finances, which posed a serious obstacle to municipal improvement despite 'steeply rising levels of rates' in the 1860s.[58] The corporation responded to these challenges by repeatedly seeking assistance from the central government in the 1850s and early 1860s, but without success.[59] Dublin Corporation's decision to take up the subject of taxation, consequently, reflected its ongoing

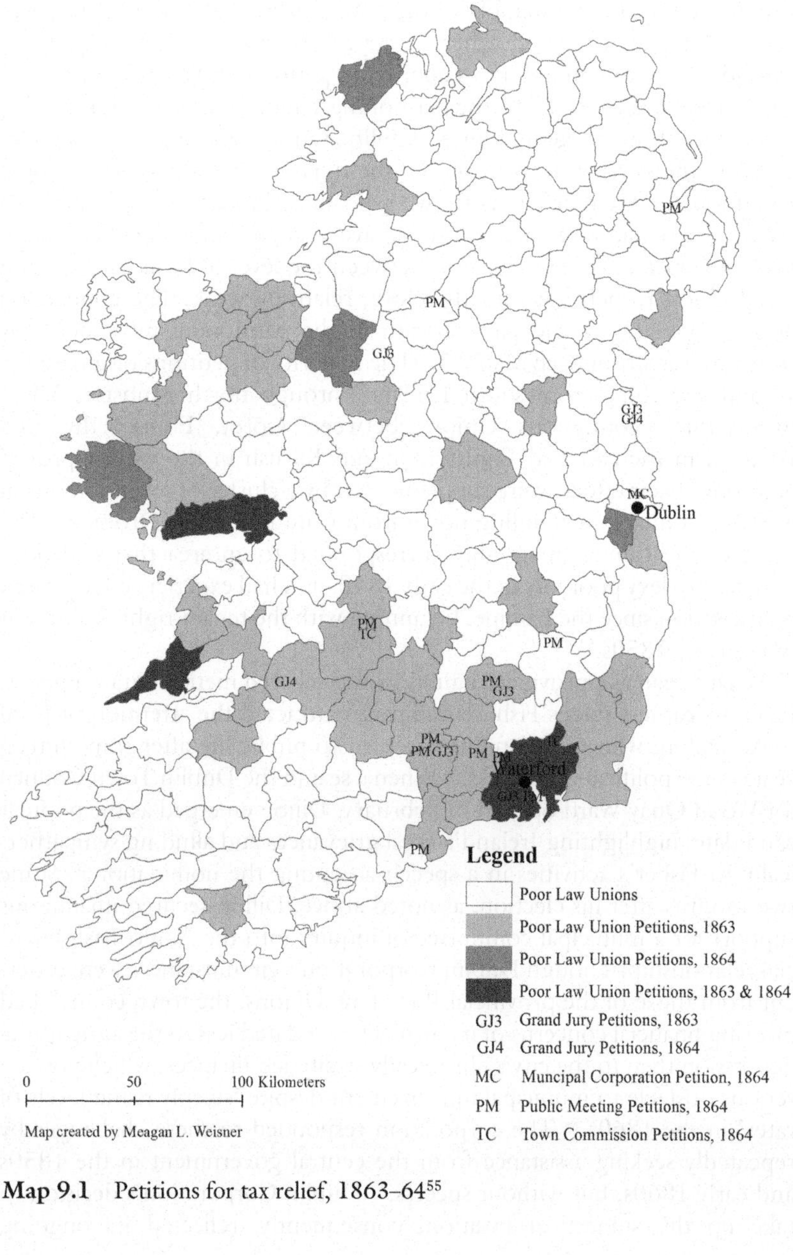

Map 9.1 Petitions for tax relief, 1863–64[55]

frustrations with the Treasury. It provided the highest profile endorsement of Fisher's cause, attracting widespread press coverage and inspiring Limerick Corporation to authorise a similar inquiry.[60] Finally, the episode paid dividends for Dillon personally, signalling his return to national prominence and helping him to secure election as an alderman in July.[61]

Despite its success in Ireland, the parliamentary influence of the agitation was limited. The campaign may have stiffened the resistance of Irish independents and Conservatives when, in February, Gladstone proposed to lower the import duty on manufactured tobacco. Irish critics of Gladstonian finance scored a rare victory on this occasion, with the Chancellor eventually conceding an altered duty that Irish tobacco manufacturers regarded as satisfactory.[62] The petitioning movement probably helped to shape the Irish provisions of the 1863 budget, as Gladstone considered but set aside plans for either an extension of the British tax on railway receipts to Ireland, or a revaluation of Irish property for the purpose of raising the assessment of taxable income.[63] When the Chancellor finally introduced his budget in April, moreover, he spoke sympathetically of Irish distress, and offered a reduction of the rate of income tax to 2.9 per cent throughout the United Kingdom. At the same time, however, Gladstone refused to consider a remission of the spirit duty, and he proposed a new legacy duty on Irish charitable bequests.[64] The limits of extra-parliamentary pressure were starkly revealed in June, when Dunne moved for a committee of inquiry into the causes of the agricultural depression and the effects of Irish taxation, in what was clearly an attempt to link the two. While indicating some support for state-assisted Irish economic development in the form of public loans, Gladstone rejected the suggestion that fiscal policy be differentiated according to geography and opposed the request for a committee. Following a brief debate in a thin House, Dunne withdrew his motion.[65]

This reverse scarcely deterred activists in Ireland, where the tax protest continued during the parliamentary recess. At the end of October, the Dublin Corporation unanimously endorsed the findings of its municipal committee of inquiry, which concluded that Irish taxation was 'excessive' and that a substantial proportion of Irish revenue was 'expended in England, or elsewhere, out of Ireland'. The report, composed by Dillon, recommended that the corporation invite 'other representative bodies throughout Ireland' to press for 'a diminution of existing taxation' and for 'the expenditure, on works of public improvement in Ireland, of a fair portion of those taxes which are now annually remitted to England'.[66] Fisher and his allies responded to Dillon's appeal by organising a public meeting at Waterford in December, which deputed a committee to draft a petition in favour of tax relief.[67] By late January 1864, this body had evolved into a more ambitious organisation, the Association for the Reduction of the Taxation of Ireland, which established several branches in southern towns over the next two months. Fisher played a key role in launching the new initiative, but local civic elites also gave it crucial support.[68] The association, in turn, provided the impetus for a renewed appeal to Parliament, with no less than twenty-four petitions for tax relief and increased central government expenditure adopted in Ireland between February and July.[69] The petitions emanated from a more diverse array of bodies than in the preceding year, with eleven approved by public meetings, eight by Poor Law boards, two by grand juries, two by town commissions, and one by Dublin Corporation. But the movement largely conformed to the geographical profile of the agitation that had been evident previously, with eighteen of the petitions originating in the regions of south Leinster, north Munster, and Connacht that had been active in 1863 (see Map 9.1).

Senior British politicians, confronting a campaign that showed little sign of abating, finally embraced a more active approach to the tax protest in 1864. Gladstone took the initiative in January after reading Dillon's report, which he believed to be 'full of errors, misapprehensions, & false assumptions'.[70] At the Chancellor's instigation, the Irish executive retained William Neilson Hancock, the prominent Irish political economist, to provide an anodyne analysis of Irish public finance.[71] Hancock's report, which was delivered to Dublin Castle in March, detailed the exemptions and abatements that Irish taxpayers had enjoyed since the Union, and emphasised that surviving exceptions—by disproportionately benefitting 'the wealthier classes'—gave a particularly regressive character to the Irish tax code. Hancock calculated that Ireland paid less than its fair share to the Treasury, even when estimates of Irish tax transfers were included in the account, and noted that local authorities in Ireland received more generous subsidies from central government than those in Britain for expenses relating to police and education. 'In the financial dealing between Great Britain and Ireland', the report concluded, 'no injustice has been done to Ireland, and … no claim exists on her part … for exemption from that equal taxation with Great Britain which is provided for by the Act of Union.'[72]

The administration also sought to redirect Irish agitation into parliamentary channels by conceding a select committee on Irish taxation when

Dunne renewed his motion in February.[73] The committee was favourably composed for Dunne's purposes, with eight of the fifteen members selected from Irish constituencies, including no less than four Conservative MPs who had previously criticised Liberal fiscal policy.[74] The government was represented by Sir Robert Peel, third baronet, the irascible Chief Secretary for Ireland; but fiscal expertise was provided by Sir Stafford Northcote, who had served as Gladstone's private secretary in the 1840s and had established his reputation as a financier with the publication of *Twenty Years of Financial Policy* in 1862. Northcote sat as a Conservative, but he could be counted on as a reliable exponent of fiscal orthodoxy.[75]

Under Dunne's auspices, the committee worked deliberately over the course of the session, meeting on nineteen occasions between March and July. Dillon, Fisher, and other proponents of Irish tax reform provided evidence, rehearsing a now familiar critique of Irish public finance which drew upon historical, political-economic, and moral arguments in an attempt to demonstrate that Ireland was overtaxed. The witnesses maintained that the initial Irish contribution to UK expenditure, established in 1800, had been set too high, resulting in the rapid escalation of taxation and debt in the early years of the Union.[76] This development, in turn, had necessitated the amalgamation of the British and Irish Exchequers in 1817, which left Ireland vulnerable to indiscriminate taxation and subject to a fiscal policy that was better suited to British than Irish economic circumstances.[77] In particular, the repeal of the Corn Laws in 1846, followed by steep increases in Irish taxation from 1853, resulted in falling land values and the impoverishing removal of capital from the country as a result of substantial tax transfers to Britain.[78] Equal taxation was unfair, the witnesses argued, in part because it contravened the Act of Union, which required Parliament to consider Irish circumstances in raising the revenue, and in part because it had a differential impact.[79] On the one hand, expenditure of the revenue raised in Ireland disproportionately benefitted Britain, with its much larger bureaucratic and military establishments.[80] On the other hand, Ireland's relative poverty made the Irish tax burden effectively heavier.[81] A more equitable Irish fiscal policy, the witnesses suggested, would entail some combination of tax remissions and increased central government expenditure in the form of public works, enlarged establishments, and more liberal access to public loans for private parties who wished to undertake agricultural improvements.[82] Dunne's draft report, submitted after the committee's hearings concluded, adroitly summarised the case for a reform of Irish public finance.[83]

Despite providing a high profile forum for critics of Gladstonian finance, the Dunne committee proved to be something of a damp squib. The Chancellor did his part to curb its appeal when he introduced his budget in April, perhaps disingenuously citing Irish complaints about over-taxation while proposing a further reduction of the income tax to 2.5 per cent.[84] The committee, moreover, failed to provide the type of clarity that tax reformers had anticipated. In the course of its hearings Fisher's credibility was damaged by his tendency, exposed under hostile questioning, to shape the historical and statistical record for polemical purposes.[85] Even after all of the witnesses had been called and a mass of financial data had been aggregated, members of the committee found agreement on policy to be elusive, as five reports were submitted for consideration and none was adopted. Pleading 'the lateness ... of the Session' for their inability to frame an acceptable report, the committee members asked to be reappointed the following year.[86] Though tax reformers were eager to claim victory as the committee completed its labours, this was a disappointing conclusion to some two years of agitation.[87]

The government, moreover, launched a counter-attack during the parliamentary recess, finally releasing Hancock's report in October. Its publication provided intellectual ballast to an Irish Liberal press that remained sceptical about Conservative and nationalist allegations of over-taxation.[88] By November, the formerly effusive Fisher was lamenting that the taxation committee's blue book was 'a bulky volume, and we fear many will either fling it aside, or rise from its perusal, tired of the subject'.[89] Dunne, too, privately bemoaned 'the apathy of all classes on the subject'.[90] Though Daunt sought to keep the flagging cause alive in nationalist circles, more nimble politicians began to seek out other causes.[91] Dillon, in particular, pivoted away from the campaign for tax relief, forming an alliance with Archbishop Cullen and making preparations to launch the National Association. Tenant right, disestablishment of the Church of Ireland, and denominational education would be the central issues in their new departure.[92] The Association for the Reduction of the Taxation of Ireland was nearly moribund by the end of the year, and activists failed to renew the petitioning drive.[93]

The Dunne committee's efforts, however, revealed one area of agreement between tax reformers and British policymakers, in the form of public loans for Irish economic development. Gladstone had alluded positively to such advances in June 1863, and Northcote indicated support for an expansion of 'improvement' loans in the draft report that he submitted to the committee the following year.[94] Peel seized on Northcote's recommendation in a November speech to the Royal Dublin Society, and within weeks Gladstone found himself pressed on the matter by the Prime Minister, Home Secretary, and Lord Lieutenant.[95] For once, supplicants to the Treasury were pushing at an open door, as the Chancellor professed himself 'friendly to ... advances for Ireland ... at low rates of interest'.[96] After Parliament reconvened in February 1865, Gladstone publicly reiterated his favourable opinion of improvement loans.[97] Northcote, taking his cue from the Chancellor, ensured that the taxation committee was instructed to consider 'advances ... for drainage and other works of public utility in Ireland' upon its reappointment in March.[98]

Dunne found himself outmanoeuvred by Northcote when the committee resumed its hearings in the spring, as the emphasis of its deliberations shifted from taxation to expenditure. The government, meanwhile, continued to adjust its approach to Irish finance. The centrepiece of Gladstone's April budget—yet another reduction of the rate of income tax, this time to 1.7 per cent, the lowest level since its reinstatement in 1842—could be seen to go some way towards meeting a central demand of Irish tax reformers.[99] Though the Chancellor did not allude to Irish considerations when announcing the remission, the *Freeman's Journal* conceded that his financial plan 'gave great satisfaction'.[100] Less than a week later, the administration began to address the matter of Irish public expenditure, introducing a bill to facilitate drainage loans in Ireland.[101]

The ministry's legislation anticipated the taxation committee's majority report, issued in June and framed by Northcote over Dunne's objections. Northcote's report was, in many respects, a model of even-handed analysis. It conceded that the initial Irish contribution to UK expenditure, established by the Act of Union, had been set too high, but echoed Hancock's findings in its insistence that Ireland had been 'favoured' in fiscal matters since 1817. The report admitted that Irish 'complaints' about taxation were 'not surprising' given 'the large increase ... in ... general taxation between 1852 and 1862', but denied that the agricultural depression had been caused by 'the pressure of taxation', attributing it instead 'to the extremely unfavourable character of the seasons'. Northcote decisively rejected proposals for a tax policy differentiated according to geography, but endorsed other forms of financial assistance. Specifically, the report recommended that Irish Poor Law Unions receive central government grants to defray certain workhouse expenses that were already charged to the consolidated fund in England, and suggested that 'extensive proprietors be allowed [additional] advances for land improvement, drainage, and labourers' cottages'.[102]

None of these concessions mollified the most committed of the tax reformers.[103] But with the return of more favourable weather finally bringing an end to the agricultural depression, most politicians were eager to move on. Though Fisher and the Association for the Reduction of the Taxation of Ireland attempted to make over-taxation a central issue at the July general election, public finance played only a minor role in the campaign.[104] Irish Conservatives generally fought shy of the subject, to Fisher's disappointment.[105] Dillon, who secured a seat for County Tipperary, exploited fiscal grievances for electoral purposes, but when he convened a meeting of Irish Liberal MPs under the auspices of the National Association in December Irish finance was omitted from the programme.[106] Fisher belatedly recognised that Dillon had abandoned the cause, lamenting that his quondam ally was 'paving the way to support the present Government'.[107] Indeed, during the 1866 session Dillon pursued a rapprochement with the British Liberal Party—a project that was sustained by others after his untimely death.[108] Acquiescence in Gladstonian finance was the price of the Liberal alliance.

Consequences, 1865–1905

The substantive fiscal achievements of the campaign against over-taxation were modest. The movement had only a limited impact on the tax code, with successive remissions of income tax between 1863 and 1865 owing less to Irish agitation than to Gladstone's ambivalence about the levy and to Britain's rising prosperity.[109] The Chancellor refused to reduce the spirit duty—a more significant source of Irish revenue—though successive rate increases between 1858 and 1860 contributed to a steep decline in Irish spirit production.[110] Tax protesters, however, probably deserve some credit for forestalling the additional Irish tax increases considered by Gladstone in 1863. Thereafter, the Chancellor tacitly accepted the remaining Irish abatements and exemptions.

Where expenditure was concerned, the results of the agitation were similarly mixed. Unfortunately, the mid-Victorian state made no systematic attempt to track the geographic distribution of government spending in its annual finance accounts. But estimates made in the 1890s suggest that Irish civil expenditure, exclusive of loans, rose by perhaps 28 per cent between 1859 and 1869, while British civil spending grew by some 20 per cent over the same decade.[111] Irish pressure played a role in extracting some of this additional money from the Treasury—in 1866 the Derby ministry agreed to meet certain Irish workhouse expenses from the consolidated fund, as recommended by the Northcote report the previous year.[112] The influence of the tax protest on broader spending patterns, however, is impossible to determine. It afforded a mild stimulus to the provision of advances for agricultural improvements, as legislation enacted in 1865–66 eased the terms on which landlords could obtain public loans and increased the total sum available to borrow. Between 1865 and 1869, the Commissioners of Public Works in Ireland more than doubled the amount annually issued for drainage, irrigation, fencing, and the construction of farm buildings; but the sums lent (under £127,000 in 1869) remained small.[113]

In the final analysis, the campaign against over-taxation failed to effect dramatic changes in the Anglo-Irish financial relationship. As noted in the introduction to this chapter, moreover, economic historians have found the central claims made by its leading figures to be unpersuasive. Yet the political and intellectual inadequacies of the movement should not be allowed to obscure the fact that the dispute over public finance was grounded in substantive disagreements over fiscal policy. Most mid-Victorian British politicians, with Gladstone to the fore, embraced a programme of 'sound' finance, entailing low levels of taxation and expenditure, free trade, balanced budgets, and the maintenance of a tax code that did not explicitly favour special interests, social classes, or regions within the United Kingdom.[114] Many Irish Liberals also subscribed to these precepts into the 1860s.[115] Proponents of 'sound' finance wished to establish a minimal and apparently neutral state, which would be insulated from accusations that it selected 'winners' and 'losers' by manipulating markets or redistributing wealth. The intent of the policymakers who championed 'sound' finance was as much political as economic: a state perceived by taxpayers to be fair in fiscal matters was also likely to be regarded as legitimate.[116] The Irish activists who agitated for tax reform, in contrast, endorsed a proto-Keynesian fiscal policy for Ireland, involving light taxation and heavy public spending—with the deficit to be made up by the largesse of British taxpayers. The criticisms of Corn Law repeal levelled by leading tax protesters, and the recommendations they offered for additional public works projects, enlarged establishments, and improvement loans, indicated a preference for an active state that would play a managerial role in the Irish economy.

This alternative conception of public finance reflected an acute awareness of the disparate economic circumstances obtaining on the two islands. Sir Edward Grogan, Conservative MP for Dublin City, called attention to the differences in 1864 when he remarked on the 'striking and ... painful contrast between the condition of England and Ireland' during a parliamentary debate on Irish taxation. 'In England', Grogan observed 'there was no end to the accumulation of wealth and the development of prosperity. Let them cross the Channel, however, and all was changed.'[117] For the tax reformers, a suitably amended system of public finance might serve as a means to address Irish poverty and underdevelopment. This view was conveyed, for example, in testimony given to the taxation committee by John Francis Maguire, a leading member of the IIP, who insisted that Ireland was entitled to 'exceptional treatment' in fiscal matters after having been 'neglected and abandoned' by Britain.[118] Robert Longfield, an Irish Conservative MP, reiterated the point during the hearings, reasoning analogically from the case of 'a proprietor in relation to his tenantry'. If 'the improvement of the country is to be effected by lightening the people's burdens and developing their capability for labour', he suggested, then it followed that 'the improvement of a population by the State may be done in the same way.'[119]

Proposals for a geographically differentiated system of public finance, however, raised fundamental questions about the nature of the Union itself. On the one hand, as Daunt perceptively recognised, the adherents of 'sound' finance sought to treat Ireland 'as if she was as integral a part of Great Britain as Dorsetshire'.[120] On the other hand, both nationalist and Conservative advocates of tax reform insisted upon Irish distinctiveness. Dunne encapsulated their position in a letter sent to Daunt after his committee concluded its labours: 'I never could assent to the proposition that Ireland was or ought to become an integral part of Great Britain and I have ever repudiated the name of "West Briton" which some Irishmen affect to adopt.' 'The nationality of Ireland', Dunne admitted, 'was in my committee as much the subject of differences as that of financial calculations.'[121] Divergent attitudes to tax reform were intimately related to discrepant understandings of Ireland's status within the United Kingdom. Unfortunately for the proponents of 'sound' finance, a fiscal policy intended to buttress the Union through the identical treatment of its constituent parts was unable to redress the regional economic inequalities that helped to foster a separate Irish identity. Indeed, because nationalists and some Irish Conservatives associated fiscal orthodoxy with Irish poverty, the refusal to reform Irish public finance undermined the legitimacy of the state and strengthened the case for a readjustment or repeal of the Union.[122]

Viewed in this light, the Irish campaign against over-taxation appears not as a historical blind alley but as one of the winding roads that led towards home rule. The most prominent figures in the earlier agitation all took part in the later movement, with Daunt formally proposing the establishment of the Home Government Association in 1870, Fisher resurfacing as a member of the organisation's 'Provisional Committee' that same year, and both Fisher and Dunne running unsuccessfully as home rule candidates at the general election of 1874.[123] Many of the actors in the little drama of 1863–65 reprised their roles on a larger stage a decade later, when Daunt chaired an inquiry into Anglo-Irish financial relations under the auspices of the Home Government Association.[124] Allegations of over-taxation continued to serve a number of useful political functions from the perspective of leading home rulers over the course of the next three decades: they provided a cause around which the nationalist and Conservative wings of the nascent home rule movement could coalesce in the 1870s; they supplied a complaint that could not be redressed by Gladstonian liberalism, which was to prove itself less amenable to financial than to constitutional, religious, and land reform between 1869 and 1894; and they could be used to prise money from the Treasury during the Conservative ministries of 1885, 1886–92, and 1895–1905. In the long run, therefore, the grievances that stimulated the campaign against over-taxation were subsumed by the home rule movement, with enduring consequences for late Victorian and Edwardian politics.

Notes

1. *Freeman's Journal* (hereafter *FJ*), 22 Apr. 1863, in Larcom Papers, National Library of Ireland (hereafter NLI) MS 7786.
2. *Irish Times*, 22 Apr. 1863; *Nation*, 25 Apr. 1863, in Larcom Papers, NLI MS 7786.
3. Thomas Kennedy, *A History of the Irish Protest against Over-Taxation, from 1853 to 1897* (Dublin: Hodges, Figgis, and Co., 1897), ix–x.
4. W. E. Vaughan, 'Ireland c. 1870', in *A New History of Ireland*, vol. 5: *Ireland under the Union, I: 1801–70*, ed. W. E. Vaughan (Oxford: Oxford University Press, 1989), 787–88.

5. David S. Johnson and Liam Kennedy, 'Nationalist Historiography and the Decline of the Irish Economy: George O'Brien Revisited', in *Ireland's Histories: Aspects of State, Society and Ideology*, ed. Seán Hutton and Paul Stewart (London: Routledge, 1991), 19; Liam Kennedy and David S. Johnson, 'The Union of Ireland and Britain, 1801–1921', in *The Making of Modern Irish History: Revisionism and the Revisionist Controversy*, ed. D. George Boyce and Alan O'Day (London: Routledge, 1996), 44, 46–48.
6. Two recent accounts have briefly examined the high politics of the movement; see Pauric Travers, 'The Financial Relations Question, 1800–1914', in *Ireland, England and Australia: Essays in Honour of Oliver MacDonagh*, ed. F. B. Smith (Canberra: Australian National University, 1990), 43; K. Theodore Hoppen, *Governing Hibernia: British Politicians and Ireland, 1800–1921* (Oxford: Oxford University Press, 2016), 160–62.
7. Martin Daunton, *Trusting Leviathan: The Politics of Taxation in Britain, 1799–1914* (Cambridge: Cambridge University Press, 2001), 12–22; Isaac William Martin, Ajay K. Mehrotra, and Monica Prasad, 'The Thunder of History: The Origins and Development of the New Fiscal Sociology', in *The New Fiscal Sociology: Taxation in Comparative and Historical Prospective*, ed. Isaac William Martin, Ajay K. Mehrotra, and Monica Prasad (Cambridge: Cambridge University Press, 2009), 18–19.
8. Article seven is reprinted in House of Commons, 'Report from the Select Committee on Taxation of Ireland', *Sessional Papers, 1864* (513), vol. 15, pp. 9–11; see also Trevor McCavery, 'Politics, Public Finance and the British-Irish Act of Union of 1801', *Transactions of the Royal Historical Society*, 6th ser., 10 (2000): 354–59.
9. McCavery, 'Politics', 373–74; Douglas Kanter, 'The Politics of Irish Taxation, 1842–53', *English Historical Review* 127, no. 528 (2012): 1124–25; Hoppen, *Governing Hibernia*, 38–40.
10. R. B. McDowell, *The Irish Administration, 1801–1914* (London: Routledge and Kegan Paul, 1964), 87–92.
11. Earl of Dunraven, *The Finances of Ireland before the Union and after: An Historical Study* (London: John Murray, 1912), 82.
12. House of Commons, 'Finance Accounts ... of the United Kingdom', *Sessional Papers, 1852–53* (275), vol. 57, pp. 12, 36, 41.
13. *Report of the Commissioners of Inland Revenue on the Duties under their Management*, C. 82 (1870), vol. 20, p. 226.
14. Except where noted, this paragraph is based upon Kanter, 'Irish Taxation', 1140–48.
15. *Inland Revenue ... Vol. II*, C. 82–1 (1870), vol. 20, p. 568. The rate was graduated between 1854 and 1863; the higher rate is provided here and

throughout. Some Irish income taxpayers, however, enjoyed a lower effective rate than their British counterparts, due to differences in the method of assessment; see Kanter, 'Irish Taxation', 1152–53.

16. *Inland Revenue*, 226.
17. House of Commons, 'Finance Accounts ... of the United Kingdom', *Sessional Papers, 1861* (326), vol. 34, pp. 10, 24–25.
18. Ibid., *Sessional Papers, 1852–53* (275), vol. 57, p. 12, *Sessional Papers, 1861* (326), vol. 34, p. 10.
19. Douglas Kanter, 'The Galway Packet-Boat Contract and the Politics of Public Expenditure in Mid-Victorian Ireland', *Historical Journal* 59, no. 3 (2016): 766.
20. On post-Famine prosperity, see R. V. Comerford, 'Ireland, 1850–70: Post-Famine and Mid-Victorian', in *New History*, ed. Vaughan, 374–82.
21. James S. Donnelly Jr., 'The Irish Agricultural Depression of 1859–64', *Irish Economic and Social History* 3 (1976): 33–54.
22. W. E. Vaughan, *Landlords and Tenants in Mid-Victorian Ireland* (Oxford: Clarendon Press, 1994), 230; *Emigration Statistics of Ireland*, C. 1700 (1877), vol. 85, p. 646; *Annual Report of the Commissioners for Administering the Laws for Relief of the Poor in Ireland*, No. 3668 (1866), vol. 36, p. 12.
23. *Hansard Parliamentary Debates*, 3rd ser., vol. 149, cols. 1743–48 (26 Apr. 1858), vol. 154, cols. 836–37 (7 July 1859), 1419 (18 July 1859); *Cork Examiner*, 30 June 1858; *Nation*, 10 Sept. 1859, 15 Oct. 1859.
24. *Hansard*, 3rd ser., vol. 156, cols. 852 (10 Feb. 1860), 1514–15, 1521 (21 Feb. 1860), 1991 (28 Feb. 1860), 2185 (2 Mar. 1860).
25. *Debt and Taxation of Ireland (Reprinted from the 'Irish Quarterly Review', for January, 1860)* (Dublin: W. B. Kelly, 1860), 21–25, 31.
26. *Hansard*, 3rd ser., vol. 157, cols. 1661–64 (30 Mar. 1860).
27. On Dunne, see Stephen Ball, 'Dunne, Francis Plunket (1802–1874)', in *The History of Parliament: The House of Commons, 1832–68; Online Preview*, ed. Philip Salmon, http://www.historyofparliamentonline.org/volume/1832-1868/member/dunne-francis-plunket-1802-1874 (accessed 27 Mar. 2018).
28. *Hansard*, 3rd ser., vol. 157, col. 1470 (28 Mar. 1860).
29. Ibid., vol. 159, cols. 1971–73 (16 July 1860).
30. *FJ*, 18 July 1860, 20 July 1860, 7 Mar. 1861; *Nation*, 28 July 1860, 1 Sept. 1860.
31. *Nation*, 8 Dec. 1860.
32. W. J. O'Neill Daunt, journal for 15 Jan. 1861, 25 Feb. 1861, O'Neill Daunt Journals, NLI MS 3041, ff. 672–73; *Cork Examiner*, 28 Jan. 1861.

33. *Nation*, 30 Mar. 1861, 7 Sept. 1861; *Hansard*, 3rd ser., vol. 162, cols. 1119–20 (25 Apr. 1861), 1423–26 (2 May 1861), 2043 (13 May 1861).
34. Kanter, 'Packet-Boat Contract', 767–68.
35. *Nation*, 24 May 1862.
36. On Fisher, see Richard S. Harrison, *A Biographical Dictionary of Irish Quakers*, 2nd ed. (Dublin: Four Courts Press, 2008), 89; Don Lehane, 'History of Kinsalebeg: Fishers of Pilltown', http://kinsalebeg.com/chapters/fishers/fishers.html (accessed 18 July 2017).
37. *Waterford Mail* (hereafter *WM*), 20 July 1853, 22 June 1863; A. P. W. Malcomson, *John Foster (1740–1828): The Politics of Improvement and Prosperity* (Dublin: Four Courts Press, 2011), xvi, 45, 383; Andrew Shields, 'Irish Conservatives, the "Patriot" Tradition and the Act of Union, c. 1829–69', in *Culture and Society in Ireland since 1750: Essays in Honour of Gearóid Ó Tuathaigh*, ed. John Cunningham and Niall Ó Ciosáin (Dublin: Lilliput Press, 2015), 144–59.
38. *WM*, 5 Jan. 1863; F. P. Dunne to Daunt, 30 May 1870, O'Neill Daunt Papers, NLI MS 8045/4.
39. Joseph Fisher, *How Ireland may be Saved* (London: Ridgway, 1862), 83–87, 95.
40. *WM*, 10 Sept. 1862, 27 Oct. 1862, 7 Nov. 1862, 14 Nov. 1862, 21 Nov. 1862, 31 Dec. 1862; Joseph Fisher, *The Case of Ireland* (London: Ridgway, 1863).
41. *Nation*, 8 Nov. 1862, 15 Nov. 1862, 22 Nov. 1862; *FJ*, 11 Nov. 1862, 30 Dec. 1862; *WM*, 21 Jan. 1863.
42. *WM*, 19 Nov. 1862.
43. Ibid., 2 Jan. 1863, 7 Jan. 1863, 27 Mar. 1863.
44. On Blake, see K. Theodore Hoppen, 'Tories, Catholics, and the General Election of 1859', *Historical Journal* 13, no. 1 (1970): 56, 65, 67.
45. *WM*, 6 Feb. 1863.
46. *Reports of the Select Committee of the House of Commons on Public Petitions, Session 1863*, app. 46.
47. *WM*, 6 Feb. 1863.
48. *Public Petitions, Session 1863*, index, xlviii, identifies twenty-nine petitioning Unions; for the remainder, see *WM*, 18 Feb. 1863, 23 Feb. 1863; *Clare Journal*, 19 Feb. 1863; *Cork Examiner*, 20 Feb. 1863; *Nation*, 28 Feb. 1863; *FJ*, 3 Mar. 1863; *Londonderry Standard*, 12 Mar. 1863.
49. William L. Feingold, *The Revolt of the Tenantry: The Transformation of Local Government in Ireland, 1872–1886* (Boston: Northeastern University Press, 1984), 14, 22; Virginia Crossman, *Politics, Pauperism and Power in Late Nineteenth-Century Ireland* (Manchester: Manchester University Press, 2006), 2, 38–40.
50. Feingold, *Revolt of the Tenantry*, 21–22, 24–25, 30–31.

51. *Relief of the Poor in Ireland*, 13.
52. *Public Petitions, Session 1863*, index, xlviii; *WM*, 20 Feb. 1863.
53. Poor rates were assessed and levied locally, so there was not a uniform rate throughout Ireland; for the rates in 1863, see *Annual Report of the Commissioners for Administering the Laws for Relief of the Poor in Ireland*, No. 3338 (1864), vol. 25, pp. 470–78.
54. For resistance to rate in the 1840s, see the chapter by Mel Cousins in this volume; for post-Famine politicisation, see Feingold, *Revolt of the Tenantry*, 70–71, 82.
55. Adapted from I. Gregory and P. Ell, *Irish Poor Law Union and Barony Boundaries, 1841–1871*, https://doi.org/10.5255/UKDA-SN-4999-1 (accessed 5 Jan. 2018).
56. Brendan O'Cathaoir, *John Blake Dillon: Young Irelander* (Dublin: Irish Academic Press, 1990), 145–47.
57. *FJ*, 12 Feb. 1863.
58. Mary E. Daly, *Dublin: The Deposed Capital; An Economic and Social History, 1860–1914* (Cork: Cork University Press, 1985), 227; Stefanie Jones, 'Dublin Reformed: The Transformation of the Municipal Governance of a Victorian City, 1840–1860', 2 vols. (PhD diss., Trinity College Dublin, 2001), 2:288–91.
59. Jones, 'Dublin', 2:323–29.
60. *Financial Wrongs of Ireland: International Taxation; Report to the Corporation of Limerick, from the Special Committee* (Limerick: Munster News Office, 1863).
61. *FJ*, 28 July 1863.
62. *Hansard*, 3rd ser., vol. 169, cols. 329–33 (13 Feb. 1863), 706–14 (23 Feb. 1863), 956–59 (27 Feb. 1863), 980–1001 (2 Mar. 1863), 1114 (5 Mar. 1863), 1208 (6 Mar. 1863), 1608–28 (19 Mar. 1863).
63. William Gladstone, memoranda for [1 Jan. 1863], 12 Mar. 1863, 8 Apr. 1863, in *The Gladstone Diaries*, ed. M. R. D. Foot and H. C. G. Matthew, 14 vols. (Oxford: Clarendon Press, 1968–94), 6:172, 188, 193.
64. *Hansard*, 3rd ser., vol. 170, cols. 207–9, 213–16, 224c–224d, 224j–224m (16 Apr. 1863); *Inland Revenue … Vol. II*, 568. The bequests duty was ultimately abandoned.
65. *Hansard*, 3rd ser., vol. 170, cols. 171, 816–36, 862 (12 June 1863); *FJ*, 16 June 1863.
66. *Report of the Special Committee of the Municipal Council of Dublin on the State of the Public Accounts between Ireland and Great Britain* (Dublin: Joseph Dollard, 1863), 9, 10, 12; *FJ*, 28 Oct. 1863.
67. *WM*, 16 Dec. 1863, 30 Dec. 1863, 11 Jan. 1864,
68. Ibid., 25 Jan. 1864, 27 Jan. 1864, 29 Jan. 1864, 8 Feb. 1864, 15 Feb. 1864, 19 Feb. 1864, 22 Feb. 1864, 18 Mar. 1864. Branches were estab-

lished in Carrick-on-Suir, Clonmel, Kilkenny, Limerick, New Ross, Waterford, and Youghal.

69. *Public Petitions, Session 1864*, index, xli–xliii, identifies twenty-one petitions; for the remainder, see *WM*, 24 Feb. 1864, *FJ*, 4 Mar. 1864, 16 Mar. 1864.
70. Gladstone to the Earl of Carlisle, 7 Jan. 1864, Larcom Papers, NLI MS 7786.
71. Gladstone to Carlisle, 11 Jan. 1864, W. N. Hancock to Sir Thomas Larcom, 19 Jan. 1864, Larcom Papers, NLI MS 7786.
72. W. Neilson Hancock, *Report on the State of Public Accounts between Great Britain and Ireland* (Dublin: Alexander Thom, 1864), 1–13, 26–33, 35, 58.
73. *Hansard*, 3rd ser., vol. 173, cols. 1199–1217 (26 Feb. 1864).
74. Kennedy, *Irish Protest*, 45–47.
75. W. D. Rubinstein, 'Northcote, Stafford Henry, first Earl of Iddesleigh (1818–1897)', in *Oxford Dictionary of National Biography*, ed. H. C. G. Matthew et al., http://www.oxforddnb.com.ezproxy.fau.edu/view/10.1093/ref:odnb/9780198614128.001.0001/odnb-9780198614128-e-20328?rskey=l2bdlV&result=2 (accessed 27 Mar. 2018).
76. Commons, 'Taxation of Ireland', 64–71, 105–24.
77. Ibid., 71, 155.
78. Ibid., 80, 89, 98, 100, 160–61, 163–64, 166, 201, 268–69, 291–93.
79. Ibid., 43–44, 90, 118.
80. Ibid., 98, 204, 218–19, 236–37.
81. Ibid., 166, 206, 268, 290, 295–96.
82. Ibid., 101–2, 179–83, 214, 239, 270, 272.
83. Ibid., 9–17.
84. *Hansard*, 3rd ser., vol. 174, cols. 588–90 (7 Apr. 1864).
85. *Daily Express*, 8 June 1864, in Larcom Papers, NLI MS 7786; Daunt, journal for 14 June 1864, O'Neill Daunt Journals, NLI MS 3041, f. 748.
86. Commons, 'Taxation of Ireland', 3, 32.
87. *WM*, 1 Aug. 1864.
88. *Daily Express*, 11 Oct. 1864; *Northern Whig*, 13 Oct. 1864; *Newry Herald*, 15 Oct. 1864; *Southern Reporter*, 15 Oct. 1864; *Londonderry Standard*, 15 Oct. 1864, all in Larcom Papers, NLI MS 7786.
89. *WM*, 2 Nov. 1864.
90. Dunne to Daunt, 21 Nov. 1864, O'Neill Daunt Papers, NLI MS 8045/4.
91. W. J. O'N. Daunt, *Publications of the Irish National League—No. 3: The Financial Grievances of Ireland* (Dublin: N. Harding, 1864).
92. O'Cathaoir, *Dillon*, 150–54.
93. *WM*, 4 Nov. 1864, 16 Nov. 1864, 30 Nov. 1864, 7 Dec. 1864.

94. Commons, 'Taxation of Ireland', 23.
95. 'Mr. Lane Joynt's Suggestions for the Amendment of the Arterial Drainage Laws', *Journal of the Royal Dublin Society* 4, nos. 32–33 (1865): 381; Lord Wodehouse to Gladstone, 14 Dec. 1864, Lord Palmerston to Gladstone, 20 Dec. 1864, Gladstone Papers, British Library Add. MSS 44224, f. 25, 44273, f. 98.
96. Gladstone to Sir George Grey, 13 Dec. 1864, Kimberley Papers, Bodleian Library MS Eng. c. 4016, f. 114.
97. *Hansard*, 3rd ser., vol. 177, col. 683 (24 Feb. 1865).
98. Ibid., 1027 (2 Mar. 1865).
99. Ibid., vol. 178, col. 1120g (27 Apr. 1865).
100. *FJ*, 28 Apr. 1865.
101. *Hansard*, 3rd ser., vol. 178, cols. 1317 (2 May 1865), 1450 (3 May 1865).
102. House of Commons, 'Report from the Select Committee on the Taxation of Ireland', *Sessional Papers, 1865* (330), vol. 12, pp. 6, 8, 10–11, 13–14.
103. Dunne to Daunt, 24 May 1865, O'Neill Daunt Papers, NLI MS 8045/4.
104. *WM*, 16 June 1865, 23 June 1865, 28 June 1865, 14 July 1865.
105. Ibid., 17 July 1865.
106. *FJ*, 11 July 1865.
107. *WM*, 13 Dec. 1865.
108. R. V. Comerford, *The Fenians in Context: Irish Politics and Society, 1848–82*, 2nd ed. (Dublin: Wolfhound Press, 1998), 142.
109. H. C. G. Matthew, *Gladstone, 1809–1898* (Oxford: Oxford University Press, 1997), 120–28; Daunton, *Trusting Leviathan*, 172–73.
110. Andy Bielenberg, 'The Irish Distilling Industry under the Union', in *Refiguring Ireland: Essays in Honour of L. M. Cullen*, ed. David Dickson and Cormac Ó Grada (Dublin: Lilliput Press, 2003), 296.
111. House of Commons, 'Imperial Revenue (Collection and Expenditure) (Great Britain and Ireland)', *Sessional Papers, 1899* (318), vol. 51, pp. 242, 244.
112. *Hansard*, 3rd ser., vol. 184, col. 822 (16 July 1866).
113. *Report from the Board of Public Works, Ireland*, No. 3676 (1866), vol. 24, p. 463, C. 154 (1870), vol. 17, p. 359.
114. K. Theodore Hoppen, *The Mid-Victorian Generation, 1846–1886* (Oxford: Oxford University Press, 1998), 118; Philip Harling, *The Modern British State: An Historical Introduction* (Cambridge: Polity Press, 2001), 84–85; Kanter, 'Packet-Boat Contract', 760–61.
115. Peter Gray, 'The Making of Mid-Victorian Ireland? Political Economy and the Memory of the Great Famine', in *Victoria's Ireland? Irishness and Britishness, 1837–1901*, ed. Peter Gray (Dublin: Four Courts Press, 2004), 151–59.

116. Daunton, *Trusting Leviathan*, 61–63.
117. *Hansard*, 3rd ser., vol. 173, col. 1209 (26 Feb. 1864).
118. Commons, 'Taxation of Ireland', *Sessional Papers, 1864*, 243–44.
119. Ibid., 288.
120. Daunt, journal for 9 Aug. 1865, O'Neill Daunt Journals, NLI MS 3041, f. 780.
121. Dunne to Daunt, 20 Nov. 1865, O'Neill Daunt Papers, NLI MS 8045/4.
122. *Nation*, 4 Nov. 1865.
123. C. J. Woods, 'Daunt (Moriarty), William Joseph O'Neill', in *Dictionary of Irish Biography*, ed. James McGuire and James Quinn http://dib.cambridge.org.proxy.bc.edu/viewReadPage.do?articleId=a2414 (accessed 27 Mar. 2018); *Nation*, 20 Aug. 1870; *FJ*, 26 Jan. 1874; Ball, 'Dunne'.
124. *Report of the Committee Appointed by the Council of the Home Government Association to Examine the Financial Relations between Great Britain and Ireland, and the Pressure of Taxation upon Irish Resources* (Dublin: Robert Chapman, 1873); Dunne to Daunt, 3 May 1873, 10 May 1873, 26 June 1873, O'Neill Daunt Papers, NLI MS 8045/4.

CHAPTER 10

Tides of Change and Changing Sides: The Collection of Rates in the Irish War of Independence, 1919–21

Robin J. C. Adams

The County Councils were re-established. Their first action was to dismiss the Austrian officials who had been planted on the counties during the Ten Years' Tyranny, their second to strike out the rate for supporting the Austrian Army, their third to order the tax-collectors to collect no taxes unless levied by authority of the Hungarian Parliament.
'What is the object sought after by the Hungarian County Councils?' asked a Vienna journal indignantly. Its answer to its own question did not convey the truth half so well as the prompt reply of the County Council of Pesth: 'To sweep away every trace of Austrian rule, and hold Hungary for the Hungarians'.
The Resurrection of Hungary: A Parallel for Ireland
Arthur Griffith, 1904

R. J. C. Adams (✉)
University of Oxford, Oxford, UK
e-mail: robin.adams@spc.ox.ac.uk

D. Kanter, P. Walsh (eds.), *Taxation, Politics, and Protest in Ireland, 1662–2016*, Palgrave Studies in the History of Finance,
https://doi.org/10.1007/978-3-030-04309-4_10

The Irish War of Independence (1919–21) is among the most studied periods in Irish historiography. However, less well documented is the quiet revolution that took place in its shadow and presaged the establishment of the Irish Free State—the revolution in local taxation. There are, of course, a number of exceptions. David Fitzpatrick's seminal *Politics and Irish Life* examined the revolution in local government in County Clare and, more recently, Marie Coleman's *County Longford and the Irish Revolution* did the same for that county.[1] A more nationwide focus has been provided by Tom Garvin in *1922: The Birth of Irish Democracy* and Mary Daly in *The Creation of the Dáil*, while Brian Hughes, in *Defying the IRA?*, provides a wide-ranging survey of the role of the IRA in the collection of rates.[2] This chapter adds to this literature by providing a more explicit focus on local taxation; how it was shaped by politics and responded to protest. More specifically, it looks at the incentives that faced local tax collectors as the balance of power shifted from the British government in Ireland to the Irish republican government-in-waiting. The role of the taxpayers is also considered, including organised opposition to the collection of rates. Turning to the latter phase of the Irish War of Independence, the chapter then explores the ways in which the collection of rates was shaped by the shifting balance of power within the republican movement. Particular focus is given to the struggle of the central, civilian authority in Dublin to control the militants in the provinces.

The 1918 UK general election resulted in a landslide victory in Ireland for the separatist Sinn Féin party, winning seventy-three of 105 seats. In line with Arthur Griffith's 1904 polemic *The Resurrection of Hungary*, the Sinn Féin representatives boycotted Westminster and formed their own assembly in Dublin. Drawing on the example of nineteenth-century Hungarian nationalists, Griffith's treatise was widely read in Sinn Féin circles and many aspects of it served as a blueprint for the party's democratic programme.[3] Named Dáil Éireann, the underground Irish republican parliament held its first session on 21 January 1919. This democratic event in Dublin was accompanied by a more violent event in the countryside. On the same day, two Royal Irish Constabulary (RIC) policemen were shot dead in County Tipperary in a raid by Irish Volunteers to capture explosives. This incident is generally regarded as opening the Irish War of Independence, a major civil conflict with between 1,200 and 1,500 fatalities, many more casualties and substantial damage to property.[4]

The Dáil selected a cabinet from its representatives, with ministries including Defence, Finance, and Foreign Affairs forming what historian

Arthur Mitchell has termed a 'counter-state'.[5] At first, this counter-state had neither international recognition nor territorial integrity, but as the war progressed, it took on more and more of the characteristics of an established state. Of course, the Dáil's pretensions to statehood came with a price tag, but its administrators came with experience of fundraising: from the Defence of Ireland fund for arming the Irish Volunteers to the Irish National Aid Association and Volunteers' Dependents' Fund to pay for their dependents, and the National Defence Fund to resist conscription in 1918.[6] However, such church-gate collections were deemed 'not in accord with [the Dáil's] dignity as the *de jure* and accepted Government of Ireland'.[7] In keeping with the Dáil's proclaimed statehood, there were initial hopes that it could raise revenue through income tax, but this was deemed impracticable for the time being.[8] Instead, it raised funds through the sale of 'bond certificates' that would be exchangeable for sovereign bonds if and when the Irish Republic had 'received international recognition, and the English have evacuated Ireland'.[9] Through these bond certificates, the Dáil's Department of Finance raised £370,165 in Ireland and nearly $6 million in America.[10]

However, these funds were only enough to sustain the Dáil's skeleton national administration, the creation of which was but one element of the counter-state envisaged in Griffith's *Resurrection of Hungary*. Following the example of the county council of Pest in 1861, it also proposed the secession of Ireland's local government bodies to provide an infrastructure through which the Dáil could implement its policies.[11] Unfortunately, with running costs of £10,039,156, local government in Ireland was beyond the fiscal capacity of the nascent Dáil administration.[12] Instead, the Dáil's administrators would have to take over the existing, British, revenue raising infrastructure. In the words of David Fitzpatrick, the Irish rebels had 'a valuable inheritance' at their disposal: 'an existing apparatus needing no dislocation but adaptation'.[13]

This 'inheritance' dated from the Local Government Act of 1898, which established county and borough councils across the country, the members of which were elected by ratepayers.[14] Under the supervision of the county and borough councils were rural district councils (RDCs) and urban district councils (UDCs) for small and medium-sized towns, and the whole system was accountable to the Local Government Board (LGB), a central coordinating and grant-aiding body based in Dublin's Custom House.[15] These local authorities provided services such as road building and maintenance, hospitals, and workhouses. Noted for their corruption, in the words of Garvin, they were 'providers of relief, employment and patronage'.[16] This was all paid for by a combination of rates raised locally, other local revenue such as tolls and dog licenses, and grants from the LGB.[17] By far the largest component of local revenue was rates, set by county councils based on the valuation of land held by the ratepayer. Totalling £5,249,380 nationwide, rates were raised annually by the councils and collected in two equal half-yearly moieties.[18]

As part of its counter-state, the Dáil established a Department of Local Government (DÉDLG), under the ministry of W. T. Cosgrave in Dublin. Decidedly less salubrious than the LGB's Custom House, the DÉDLG moved from office to office, from Harcourt Street to Clare Street, Parnell Square, O'Connell Street, and finally Wicklow Street.[19] Rather fittingly, in one of these locations, it used the cover of a company providing advice on taxation.[20] In common with most of the 'departments' set up by the Dáil, at first the DÉDLG was a department in name only. However, as the electoral cycle progressed, it became one of the most significant.

The first phase of local elections came in January 1920, when Ireland's 126 urban centres voted under a proportional representation system designed to harm Sinn Féin's chances of success.[21] Based on a 70 per cent turnout, 550 seats were won by Sinn Féin, while Labour won 394, unionists 355, nationalists 238, independents 161, and municipal reformers 108.[22] The Dáil requested that all UDCs and county boroughs give it their allegiance, but they were reluctant to take this risk while the county councils and RDCs had not yet been elected and remained outside Sinn Féin's control.[23]

In June 1920, came the second phase of local elections: those for the rural areas. This resulted in another Sinn Féin landslide, particularly in Munster and Connacht, where it won 258 of the 263 council seats.[24] Overall Sinn Féin won control of 338 of the 393 local bodies, county councils, boards of guardians, and RDCs across the island of Ireland.[25] In the words of the RIC county inspector for Longford, 'the local councils in this county are now in the hands of the rabble.'[26]

Notwithstanding Griffith's outline in the *Resurrection of Hungary*, the DÉDLG was surprisingly unprepared for this landslide. By the time of the rural elections, Assistant Minister for Local Government Kevin O'Higgins had already concluded that a 'clean break' with the LGB, although dignified, would be disastrous. The loss of LGB grants to Dublin Corporation for example would be £164,674 and, while an increased rate of 3s. 2d. would cover this loss, O'Higgins considered the enforcement of such an increase would be extremely difficult.[27] There was also the danger that the British government might move to seize councils' funds, as they had tried to do to the Dáil's own funds two months earlier.[28] Instead, O'Higgins recommended that the DÉDLG wait for the British to make the first move.[29] While the DÉDLG issued instructions to incoming county councils to pass resolutions of allegiance to 'the authority of Dáil Éireann as the duly elected Government of the Irish People', it also advised 'no drastic action' with regard to the LGB's authority until further notice.[30]

While the DÉDLG was deliberating on what policy to follow, developments on the ground forced county councils to take the initiative themselves. A key issue was how to prevent the local authorities' funds from being seized by the LGB to pay claims for malicious injuries committed by the IRA or Crown forces.[31] In the absence of firm direction from the DÉDLG, Clare County Council took the initiative and appointed a special committee to determine how to deal with the problem.[32] As a first step, on 25 June 1920, the council instructed its treasurer, the Provincial Bank of Ireland Ltd, not to disclose the state of its finances to anyone but the 'duly accredited officers' of the council itself. It also instructed the bank to refuse payment of all decrees for the Criminal Injuries Act.[33] Then, in August 1920, it took the further step of dismissing the Provincial Bank as treasurer altogether and requesting that the bank manager publish the fact accordingly.[34]

To take the place of the bank, a system was devised that council funds would be held by council-nominated trustees and administered by a paymaster.[35] The trustees received warrants from the county council and sent demand notes to the ratepayers.[36] The rate collectors would wait until substantial amounts had been collected before handing the money on to the paymaster.[37] In one case, the amounts totalling £4,800 were stored in tins and boxes concealed in hedges, before being handed over to the paymaster in instalments.[38] The paymaster, having given a receipt to the rate collector, handed the funds over to the designated trustee.[39] The designated trustee would then lodge the money in his account and clear it almost immediately by issuing cheques to the other five trustees.[40] The Clare paymaster, Art O'Donnell, was appointed on a salary of £5 a week.[41] He took up duty on 20 August 1920, and by the time he was arrested by the RIC, on 22 November 1920, he had received £108,000 from rate collectors and other sources and paid out almost £100,000.[42]

Although Clare was an early mover, many other counties followed when, as expected, on 29 July 1920, the LGB responded to the local authorities' disloyalty. As feared, it announced that annual grants-in-aid would be withheld from any local authorities that refused to recognise the authority of the LGB by submitting their accounts for audit.[43] Since the grants constituted 19 per cent of gross revenue for the public bodies in Ireland, this was a severe threat.[44] However, by now the opportunity cost of losing LGB grants was significantly diminished by that body's insistence that local authorities pay for malicious injuries.[45] Consequently, the ultimatum resulted in most local authorities severing links with the LGB.[46] By September 1920, only Antrim, Armagh, and Derry had given a formal assurance to the board.[47] In some cases, the LGB circulars were burnt by the councils, while the minutes of other council meetings recorded councillors throwing them in the bin.[48] The scheme developed in Clare was adopted by the DÉDLG, which recommended it to other local authorities across the country.[49] By 18 December 1920, the *Freeman's Journal* reported that some nineteen county councils were operating without a bank as treasurer.[50]

This was the 'clean break' considered by O'Higgins and predicted by Arthur Griffith. On examining documents outlining the DÉDLG's plan, Nevil Macready, General Officer Commanding-in-Chief of British forces in Ireland, was astonished. 'It is almost word for word what Arthur Griffith foreshadows in that book of his, "The Resurrection of Hungary".'[51]

There was, however, a major weakness in the DÉDLG's plan, as noted in the minority report of the Dáil commission of enquiry into local government, 27 August 1920: 'The scheme for protecting the County funds is very perfect, but the difficulty most to be dreaded is the conduct of the Rate Collectors.'[52] Once the republican local authorities had severed their links with the LGB, the rate collectors of Ireland found themselves at the centre of a tug of war between two rival governments. In the words of the *Dundalk Democrat*, they were 'between the devil and the deep sea'.[53]

To understand the rate collectors' predicament fully, it is necessary to consider the incentives they faced in their role. In order to become a rate collector, the candidate had to offer a bond, calculated based on the potential earnings from the role. This gave the county council some collateral, providing a disincentive for the rate collector to sequester funds collected. These bonds ranged from £1,000 in County Kildare to £3,000 in Tipperary North Riding.[54] Typically, candidates were also asked to provide the names of two solvent ratepayers who would be willing to enter into a joint bond with them as sureties.[55] Alternatively or additionally, they could nominate a Guaranty Society to provide surety.[56]

Another crucial point to note was that the rate collectors were paid not by salary, but by poundage. Essentially, they were entitled to a cut of the amount they had collected and lodged with the county council. This percentage varied from county to county but typically was in the region of 8d. for every pound lodged.[57] Payment of poundage was dependent on a certain amount of rates being lodged with the county council by certain dates.[58] However, for most rate collectors, their poundage from rate collection was not their only source of income and, as noted in the minority report of the Dáil commission of enquiry into local government, this gave them considerable power: 'Their position is very powerful as they are not wholetime officers and most of them have other means of livelihood. If any of them wish they can raise trouble and seriously obstruct the working of the scheme requiring considerable diplomacy on the part of the Councils to get the Rate Collectors to perform their duties to the Councils.'[59]

Poundage was not the only remuneration offered for the collection of rates. The rate collectors were also entitled to superannuation, providing for a pension after retirement.[60] As recalled by the brigade commander of the East Clare IRA, the rate collectors were 'nearly all fairly old men', so the risk of losing their pensions must have been a real concern.[61] Moreover, another peculiarity of the rate collector's job was the extent to which it could, in practice, be hereditary. It was not uncommon for sons to be appointed rate collectors on the retirement of their fathers.[62] Indeed, in Sligo County Council, it was considered a 'general rule' that a family member would take over after a rate collector retired.[63] In this context, if the rate collector resigned on bad terms, he would not only be losing his pension but potentially also a position for his son.

As the tussle between the LGB and DÉDLG intensified, so did the pressure on the rate collectors. On 11 November 1920, the LGB issued a reminder to rate collectors that they would be liable for any money lodged with 'unauthorised persons'.[64] It was a legal obligation for the rate collectors to lodge the money they had collected in a bank that had been officially designated by the Lord Lieutenant, and a rate collector who failed to do this ran the risk of losing the surety he had pledged on taking the job.[65] The LGB gave three options to the rate collectors: resign on a retiring allowance; lodge the rates in their personal accounts until the banks were reinstated as treasurers; or, if they followed orders from the republican local authorities, be dismissed without pension.[66] The predicament of the rate collectors was neatly summed up in the *Dundalk Democrat*:

> The county councils want them to collect rates and lodge them with the illegally appointed private treasurers, so that the councils may carry on. The Local Government Board says that if they do so they and their sureties will be held responsible for the money so collected and disposed. The councils—in most cases, we are glad to believe, unwillingly—threaten dismissal. The Local Government Board says that dismissal will be invalid.[67]

The LGB's ultimatum seems to have had an effect, as rate collectors who previously acquiesced to the Dáil's instructions became reluctant to cooperate.[68] According to a DÉDLG official, in November and December 1920, the rate collectors in Clare 'got "funky" to such an extent that they actually refused to collect' rates for the county council unless the bank was reinstated as treasurer.[69] All the Clare rate collectors, with the exception of one, who was an IRA member, refused to lodge their collections with the county council.[70] Elsewhere, in Tipperary North Riding, the rate collectors notified the council that they were not prepared to carry out their duties unless the banks were reappointed as treasurers.[71]

The Dáil softened its demands on the rate collectors in early December 1920 and instructed them simply to lodge the money they had collected in a local bank and write a crossed cheque to the county council for the amount lodged.[72] It also instructed local authorities to indemnify rate collectors against any financial loss sustained as a result of following the Dáil's instructions.[73] These concessions had little effect however and, in the words of David Fitzpatrick, 'many collectors retreated into canny inactivity'.[74]

The intransigence of the rate collectors became formalised on 17 December 1920, when their representative body, the Rate Collectors' Association, called an All-Ireland meeting to decide a policy response.[75] Acting on legal counsel, the association advised its members to hold the money already collected in their private accounts and collect no more money until the matter of treasurers was settled between the county councils and the LGB.[76] This decision, enabling collective action, strengthened the bargaining position of the rate collectors. The *Dundalk Democrat* viewed this as a sensible course to take, but in the view of a columnist at the *Nationalist and Leinster Times*, it was akin to 'deciding to commit suicide'.[77]

Kevin O'Higgins responded with a circular to the rate collectors, which was published in newspapers across the country on 26 December 1920. He pointed out that the hoarding of rate money would be against the terms of the rate collectors' position, as they were only allowed to hold a maximum of £100 in their personal bank accounts. He also reminded the collectors that pensions were paid not by the LGB but by the county councils. Finally, he gave a warning: 'Any rate collector who throws his lot in with the enemy, and endeavours to force his Council to conform to enemy regulations by a refusal to resign or collect the rates is warned that in so doing he is acting as a public enemy, and will be appropriately dealt with.'[78] This pronouncement was formalised in January 1921, when the Dáil cabinet decided that rate collectors deemed negligent should be fired, and ordered that a list of defaulters be sent to the DÉDLG so that those could 'be dealt with by the Defence Department where necessary'.[79] As both a backstop and an incentive, the Dáil also made £100,000 available for bridging loans to county councils who managed to collect 75 per cent of their rates.[80]

A series of pre-arranged IRA raids were carried out across County Dublin on the morning of 4 January 1921. The objective was to secure the books and money of eight rate collectors who had resigned from Dublin County Council due to its repudiation of the LGB.[81] According to the *Skibbereen Eagle*:

> In every case the procedure followed was almost the same. Armed men called at the residence of the collector, seized his books and documents, and compelled him to sign a cheque, transferring to one of the raiding party the amount of his collection of the poor rate lodged in the bank. Receipts were given to the collectors for the documents and money seized. Some of the raiders then went to the bank and cashed the cheques, the collectors meantime held in their houses by armed guards.[82]

The cheques, ranging from £500 to over £1,000, and totalling £10,000, were all cashed at the same time, to avoid word spreading to the British authorities.[83] According to one of the rate collectors, the raiders 'were very courteous and well-behaved young men, and during their stay they partook of tea, which they insisted on paying for'.[84]

In all, Dublin Castle recorded twenty-two raids of rate collectors' houses in the first week of 1921.[85] The variation in responses to these raids illustrates the differing attitudes of rate collectors around the country. The raids of eight rate collectors in County Wexford between 5 and 7 January 1921 generated a particularly fierce response.[86] The secretary of Wexford County Council received an anonymous letter, signed 'Anti-Murder

Gang', warning, 'if anything happens to any one of them you and your son will pay the supreme sacrifice.'[87] In contrast, on 14 January 1921, when the IRA seized the books of a rate collector sympathetic to the IRA in Kilfenora, County Clare, the seizure was only a matter of form.[88] At the other end of the spectrum, later in January, a rate collector in Duleek, County Meath, was kidnapped and held for two days by armed men who tried to compel him to hand over rate money.[89]

The raids continued in February, and the Clare IRA was particularly active.[90] Masked men raided the house of a rate collector in Ennistymon district and took £765 and rate books.[91] Another rate collector was compelled to write a cheque for £207, and his son was sent to cash it.[92] In one case, a rate collector was forced to sign not only a cheque for £352 but also his own letter of resignation.[93] Two Clare rate collectors took the option of retiring in February 1921 and, although both were given generous pensions for their years of service, it is hard to imagine the turmoil around them had no influence on their decisions to leave the stage.[94] When raiders came to the house of a rate collector in Ennis, they found he had already made arrangements to hand over the rate books and undeposited rate moneys totalling £1,013 to the IRA.[95] Together with another raid in Ennis, the IRA secured £2,068 for the republican county council.[96] The *Freemans Journal* reported similar scenes across the county, with amounts taken ranging from £200 to £1,400.[97] In North Clare, some of the raiders were apprehended and arrested by the RIC but, demonstrating the power of the IRA in that area, the rate collector testified in favour of their innocence.[98]

Seizures such as these laid the groundwork for the collection of rates by the IRA.[99] Clare County Council decided to dismiss all but one of the rate collectors and to replace them with IRA Volunteers.[100] The one rate collector who kept his job was himself a member of the IRA.[101] Through official orders, it became the duty of every IRA battalion commanding officer (O/C) in Clare to ensure that ratepayers paid their dues.[102] Clare was divided into nine rural districts, covered by thirty-two rate collectors, all of whom were members of the IRA or Irish Republican Police.[103] Each company captain was responsible for the collection of rates in his district, and the funds collected were then handed to the battalion headquarters, where they were handed over to someone nominated by the brigade council.[104] The RIC observed IRA agents collecting rates throughout County Clare in March 1921, and by April, the collection of rates that year was practically complete.[105] According to Michael Gleeson of the East Clare Brigade, even well-known unionist ratepayers paid their rates to the local IRA.[106]

Another wave of raids came in April 1921.[107] The financial year had just ended, and many of the local authorities' finances were in dire straits.[108] The IRA in Louth raided rate collectors' houses across the county, and five of them were compelled to sign cheques for the rates collected but not yet lodged with the treasurer.[109] In every case, the raiders knew exactly how much was held by the collectors: in one case £3,000 and in another £5,000.[110] A total of £16,000 was lodged in the Drogheda and Dundalk branches of the Hibernian Bank and withdrawn by the council chairman the same day.[111] According to the *Meath Chronicle*, the raiders ordered the collectors to provide breakfast, and some of them remained until after banking hours.[112]

In one case, according to the *Drogheda Independent*, the rate collector was driven 'at a rapid pace' to a churchyard out of town, where he was made to sign away £2,582 'at the point of a revolver'.[113] The rate collector in question, a shopkeeper named Gannon, provided rations to the Black and Tans, who called at his shop every morning at 9 a.m. In order to avoid the Tans, the raiders planned to call at Gannon's shop at 8:45 a.m., but one of them was late, delaying the raid till 8:50 a.m.[114] The panic this caused was recalled in vivid detail by one of the raiding party:

> In the shop we met an assistant whom we asked for Mr. Gannon. This man appeared to be antagonistic and I had to force him with a gun to take us upstairs to Gannon's bedroom. On the stairs we met Mrs. Gannon and she became hysterical which created a dangerous situation if the Tans had then arrived. We got Gannon and all his papers and vouchers and took him down the stairs by a back passage and out to a car we had waiting for us in the side street.[115]

The following month, the *Irish Independent* reported more raids of rate collectors in counties Mayo and Sligo, one of which involved the kidnapping of a rate collector.[116] The rate collector, who refused to hand over the rate monies to the Sinn Féin controlled council, was brought to an unknown location where, according to one of the raiders, he was detained for several months.[117] He finally changed his mind and signed a cheque for £14,000, at which point he was released.[118]

Of course, coercion of rate collectors was not the sole preserve of the IRA. In Carlow, a Dáil rate collector received eighteen months in prison from the British authorities in March 1921.[119] Police and military arrested a County Wexford rate collector in April 1921 and seized the rate books in his possession.[120] The RIC also arrested a number of unauthorised rate collectors in County Wicklow the following month, and the house of another was raided in Youghal, County Cork.[121] However, as the armed campaign progressed, in more and more of the country the power to coerce shifted in favour of the IRA, hastening the demise of the LGB. This was most graphically illustrated on 25 May 1921, when the IRA attacked and burnt the Custom House in Dublin, destroying the LGB's head office.[122]

On 1 July 1921, the DÉDLG delivered a report on the state of local government in Ireland, and its findings were telling. By April 1921, despite the chaos of the previous nine months, rate collection had closed in nine counties: Cavan, Galway, Kildare, Kilkenny, King's, Mayo, Queen's, Tipperary North, and Westmeath.[123] Collection was practically closed in a further seven counties: Carlow, Clare, Donegal, Limerick, Tipperary South, Waterford, and Wicklow.[124] Remarkably, Mayo, Queen's, and Tipperary North managed to close their collections without reinstating their banks as treasurer.[125]

However, a number of counties were not doing so well. The situation in Leitrim was particularly bad and was a lost cause in the eyes of some Dáil officials.[126] The poorest of the twenty-seven administrative counties that would form the Irish Free State, there were even suggestions to expel Leitrim from the republic as it was more trouble than it was worth.[127] To make matters worse, according to Garvin, the Leitrim IRA 'resembled a criminal gang more than a disciplined guerrilla army'.[128] As for the county council, it had no treasurer since dismissing the Northern Bank, the paymaster was in prison, and the chairman was on the run.[129] The secretary of Leitrim County Council was not even able to give a summary of the state of rate collection in the country, as the rate collectors had refused to have their books checked pending reinstatement of a bank as treasurer.[130]

In Monaghan, the collection was hampered by the seizure of rate books by Crown forces in January 1921 and later by the arrest of a republican rate collector, but a more systemic problem was the county's large unionist population. A bloc of unionists refused to pay their rates to a collector not sanctioned by the LGB, resulting in a shortfall amounting to £10,000, some 25 per cent of rates due in the year to 31 March 1921.[131] This organised unionist resistance seems exceptional, however, and was a function of Monaghan's particular demographics. Elsewhere, as noted in Clare, smaller unionist populations realised they had no alternative but to pay rates to the IRA.[132] In Kerry, for example, the county council considered that 'the citizens of this country who did not see eye-to-eye with their Republican fellow-countrymen deserve credit for their punctuality in paying their rates last year.'[133]

Other resistance came from the farmers, who formed the bulk of the provincial rate-paying population.[134] An agricultural recession, combined with an increase in rates in many counties and cuts in services provided by the cash-strapped county councils, offered ample incentive for non-payment of rates.[135] At the centre of this organised resistance was the Dublin-based Farmers' Union, which openly defied the Dáil's rate collection and challenged the legality of rate struck in July 1921.[136] The union encouraged non-payment of rates across the country, and its influence was particularly strong in County Meath, which, according to the DÉDLG's report, had £30,000 in rates outstanding.[137] Ratepayers' associations were also active in protesting against rates, highlighting as unjustifiable the high rates struck by the councils and their poor management of funds.[138] The County Dublin ratepayers' association wrote to the county council demanding an enquiry into the rate struck that year.[139] Although a thorn in the side of the DÉDLG, the fact that these anti-rates groups petitioned the DÉDLG and not the LGB was testament to the extent to which the latter's authority to collect rates had been defeated. Indeed, indicative of its supremacy in the administration of local government, Cosgrave's office began receiving a large volume of correspondence from various organisations lobbying for their interests.[140]

However, when it came to enforcing the DÉDLG's authority to collect rates, it was the IRA that held the power, and the DÉDLG's control over the local IRA Volunteers was neither perfect nor universal. Moreover, the incentives facing local IRA Volunteers were not always aligned with those of the DÉDLG. As noted by Garvin, members of the IRA 'felt that they had far better things to be doing than enforce an unpopular levy'.[141] Indeed, the collection of rates and other fundraising duties occupied more and more of the IRA Volunteers' time. In addition to rate collection, IRA Volunteers imposed a toll for pilgrims visiting a shrine in Tipperary and a tax on alcohol in Mayo, and were also observed collecting dog license fees in Cavan, Clare, Kildare, Kilkenny, Longford, and Wexford.[142] More forcefully, the IRA was also engaged in collecting for its 'Arms Fund Levy', which was essentially organised extortion levied on farmers and businessmen in their brigade area.[143] Where there was a refusal to pay on the first request, a second request was made later on, with the threat of seizures as a sanction.[144] If the second request were met with refusal to pay, IRA Volunteers would seize cattle or stock to the value of the levy imposed.[145] Beyond seizure of assets, enforcement could also take a violent character. The RIC county inspector for Leitrim, for example, reported a Protestant being dragged from his house in the dead of night and shot for not subscribing to the levy, his body later found mutilated.[146]

Unlike the Arms Fund Levy, the proceeds of which went straight to the IRA, the time-consuming collection of rates had no clear benefit to the ordinary Volunteer. This sentiment was observable in Sligo, for example, where the IRA demanded payment in return for enforcing the collection of rates.[147] The IRA's obstruction of rate collection went further than lack of interest, however. Much of the resistance to Dáil rate collection came from areas with an active IRA and, according to Garvin, the Volunteers were often in sympathy with defaulting ratepayers and helped organise resistance to the collection of rates.[148] Indeed, in Donegal and Galway, the IRA officers were actually the leaders of the anti-rates movement.[149]

The IRA's monopoly on the use of violence in much of the country was copper-fastened on 9 July 1921 when the Dáil signed a truce with the British government, effective 12 July. The months that followed saw a dramatic expansion in the Dáil's activities, and its total gross outlay increased from £106,137 in the first half of 1921 to £204,429 in the second.[150] Part of this expansion constituted an attempt by the Dáil to assert its authority over the IRA and, on 15 September 1921, the Dáil cabinet agreed on what the historian Charles Townsend has termed 'a radical rebranding exercise', by reconstituting the IRA as the army of the Dáil.[151] This move was designed to clarify the IRA's position as a legitimate army that was answerable to the Dáil.[152] A similar centralisation drive can be seen in the DÉDLG, the outlays of which shot up from £3,858 in the first half of 1921 to £12,074 in the second.[153] By August 1921, in addition to a number of auditors, the DÉDLG employed 20 inspectors who travelled around the country, attending county council meetings and trying to improve local administration.[154] These inspectors then held monthly meetings with either Cosgrave or O'Higgins, ensuring the Dáil had a clear picture of what was happening in the country.[155]

Troublesome counties like Leitrim became the focus of this centralisation project. The DÉDLG inspector for that county made it known that he had the department's sanction to take 'any action which I find it might be necessary' against rate collectors who failed to close the previous year's collection before 1 September 1921.[156] He gave instructions to the Leitrim county secretary to summon rate collectors once they had closed their collections and take possession of their new books so that the next collection could begin.[157] Matters did not improve, however, despite the appointment of the Munster and Leinster Bank as treasurer.[158] Widespread personal enmity towards one rate collector and heated arguments over whom the council would appoint to replace him further retarded the collection in the county.[159] Organised resistance to paying was also present in Leitrim, and anti-rate meetings were held across the county in September and October 1921.[160] Feelings were so strong that when the DÉDLG inspector tried to reason with the ratepayers at an anti-rate meeting, he had to fire over the heads of the crowd in order to defend himself.[161]

On 7 October 1921, the DÉDLG inspector requested that forty young men be sent from Dublin 'with full powers to collect the current and outstanding Rates by any means they deem necessary'.[162] The county would be divided into sections, with each section served by five or six men jointly.[163] Outside help was particularly necessary as it was suspected that members of the Leitrim IRA were among those in opposition to the payment of rates.[164] In Garvin's words, 'Leitrim's only chance was to be, in effect, conquered by the Dublin government.'[165] The DÉDLG endorsed the inspector's recommendation and sent out an expedition of forty active, intelligent men. In order to cover the cost of this expedition, an additional levy was placed on defaulters.[166]

The centralising drive of the DÉDLG was also felt elsewhere. Although Clare began as an exemplar of rate collection, by the autumn of 1921 it was listed alongside Leitrim as one of the worst-performing county councils in the country. Not a penny of the 1922 rate had been collected by September 1921, and £26,000 was still outstanding from the 1921 rate.[167] In Kilrush, the UDC simply gave up its rate collection duties and handed over its street-cleaning functions to the local ratepayers' association.[168]

Desperate for funds, Clare County Council appointed forty-one temporary rate collectors on 20 September 1921.[169] All of them were nominees of county councillors and, according to the RIC county inspector, the appointments were a compromise resulting from 'a heated dispute' between two factions of the council.[170] When the county council wrote to the DÉDLG to sanction the appointments, the response on 10 October 1921 was damning. The DÉDLG noted that eighteen of the council's nominees were appointed 'under a threat from the local brigade of the IRA that any Collector other than the one nominated by them would be shot'.[171]

The terms on which the IRA collectors in Clare were appointed also drew sharp criticism from the DÉDLG, in particular, the lack of a guarantee that the rates would be collected in full or by a certain date.[172] Unlike previous appointments, the new rate collectors were not required to provide a surety for their positions, as the county's IRA brigade officers took responsibility for the work.[173] However, Chairman Michael Brennan, who also happened to be IRA O/C in East Clare, claimed the brigade commandants had given no guarantee that the rates would be collected *in full*.[174] A further remark by Brennan that the councillors would consider themselves lucky if only 60 per cent of the rates were collected 'leaves this Department gasping', wrote Cosgrave.[175]

This kind of IRA interference in local government appointments was not unique to Clare. The historian Michael Farry has found similar meddling in Sligo County Council appointments, while Fearghal McGarry and Brian Hughes have identified interference in Monaghan and Limerick county councils, respectively.[176] However, in order to assert its authority, the DÉDLG had to act, and it informed Clare County Council that the appointments would be deferred pending investigation by the Dáil Department of Defence.[177] With its finances in dire straits, the council pleaded that the rate collectors be allowed to proceed with collections.[178]

A representative of the Department of Defence went to Clare in late October and reached a satisfactory settlement with the council, but this did not bring the county's rate collection problems to an end.[179] The Farmers' Union in Dublin requested a meeting with Clare County Council on 14 October 1921, stating that unless a deputation from the union was met by council officials, it would recommend its members not pay rates.[180] Representing the road workers employed by the council, whose wages depended on the collection of rates, the Transport Workers' Union added pressure on the other side. On 17 October 1921, it requested that the council apply to the Dáil Department of Finance for permission to confiscate money on deposit belonging to defaulting ratepayers 'in the name of the Country'.[181] Only from 12 November 1921 when, with the help of the Dáil, the county council came to an agreement with the Farmers' Union, did the collection of rates in Clare commence in earnest.[182]

The Dáil's control of local taxation in Ireland, although incomplete and imperfect, was a key part of its mission to take on the attributes of a state. It was a clear manifestation of the shifting balance of power, first from the LGB to the DÉDLG and then from the DÉDLG to the IRA. However, as observed by Griffith in his analysis of Hungary, 'for a little time, something like anarchy prevailed in the land', and many ratepayers took advantage of this to evade paying tax to either administration.[183] The Irish War of Independence came to an end on 6 December 1921 with the signing of the Anglo-Irish Treaty, but this did not end the Dáil's problems with rate collection. Although local authorities across the country passed resolutions in favour of the Treaty, its terms split both the Dáil and the IRA into pro-Treaty and anti-Treaty factions. The centrifugal forces experienced between the Dáil and the local IRA units in the War of Independence also faced the Provisional Government that took its place on 7 January 1922. Opposition to the payment of rates continued well into 1922 and the Provisional Government viewed the anti-Treaty IRA as responsible for encouraging default.[184] Tax collection remained dysfunctional as the state found its feet, and in Cork, income tax was still being collected by the IRA as late as August 1922.[185] The extent of tax evasion was such that, at the suggestion of the Provisional Government, on 10 November 1922, Roman Catholic bishops sent out a statement urging their parishioners to pay their taxes.[186] Nevertheless, the extent to which the Dáil gained control of local taxation during the war of independence was crucial in determining the direction of the war and was an important part of that story.

Notes

1. David Fitzpatrick, *Politics and Irish Life, 1913–1921: Provincial Experience of War and Revolution* (Dublin: Gill and Macmillan, 1977); Marie Coleman, *County Longford and the Irish Revolution, 1910–1923* (Dublin: Irish Academic Press, 2003).
2. Tom Garvin, *1922: The Birth of Irish Democracy* (Dublin: Gill and Macmillan, 1996); Mary Daly, 'Local Government and the First Dáil', in *The Creation of the Dáil: A Volume of Essays from the Thomas Davis Lectures*, ed. B. Farrell and M. Littleton (Dublin: Blackwater, 1994); Brian Hughes, *Defying the IRA? Intimidation, Coercion, and Communities During the Irish Revolution* (Liverpool: Liverpool University Press, 2017).
3. Michael Laffan, *The Resurrection of Ireland: The Sinn Féin Party, 1916–1923* (Cambridge: Cambridge University Press, 1999), 3.
4. Michael Hopkinson, *The Irish War of Independence* (Dublin: Gill and Macmillan, 2002), 26.
5. Arthur Mitchell, *Revolutionary Government in Ireland: Dáil Éireann, 1919–1922* (Dublin: Gill and Macmillan, 1995).

6. *Donegal News*, 11 July 1914; Caoimhe NicDháibhéid, 'The Irish National Aid Association and the Radicalization of Public Opinion', *Historical Journal* 55, no. 3 (2012): 705–29; RIC Inspector General's Report, Apr. 1918, The National Archives (hereafter TNA): CO 904/105/862.
7. Ard Chomhairle of Sinn Féin, 20 Feb. 1919, National Library of Ireland (hereafter NLI) MS 8786 (i), 2.
8. Fitzpatrick, *Politics and Irish Life*, 17.
9. Ronan Fanning, *The Irish Department of Finance, 1922–58* (Dublin: Institute of Public Administration, 1978), 15–16.
10. Francis M. Carroll, *Money for Ireland: Finance, Diplomacy, Politics, and the First Dáil Éireann Loans, 1919–1936* (Westport, CT: Praeger, 2002), 9, 15.
11. Arthur Griffith, *The Resurrection of Hungary: A Parallel for Ireland* (Dublin: James Duffy, 1904), 94.
12. *Returns of Local Taxation in Ireland for the Year 1918–1919*, Cmd. 799 (1920), vol. 40, p. 851.
13. Fitzpatrick, *Politics and Irish Life*, 154.
14. Garvin, *1922*, 64.
15. Ibid., 64–65.
16. Ibid., 65.
17. *Returns of Local Taxation*, 851.
18. Ibid., 860, 851.
19. Michael Laffan, *Judging W. T. Cosgrave* (Dublin: Royal Irish Academy, 2014), 66.
20. Ibid.
21. Laffan, *The Resurrection of Ireland*, 326.
22. Ibid., 327.
23. Daly, 'Local Government and the First Dáil', 125.
24. Laffan, *The Resurrection of Ireland*, 327.
25. Hopkinson, *The Irish War of Independence*, 28.
26. Coleman, *Longford*, 91.
27. T. J. McArdle Witness Statement, National Archives of Ireland, Bureau of Military History (hereafter NAI, BMH)/WS0501, 10.
28. David Nelligan Witness Statement, NAI, BMH/WS0380, 5.
29. McArdle Witness Statement, NAI, BMH/WS0501, 10.
30. Fitzpatrick, *Politics and Irish Life*, 154–55.
31. Daly, 'Local Government and the First Dáil', 127.
32. Art O'Donnell Witness Statement, NAI, BMH/WS1322, 54.
33. Clare County Council Minutes, 25 June 1920, Clare County Archives (hereafter CLCA), CC/MIN/5/393.
34. Clare County Council Minutes, Aug. 1920, CLCA, CC/MIN/5/414.
35. O'Donnell Witness Statement, NAI, BMH/WS1322, 54.

36. Ibid., 55
37. Ibid.
38. Anthony Malone Witness Statement, NAI, BMH/WS1076, 13.
39. O'Donnell Witness Statement, NAI, BMH/WS1322, 55.
40. Ibid.
41. Clare County Council Minutes, Aug. 1920, CLCA, CC/MIN/5/414.
42. O'Donnell Witness Statement, NAI, BMH/WS1322, 56.
43. Garvin, *1922*, 67; Daly, 'Local Government and the First Dáil', 126.
44. Dáil Commission of Enquiry into Local Government in Ireland, NAI, BMH/WS1413.
45. Joost Augusteijn, *From Public Defiance to Guerrilla Warfare: The Experience of Ordinary Volunteers in the Irish War of Independence, 1916–1921* (Dublin: Irish Academic Press, 1996), 303.
46. Daly, 'Local Government and the First Dáil', 126.
47. Ibid.
48. Ibid.
49. McArdle Witness Statement, NAI, BMH/WS0501, 24.
50. *Freeman's Journal*, 18 Dec. 1920.
51. Nevil Macready to John Anderson, Aug. 1920, TNA: CO 904/188/1, cited in Laffan, *The Resurrection of Ireland*, 330.
52. Dáil Commission of Enquiry into Local Government in Ireland: Minority Report, 27 Aug. 1920, NAI, BMH/WS1413.
53. Quoted in *Connacht Tribune*, 1 Jan. 1921.
54. *Leinster Leader*, 30 July 1921; *Nenagh Guardian*, 4 Dec. 1920.
55. *Anglo-Celt*, 10 July 1920; *Leinster Leader*, 30 July 1921; *Leinster Express*, 26 June 1920; *Nenagh Guardian*, 4 Dec. 1920.
56. *Leinster Express*, 26 June 1920; *Nenagh Guardian*, 4 Dec. 1920.
57. *Leinster Leader*, 30 July 1921; *Leinster Express*, 26 June 1920; *Anglo-Celt*, 2 Apr. 1921.
58. *Leinster Express*, 26 June 1920.
59. Dáil Commission of Enquiry into Local Government in Ireland: Minority Report, 27 Aug. 1920, NAI, BMH/WS1413.
60. *Nationalist and Leinster Times*, 3 Dec. 1921.
61. Michael Brennan Witness Statement, NAI, BMH/WS1068, 58.
62. Leitrim County Council Minutes, 14 Sept. 1921, NAI, DELG/16/9; Clare County Council Minutes, 11 May 1921, CLCA, CC/MIN/5/375; Longford County Council Minutes, 19 May 1920, Longford County Archives, LCC/1/3/309; *Fermanagh Herald*, 24 Sept. 1921.
63. *Sligo Champion*, 4 Sept. 1920.
64. Fitzpatrick, *Politics and Irish Life*, 161.
65. Daly, 'Local Government and the First Dáil', 127.
66. Fitzpatrick, *Politics and Irish Life*, 161.

67. Quoted in *Connacht Tribune*, 1 Jan. 1921.
68. *Freeman's Journal*, 18 Dec. 1920.
69. Clare DÉDLG Inspector's Report 9782, 28 Oct. 1921, NAI, DELG/5/18.
70. Hugh Hehir Witness Statement, NAI, BMH/WS0683, 12.
71. RIC Inspector General's Report, Nov. 1920, TNA: CO 904/113/301.
72. Hughes, *Defying the IRA?*, 63.
73. Ibid.
74. Ibid.; Fitzpatrick, *Politics and Irish life*, 161.
75. *Freeman's Journal*, 18 Dec. 1920.
76. Ibid.
77. *Nationalist and Leinster Times*, 1 Jan. 1921.
78. *Nenagh Guardian*, 1 Jan. 1921.
79. Mitchell, *Revolutionary Government in Ireland*, 161.
80. Ibid.
81. *Irish Independent*, 6 Jan. 1921.
82. *Skibbereen Eagle*, 8 Jan. 1921.
83. George Joseph Dwyer Witness Statement, NAI, BMH/WS0678, 9; *Skibbereen Eagle*, 8 Jan. 1921.
84. *Irish Independent*, 6 Jan. 1921.
85. Ibid., 15 Jan. 1921.
86. *Freeman's Journal*, 10 Jan. 1921.
87. *Irish Independent*, 13 Jan. 1921.
88. Andrew O'Donohoe Witness Statement, NAI, BMH/WS1326, 42.
89. *Irish Independent*, 26 Jan. 1921.
90. RIC Inspector General's Report, Feb. 1921, TNA: CO 904/114/317.
91. *Freeman's Journal*, 10 Feb. 1921.
92. Ibid.
93. *The Liberator*, 24 Feb. 1921.
94. Clare County Council Minutes, 28 Feb. 1921, CLCA, CC/MIN/6/14.
95. Peter O'Loughlin Witness Statement, NAI, BMH/WS0985, 8–9.
96. *Freeman's Journal*, 10 Feb. 1921.
97. *Freeman's Journal*, 9 Feb. 1921.
98. Ibid.; T. S. McDonagh Witness Statement, NAI, BMH/WS1540, 10–11.
99. O'Donohoe Witness Statement, NAI, BMH/WS1326, 42.
100. Joseph Barrett Witness Statement, NAI, BMH/WS1324, 56.
101. Ibid.
102. Sean McNamara Witness Statement, NAI, BMH/WS1072, 10.
103. O'Donnell Witness Statement, NAI, BMH/WS1322, 55; McArdle Witness Statement, NAI, BMH/WS0501, 88–89.
104. Michael Gleeson Witness Statement, NAI, BMH/WS1288, 13.

105. RIC Inspector General's Report, Mar. 1921, TNA: CO 904/114/623; McArdle Witness Statement, NAI, BMH/WS0501, 88–89.
106. Gleeson Witness Statement, NAI, BMH/WS1288, 13.
107. Joseph O'Higgins Witness Statement, NAI, BMH/WS0507, 12.
108. Mitchell, *Revolutionary Government in Ireland*, 234.
109. RIC Inspector General's Report, Apr. 1921, TNA: CO 904/115/11; *Meath Chronicle*, 16 Apr. 1921.
110. *Freeman's Journal*, 14 Apr. 1921.
111. RIC Inspector General's Report, Apr. 1921, TNA: CO 904/115/11.
112. *Meath Chronicle*, 16 Apr. 1921.
113. *Drogheda Independent*, 16 April 1921.
114. O'Higgins Witness Statement, NAI, BMH/WS0507, 12.
115. Ibid.
116. *Irish Independent*, 11 May. 1921.
117. Patrick Cassidy Witness Statement, NAI, BMH/WS1017, 17.
118. Ibid.
119. Garvin, *1922*, 74.
120. *Freeman's Journal*, 4 Apr. 1921.
121. *Cork Examiner*, 19 May 1921; RIC Inspector General's Report, May 1921, TNA: CO 904/115/378.
122. Mitchell, *Revolutionary Government in Ireland*, 277.
123. McArdle Witness Statement, NAI, BMH/WS0501, 88.
124. Ibid.
125. Ibid., NAI, BMH/WS0501, 97.
126. Garvin, *1922*, 75.
127. Ibid., 76.
128. Ibid., 75.
129. DÉDLG Report 3059, on Leitrim County Council, NAI, DELG/16/9.
130. Leitrim County Council Minutes, 4 May 1921, NAI, DELG/16/9.
131. McArdle Witness Statement, NAI, BMH/WS0501, 88–89.
132. Gleeson Witness Statement, NAI, BMH/WS1288, 13.
133. Hughes, *Defying the IRA?*, 82.
134. Fitzpatrick, *Politics and Irish Life*, 221.
135. Ibid., 161.
136. Hughes, *Defying the IRA?*, 60.
137. Garvin, *1922*, 75; McArdle Witness Statement, NAI, BMH/WS0501, 89.
138. Hughes, *Defying the IRA?*, 60.
139. Ibid.
140. Representations to Minister for Local Government from Institutions, Associations, Trade Unions, etc., NAI, DELG/34/1.
141. Garvin, *1922*, 74.

142. Diarmaid Ferriter, *A Nation and not a Rabble: The Irish Revolution, 1913–23* (London: Profile Books, 2015), 225; Sean Scott Witness Statement, NAI, BMH/WS1486, 7; RIC Inspector General's Report, Apr. 1921, TNA: CO 904/115/5, 245, 10, 149, 14; RIC Inspector General's Report, Mar. 1921, TNA: CO 904/114/615.
143. Jeremiah Keane to 'Ned', 30 Sept. 1928, NLI MS 31,325.
144. Dan McCarthy Witness Statement, NAI, BMH/WS1697, 12.
145. Tadhg O'Sullivan Witness Statement, NAI, BMH/WS0792, 9–10.
146. Laffan, *The Resurrection of Ireland*, 294.
147. Garvin, *1922*, 77.
148. Ibid., 70.
149. Ibid., 74.
150. Total Outlay from Home Funds, 1921, NLI MS 17,152 (i).
151. Charles Townsend, *The Republic: The Fight for Irish Independence, 1918–1923* (London: Penguin Books, 2013), 328–29.
152. Ibid.
153. Total Outlay from Home Funds, 1921, NLI MS 17,152 (i).
154. Laffan, *Judging W. T. Cosgrave*, 67.
155. Ibid.
156. Leitrim DÉDLG Inspector to Leitrim County Council, 26 Aug. 1921, NAI, DELG/16/9.
157. Ibid.
158. *Fermanagh Herald*, 13 Aug. 1921.
159. Patrick Doherty Witness Statement, NAI, BMH/WS1195, 11–12; Additional Comments on Leitrim County Council Minutes, 24 Aug. 1921, NAI, DELG/16/9.
160. Hughes, *Defying the IRA?*, 72.
161. Memo from DÉDLG to Cabinet Members re: Co. Leitrim, Non-Payment of Rates, 10 Oct. 1921, NAI, DE/2/466, 1.
162. Report of DÉDLG Inspector re: Co. Leitrim, Non-Payment of Rates, 7 Oct. 1921, NAI, DE/2/466, 2.
163. Ibid.
164. Memo from DÉDLG to Cabinet Members re: Co. Leitrim, Non-Payment of Rates, 10 Oct. 1921, NAI, DE/2/466, 1.
165. Garvin, *1922*, 76.
166. Memo from Cosgrave and O'Higgins to each Member of the Cabinet, 10 Oct. 1921, NAI, DE/2/466, 2.
167. Fitzpatrick, *Politics and Irish Life*, 161.
168. Garvin, *1922*, 74.
169. Clare County Council Minutes, 20 Sept. 1921, CLCA, CC/MIN/6/32.
170. Ibid.; Clare RIC County Inspector, Sept. 1921, TNA: CO 904/116/763.

171. Clare County Council Minutes, 17 Oct. 1921, CLCA, CC/MIN/6/36–37.
172. W. T. Cosgrave to Minister of Defence, 18 Oct. 1921, NAI, DELG/5/18.
173. Clare County Council Minutes, 20 Sept. 1921, CLCA, CC/MIN/6/34.
174. Cosgrave to Minister of Defence, 18 Oct. 1921, NAI, DELG/5/18.
175. Ibid.
176. Michael Farry, *The Aftermath of Revolution: Sligo, 1921–23* (Dublin: UCD Press, 2002), 20–21; Fearghal McGarry, *Eoin O'Duffy: A Self-made Hero* (Oxford: Oxford University Press, 2005), 50; Hughes, *Defying the IRA?*, 74 (all cited in Hughes, 74).
177. Clare County Council Minutes, 17 Oct. 1921, CLCA, CC/MIN/6/37.
178. Ibid.
179. Cosgrave to Chief of Inspection, 29 Oct. 1921, NAI, DELG/5/18.
180. Clare County Council Minutes, 17 Oct. 1921, CLCA, CC/MIN/6/40.
181. Clare County Council Minutes, 31 Oct. 1921, CLCA, CC/MIN/6/46.
182. Fitzpatrick, *Politics and Irish Life*, 161.
183. Arthur Griffith, writing in the *Connaught Telegraph*, 8 Jul. 1905.
184. Hughes, *Defying the IRA?*, 82; Gavin Maxwell Foster, *The Irish Civil War and Society: Politics, Class and Conflict* (Basingstoke: Palgrave Macmillan, 2015), 128, 135.
185. Bill Kissane, *The Politics of the Irish Civil War* (Oxford: Oxford University Press, 2005), 153.
186. *Irish Times*, 10 Nov. 1922, cited in Kissane, *The Politics of the Irish Civil War*, 160.

CHAPTER 11

Taxation and the Revolutionary Inheritance: Tax Proposals, Legitimacy, and the Irish Free State, 1922–32

Jason Knirck

Kevin O'Higgins told the Dáil in 1923, 'I am not a profound economist. I can make that admission now. I could not make it when I was Minister for Economic Affairs. When I pass out from the Home Affairs Ministry I shall have equally interesting revelations to make.'[1] None of O'Higgins's colleagues proved to be profound economists either, and they have received much criticism for their inability to create a thriving economy after independence. Neither this failure nor historians' frequent focus on political differences over the Treaty should obscure the central role economic disputes played in the creation of the Free State political system. Such disputes were central indicators of political difference and fuelled the creation of the state's first two parliamentary opposition parties, the Labour and Farmers' parties. Economic policy was also a crucial benchmark by which Irish politicians assessed the state's legitimacy and advanced their interpretations of the Revolution. Most politicians framed their economic analysis with reference to the legacies of the colonial period and sought ways to overcome what were generally perceived as colonial

J. Knirck (✉)
Central Washington University, Ellensburg, WA, USA
e-mail: jason.knirck@cwu.edu

D. Kanter, P. Walsh (eds.), *Taxation, Politics, and Protest in Ireland, 1662–2016*, Palgrave Studies in the History of Finance,
https://doi.org/10.1007/978-3-030-04309-4_11

restrictions on Irish economic development. Cumann na nGaedheal argued that a postcolonial state must demonstrate its fitness to govern by balancing its budget and maintaining its credit. Party leaders also recognised the practical advantages in maintaining trade connections with England. Anti-Treatyite republicans sought to break those connections and thereby legitimise the Revolution by implementing Arthur Griffith's policy of economic self-sufficiency behind tariff walls. The Labour Party worried about capital flight to the former metropole and wanted to create structures that mandated the use of Irish wealth for Irish purposes. Labour also argued that the Revolution needed to transcend mere political aims by implementing a greater array of social services and a fairer redistribution of wealth. Finally, the Farmers' Party sought a post-revolutionary state that embraced the centrality of the farmer while reducing taxation. An analysis of the early Free State that includes the minor parties and goes beyond Treaty differences provides a fuller picture of its political development and the centrality of economic questions to that development.

While contemporary economists and financiers largely approved of Cumann na nGaedheal's economic orthodoxy, historians have been less kind. The government's general approach is well known—a balanced budget, reduced spending, lower taxes, moderate tariffs—as are the financial constraints under which it operated, such as a backlog of unpaid taxes, an expensive Civil War, and an international agricultural slump. Cormac Ó Gráda conceded the government's 'modest' economic achievements, but Mary Daly's criticism of its economic inaction is probably more typical.[2] Daly argues that the driving force behind government economic policy was Minister for Agriculture Patrick Hogan, whose commitment to free trade and hostility to industrial tariffs generally prevailed in internal Cumann na nGaedheal disputes.[3] Egged on by Finance bureaucrats, the government used commissions of experts to stall requests for economic change and, instead, pursued what Daly called the 'Triumph of Continuity', a predominantly free trade approach focused on maintaining economic connections with England.[4]

Ronan Fanning's study of the Irish Department of Finance also emphasises continuity and conservatism but with the Finance Ministry as the key institution. Fanning argues that the government was initially hesitant on financial matters, which allowed Finance officials to institute their ideas of efficiency, cost reduction, and free trade. By the mid-1920s, it was clear that 'the administration of the new state would continue to be run in the future, not in accordance with the aspirations of those men who had taken up arms in 1919–21 … but in accordance with the administrative principles of the civil servants who had come to power with the provisional government and within whose councils the representatives of Finance were pre-eminent.'[5] Mike Cronin also has focused on the abandonment of revolutionary economic ideals—which he calls 'the golden dream of national freedom, self-sufficiency and protectionism'—in favour of an acceptance of the 'harsh reality that Ireland had little real freedom in the economic realm as a result of dependence on the British market and an overriding belief in the orthodoxy of British economic thinking'. Cronin also uses Gallagher and Robinson's concept of a British 'informal empire', drawn together by financial ties more than formal political control, as a way of describing the Free State's lingering connection to the former metropole.[6] Andy Bielenberg and Raymond Ryan similarly point to 'a greater degree of continuity with pre-independence monetary arrangements', as well as the dominant role of the Department of Finance, in explaining Irish post-independence financial caution.[7]

There have been some historians who have pointed to factors other than slavish adherence to British values as explanatory factors in Irish economic decision-making. T. K. Daniel also notes the 'triumph of pragmatism over dogma' among Cumann na nGaedheal leadership. This pragmatism was rooted in concern over capital flight to British investment opportunities, a recognition of the centrality of agricultural exports to Britain, and a need to hold down costs to farmers. Daniel thus portrays Cumann na nGaedheal ministers as rationally responding to internal Irish concerns rather than blindly following British precedents. The result was 'a substantial, if unspectacular, measure of success'.[8] Similarly, Kevin Hjortshøj O'Rourke argues that Irish economic decisions generally mirrored those in the rest of Europe: most other European governments desired balanced budgets and low levels of taxation, and by the late 1920s and early 1930s, most had switched to a system of protection. O'Rourke does note the persistent—and, in his view, damaging—tie to the British economy but sees both Cumann na nGaedheal and Fianna Fáil as following general European patterns, rather than embodying idiosyncratic consequences of the Irish Revolution. O'Rourke also contends that the Irish economy performed just about as should have been expected during the 1920s and 1930s.[9]

Beyond assessments of Irish economic performance, historians have also investigated the British system of taxation that the Free State inherited. One of the most useful analyses is contained in Martin Daunton's two-volume study of British taxation and finance.[10] Daunton emphasises that 'consent, trust, and legitimacy are crucial to the history of taxation', as the government had to convince the electorate that economic policies were fairly balanced between interest groups.[11] The British government's successful creation of legitimacy allowed it to rely on greater direct taxation throughout the nineteenth century and eventually pursue what historian Roy Douglas calls 'constructive taxation' designed to produce social change.[12] Daunton also claims that economic interest groups were discursively created: 'politicians did not simply devise fiscal policies to appeal to existing social categories with economically rational, self-interested attitudes toward taxation; interests and identities were imagined or constructed by politicians and the public at least in part through the rhetoric of taxation.'[13] Following Daunton's broad approach, this chapter aims to investigate the political debates over economic policy, paying particular attention to how various parties related their economic goals to the Revolution, the legacies of colonialism, and the portions of the electorate that they felt would be receptive to their economic ideas.

As a new state, the Free State lacked the legitimacy of the British government and had to build up respect for its fiscal institutions in the face of long-standing suspicion of government as a foreign and repressive entity. Cumann na nGaedheal also inherited British colonial structures and Sinn Féin arguments attacking those structures. One of the most prominent of the latter was Arthur Griffith's notion that an independent Ireland should protect nascent Irish industries from British dumping, which drew on a wider assumption that colonialism had deliberately hindered Irish economic growth through over-taxation and revenue confiscation. An American prospectus for the 1919 Dáil loan noted that Ireland's government had cost US$65,000,000 the past fiscal year, while England had collected US$170,000,000 in Irish revenue. After noting that government only cost between US$6 and US$15 annually per capita in other small European countries, while 'British militarism costs about $40 per capita' in Ireland, the writer concluded 'it is cheaper to be free than in slavery.'[14] Independence would therefore automatically improve the Irish economy by removing colonial restrictions on Irish economic performance. Such promises were central to the Sinn Féin message. Michael Collins pledged that 'the Elected Government of Ireland stood for Social and Economic Deliverance no less than for Political Deliverance.'[15] Eamon de Valera similarly said that 'Republican policy today is … a grafting … of the constructive industrial policy of the Arthur Griffith Sinn Féin school … on to the old Fenian stock.'[16]

There also was the assumption that this economic revival would result from a particularly 'Gaelic' or 'Irish' economic and fiscal policy. Collins mused during the Civil War that 'we want a modern edition of our old Gaelic Social policy', and even Patrick Hogan hoped for 'some Gaelic social and economic ideals'.[17] The problem was that no one ever really defined what was meant by a Gaelic fiscal system. Most often, it was used as shorthand for one distinct from British colonial policy and constructed around Irish interests. Most politicians at least attempted to explain the 'Irish' origins or contexts of their economic proposals, but the overall lineaments of the Gaelic fiscal state were generally left vague.

The Cumann na nGaedheal government initially tasked with creating this fiscal state was internally divided on economic policy, but those arguing for efficiency, low taxes, and free trade generally prevailed in the state's early years. Much of this stemmed from the influence of the bureaucrats in the Ministry of Finance and the policy that Finance had to approve spending plans originating in any other department. As the state took shape, Finance officials generally took a conservative line. A Finance memo from May 1923 noted that 'the country is not in a position to stand increased taxation and the maintenance for any length of time of the present conditions under which our taxation is at higher rates than the British will tend to become embarrassing ... strict economy, therefore, becomes imperative.'[18] The most well-known manifestation of this urge was the government's decision to cut old-age pensions in the 1924 budget, a decision that was initially proposed by Finance officials.[19]

The government, W. T. Cosgrave in particular, also repeatedly expressed disdain for excessive borrowing, claiming that it would hurt Ireland's credit. The general principle by which the government operated was that recurring expenses had to be paid out of ordinary revenue, with loans only used for extraordinary costs such as the Civil War, the Shannon Scheme, and land purchase. As Cosgrave told the Dáil, 'I have no particular penchant for National Debt. If you can show value for it, and that the country benefits by whatever it has purchased, and that it makes the country richer, and gives it greater possibilities to stir up and develop its potentialities, then there is a case for raising money for that particular purpose.'[20] The government and Finance officials rejected a new court system, afforestation schemes, improving the Gaeltacht, and old-age pensions as unworthy of debt. As Cosgrave said in frustration, 'deputies come here repeatedly, time after time, asking for an extension of this service and of that ... but when it comes to a question of raising the money nobody can make a suggestion as to how it is to be got. Get it from somebody else is always the story.'[21]

On the revenue side, Cumann na nGaedheal decided initially to retain the taxation system from the final years of British rule, claiming it did not want to make piecemeal fiscal changes in the state's infancy pending greater study. As Cosgrave explained, 'I am not very keen on the reconsideration of the whole fiscal system until there is an opportunity of considering it in the widest aspect. It is not a matter that can be dealt with with any degree of satisfaction in a haphazard way. We have not been able to give it any such consideration as it deserves, and it is not wise to make experiments.'[22] As revolutions are nothing if not experiments, this proved unsatisfying to many inside and outside of the party. The Free State started with an income tax rate of 5s. in the pound in 1922, but as it reduced that throughout the decade to make Irish investments more attractive, it ended up deriving a disproportionate amount of its revenue from regressive sin taxes, a system widely seen as favouring the wealthy over the poor.[23]

The government depicted this not as a disappointing retreat from revolutionary goals, but as the exercise of responsibility necessary to a new state. Even after unpopular cuts to old-age pensions, Finance Minister Ernest Blythe confidently asserted, 'we are not afraid of doing anything necessary for the welfare of the country. We are able to face any unpopularity that may be necessary for the purpose of balancing the Budget.'[24] Ministers, Cosgrave in particular, liked to depict themselves as resisting pressure and accepting criticism in the face of other parties' irresponsible spending plans. Cosgrave said, 'this Dáil is so popularly constituted that the one enemy of the people in this Dáil is the Minister for Finance. He must be. He has to stand out against claims coming in, and suggestions coming from different sides of the Dáil that this person has suffered, that that person must be compensated, and that that local authority must get something else, and that we require the development of industry and commerce and fisheries, and other things in every part of the country.'[25] According to Cosgrave, other deputies could be swayed by such factors, but the Minister for Finance could not: 'I have not got the happy knack … of leaving my conscience outside the door when I come in here. I have to bring it along with me, and I cannot close my eyes to facts.'[26] Civil War lawlessness, and the debt that came in its wake, jeopardised Ireland's credit rating, and there was a time in early 1923 when the government was unsure of its ability to meet its costs.[27] The fact that the government overcame this crisis and maintained its solvency and creditworthiness was a great source of pride to Cumann na nGaedheal and was often used to defend subsequent fiscal caution.

It is easy to reduce this concern with debt, credit, and expenditure to a caricature of Cosgrave's oft-cited 'business' principles and experience managing a public house. However, the international and postcolonial dimension to this attitude renders it more interesting. Ireland needed to demonstrate that it was indeed fit for self-government, and financial prudence was one of the key markers of this for Cumann na nGaedheal. A party appeal for donations in 1924 noted 'the Government has established our National Credit on a solid basis of native brains, industry, and resources, without any foreign aid or foreign Commitments. It has secured by careful finance that the good name of Ireland shall stand untarnished in the markets of the world and that the disorganisation caused by years of revolution and civil war shall be made as brief in its effects as possible.'[28] Ministers also cited the performance of Ireland's internally floated loan as a source of national pride. Blythe's New Year's message as Minister for Finance for 1927 boasted, 'Our National Loan has in recent weeks stood as high as [the] British War Loan', while Hogan echoed, 'our National Loan [is] standing higher than the price of issue and practically at par.'[29] International money markets proved Irish fitness for self-government. A key element of this was Ireland's willingness to assume what were perceived as rightful debts, such as the land annuities, and to treat all sections—including unionists—fairly and responsibly. This was laid out by Patrick Hogan in his initial explanation of the payments to landlords for land expropriated under the 1923 Land Act: 'in fixing these terms the Government have kept in mind our financial credit, and they have also kept in mind something that is much more important—what I will call our national credit. They wish to be fair both to the landlord and tenant.'[30] International reputation mattered as much as accounting ledgers.

Ireland's economic and fiscal problems were blamed on groups external to the government. Taxes could not be lowered because republicans initiated an expensive Civil War. Revenues slumped because unionists and others had used the Revolution to evade taxes. Irish industry struggled because of its inefficiency and incompetence. The suggested remedy was for the Irish people to make better economic choices. They had to pay their taxes, strengthen their companies, and respect order. Cosgrave informed the Dáil in 1922, 'there has been all through the history of this country a general design to place practically every citizen in the community dependent upon the Government. That is a false basis—a wrong basis.'[31] Eoin MacNeill told the Cumann na nGaedheal convention in 1924 'this condition of dependence on the Government must be replaced by an attitude of self-help which would grow with greater experience of liberty.'[32] This transferred the Sinn Féin notion of self-reliance from the community to the individual. While it was presented as a way of weaning the Irish from colonial notions of the omnipotent state and could also be pitched to an international audience expecting profligacy and irresponsibility from a postcolonial government, it ultimately proved a sharp distinction from the aspirational rhetoric of the Revolution and lacked appeal to Irish voters.

In one of the few analyses of Ernest Blythe as Finance Minister, Ryan McCourt has argued that Blythe did not face significant criticism for his policies until Fianna Fáil entered the Dáil.[33] This simply is not true, as the government's perceived failure to adhere to the economic ideas of the Revolution drew considerable opposition from within the Dáil chamber before 1927, including from those who otherwise supported Cumann na nGaedheal. Much of the early criticism came from Darrell Figgis, who consistently lobbied for the implementation of Griffith's economic plans. Figgis was a well-known author and long-time Sinn Féiner who had chaired the Commission of Inquiry into the Resources and Industries of Ireland set up by the First Dáil. As a result, he considered himself something of an expert on economic policy. After hearing that Cumann na nGaedheal was going to continue the British fiscal system, Figgis said, 'I feel regret that the Minister for Finance did not bravely throw the entire English system that we have taken over into the melting pot. It was drafted for conditions that were not suitable for this country. They are not applicable to this country, as they were never intended for conditions here.'[34] George Gavan Duffy, another Sinn Féiner and frequent Cosgrave critic, similarly demanded that the next Irish budget be 'a purely Irish budget independent of the traditions of the past and of our fiscal system being tied up with England'.[35] Figgis spoke frequently about why he thought the British fiscal system was not applicable to Ireland, citing the example of the 33 per cent duty on motor cars, which served no protective purpose in Ireland because there were no native car manufacturers. Similar arguments were advanced about the taxes on white glass, films, and medical chloroform. As Figgis said, 'a large number of taxes that we have taken over have no earthly kind of applicability or application whatever to this country. They were drafted to safeguard English industries, many of which do not exist in this country at all.' The Irish government was using them to increase revenue, which was contrary to their purpose in England.[36] In addition, Figgis claimed that 'Ireland is bearing a scale of taxation first introduced by a foreign Parliament because of its own operations in the European War ... If the present heavy taxation should remain it would cripple our productive power for the future.'[37] Figgis favoured lower taxes, tariffs more suited to Irish manufacturers, and greater borrowing. Gavan Duffy proposed a non-party tariff committee and cuts to the civil service: 'I think it is within the recollection of Deputies that in the pre-Free State days very considerable propaganda used to be carried on about the corruption of Dublin Castle, its unnecessary departments, its inefficiency, its waste, and its large salaries.'[38] Sean Milroy, another committed Griffithite initially within Cumann na nGaedheal, echoed Figgis in claiming that Irish duties were useless as they were not protecting goods made in Ireland. He also wanted taxation to be 'reproductive, so that, instead of diminishing the wealth of those who contribute to the revenues of the State, it increases it, and, consequently, increases the wealth of the State'. Instead, he did not see 'any glimmer of comprehension that taxation had any relation to the production of wealth in the state'.[39] What these critics wanted was what the government eventually adopted—a targeted system of tariffs applied after investigation of the particular Free State conditions—but they wanted to move more quickly towards that goal than did the government and rejected the imposition of non-protective duties solely for the raising of revenue. These critics also believed that such a policy would legitimise the state by tying it more closely to the Revolution, in terms of both implementing Griffith's ideals and rooting out the sins of Dublin Castle.

The government also faced criticism from the Farmers' and Labour parties. The Farmers' Party newspaper lamented the dominance of political questions at the polls: 'we would suggest that the next political election be contested on issues of protection or free trade, and similar matters affecting the private purse of every citizen ... we urge upon the farming community ... that they be guided in their choice of representatives largely by the economic policy and programme outlined by the various Party leaders.'[40] The Farmers aggressively promoted their economic vision—free trade, low taxes and rates, and reductions in public services—because they felt the unnatural dominance of Sinn Féin had excluded farmers from their rightful position in the Free State. Farmers constituted approximately two-thirds of the population and controlled almost 85 per cent of the country's wealth but 'find themselves debarred from the councils of the nation'.[41] Farmers hoped that the Revolution would usher in an era in which agrarian issues dominated government policy, reversing what they saw as years of British neglect.[42] Instead, the Revolution brought irresponsible spending, crushing taxation, and local councils run by Sinn Féiners with no agrarian connection, who presided over high levels of spending subject to low levels of oversight. A Farmers' editorial condemned 'a county council … composed entirely of guerrilla chiefs, whose energies were unnaturally divided between attention to functions of war and administration of affairs of peace—with injustice both to themselves and the general community'.[43] Another charged that 'its [Sinn Féin's] nominees took office in a land of plenty, and they bequeathed a desert.'[44] This attitude partially stemmed from class prejudices, as it was implied that Sinn Féin's 'guerrilla chiefs' came from a class that did not pay local rates. In contrast, the Farmers believed themselves to be 'well-known respectable citizens … who … could be relied on to carry on the affairs of the country both efficiently and economically'.[45] The party argued that the centrality of agriculture meant that the farmers should actually bear the lowest burden of taxation, for fear of 'killing the goose that lays the golden egg'.[46] Farmers' deputies specifically complained about the costs of hospitals, sanatoria, and the Board of Health and repeatedly requested a greater portion of road repair costs be charged to the state rather than the local rates, so as to spread the burden more evenly across the population. They also invoked class-based language, as much of the damage to the roads—outside of Civil War residue—was blamed on 'the wealthy man's heavy touring car used principally for joy-riding, and travelling through many counties besides that in which it was taxed'.[47]

The Farmers saw little accountability at the national level either. Whereas county councils were in the hands of non-rate-paying local Sinn Féiners, the central government was perceived as a playground for urbane educated elites who cared little about the land. The always-quotable Denis Gorey, parliamentary leader of the Farmers' Party until 1927, said:

> We got into the spending habit during the war and we have not got out of it yet. This is most remarkable among our professional, business, and official people. … The fault is not of agriculture, but of the parasites living on the back of agriculture. … The Dublin picture-houses and theatres are overflowing night and day, and they are building more of them. … And who is paying for it all? Does it need any answer—the cart-horse of the country, the farm labourer and the farmer.[48]

A speaker at a Farmers' Union meeting in 1925 blamed taxation for the agricultural depression and said 'all the public offices and institutions were over-staffed and the officials over-paid. Reductions all round would have to be made in that sphere.'[49] Gorey at times claimed that there was rampant overstaffing in the railroads ('the workers are for the most part of the day doing nothing'), the Seanad ('I think the place is overstaffed doing nothing'), the Post Office ('it is quite a common thing in the west and rural districts ... that a postman should not deliver more than one letter in the whole week. The rural districts of Ireland are not inhabited by letter-writing people'), and in the army ('probably there are too many typists employed. I have seen some of them sometimes dancing instead of typing').[50] He also complained bitterly about the cost of education, claiming that 'we have too much education in Kilkenny' because 'it is costing them [taxpayers] more than any other people in the world.' The result was an overeducated non-agrarian elite: 'We have practically got rid of the landlord class, but now we are establishing what may be called the mental lords, the educational lords—another new system of aristocracy.'[51] Conor Hogan, a Farmers' Teachta Dála (TD), made the disturbing claim that 'they were being literally blood-sucked by this mass of officials.' Less distressingly, another supporter said the Free State was 'a paradise for officials'.[52]

The suggested remedies included cuts to salaries, staffing, and services. At the 1926 party congress, the Waterford branch proposed a sliding scale of reductions to salaries over £200. Another supporter proposed a committee of experts to reduce the ranks of the bureaucrats, the Irish equivalent of Britain's Geddes Axe.[53] Economy and efficiency in government were key planks of the Farmers' platform, and one way that they hoped the interests of farmers—a group they saw as synonymous with ratepayers—could be foregrounded in the new state.

Party spokesmen also blamed organised labour, which they claimed drove up wages, lowered productivity, and disturbed industry. The *Irish Farmer* wrote that 'the unskilled Dublin street labourer is one of the most pampered workers in Europe.'[54] In Gorey's words, 'in the City of Dublin, it is nothing but "go slow and take it easy", one holding up a crowbar, while another hits it with a hammer; one stroke every ten minutes. Why you would want a microscope to watch their movements.'[55] One of the most interesting things about the Farmers' diagnosis of Ireland's economic ills was that they scarcely referenced colonialism. Instead, the roots of the problem were found within Ireland: a free-spending government with little regard for farmers, local authorities unmoored from a sense of fiscal responsibility, and a lack of work ethic among the population. Gorey said, 'it is no use trying to expect prosperity in a nation if we are all going to be a nation of go-slows and born-tireds.'[56] Farmers' TD Richard Wilson detected

> a little over-appreciation of our own abilities. No man in Saorstát Éireann at the present time considers what is paid to another man similarly employed in any other white country would be sufficient for any personage dignified by being a member of Saorstát Éireann. ... A member of the 'wee country' [Northern Ireland] is willing to produce flour at a certain wage, and we are asked then to put up a barrier so as to prevent the man who gives value for the money. ... We consider that we are the sons of Saorstát Éireann, and by that means that we are entitled to more than anyone else.[57]

The Farmers imagined an ideal economic citizen who was agrarian, rate-paying, and self-made. Their views intersected broadly with Cumann na nGaedheal attitudes, although without the Gaelicism and statism of many ex-revolutionaries. Gorey summed it up by asking, 'What has enabled any country to carry on? There is one thing—and that is individual effort, and the moment you sap or tamper with individual effort, you sap the spring of the nation's life.'[58] The Farmers responded similarly when Labour proposed a mandatory tillage resolution—such policies would violate the notions of liberty with which they associated the Revolution. Gorey said, 'there is no free choice in his suggestion. It is coercion and slavery, and nothing else.' Deputy Wilson said, 'We are experts in our own line. There is nobody here who can tell us anything about agriculture.'[59] At times, the Farmers requested state funding for agricultural marketing and technical education, but they most often posited the state as a baneful influence. While Cumann na nGaedheal leaders shared many of these laissez-faire assumptions in the realm of economics—particularly minimising the state's role in and responsibility for job creation—they had more of a statist approach in non-economic realms.

The Labour Party, in contrast, remained concerned about colonial legacies, particularly the continued attraction of British investments and emulation of British Treasury attitudes towards finance. They envisioned an economically interventionist state, a different package of taxes, and a commitment to using Irish wealth to fund Irish prosperity rather than seeing profits siphoned off to London. Daunton argues that one of the main tasks of the nascent British Labour Party was to show that its sectional concerns overlapped with the concerns of the British public in general.[60] This was an even more imperative task for Irish Labour, operating in a demographic context with relatively few urban workers and a political context that had emphasised unity and 'national' concerns during the Revolution. As a result, the party tried to broaden its message. Labour leader Thomas Johnson repeatedly denied that his party aimed for nationalisation of all industry, although admitting its appeal for particular industries.[61] He also denied that he argued for an equal distribution of wealth.[62] He did, however, assert that workers expected to get more than a parliament out of the Revolution. They expected 'an improvement in the position of the worker relative to the position of the wealthier class in the community'.[63]

Labour called for a higher amount of social spending than did Cumann na nGaedheal or the Farmers, emphasising in particular education, housing, unemployment insurance, and pensions. As for funding those programmes, Labour rejected assumptions that recurrent expenses should come out of ordinary revenue. For example, Labour deputies proposed that money be borrowed for public works and to construct houses for working-class men discharged from the National Army.[64] These debts were acceptable to Labour because they served socially, economically, and morally good purposes. Johnson claimed, 'you will get value for it. You will get material value for it. … you can utilise the labour of these men [ex-soldiers] and the labour of the men who are at present unemployed in such a matter as will add to the national wealth, and even make it possible for ordinary economic processes in future years to be more productive and beneficial to the individuals who are responsible for the running of the economic machine.'[65] This critique was similar to that expressed by Sean Milroy—that the government was unable to see a tax system as good for anything but revenue creation—but Labour had a different group of beneficiaries in mind.

Labour looked at taxation through this same lens of broad social and economic utility rather than as a loss to an individual taxpayer. When initiating discussion on the first formal financial estimates of the new state, Johnson urged the Dáil 'to consider, not the amount of taxation, but the value that is received from it'.[66] In so doing, he frequently compared the waste of Civil War spending—for which money was borrowed—with the remunerative and socially useful programmes proposed by Labour. The goal was to use taxation policy to achieve both a redistribution of wealth and a greater domestic market for Irish goods. As Johnson told the Dáil in 1923, 'the weight of taxation is not the only consideration, and if we can ensure that the taxes that are paid to the public Exchequer are to be circulated within the country the loss will not be felt by the normal workmen of the town or the normal working farmers of the country. The people who will be hit no doubt will be that considerable section of the community that is living on unearned incomes for which they give no service.'[67] Labour thus did not attack private property as a concept but instead argued for social utility and social contribution as standards by which to judge the legitimacy of property.

This approach can be seen in Labour's position on the question of double taxation. Cosgrave's government proposed a bill that allowed Irish citizens to escape full rates of Irish and British income tax on investments lodged in Britain. Johnson criticised this, hoping to remove an incentive for capital flight: 'The effect of this relief is to encourage Irish investors to send their investments over the water. I think the policy should be just the contrary—to encourage or induce or prevail upon Irish investors, by a fiscal provision, to invest their moneys in Irish undertakings.' The goals would be to increase money in the Irish Exchequer and to use the fiscal system to promote a greater sense of Irishness: 'It is said "where your treasure is there will your heart be also", and if we encourage, by [Cosgrave's] system of relief, investors to invest their money in British securities we shall find that the minds and the thoughts and the ambitions of the said investors will follow their investments and that they will take more interest in British affairs than they will take in Irish affairs.' Johnson proposed an even higher tax on profits from investments external to Ireland.[68] He thought the additional revenue could be used to reduce the sugar tax, 'the one tax that touches in a direct way every child, every woman, and every man in the community'.[69]

This dispute, which Labour lost, gets to the heart of Labour's view on taxation. The party judged wealth by its social utility, finding little such utility in money invested overseas. In supporting Johnson's proposal, Labour TD Sean Lyons said, 'we in this country have no longer any room for drones who simply lodge their money in the banks and do not utilise it for the benefit of the people, or for the advancement of the interests of the country.' Lyons argued that interest income should have its tax doubled 'or else these people should be made take the money from the banks and utilise it for the development and benefit of the country'.[70] Johnson made the same argument about penalising useless wealth in discussing compensation to landlords under the Land Act: 'So far as there are legal rights on the part of the landlord, they ought be conditioned by the services he renders in his connection with the land, and I am not going to admit any right to compensation ... to any landlord who is simply a rent receiver.'[71]

This mirrored the position of the British Labour and Liberal reformers who attacked unearned income during Lloyd George's overhaul of the British tax code, but the issue was altered in Ireland by the postcolonial context.[72] In the Irish case, the critics of unearned wealth wanted not only to tap that wealth to fund social programmes but also to prevent it from returning to the former metropole. The implicit assumption here was that many such investors were unionists who had to be made to help Ireland through financial incentives rather than sentiment. This proposal also tied into a larger aspect of Labour's views on taxation: the party wanted to use the tax code to promote a greater sense of Irishness and community. Unlike Fianna Fáil, Labour generally did not want to do this through tariffs, but instead through restrictions on the spending of government moneys, as well as taxing externally derived income. This was evident in the party's promotion of a 'buy Irish' campaign through proposed changes to the fiscal system. Johnson suggested that a portion of unemployment benefits and army salaries must be used for Irish goods.[73] He made the same proposal regarding compensation to property owners for revolutionary damages.[74] These proposals reveal Labour's general economic vision: that the government would provide generous benefits paid for by higher direct taxation, but those benefits would circulate in the Irish economy, creating more jobs and more demand.

Labour also wanted to reduce the amount of indirect taxation in Ireland. Ireland derived a higher proportion of its revenue from indirect taxation than did Britain and other Dominions—Johnson particularly cited New Zealand—and Labour believed this particularly regressive tax code to be profoundly unjust.[75] The tea and sugar duties were 'a tax upon the housewife' and 'taxes upon women', and Johnson claimed that the amount of these taxes was 'unconscionably large'. Johnson made a number of financial arguments about the state's undue reliance on indirect taxation, but Labour's proposals for reduction in such taxes fundamentally rested on a moral argument. Johnson proposed to reduce the duty on sugar to give the Dáil 'an opportunity of indicating its intention in regard to taxation of the poor'. He said, 'I lay down that the principle we should follow in respect of taxation is that it should not leave the taxpayer in a position of destitution. It should be so modulated as to leave the citizen with a sufficiency to lead a reasonable life according to civilised standards.'[76]

Like Cumann na nGaedheal, Labour believed the remnants of colonialism still had a deleterious effect on Ireland's economy. But whereas Cumann na nGaedheal tended to defend efficiency measures as a way of overturning colonial stereotypes, Labour was more concerned about the continued pull of the London financial market and the government's emulation of the British financial system. Johnson claimed that Cosgrave's stance on double income tax demonstrated 'that he had been completely caught up with the British ideas of finance and economics and commerce, and I think it is a bad look out for the future of the country'.[77] Unlike the Farmers, though, Labour tended to see economic underperformance as rooted in structural difficulties, particularly a taxation system that did not reward investment in Ireland, as well as low wages and insufficient jobs that did little to build up Irish demand for Irish-made products. Labour proved a persistent critic of the government's financial policy, charging it with ignoring both the economic promise of the Revolution and the reams of documents produced by revolutionary propagandists about Ireland's colonial underdevelopment. In so doing, it assumed that its economic public consisted of male, largely urban, workers, who would benefit from a reduction in indirect taxation and the variety of mostly urban amenities—parks, libraries, and unemployment benefits—for which Labour argued.

Anti-Treaty Sinn Féin also articulated an alternative economic and fiscal vision for Ireland, using its time in abstention to hone the economic focus that would ultimately bring republicans to power in 1932. As Tim O'Neil has argued, the end of the Civil War touched off a debate within the republican movement about the role of economic proposals in the republican platform. O'Neil's 'negotiable republicans'—those who wanted to achieve the republic through the institutions of the Free State if necessary—'increasingly re-framed their republic in socio-economic terms'.[78] In 1926, these republicans formed Fianna Fáil, and the new party's economic platform echoed Griffith's vision, including extensive industrial tariffs, an increase in tillage, and a loan-funded infrastructure and reconstruction programme.[79] Fianna Fáil also emphasised the interests of smaller farmers, calling for a more rapid redistribution of land to the landless and uneconomic holders. Additionally, republicans hearkened back to Sinn Féin's claim that Ireland was overtaxed, criticising the government's failure to press this claim. Fianna Fáil's pamphlet attacking the 1926 Ultimate Financial Settlement estimated that Irish over-taxation since 1870 was in the neighbourhood of £169,000,000, a figure then used to argue for the non-payment of land annuities to Britain.[80] Republicans also claimed that the Free State was simply a continuation of British economic and political domination. Countess Markievicz, for example, wrote that by accepting the Treaty, the Cumann na nGaedheal ministers 'were part of the machinery of the British Empire; they had sold themselves to Imperialism, capitalism and graft. The economic ruin of Ireland was begun.'[81] Anti-Treatyites also blamed unemployment on 'the British policy (which dominates Ireland)' of placing 'the interest of bankers and financiers first and ... sacrific[ing] the people to reactionary financial interests ... The Anglo-Irish financiers who place British financial and political domination first and last are too strong for the Free State leaders.'[82]

Although Cumann na nGaedheal had faced significant criticism of its economic plan during its first five years, the combination of Fianna Fáil's assertive socio-economic focus with the onset of the depression meant that economic issues assumed even greater importance once Fianna Fáil entered the Dáil. Even though many of its criticisms of the government had been raised before 1927 by the Farmers' and Labour parties, Fianna Fáil had a talented leadership group and a national newspaper, the *Irish Press*, both of which the small parties lacked. The party also tapped into genuine dissatisfaction with the Free State's economic performance, even before the onset of depression. The government's ability to explain its apparent neglect of economic issues withered as the Civil War receded, and its inactivity began to look less like an ad hoc response to the state's difficult birth and more like a governing philosophy as the decade wore on. As a result, Fianna Fáil set the tone of the economic discussion after 1927, and this was most evident in the critical election campaign of 1932.

In seeking its first electoral majority, Fianna Fáil blasted the government for its neglect of economic issues, specifically its failures in breaking the economic connections with England, implementing efficiencies, and developing native industry. De Valera said, 'the present government has had ten years to work out its policy and the result is that 26 counties of this country with their three million people buy more from Britain than any country in the world.'[83] An *Irish Press* editorial noted that 'if Mr. Hogan has his way, he will land us back to the economic union with Great Britain, which in the seventy-four years preceding 1921 reduced the population of Ireland by half.'[84] Sean Lemass, Fianna Fáil's most effective campaigner on economic issues, said, 'the Saorstát was the only country in the world inhabited by the white race where the population had declined as it had here in the last nine years', implying that economic underperformance and emigration were now seen as badges of the non-white world.[85] Fianna Fáil also ridiculed Cumann na nGaedheal's claims to be running the country on business lines, with the expense of the Shannon Hydroelectric Scheme generally cited as evidence of the government's managerial ineptitude.[86] Lemass called Cumann na nGaedheal 'an unmitigated disaster for the people' and Robert Briscoe said, 'the record of the present Government showed a continual surrender, nationally and economically, to England.'[87] A Fianna Fáil advertisement tagged Cumann na nGaedheal as 'the Greatest Failure in Irish History' and a Fianna Fáil candidate memorably predicted, 'if there were a Cumann na nGaedheal Government in power for another five years the country, at the end of the term, would be half an internment camp and the other half a poorhouse.'[88]

Fianna Fáil also questioned the government's spending priorities. The government had just announced unpopular cuts to Garda and teachers' salaries, and Fianna Fáil responded by claiming it would trim those of elite civil servants. De Valera argued that those making £1,000 annually should face reductions because 'we could always feel certain that those smaller salaries are being spent inside the community for necessaries, while much of the larger salaries were spent outside the community and often on luxuries.'[89] The party wanted increased domestic spending and a greater homogenisation of incomes, what de Valera memorably termed 'frugal comfort'.

Fianna Fáil also censured the government's handling of the land annuities due to Britain for land purchased under pre-independence Land Acts, claiming that the Free State government's willingness to collect the annuities and transfer them to Britain reduced it to a British tool. Referencing the annuities, Sean MacEntee said, 'the Government which resigned rather than find money for the Old Age Pensioners was prepared to spend thousands in an attempt to maintain and enforce British claims against this country.'[90] The government's acceptance of the annuities' legality and legitimacy—an issue settled by secret agreements with Britain in 1923 and 1926—was blamed for burdening the Irish people with a debt higher than that of German reparations. De Valera claimed that for every £100 collected in Ireland, £24 went to England to pay annuities, damage claims, and Royal Irish Constabulary (RIC) pensions, while only £20 of such funds went to reparations in Germany.[91] The implication was clear: if a cessation of reparation payments was being discussed for 'guilty' Germany, a similar cessation would be acceptable for victimised Ireland. De Valera, however, was careful to state that Fianna Fáil still wanted the annuities to be collected, but his party would retain them in Ireland so as to reduce taxation and rates.[92]

The main subject about which Fianna Fáil condemned the government, though, was its unwillingness to implement widespread tariffs. Fianna Fáil thought Cumann na nGaedheal's approach to tariffs had been both too narrow and too slow. By 1932, Fianna Fáil speakers regularly claimed that Cumann na nGaedheal's unwillingness to extend its tariff policy led to '80,000 workers ... employed in various other countries making goods to be sent to this country which could be produced at home'.[93] Eighty thousand was also conveniently the number of registered unemployed in the Free State.

The solution was to return to the old Sinn Féin programme. De Valera said, 'the cure for unemployment was the old Sinn Féin policy of making themselves as self-supporting as possible, but the very men who had preached it on the same platforms as he in 1917 and 1921, when they had an opportunity of working it turned their backs upon it and sneered.'[94] Fianna Fáil frequently invoked the memory of Arthur Griffith in making this argument: a 1902 quote from Griffith railing against British dumping was highlighted in a 1932 election issue of the *Irish Press*, and an editorial claimed that 'Griffith spent his life trying to break the economic union with Great Britain. Mr. Cosgrave's dearest ambition would seem to be to restore it in some measure.'[95] As Lemass told an election meeting, protection could 'build up their wasted resources, repair the damages of misgovernment, and get a sustained effort to solve economic and social problems. Unemployment was the key of the whole position. Unemployment in the Free State need not exist and the reason it did was the failure of the Government to deal with it.'[96] Fianna Fáil blamed the government for Ireland's economic underperformance and saw that government as a continuance of British colonial rule. In making this argument, the party also turned the government's extolling of the powers of the Treaty against it. De Valera said the government 'had at least the power to put their [Sinn Féin's] economic policy into force, but they were no more true to that economic programme than they were true to the political programme'.[97] Fianna Fáil even claimed that its tariff policy would not harm export farmers. De Valera blithely asserted that 'England was not going to war with her best customer', but the party also expressed willingness to negotiate an overall trade deal with England.[98] In addition, Fianna Fáil speakers argued that protection would build up the Irish market for agricultural producers and reduce farmers' relative tax burden by increasing the general population and the ranks of property holders.[99] Lemass called this 'a constructive alternative to Communism'.[100]

The smaller parties were often left in Fianna Fáil's wake, having had many of their issues co-opted by their larger rival. Labour, however, distinguished itself from Fianna Fáil by being considerably more sceptical regarding tariffs. As the party's official election statement read:

> The Labour Party favours the active use of the power of the State to foster existing industries and promote such new industries as are suited to the country and are capable of development. For these purposes we would control imports where necessary, and would use the instrument of tariffs, or the more direct method of prohibition or licence, whichever seemed best calculated to help the industries at the lowest cost to the consumer. The Labour Party does not stand for high tariffs without discrimination; nor do we believe in sheltering inefficient manufacturers behind tariff walls. ... We are not prepared to protect manufacturers against foreign competitors without imposing upon them an obligation to pay fair wages to their employees.[101]

Labour's position on tariffs, other than its attempt to link them to a guarantee of fair wages, did not differ substantially from Cumann na nGaedheal's. Labour's scepticism derived in part from an assumption that the problems with Irish industry were rooted in the failures of Irish industrialists to modernise. Senator T. J. O'Farrell argued that 'the backward condition of Irish industry was largely accounted for by the absence of organisation, modern machinery, modern marketing methods and a proper sense of the requirements of a modern community in a world of competition. Tariffs of themselves were proving an absolute failure.' O'Farrell then cited industries that had been protected but were still unable to compete with imports, such as overcoats and boots. He and other Labour candidates proposed that funds from approved tariffs be used to establish a 'National Development Commission [for] Irish industrialists, with a view to re-organising and modernising their factories and their methods ... so as to ensure that Protection was not being utilised to cover up laziness and inefficiency'.[102] Overall, Labour sought to hold the balance of power in the Dáil and restrict what it considered a dangerously broad tariff policy.

The Farmers' Party lost a great deal of coherence after 1927, when a number of its members, including Gorey, joined Cumann na nGaedheal. In the September 1927 election, the Farmers' position still stressed

'Reduced Taxation, Easy Credit Facilities, State Stability, Free Trade and all round Fair Play for Farmers'.[103] But, as Daly notes, certain non-cattle farmers were already starting to agitate for limited protection, and the governing party was receptive to their concerns in a way that it was not to those raised by manufacturers. Already in February 1927, the Cumann na nGaedheal Ard Comhairle directed the government 'to examine in detail the suggestion for Protection for Agricultural Produce generally'.[104] In the 1932 election, the remaining Farmers' candidates continued to emphasise the need to cut rates, taxes, and expenses; the desire to transfer road expenses to the national government; and the necessity of creating more agricultural jobs. Candidate John Cuffe expressed many of the same concerns about tariffs as Labour but promised to keep an 'open mind', explaining 'on principle he was opposed to conferring favours on any small section of the community at the expense of the general ratepayer and consumer, but where tariffs could be shown to do more good than evil, he had no objection to a fair measure of protection for Irish industry.'[105] Like Labour and Cumann na nGaedheal, the emphasis was on deciding the question industry by industry rather than across the board.

For its part, the government seemed confident in its economic record as the 1920s closed. In 1929, Blythe told the Dáil 'there is now no serious cause for alarm', and he remained cautiously optimistic in 1930.[106] In a 1929 article called 'Eight Years of Progress', Cosgrave boasted that 'the total dead-weight national debt amounts to less than one year's revenue', and that taxation per head had been reduced over 25 per cent since 1920–21, earned income tax had been reduced 50 per cent, and the duties on tea, coffee, and cocoa had been abolished.[107] By 1931, though, the situation had worsened and the government had to pass supplemental estimates and an income tax increase. An internal Finance memo bemoaned the fact that departments had not cut costs sufficiently, revenue was down from projected amounts, and the government had been living beyond its means for years.[108]

Despite these difficulties, ministers hit the campaign trail in 1932, exuding optimism about their economic record. Blythe's pamphlet for Monaghan voters publicised the government's protection of 'over twenty-three industries', its reorganisation and standardisation of the agricultural industry, its reduction of taxation, its floating of three internal loans, and even its relief of double taxation obligations. Voters were also told the government had 'won for the Irish Free State a high reputation in every country for honesty of dealing and sound business Government'.[109]

This latter was a major point of pride. The 'Fighting Points' given to Cumann na nGaedheal speakers in 1932 said, 'our National Credit is good because the Government has made it good.'[110] Cosgrave praised the 'very sound financial system' they had created that was 'the envy of other countries'.[111] As Cosgrave said, 'they had shown a relatively lower fall in their business, in their wealth, in their credit, and in the number of unemployed persons than any of the great nations.'[112] The government had brought about this relatively happy state of affairs by balancing the budget for eight straight years and cutting costs.[113]

The government also defended its record on tariffs. First, it tried to decouple Fianna Fáil's proposals from those of Griffith, generally seen as a Treatyite icon. Blythe told a nominating convention in Cavan that 'Griffith always believed in discrimination in tariffs and was not in favour of giving protection to any manufacturer if the latter was going to make undue profits at the expense of the consumer.'[114] Eoin MacNeill called this 'selective protection' that would only be imposed after 'full inquiry showed that the imposition of a tariff would lead to increased employment without a disproportionate rise in the cost of living'.[115] Patrick Hogan said that a tariff, with some exceptions, was merely 'a tax on the consumer in favour of particular industries. Tariffs, in the main, with very few exceptions, mean taking the money out of the pockets of the consumer and giving it to specially protected industries.'[116] Blythe dismissed large-scale protection by pointing to the ongoing difficulties of the pro-tariff United States.[117] The best path for the Free State was to continue preferential access to the British market. Hogan made this point most frequently: 'the country was not going to be made rich quickly with tariffs. There was a tariff on bacon and butter and the prices of the latter commodity did not advance until it became scarce in the home market. He wanted to see co-operation between this country and England economically; he wanted to see Ireland get a better slice of the British market and a better price for Irish goods.'[118]

The government presented this approach as something other than Anglophilia, as its opponents charged. Blythe said they were willing to fight England when necessary but were also prepared to cooperate with Britain when the situation so demanded: 'we don't care a d___ about England … but we want good relations in the interests of our own people and in the interests of trade, and we want a better place in the English market. We will not put our heritage in pawn for that, but we know that good trade is for the advantage of everyone.'[119] In essence, members of the government refused to increase social spending and promoted the same go-slow export-based approach that they had followed throughout the decade. They depicted this as pragmatism rather than a lack of concern for the promise of the revolutionary years. As Cosgrave said in 1930, 'other Deputies went so far as to say that we were legislating entirely for the rich and we were indifferent to the poor. That is not a true charge. … We have been responsible for as intensive a social programme as the county was able to afford.'[120]

Late in life, two former Cumann na nGaedheal stalwarts mused that the party lost power because it refused to focus on economic issues. Michael Hayes praised Lemass for supplying 'the bread and butter argument' that 'Kevin O'Higgins refused to allow'. Richard Mulcahy thought that having most of the government isolated for security reasons in 1922 meant the ministers focused on abstractions and constitutions instead of 'constructive economic work'.[121] Although debates over the Treaty certainly never disappeared, economics assumed a prominent position in political discourse as the 1920s proceeded. Fianna Fáil, Labour, and the Farmers argued the economic promise of the Revolution had not been met, although each had a different diagnosis of the problems and different prescriptions for their solutions. Farmers thought the Revolution presented an opportunity to create an agrarian state and felt deeply disappointed that the position of agriculture worsened after independence. Labour believed the Revolution would bring about an improvement in the workers' standard of living and opposed the government's excessive reliance on indirect taxes and a fiscal system otherwise inherited from the former colonial master. Fianna Fáil wanted a return to Griffithite protectionism, while co-opting Labour's criticism of the government's catering to the rich, as well as the Farmers' criticism of the excessive salaries of bureaucrats. Cumann na nGaedheal generally defended its fiscal conservatism, claiming that the government needed to show its detractors that the Irish were fit for self-government. Often, politicians judged the legitimacy of the state by its ability to deliver on revolutionary promises and on the economic separation it had gained from Britain. Competing evaluations of the Irish economy have not always received the attention given to issues such as the oath but raised fundamental questions about the nature of the postcolonial Irish state, the lingering effects of colonialism on the Irish economy, the role of opposition in the new Free State Dáil, and the responsibility the government had towards its citizens.

Notes

1. Dáil Éireann, 3 Jan. 1923. The Dáil debates (hereafter DD) are available at http://www.oireachtas.ie/parliament/oireachtasbusiness/parliamentarydebates/.
2. Cormac Ó Gráda, *Ireland: A New Economic History, 1780–1939* (Oxford: Clarendon Press, 1994), 389.
3. Mary Daly, *Industrial Development and Irish National Identity, 1922–1939* (Syracuse: Syracuse University Press, 1992), 45, 47, 55.
4. This is the title of Daly's chapter covering the years 1922–27.
5. Ronan Fanning, *The Irish Department of Finance, 1922–58* (Dublin: Institute of Public Administration, 1978), 119.
6. Mike Cronin, 'Golden Dreams, Harsh Realities: Economics and Informal Empire in the Irish Free State', in *Ireland: The Politics of Independence, 1922–49*, ed. Mike Cronin and John M. Regan (New York: St. Martin's Press, 1999), 145, 146–47.
7. Andy Bielenberg and Raymond Ryan, *An Economic History of Ireland Since Independence* (London: Routledge, 2012), 9–10.
8. T. K. Daniel, 'Griffith on his Noble Head: The Determinants of Cumann na nGaedheal Economic Policy, 1922–32', *Irish Economic and Social History* 3 (1976): 55, 58, 63, 65.
9. Kevin Hjortshøj O'Rourke, 'Independent Ireland in Comparative Perspective', *Irish Economic and Social History* 44 (2017): 30, 20.
10. Martin Daunton, *Trusting Leviathan: The Politics of Taxation in Britain, 1799–1914* (Cambridge: Cambridge University Press, 2001); idem, *Just Taxes: The Politics of Taxation in Britain, 1914–1979* (Cambridge: Cambridge University Press, 2002).
11. Daunton, *Trusting Leviathan*, 7.
12. Roy Douglas, *Taxation in Britain since 1660* (London: Palgrave Macmillan, 1999), 75.
13. Daunton, *Trusting Leviathan*, 19.
14. Bond Certificate Campaign, 1919, Thomas Clarke Collection, Boston College Burns Library MS 2001–07 (Folder 2/13).
15. Michael Collins to Eamon de Valera, 19 Feb. 1920, Eamon de Valera Papers, University College Dublin Archives (hereafter UCDA) P150/726.
16. Eamon de Valera, Notes for Speech in America, c. 1919–20, de Valera Papers, UCDA P150/674.
17. Notes by Michael Collins 'Change of Situation and Outlook', c. summer 1922, Richard Mulcahy Papers, UCDA P7/B/28; DD, 12 Sept. 1922.
18. Joseph Brennan, Memorandum on General Financial Situation, 27 Apr. 1923, Mulcahy Papers, UCDA P7/B/253.
19. Fanning, *Department of Finance*, 112–14.

20. DD, 17 Apr. 1923.
21. Ibid., 23 Mar. 1923.
22. Ibid.
23. Daniel, 'Griffith on his Noble Head', 59–60.
24. Bryan Cooper, 'Our Rulers—III, Mr. Ernest Blythe', 9 Feb. 1924, Mulcahy Papers, UCDA P7/B/440.
25. DD, 8 Feb. 1923.
26. Ibid., 20 Apr. 1923.
27. Fanning, *Department of Finance*, 91–93.
28. Cumann na nGaedheal Appeal for Funds, c. Dec. 1924, Desmond FitzGerald Papers, UCDA P80/1103.
29. Blythe, New Year Message from the Minister for Finance and Hogan, New Year Message from the Minister for Agriculture, Dec. 1926, Mulcahy Papers, UCDA P7b/61.
30. DD, 28 May 1923.
31. Ibid., 20 Oct. 1922.
32. Minutes of National Convention, 29 Jan. 1924, Cumann na nGaedheal Papers, UCDA P39/1.
33. Ryan McCourt, 'Ernest Blythe as Minister for Finance in the Irish Free State, 1923–32', *Parliamentary History* 33, no. 3 (2014): 485.
34. DD, 17 Apr. 1923.
35. Ibid.
36. Ibid., 17 May 1923.
37. Ibid., 17 Apr. 1923.
38. Ibid.
39. Ibid., 2 May 1923.
40. *Irish Farmer*, 18 Dec. 1925.
41. Ibid., 5 Mar. 1926, 28 Aug. 1925.
42. DD, 19 Sept. 1922.
43. *Irish Farmer*, 19 June 1925.
44. Ibid., 5 Mar. 1926.
45. Ibid., 19 June 1925.
46. *Farmers' Gazette*, 2 Apr. 1927.
47. Co. Clare Farmers' Association—Irish Farmers' Union, Memo on 'Local Taxation and Local Government', c. 1925, George O'Callaghan-Westropp Papers, UCDA P38/4(482).
48. *Irish Farmer*, 29 Oct. 1926.
49. Ibid., 27 Nov. 1925.
50. DD, 3 Jan. 1923, 9 Mar. 1923, 30 Nov. 1922, 7 June 1923.
51. Ibid., 31 May 1923.
52. *Irish Farmer*, 26 Mar. 1926.

53. *Farmers' Gazette*, 9 July 1927. The Geddes Axe refers to a British government committee chaired by Sir Eric Geddes in the 1920s that recommended significant cuts in state expenditure.
54. *Irish Farmer*, 6 Nov. 1925.
55. DD, 19 Nov. 1922. Labour Deputy William Davin noted that this speech caused much laughter in the Dáil.
56. Ibid., 14 Dec. 1922.
57. Ibid., 12 Dec. 1922.
58. Ibid., 14 Dec. 1922.
59. Ibid., 19 Sept. 1922.
60. Daunton, *Just Taxes*, 61.
61. DD, 20 Oct. 1922, 3 Jan. 1923.
62. Ibid., 13 Apr. 1923.
63. Ibid., 3 Jan. 1923.
64. Ibid., 13 Apr. 1923, 4 May 1923.
65. Ibid., 13 Apr. 1923.
66. Ibid., 26 Mar. 1923.
67. Ibid., 13 Apr. 1923.
68. Ibid., 20 Mar. 1923.
69. Ibid., 18 Apr. 1923.
70. Ibid.
71. Ibid., 28 May 1923.
72. For the British case, see generally Daunton, *Just Taxes.*
73. DD, 20 Oct. 1922.
74. Ibid., 27 Mar. 1923.
75. Ibid., 25 Apr. 1923. Johnson claimed that only 25 per cent of Irish revenue came from direct taxation; idem, 20 Apr. 1923.
76. Ibid., 25 Apr. 1923.
77. Ibid., 18 Apr. 1923.
78. Timothy M. O'Neil, 'Reframing the Republic: Republican Socio-Economic Thought and the Road to Fianna Fáil, 1923–26', in *A Formative Decade? Ireland in the 1920s*, ed. Mel Farrell, Jason Knirck, and Ciara Meehan (Dublin: Irish Academic Press, 2015), 157.
79. O'Neil, 'Reframing the Republic', 169.
80. Fianna Fáil pamphlet, The Free State Government's Secret Financial Agreement with Britain, c. summer 1926, Clarke Papers, Boston College Burns Library Archives MS 01–07 (Folder 2/29).
81. *Sinn Féin*, 15 Nov. 1924, Canon Rogers Papers, Boston College Burns Library Archives Box IV, Folder 18.
82. *Sinn Féin*, 20 Dec. 1924, Canon Rogers Papers, Boston College Burns Library Archives Box IV, Folder 18.

83. *Irish Press* (hereafter *IP*), 4 Jan. 1932.
84. Ibid., 16 Jan. 1932.
85. Ibid., 25 Jan. 1932.
86. See, for example, ibid., 29 Jan. 1932.
87. Ibid., 22 Jan. 1932, 23 Jan. 1932.
88. Ibid., 29 Jan. 1932, 22 Jan. 1932.
89. Ibid., 2 Feb. 1932.
90. Ibid., 18 Jan. 1932.
91. Ibid., 11 Jan. 1932.
92. Ibid., 4 Feb. 1932.
93. Ibid., 4 Jan. 1932.
94. Ibid., 3 Feb. 1932.
95. Ibid., 18 Jan. 1923, 11 Jan. 1923.
96. Ibid., 23 Jan. 1932.
97. Ibid., 4 Jan. 1932.
98. Ibid., 25 Jan. 1932.
99. Ibid., 11 Jan. 1932.
100. Ibid., 3 Feb. 1932.
101. Ibid., 29 Jan. 1932.
102. Ibid., 1 Feb. 1932.
103. *Farmers' Gazette*, 10 Sept. 1927.
104. Minutes, Cumann na nGaedheal Ard Comhairle, 22 Feb. 1927, Cumann na nGaedheal Papers, UCDA P39/MIN/1.
105. *IP*, 25 Jan. 1932.
106. DD, 24 Apr. 1929, 30 Apr. 1930.
107. *The Star*, Mar. 1931, in Mulcahy Papers, UCDA P7/D/170.
108. J. J. McElligott, 'Financial Position', 9 Sept. 1931, Ernest Blythe Papers, UCDA P24/99(2).
109. Facts for Intelligent Voters, c. Jan. 1932, Blythe Papers, UCDA P24/622(b).
110. Fighting Points for Cumann na nGaedheal Speakers, 1932, Mulcahy Papers, UCDA P7/C/42.
111. *IP*, 5 Feb. 1932.
112. Ibid., 1 Feb. 1932.
113. Ibid., 1 Feb. 1932.
114. Ibid., 11 Jan. 1932.
115. Eoin MacNeill, 'Ten Years of the Irish Free State', *Foreign Affairs* 10, no. 2 (1932): 238, 242.
116. DD, 19 Nov. 1930.
117. *IP*, 4 Jan. 1932.
118. Ibid., 16 Jan. 1932.

119. Ibid., 29 Jan. 1932.
120. DD, 3 Apr. 1930.
121. Talk Between Mulcahy and Senator Hayes about Certain Aspects of de Vere White's biography, 22 Oct. 1964, Mulcahy Papers, UCDA P7b/183(55); Conversation between Risteard and Richard Mulcahy, 18 Sept. 1963, Mulcahy Papers, UCDA P7/D/105.

CHAPTER 12

The Economic War and the Pamphlet War

Aidan Beatty

This chapter studies public debates around the issues of taxes and annuities during the late 1920s and early 1930s. Article 5 of the Anglo-Irish Treaty of 1921 had stipulated that the new Irish Free State would continue to contribute to the 'Public Debt of the United Kingdom … in such proportion as may be fair and equitable'. The language of the article's single paragraph was frustratingly vague, not least in its simultaneous recognition that 'any just claims on the part of Ireland by way of set-off or counter-claim' would also be taken into consideration.[1] What all this exactly meant was left to a later date. And in the early years of the Free State, the new government's Department of Finance had a protracted negotiation with the British Treasury to come to a final agreement on how much the Free State would owe. The negotiations had to contend with a series of thorny issues: the Irish contribution to British military pensions, compensation for property damaged during the War of Independence, mortgage repayments (annuities) arising out of the Land Acts of the early twentieth century, and the problem of dual residents and their liability for income taxes in both jurisdictions. An interim agreement on all this was reached on 3 December 1925, which was then finalised with an Ultimate Financial Settlement in March of the following year.[2] The settlement was

A. Beatty (✉)
University of Pittsburgh, Pittsburgh, PA, USA
e-mail: ajbeatty@tcd.ie

D. Kanter, P. Walsh (eds.), *Taxation, Politics, and Protest in Ireland, 1662–2016*, Palgrave Studies in the History of Finance,
https://doi.org/10.1007/978-3-030-04309-4_12

itself highly technical. But it quickly proved controversial, particularly because of the provisions outlined in Article 1: 'The Government of the Irish Free State undertake to pay to the British Government at agreed intervals the full amount of the annuities accruing due from time to time under the Irish Land Acts, 1891–1909, without any deduction whatsoever whether on account of Income Tax or otherwise'.[3] The Irish state would continue to collect in full the mortgage annuities from Irish farmers and hand them over to the British Treasury.

Anti-Treatyites seized on this as evidence of the perfidy of Cumann na nGaedheal, and there was strong opposition to paying the annuities, which were seen as an undue tax on Irish land; indeed, Article 1 of the 1926 settlement stipulated that the size of a farmer's income tax bill could not be used to mitigate the level of the annuity payments. By the 1930s, the annuity repayments absorbed 3 per cent of Irish national income and, between 1932 and 1938, the newly elected Fianna Fáil government intentionally defaulted on these annuities (though it still continued to collect the repayments themselves). When, in the summer of 1932, the Fianna Fáil government refused to hand over the payments, the British government imposed tariffs of 20 per cent on Irish livestock imports. When the British tariffs proved insufficient to raise the necessary moneys owed, they were raised to 40 per cent on Irish livestock imports and 30 per cent on other agricultural imports. The Irish government had already responded in kind, introducing tariffs on British imports into Ireland.[4] The tit-for-tat imposition of tariffs, lasting until 1938, has since become known as the Economic War or, more formally, the Anglo-Irish Trade War.

This chapter is a study of the Economic War. But rather than focus on the technical details—annuity rates, the extent of Ireland's 'debt' to the United Kingdom's Exchequer, levels of tariffs—I instead offer an ideological and cultural history of this moment. This chapter analyses the tone and content of the various pamphlets written by the boosters of Fianna Fáil's policies during the Economic War, as well as pamphlets written by their detractors in Cumann na nGaedheal and that party's successor, Fine Gael. I also examine the writings of Peadar O'Donnell, a key figure in fomenting the initial protests against annuity payments. I have elsewhere argued that what motivated Fianna Fáil during the Economic War was the possibility of building a nation of independent, male property owners; the broad popularity of this gendered nationalist vision was, I have suggested, a major reason for Fianna Fáil's electoral successes in the 1930s.[5] In this chapter, conversely, I focus on the differing visions of the Irish economy that were presented in the various pamphlets that accompanied the start of the Economic War. Across the ideological spectrum of Irish politics in the early 1930s, there were drastically different visions of what Irish society and the Irish economy should look like. Most obviously, there were socialists like O'Donnell who wished to create a 'Workers' and Working Farmers' Republic!'[6] O'Donnell's views were in clear contrast to 'capitalists' who wished to preserve the sanctity of private property and who saw nothing necessarily wrong with the profit motive. Yet, within this capitalist camp, there were profound divisions. On the one hand, there were those who wished to preserve Ireland's status as a supplier of agricultural raw materials for British markets;[7] the people that a Marxist might ungenerously call a *comprador* class. On the other hand, Fianna Fáil advocated an essentially developmentalist approach to national economics, hoping to use the machinery of the state to develop the economy rapidly. These 'capitalist' viewpoints were themselves all at work in the differing arguments advanced about the annuities: about whether Irish farmers should pay them in the first place, whether they were an unjust tax, and whether the Irish government should hand them over to its British counterpart. The debates that accompanied the start of the Economic War were, quite obviously, debates about economics and about taxes. They were also debates about economic ideology; my aim in this chapter is to uncover and analyse those different ideologies.

There has been a remarkable spate of recent works on the history of capitalism, themselves often influenced by the global financial crash of 2008. While some of these works operate within a conventional econometric register,[8] the most interesting of them mix economic analysis with a cultural studies approach.[9] Mainly focused on America, questions of race have been central concerns in several of these studies (though discussions of gender are often surprisingly absent).[10] This renascent historiography of capitalism has been paralleled by a number of innovative Marxist analyses of capitalism.[11] Again, the best of this new field moves beyond a strictly economic focus to incorporate broader issues of culture, ideology, race, and gender, as well as the spatial and ecological dynamics of capitalism; there is indeed a long tradition of Marxist and 'Marxish' works in this mould.[12]

This broad body of literature provides an apposite model for studies of capitalism in Ireland. Economic history-writing in Ireland is often of the more conventional econometric and cliometric variety.[13] In general, cultural studies of Irish economics remain rare.[14] Some Marxist-influenced works have shown an innovative approach to studying Ireland and its place in the global economy.[15] Other works have drawn on Marxist methodologies to unpack the economic biases at the heart of Irish party politics or religion,[16] though some Marxist studies of Irish politics and economics, it must be said, are overly polemical and retrograde in their approach.[17] To my knowledge, there has been practically nothing written on Ireland in the mould of the type of innovative Marxist cultural history pioneered by David Roediger or Stuart Hall.[18] And the age of Brexit and Trump is an apposite time for such serious analyses of the culture(s) of protectionism, trade wars, and nationalism.

Long Live the Workers' and Working Farmers' Republic!

The anti-annuities campaign has been described as a 'one-man revolution' led by the prominent radical Peadar O'Donnell.[19] A novelist, public intellectual, and well-known anti-Treatyite, O'Donnell had long worked to combine nationalism with a kind of peasant communism.[20] O'Donnell's autobiography, written almost four decades after the anti-annuities campaign, presented the agitation against annuities as a continuation of the social conflict that he believed underpinned the Civil War. Moreover, he presented the anti-annuity agitation as emerging from a groundswell of radical peasant sentiment. As O'Donnell recalled it, he merely gave a platform in *An Phoblacht* (The Republic), Sinn Féin's newspaper, to this already extant set of sentiments.[21] And curiously, he said nothing in his memoirs about the 1926 agreement between the Free State government and the British Treasury.

As Timothy O'Neil has shown, though, from the Civil War onwards, O'Donnell had been advocating for social agitation within the Irish Republican Army (IRA) and the broader republican movement. When the Ultimate Financial Settlement was publicly released, and, most importantly, when it was publicly revealed that the Irish government would make yearly land annuity payments of £3 million for the next 60 years, 'O'Donnell believed he had found the issue from which he could launch a social revolution and smash the Free State.'[22] Recognising 'the need to sink sturdy, rural roots if his political project was to have any hope of success', he began to organise committees in his native Donegal that would co-ordinate a non-payment campaign.[23] These committees soon spread around the country, in a campaign led by O'Donnell but also tapping into existing economic grievances. This was ultimately to be 'his most influential political campaign'.[24]

O'Donnell's statements on the annuities issue mixed conventional nationalist tropes with more radical ideas, a synthesis that was viewed with trepidation by both Fianna Fáil and Cumann na nGaedheal/Fine Gael. A 'catechism' produced by Fr John Fahy, a leftist priest and supporter of O'Donnell's in Bullaun, a village outside Loughrea in East Galway, laid out some of their claims about the nature of the annuities:

> How did England establish a claim to the land of Ireland? By robbery.
>
> What is rent? Rent is a tribute of slavery enforced by the arms of the robber-landlord.
>
> What is a landlord? A landlord is a descendant of a land robber.
>
> Who pays rents to landlords? Only slaves.[25]

The annuities were depicted here as a form of thievery by the British state and thus situated in a longer history of Irish national humiliation. Writing in *An Phoblacht* in the summer of 1926, O'Donnell spoke of the need for 'defence of peasant farmers' in opposition to annuities. He described the annuities as a 'robbery of children to meet the call of British interests', thus suggesting that the annuities were an invasion not just of the land but also of the family home.[26] O'Donnell later described the annuities as a 'tax directly payable to Britain: A tax devoid of any vestige of moral sanction.'[27] These were nationalist ideas with obvious similarities to those of the emergent Fianna Fáil, which also spoke of undoing national economic humiliation. In an article for *An Phoblacht* the following year, though, O'Donnell nailed his ideological colours more firmly to the mast. National economic salvation would be achieved 'not by appeasing hunger by crusts of bread, nor relieving cold by doled out cast-off clothing, but by the organizing of the people to seize power to make bread and clothing available, according as the labour of the nation and our resources can afford them. That, then is our task—to seize power, so that the people may be worthy of themselves.'[28] O'Donnell described the campaign against the annuities as a social project which would also finish the national revolution:

> Here was what [Fintan] Lalor sighed for: a tax directly payable to Britain: a tax devoid of any vestige of moral sanction. Refuse this tax, have the people take their stand on that refusal, and you faced [*sic*] the government with a

> challenge it could not refuse and a fight it could not win. Republicans could roast the Treaty in the fire from this kindling.[29]

For O'Donnell, opposition to the annuities was to be part of a much broader, much more radical restructuring of Irish property-relations, albeit one still couched in the same language of agrarianism and the reversal of national economic humiliation.[30] What O'Donnell sought to achieve was clearly expressed in his pamphlet, *For or Against the Ranchers?*, published in the early years of the Economic War: 'The youth of the small farmer areas must get into the fray quickly. All that they have a right to demand of life this country can give them ... Take over the ranches; they are yours. Workers and Working Farmers—Unite! Long live the Workers' and Working Farmers' Republic!' While Fianna Fáil's pamphlet writers would proffer an image of cross-class national unity, O'Donnell was less amenable. He discursively placed large 'rancher' farmers outside of the nation, labelling them as 'rancher-capitalists' whose interests were diametrically opposed to those of poorer peasant farmers. He thus advocated 'taxation of the rich' as a first step towards achieving his working farmers' republic. O'Donnell also claimed that through his actions he was able to circulate 'The News Bulletin of the European Peasant Committee', the agrarian branch of Comintern, throughout the west of Ireland.[31] Certainly, his vigorous campaign against the annuities was attracting enough attention by the late 1920s for his public appearances to be monitored by An Garda Síochána.[32] He was arrested in March 1927 and was in and out of prison in 1927 and 1928.[33] The Garda Commissioner, Eoin O'Duffy—for sure not always a calm voice—did warn of a 'Red Terror' in the Irish countryside, led by O'Donnell and the IRA.[34] The support given to O'Donnell's protests against the annuities certainly revealed the unpopularity of these payments to the British Exchequer.

O'Donnell's hope had been that the IRA would offer its support to the campaign, but more conservative elements baulked at supporting anything that smacked of communism. O'Neil points out that this vacuum was filled by Fianna Fáil. Eamon de Valera had resigned from Sinn Féin in March 1926, having failed to convince the party to abandon the policy of abstention from Dáil Éireann. De Valera and the more moderate republicans orbiting him founded their new party later that month:

> Fianna Fáil clearly intended to make economic issues central to its electoral appeal, as five of the seven points in its program dealt with such issues. Yet,

> no mention of land annuities appeared in Fianna Fáil's platform. In 1927, O'Donnell approached both Fianna Fáil and Sinn Féin and invited them to join the non-payment of annuities campaign. De Valera remained cautious about joining the agitation, believing he needed more time to gauge public opinion. Meanwhile, he appointed a Fianna Fáil committee to explore the issue. Sinn Féin's response was more one of confusion than caution, as its leadership remained divided over the issue. The party had actually passed a resolution condemning the government's payments of land annuities in 1925, only to quickly retract it when the executive caught its error: 'We cannot recognise Free State legislation.'[35]

The economic policies of the newly established Fianna Fáil would adeptly tap into the same growing sense of disillusionment as O'Donnell, particularly the disillusionment with a Cumann na nGaedheal government that was increasingly seen as arrogant, insensitive, and out of touch with the 'plain people'. Shortly after ending his policy of abstention and taking his seat, de Valera declared in the Dáil in October 1927 that Irish workers 'should not merely be wage slaves or simply spending their lives to make money for somebody or other'. In contrast to this 'wage slavery', there was 'a vague suggestion that one day they might be working for themselves, possibly in rural Ireland, where the sturdy self-sufficient farmer was held up as the ideal'.[36] By October 1928, Fianna Fáil had passed a resolution that stated that handing over the annuities to the British Exchequer violated the Government of Ireland Act of 1920 and was thus unconstitutional; the 'slightly constitutional party' could have recourse to the constitution when it was politically useful. The following year, de Valera moved a motion in the Dáil for the Free State to retain the annuities. This was condemned as 'dishonest' and 'embezzlement' by the Cumann na nGaedheal Agricultural Minister, Patrick Hogan.[37] In 1930, Sean Lemass, one of Fianna Fáil's leading economic voices, said his politics were concerned with 'the plain, good, honest-to-God working men whose interests were neglected' by Cumann na nGaedheal.[38] Acquiring land had been, since the 1880s, the only guaranteed access to social status in rural Ireland[39] and had overtly masculinist overtones. While Cumann na nGaedheal acted as the party of the already established grazier farmers, Fianna Fáil positioned itself as 'the vehicle for the economic and social advancement of the "small man"', much as Sinn Féin's economic policy during the War of Independence had 'offered the small man the possibility of becoming a slightly bigger man if only he would bide his time, and fall in behind the national independence struggle'.[40]

When Fianna Fáil and its fellow travellers began to agitate on this issue and to produce pamphlets outlining the party's opposition to the annuities, they articulated a pronounced radical rhetoric that appealed to a similar demographic and set of popular emotions as did O'Donnell.[41] But Fianna Fáil also evinced a cautiousness and a certain kind of economic conservatism. One example of this is *British Plunder and Irish Blunder*, a 1928 pamphlet produced by Maurice Moore.

Status Quo Anti-Capitalism

Maurice Moore (1854–1939) was an unusual candidate to provide an intellectual grounding for Fianna Fáil's radical economic policies in the late 1920s and early 1930s. A scion of a landed Liberal family (his father, George Henry Moore, had intermittently sat in Parliament as a Liberal for counties Mayo and Kilkenny after the Famine), Moore had been educated at Sandhurst before embarking on an imperial military career with the Connaught Rangers in South Africa. His experiences during the Boer War fuelled a criticism of British imperialism and by 1906 he had retired from the British army. An interest in the Irish language led him to involvement with the Gaelic League and then with the broader nationalist movement. By 1913, he was active in the newly formed Irish Volunteers and supported John Redmond's faction in the split of 1914. By 1917 he had become a supporter of Sinn Féin and remained in that orbit through the War of Independence. Yet in the aftermath of the Treaty, he supported the nascent Cumann na nGaedheal and indeed was briefly a representative of the party in the Free State Senate. 'Opposition to the boundary agreement and the ultimate financial settlement between the Irish Free State and Great Britain' caused Moore to abandon the Treatyites in favour of Clann Éireann (Family of Ireland). When that small party disintegrated in 1928, he joined Fianna Fáil.[42] It was shortly after this that he published his first contribution to the debates over annuities, *British Plunder and Irish Blunder*.

Moore's pamphlet was written at the request of the leadership of Clann Éireann. The scale of the annuities—'about £5 millions a year, or one fifth of the total revenue of the country'[43]—as well as Cumann na nGaedheal's secretive approach and the possibility that the annuities were unconstitutional, had all precipitated this intervention by Moore and Clann Éireann.

The claim that the annuities were a 'tribute', with the implied suggestion that their payment entailed Ireland's continued subjugation to London, presumably also touched a nationalist nerve. Indeed, Moore alleged that Ernest Blythe—the Free State minister who had signed the Ultimate Financial Settlement in March 1926, along with 'Mr. Churchill'—'regards the former United Kingdom as consisting of a dominant Britain and a subsidiary Ireland'. The continued payment of these 'tributes' represented a form of 'overtaxation' of the Irish people. Six years of self-government, 'from which so much was hoped', had thus only brought about poverty 'and the depression of agriculture and commerce'. *British Plunder* was unsurprisingly dismissive of Cumann na nGaedheal's approach to the annuities issue; Moore accused government ministers of being poor negotiators[44] and of being content for Ireland to remain 'a subsidiary' to a 'dominant Britain'.

Moore saw high taxation as part of an intersecting set of other economic forces, namely declining rates of bank deposits, a poor balance of trade, and a surfeit of imported goods that edged out domestic producers. It was this constellation of economic forces, he said, which caused the 'poverty of the people'. 'It is not necessary to pursue this further, because everyone knows, rich and poor, manufacturer and trader, farmer and worker, that his pocket is light and his purse empty. Only Ministers pretend the opposite.' Moore contended that Free State taxation was 'twice as high as Britain', though in making this argument he was collapsing together the annuities with conventional taxation and suggesting that both were politically suspect.[45]

While the print media and the general public 'cry out for a reduction of expenses and reduction of taxation', the ministers of Cumann na nGaedheal refused to make anything more than desultory changes to Ireland's tax bills. This led Moore to a loaded claim, that if a reduction in taxation was not made, 'we will move, slowly perhaps, but inevitably into a financial position similar to other bankrupt nations, such as Egypt fifty years ago, when it became economically and politically a tributary of England.' If the taxation problem could not be solved, if alternative government revenue could not be secured to alleviate Irish citizens' supposed tax burdens, 'we must humbly bow our necks to a foreign yoke, and bury our hopes of nationhood alongside the graves of all the great martyrs of Irish freedom.' In other words, taxation and annuities were not just issues of pounds and pence, but were intimately connected to the question of national freedom and Ireland's (post-)colonial status. Some of Moore's rhetoric here was standard nationalist fare; Ireland had been irreparably damaged by '700 years of plunder and war', and yet now that Ireland was nominally free, 'is it credible that when at last Ireland has driven out the invader by force of arms, she should be obliged to pay huge tribute to the aggressors?' Moore claimed that ministers who negotiated Ireland's payments 'did not adopt any sane line of defence, or, indeed any defence or attack; they went to London without any account, without any documents or even ideas on which to base a set off and a counter-claim. They were beaten men before they got there.' Moore was subtly implying here that the wrong kind of pro-British politician was the wrong kind of man. Cumann na nGaedheal was led by toadying Seoiníns and national traitors. These were obviously charged accusations to use against the Treatyite wing of Irish politics.

And yet Moore also showed some unwillingness to follow through on his seemingly anti-imperial sentiments.

> Ireland was a full partner in the United Kingdom for 121 years before the Treaty, and a partial partner for some years prior to that period; at least she contributed to the expenses of wars, to the brains and the blood by which the Empire was created during the whole period of the building of the Empire. Like any other business partner, she is entitled to a proportioning of the assets of the Empire when the Union was dissolved.

There was a certain knowing sarcasm at work here as well as a conscious recognition of the violence endemic to the British imperial project. But Moore was, nonetheless, calling for Ireland to receive due recompense from imperial profits. Indeed, he explained Irish poverty as being a function of Ireland not enjoying 'her' fair share of the imperial 'swag'.[46]

Moore's ideas were echoed in the contemporaneous publications of Henry Harrison (1867–1954), another unconventional Fianna Fáil voice. Like Moore, Harrison came from a landed and Liberal family background. As an undergraduate at Oxford in the late 1880s, he had gravitated to the university's Home Rule Club. By the 1890s, he had sided with the Parnellites and had overt sympathies for agrarian agitation. After unsuccessful attempts to get elected on a Parnellite ticket, he began working for Lloyds of London. Harrison saw active duty on the Western Front during the Great War and was a supporter of both Horace Plunkett's Irish Dominion League in 1920 and of the Treatyites during the Civil War. He would seem to have positioned himself firmly on the softer, more pro-British end of Irish nationalism. That he worked as the Irish correspondent for the *Economist* through the 1920s and had also been a leading member of Cumann na nGaedheal ostensibly confirmed this.[47] As with Moore, though, his frustration over the annuities issue drew him into the orbit of Fianna Fáil.

Harrison wrote three pamphlets outlining his attitudes towards the annuities issue: *The Strange Case of the Land Purchase Annuities* (1932), and *Spotlights on the Anglo-Irish Financial Quarrel* and *The Game of 'Beggar-My-Neighbour': Who Wins?*, both in 1934. Collectively, the three short works provide an overview of pro-Fianna Fáil thinking in the first two years of the Economic War.

In the first of these pamphlets, Harrison began by telegraphing his Treatyite background as well as his one-time support for 'Dominionism'; he had a long track record of working for harmonious Anglo-Irish relations. The Treaty, however, had left over two unsolved issues. One was the constitutional status and territorial adjustment of Northern Ireland, which had been addressed by the Boundary Commission. The annuities were the second issue. And since no comparable commission had dealt with this issue, Harrison sided with Fianna Fáil's position that there was no legal need to pay the annuities. His stance, though, stemmed from a desire to reach an agreement that would allow for a more harmonious relationship to (re-)emerge between the two countries, rather than deriving from a conventional anti-British nationalist perspective. It was only natural, he claimed, that the Irish government would closely scrutinise the Free State's legal obligations. He did, however, blame the United Kingdom for the impasse: 'Great Britain, if she has the will to do so, can hang the door thus left open—and bar and bolt it against all chances of elucidation, understanding and reconciliation.' The UK Treasury, Harrison said, in an effective turn-of-phrase, 'has invariably dealt out to Ireland a step-child's portion'.[48]

His two 1934 pamphlets built on these strands of thinking. By the time he wrote *Spotlights on the Anglo-Irish Financial Quarrel*, Harrison had become more assertively nationalist, if also overly verbose: 'There can be no question that the War Guilt in this traffic affair lies with Great Britain. It inaugurated its tariff offensive against the Irish Free State for the enforcement of its own view of a justiciable dispute which the Irish Free State has been willing, from the outset, to submit to an unrestricted arbitration.'[49] Conversely, *The Game of 'Beggar-My-Neighbour': Who Wins?* began by striking a gentler and more ecumenical note. Harrison described himself here as 'an Irishman who has always worked for peace between Ireland and Great Britain—not, of course, a peace by mere surrender, but an honourable peace based upon mutual advantage and mutual understanding, a peace consistent with national self-respect'. But Harrison then proceeded to advance a more nationalist analysis. Britain, he stated, had intentionally started the Economic War in July 1932 and thus bore responsibility for it. Britain was the aggressor, refusing to acknowledge the legitimate legal disputes in existence here. Britain, Harrison said, would be happy to 'cause the overthrow of the uncompliant [*sic*] Mr. de Valera and secure the return of the less uncompliant Mr. Cosgrave'.[50] In fact, he claimed, de Valera has risen in popularity, and Ireland had begun to restructure its economy 'so that she [Ireland] may never be caught at such disadvantage again'. And, he asserted, 'few people in Britain appear to realise how much Britain has already lost and how much Britain still stands to lose.' He laid out an itemised list of reasons why Britain would be hurt by the Economic War: inter alia, the loss of its best customer; the loss of a destination for exports which benefited the British balance of trade; the loss of a trading partner which still kept its liquid capital in British banks; and the damage done to British shipping by a drop in Anglo-Irish trade, which was carried on with British ships. He seemed to recognise that the Economic War was an attempt to redefine Anglo-Irish relations within a broader capitalist world-system itself going through important realignments: 'If peace is delayed, each day's delay tends to consolidate and perpetuate the commercial relations which she [Ireland] is now establishing with Continental Europe and America. For every day Ireland is learning to revolve in a new orbit.' Harrison ended his pamphlet with two suggested contingent events that might come out of the Economic War: Ireland might break its links to sterling and withdraw its capital holdings from British financial institutions; and, in the event of 'another Great War', Ireland might have moved away sufficiently from the British economic orbit that it would no longer provide the 'copious food supplies' that would allow Britain to overcome the threat of the 'submarine menace'.[51]

Harrison's three pamphlets were oddly contradictory. He was radically nationalist and with more than a whiff of anti-British rhetoric. He was willing to talk about Ireland repositioning itself within the global economy, yet also sought a harmonious and mutually beneficial economic partnership between Ireland and the United Kingdom that would last well into the future. Such tensions and contradictions were reflected in how Fianna Fáil discussed economic questions in its contemporaneous literature.

The party's 1926 constitution contained a list of strongly worded economic goals, among which were 'To make the resources and wealth of Ireland subservient to the needs and welfare of all the people of Ireland' and 'To make Ireland, as far as possible, economically self-contained and self-sufficing'.[52] Proposed amendments to the original party constitution called for Irish capital invested in Irish industries to be made exempt from income tax and for incomes under £200 (per annum, presumably) to be also made exempt.[53] Party literature produced for the 1932 general election accused Cumann na nGaedheal of paying a £5 million annual 'Tribute' to the British Exchequer and thus urged former supporters of the party to switch their allegiances to Fianna Fáil. If elected, de Valera's party would reduce taxation and create tens of thousands of new jobs. The republicans also promised to eliminate unemployment.[54] In an open letter to his constituents in North Dublin, Fianna Fáil's Oscar Traynor accused the Treatyites of sacrificing 'the economic interests of our people to a blind adherence to the theory of so-called Free Trade, which during seventy years made the export of human beings our most profitable business and reduced the population of our country to a mere fraction of what it could support if properly developed'. Traynor promised that a 'native government'—one not beholden to British interests like Cumann na nGaedheal—would end this national economic misery.[55] A certain economic radicalism clearly still percolated within Fianna Fáil.

Yet Fianna Fáil's radicalism in the 1930s was always defined by its contradictory nature. Richard Dunphy has aptly spoken of the party's 'status-quo anti-capitalism' in a cogent analysis indebted to the work of the Greek Marxist theorist, Nicos Poulantzas.[56] Fianna Fáil's stated desire for an interventionist state that could economically develop the country was belied by its promise to reduce taxation; how to fund these grand projects without substantial tax revenue? The party's economic rhetoric appealed to those small farmers who felt that they had been economically dispossessed by British rule, but party members also wanted to ensure that anti-annuity protests would stay within strictly defined boundaries, and they had scant praise for O'Donnell's desire to tax the rich at high levels.

Indeed, Sean Lemass, Minister for Industry in de Valera's first government, supposedly told O'Donnell that Fianna Fáil would only take up the annuities issue provided doing so would not undermine the right to private property.[57] O'Donnell's hoped-for revolution would harm Fianna Fáil's vision of a nation of male owner-occupiers, 'bread-winners', rooted in their own land and able to provide for their wives and children in frugal—but still capitalist—self-sufficiency. Despite the view that 'the Irish land purchase annuities are nothing more or less than the old rents imposed by landlords and their predecessors', the Fianna Fáil government continued to collect the annuities from farmers, even if they were not subsequently handed over to the British state.[58] An internal government memorandum from late 1932 identified various proposals for what to do with the land annuities and also discussed why the annuity payments themselves should still be collected:

> The introduction of such legislation [to cancel the annuities outright] will immediately raise in an acute form the problem of the landless men. It will give point in purpose to the agitation which is being carried on by Peadar O'Donnell's Organisation for the non-payment of Annuities. It is possible that behind the ostensible objective of this Organisation there may be a further purpose, that of creating that insecurity of title which would justify a demand for the ultimate appropriation of all land by the State. In the position which would be created by the introduction of the legislation referred to, every labourer would be demanding his five or ten acres, and the question of land distribution would certainly arise in a revolutionary form.[59]

The danger with O'Donnell was that he de-emphasised the status quo of male property ownership in favour of a radical anti-capitalism. Fianna Fáil's policies required a delicate balancing act, as the party sought to tap into the same economic grievances as O'Donnell, but with fundamentally different goals in mind.

The pamphlets discussed here echo this caution and these internal contradictions. Maurice Moore aggressively pitched the annuities as a form of national robbery but still demurred from following through on the more overtly anti-imperialist implications of his argument. Henry Harrison was similarly strident in his nationalist tone but also sought to preserve Ireland's economic relationship with Britain. Fianna Fáil's economic policies never fully broke from the idea that Ireland's natural status in the global economy was to be a supplier of agricultural goods for Britain.[60] The party remained conservative *and* radical at the same time.

The Ignorant and Irresponsible Chorus

Fine Gael's economic ideas were reactionary in both senses of that word; politically right wing but also formed in reaction to Fianna Fáil and to more radical figures like Peadar O'Donnell. Already in the 1920s, there was a growing realisation within certain Cumann na nGaedheal circles that the party's economic policies were out of step with popular sentiments. The rank and file of Fine Gael's predecessor, more in tune with Irish social realities, did seek to change party policy accordingly. The October 1924 'Statement of Views' of the party's Standing Committee highlighted the continued popularity of autarchic, Sinn Féin-style, economics. The party leadership was reminded that the 'brief of Cumann na nGaedheal is for the common people of Ireland, and what the common people want under the Free State is to abolish ascendancy, to undo the Conquest and resume the course of their national life *as masters in their own land*'. The document admitted, however, that the party members' 'influence on Government policy and its power to effect patronage has been negligible if not nil'.[61] When the Minister for Post and Telegraphs, J. J. Walsh, resigned from Cumann na nGaedheal in protest against the party's refusal to implement protectionist tariffs, he alleged that the party 'has gone bodily over to the most reactionary elements of the state who will henceforth control its policies. Followers of Arthur Griffith's economic teaching will now be forced to subordinate their life-long conviction to the dictates of people whose only concern appears to be the welfare of England.'[62] These were exactly the kinds of sentiments to which Fianna Fáil would soon appeal. The Cumann na nGaedheal Minister for Finance, Ernest Blythe, however, felt grassroots criticism reflected 'the state of mind which is responsible for a good deal of harm in this country' and was due to members joining in the 'ignorant and irresponsible chorus' of the rest of the country.[63] Infamously, Patrick McGilligan, Minister for Industry and Commerce, confessed that 'people may have to die in this country and may have to die through starvation' if it meant the government could balance its budget.[64]

As the Economic War began, this kind of thinking continued to predominate in the Treatyite wing of Irish politics, though with a new 'red scare' flavour. In 1933, Fine Gael was formed when Cumann na nGaedheal merged with the National Centre Party, a small centre-right party, and the National Guard, a fascist group conventionally known as the Blueshirts. In an unimaginatively titled 1934 pamphlet, Eoin O'Duffy provided *An Outline of the Political, Social and Economic Policy of Fine Gael*. O'Duffy labelled supporters of Fianna Fáil as communists and promised that Fine Gael

> shall utilise our position to cause this old country to pulsate with hope, confidence and joy. We shall endeavour to compose international differences; to give back to our farmers their peace of mind and old time pride; to provide work for every man who is willing to work; to secure that there shall be a fair day's pay for a fair day's work in our industry, and to encourage a spirit of civic service—service to the nation in the interests of all the people.

Yet, lest anyone misinterpret his arch anti-communism, 'I ask the decent workers of Ireland not to be misled by the Communist ranters who say that we are out to establish a capitalist dictatorship. We are out to establish a dictatorship of the people of Ireland. The people of Ireland include the capitalist as well as the worker, the farmer as well as the industrialists, the farm-labourer as well as the factory worker.' O'Duffy's ideal Ireland—and presumably Fine Gael's also—would be anti-communist, implicitly capitalist, but harmonious and built on a cross-class national unity. Fine Gael would also seek to maintain Ireland's 'partnership' with the Commonwealth, not break from Britain as Fianna Fáil supposedly wanted. Fianna Fáil, he alleged, had damaged the standard of living in Ireland and had damaged the standing of farming in the country. Agriculture had become 'an industry hampered by tariffs and aided by bounties and subsidies struggling for existence in an unnecessary and unnatural atmosphere that tends to make it utterly useless as a State asset and to reduce all directly and indirectly dependent on it to a state of poverty inexperienced in this country in the days of her darkest history'. O'Duffy promised to end the Economic War with an 'honourable and fruitful settlement', but any British role in fomenting this 'post-colonial wrangle'[65] was left strategically unstated.[66] The same year O'Duffy lamented that Ireland's 'national credit' had been 'undermined' and 'our privileged place in the world's best agricultural market' had been 'abandoned' by Fianna Fáil. O'Duffy's other tack, more particular to his nascent fascism, was to advocate for a corporatist state, 'which one country after another is recognising as the only one that gives reasonable hope of steady progress and well-spread prosperity, prosperity that will be shared by all classes, farmer and industrialist labourer, factory worker and shopkeeper'. In O'Duffy's not always clear prose, a corporatist state would preserve capitalism whilst also ameliorating all those 'new evils of unregulated Capitalism' which threatened 'the peace and happiness of the world at the present juncture'. He presented this cross-class harmony as being of a piece with the 'comradeship' and 'brotherly love' of the Blueshirts, an organisation that also, O'Duffy claimed, promoted national unity across otherwise divisive class lines.[67]

Fianna Fáil certainly found it easier to situate its economic policy as the truly nationalist one; it is hard to imagine a full-throated nationalist case for paying the British state for Irish land. Perhaps in response, Fine Gael instead focused on the undue levels of taxation supposedly being imposed by de Valera's government or on its ostensible communism. As O'Duffy proclaimed in 1934: 'We have had two years' experience of a sort of watery, diluted Communism. What has it given us? It has given us riotous disorder and cowardly intimidation. It has given us highway murder, unemployment and economic destitution. It has left our rural districts as derelict as they were in the days of the famine.'[68] Given the obvious popularity of the anti-annuity campaign—Fianna Fáil had won a strong national endorsement in a snap election in 1933—this kind of rhetoric fell flat. So too did the sometimes racially charged vocabulary to which Fine Gael had recourse. At a Fine Gael meeting in August 1934, W. T. Cosgrave claimed an end to law and order in Ireland was being 'brought about by a son of Mexico'.[69] O'Duffy—more overtly racialist—said de Valera embarked on the annuities issue because he 'does not understand the people of this country because he is a half-breed'.[70] Perhaps more politically useful was the attempt, before and after the 1933 election, to present Cosgrave as a paragon of bourgeois virtue. Members of Fine Gael foregrounded their leader's honesty, straightforwardness, and candour. Refusing to pay the annuities was presented as a dishonest and dishonourable act that sullied the name of Ireland internationally.[71] Cosgrave, an honest man and an honest Irish leader, was the trope that replaced anti-communism in party propaganda: 'COSGRAVE WILL END THE [ECONOMIC] WAR. COSGRAVE will give you peace with honour and without more sacrifice. COSGRAVE is the only man in Ireland who can save Ireland and save you … A win for Cosgrave is a win for you.' By claiming that he would end the Economic War and the dastardly and dishonest politics of Fianna Fáil, 'Cosgrave's reelection was thus presented as a necessary step in the restoration of the nation's honour.'[72] This politics of respectability and bourgeois normality also came to the fore as the more overt fascists like O'Duffy were falling out of favour within Fine Gael.

There were clearly stark differences between Fianna Fáil and Fine Gael. Yet both parties shared a hostility to the type of agrarian social radicalism represented by O'Donnell. For Fine Gael, this antipathy was expressed in an overt anti-communism and a red scare that also sought to tarnish their electoral opponents in Fianna Fáil. For Fianna Fáil, there was a desire to benefit from O'Donnell's protests, to incorporate them into its movement, and, ultimately, to defang them. In differing ways, Fine Gael and Fianna Fáil wanted to ensure that O'Donnell's protests would not undermine property relations in Ireland. There were grounds for a certain economic consensus here between the Treatyites and anti-Treatyites. It is also worth noting that O'Donnell, O'Duffy, and Maurice Moore—for all their manifest ideological differences—each expressed a certain hostility to taxation itself (or at least taxation of all but the rich, in the case of O'Donnell); the ubiquity of this feeling reflected broader attitudes, as other chapters in this anthology reveal. And this perhaps fits with Tom Garvin's assessment that being 'agin the government' lingered as a 'bad habit' inherited from the experiences of British colonial rule.[73]

There Will Be Another Day

A series of coal-cattle pacts from 1935 onwards marked the beginning of the end of the Economic War.[74] The Anglo-Irish Trade Agreement in 1938, which allowed Irish farmers again to have free access to British markets, was the final act of the 'war'.[75] Even by 1937, when the 'war' was supposedly still extant, 50 per cent of Irish imports were coming from Britain, with 97 per cent of Irish exports going in the opposite direction.[76] In 1938, Irish cattle exports to Britain were worth £8.4 million. By 1939, they were over £10 million, less than what they had been in 1931 but double their value for 1934. Under the terms of the 1938 agreement, though, the British could intervene at any time with import quotas if they felt that British farmers' interests were threatened. As Mary Daly observes, the 'wording of this clause indicates that the balance of advantage rested with Britain; the key consideration was the stability of the British market, not market stability for Irish farmers'.[77] Yet Daly has also said that the conclusion to the Economic War should be deemed an 'Irish victory' because 'the overall package brought consensus among the dominant forces in Irish politics and society. This consensus marked the end of Fianna Fáil economic radicalism, demonstrated by the 1938 founding of Clann na Talmhan [Family of the Land], a party representing small farmers of the west.'[78] Daly's observation raises the obvious question, if this was an 'Irish victory', which Ireland exactly was victorious? Certainly, large cattle farmers, again granted privileged access to British markets, gained much from this settlement. But those smaller farmers who felt the need to form Clann na Talmhan clearly did not think their interests had won out.[79] Nor, in general, did those who supported Fianna Fáil out of a wish to see Ireland slough off its peripheral economic status as part of the broader movement towards independence find that their goals were achieved. As Daly herself says it was 'the dominant forces in Irish politics and society' who were happy with the 1938 settlement because it was this elite who primarily gained from it.[80]

This, though, was an unsurprising conclusion to the Economic War.[81] Fianna Fáil's enthusiasm for self-sufficiency and smallholders had been gradually waning since the mid-1930s. Sean Lemass, Minister for Industry and Commerce and never a strong supporter of de Valera's vision for rural Ireland,[82] 'secretly wished for a way of removing incompetent farmers from the land'.[83] Fianna Fáil had sought to implement a popular set of policies but ended up trapped in an ideological cul-de-sac. Its ideology was partially anti-capitalist and yet also conservative. The party attacked how large farmers used their land whilst also seeking to grant more Irish men the dignity of private land-ownership. And it sought to do all this in a relatively small island with a finite supply of agricultural resources. Fianna Fáil sought to be radical and conservative at the same time, and was ultimately more of the latter than the former, settling for the status quo and a loose consensus with Fine Gael.[84]

Twenty-five years later, Peadar O'Donnell's autobiography, *There Will Be Another Day* (1963), recalled the end of the Economic War with an ellipsis:

> Fenian Ireland, the Ireland of the poor, came to the very doorstep of a struggle for power twice in ten years; in 1922 and again in 1931. In each case it failed to achieve a leadership to correspond with its needs and was driven back in confusion … Other men, in other days, will contemplate those mistakes, for of course the Ireland of the poor will be back. There will be another day…[85]

For O'Donnell, the protests against the annuities were a kind of frustrating, open-ended failure. He had managed to lead a campaign that targeted property and class hierarchies but had not succeeded in pushing this agitation to its potentially socialist conclusion. The title of his autobiography and that open-ended final sentence, though, telegraphed O'Donnell's desire to continue the class struggle. The annuities campaign, for O'Donnell, was a failure but one that could lead to a future success.

Notes

1. 'Treaty Between Great Britain and Ireland', 6 Dec. 1921, National Archives of Ireland (hereafter, NAI) TSCH/5 2002/5/1.
2. For the background to the negotiations, see Ronan Fanning, *The Irish Department of Finance, 1922–58* (Dublin: Institute of Public Administration, 1978), 155–74.
3. 'Heads of the Ultimate Financial Settlement between the British government and the government of the Irish Free State', 19 Mar. 1926, in *Documents on Irish Foreign Policy*, ed. Ronan Fanning et al., http://www.difp.ie/docs/1926/Settlement-of-financial-obligations-between-Britain-and-the-Irish-Free-State/721.htm (accessed 27 July 2018).
4. Cormac Ó Gráda, *Ireland: A New Economic History, 1780–1939* (Oxford: Clarendon Press, 1994), 412.
5. Aidan Beatty, *Masculinity and Power in Irish Nationalism, 1884–1938* (London: Palgrave Macmillan), chap. 6.
6. Peadar O'Donnell *For or Against the Ranchers? Irish Working Farmers in The Economic War* (Westport: Mayo News, n.d.), 9.
7. As Mary Daly observes, Ireland did not produce 'food', it mainly produced unfattened cattle that were then exported to Britain where they were fattened, slaughtered, and processed, with the value added going to British producers instead of Irish farmers; Mary Daly, *Industrial Development and Irish National Identity, 1922–1939* (Syracuse: Syracuse University Press, 1992), 16.
8. Sven Beckert, *Empire of Cotton: A New History of Global Capitalism* (London: Penguin Books, 2015); Robert J. Gordon, *The Rise and Fall of American Growth: The U.S. Standard of Living since the Civil War* (Princeton: Princeton University Press, 2016); Thomas Piketty, *Capital in the Twenty-First Century* (Cambridge, MA: Harvard University Press, 2014).
9. Edward E. Baptist, *The Half Has Never Been Told: Slavery and the Making of American Capitalism* (New York: Basic Books, 2014); Jonathan Levy. *Freaks of Fortune: The Emerging World of Capitalism and Risk in America* (Cambridge, MA: Harvard University Press, 2012).
10. An important exception is Bethany Moreton, *To Serve God and Walmart: The Making of Christian Free Enterprise* (Cambridge, MA: Harvard

University Press, 2010), a perceptive study of race, class, *and* gender in late twentieth-century American consumer capitalism.

11. Jonathan Crary, *24/7: Late Capitalism and the Ends of Sleep* (London: Verso, 2013); Mark Fisher, *Capitalist Realism: Is There No Alternative?* (Winchester: Zero Books, 2009); Andreas Malm, *Fossil Capital: The Rise of Steam Power and the Roots of Global Warming* (London: Verso, 2016); Jason Moore, *Capitalism in the Web of Life: Ecology and the Accumulation of Capital* (London: Verso, 2015); Kohei Saito, *Karl Marx's Ecosocialism: Capital, Nature, and the Unfinished Critique of Political Economy* (New York: Monthly Review Press, 2017).
12. Stuart Hall, 'The Great Moving Right Show', in *The Politics of Thatcherism*, ed. Stuart Hall and Martin Jacques (London: Lawrence and Wishart, 1983), 19–39; David Harvey, *Spaces of Capital: Towards a Critical Geography* (London: Routledge, 2001); Maria Mies, *Patriarchy and Accumulation on a World Scale: Women in the International Division of Labour*, 2nd ed. (London: Zed Books, 1998); Ellen Meiksins Wood, *The Pristine Culture of Capitalism: A Historical Essay on Old Regimes and Modern States* (London: Verso, 1991); David Roediger, *The Wages of Whiteness: Race and the Making of the American Working Class* (London: Verso, 1991); Immanuel Wallerstein, *The Modern World System I: Capitalist Agriculture and the Origins of the European World Economy in the Sixteenth Century*, 2nd ed. (Berkeley, CA: University of California Press, 2011).
13. See, for example, Cormac Ó Gráda, *A Rocky Road: The Irish Economy since the 1920s* (Manchester: Manchester University Press, 1997).
14. For three exceptions, see: Mike Cronin, 'Golden Dreams, Harsh Realities: Economics and Informal Empire in the Irish Free State', in *Ireland: The Politics of Independence*, ed. Mike Cronin and John M. Regan (London: Palgrave Macmillan, 2000), 144–63; Daly, *Industrial Development*; Trisha Kessler, 'Rethinking Irish Protectionism: Jewish Refugee Factories and the Pursuit of an Irish-Ireland for Industry', in *Irish Questions and Jewish Questions: Crossovers in Culture*, ed. Aidan Beatty and Dan O'Brien (Syracuse, NY: Syracuse University Press, 2018), 107–23.
15. Maurice Coakley, *Ireland in the World Order: A History of Uneven Development* (London: Pluto Press, 2012); Denis O'Hearn, *The Atlantic Economy: Britain, the US and Ireland* (Manchester: Manchester University Press, 2001).
16. Richard Dunphy *The Making of Fianna Fáil Power in Ireland, 1923–48* (Oxford: Clarendon Press, 1995); Peter O'Neill, *The Famine Irish and the American Racial State* (New York: Routledge, 2017). Both O'Neill and Dunphy make excellent use of the theories of the state of the Marxist sociologist Nicos Poulantzas.

17. See, for example, Kieran Allen, *1916: Ireland's Revolutionary Tradition* (London: Pluto Press, 2016).
18. Roediger, *Wages*; Hall *Great Moving Right Show*.
19. Michael McInerney, *Peadar O'Donnell: Irish Social Rebel* (Dublin: O'Brien Press, 1974), 119; quoted in Timothy O'Neil, 'Handing Away the Trump Card? Peadar O'Donnell, Fianna Fáil, and the Non-Payment of Land Annuities Campaign, 1926–32', *New Hibernia Review* 12, no. 1 (2008): 27.
20. Richard English says that 'the leitmotiv of O'Donnell's political career was that social struggle and national struggle must be interwoven'; Richard English, 'Green on Red: Two Case Studies in Early Twentieth-Century Irish Republican Thought', in *Political Thought in Ireland since the Seventeenth Century*, ed. D. George Boyce, Robert Eccleshall, and Vincent Geoghegan (London: Routledge, 1993), 175.
21. Peadar O'Donnell, *There Will Be Another Day* (Dublin: Dolmen Press, 1963), 38–39 and *passim*.
22. O'Neil, 'Handing Away the Trump Card', 23–24.
23. English, 'Green on Red', 179; O'Neil, 'Handing Away the Trump Card', 23–24.
24. English, 'Green on Red', 175.
25. Quoted in O'Donnell, *There Will Be*, 95; for information on Fahy, see Jim Madden, *Fr. John Fahy, 1893–1969: Radical Republican and Agrarian Activist* (Dublin: Columba Press, 2013).
26. *An Phoblacht*, 4 June 1926; quoted in Richard English, *Radicals and the Republic: Socialist Republicanism in Ireland, 1925–1937* (Oxford: Clarendon Press, 1994), 90.
27. O'Donnell, *There Will Be*, 34.
28. *An Phoblacht*, 25 Mar. 1927; quoted in English, *Radicals*, 82.
29. Quoted in Donal Ó Drisceoil, 'When Dev Defaulted: The Land Annuities Dispute, 1926–38', *History Ireland* 19, no. 3 (2011). The Young Irelander James Fintan Lalor (1807–1849) was a recurring reference point for not only O'Donnell but for socialist republicans more broadly. Lalor was assumed to be a progenitor for the synthesis of separatism and leftist economics, though ironically, as Richard English points out, he held to an essentially bourgeois economics; English, 'Green on Red', 178–80.
30. Terence Brown, for example, has said that implicit in O'Donnell's work was 'a sense that Gaelic Ireland in the west is the authentic heroic Ireland in a way that confirms rather than contradicts the conventional image of the west as "certain set apart". The power of this conventional image was perhaps so great that it affected as intelligent a social commentator as Peadar O'Donnell'; Terence Brown, *Ireland: A Social and Cultural History, 1922–85*, 2nd ed. (London: Fontana, 1985), 94; English,

Radicals, 83. See also Charles Travis, '"Rotting Townlands": Peadar O'Donnell, the West of Ireland, and the Politics of Representation in Saorstát na hÉireann (Irish Free State), 1929–1933', *Historical Geography* 36 (2008): 208–24.

31. Peadar O'Donnell, *For or Against the Ranchers*, 1, 3, 5, 7, 9.
32. Land Annuities: Non-Payment Campaign, 1928–31, Confidential Memorandum from Garda Superintendent, Kinsale, 17 May 1928, NAI TAOIS/S 8336; Land Annuities: Non-Payment Campaign, 1928–31, Secret Memorandum from Garda Chief Superintendent, Letterkenny, 12 Feb. 1929, NAI TAOIS/S 8336.
33. As an anti-Treatyite he refused to recognise the court's right to prosecute him. He told the jury that he would recognise them but not the 'lad in the wig'; O'Neil 'Handing Away the Trump Card', 27.
34. Ó Drisceoil, 'When Dev Defaulted'.
35. O'Neil, 'Handing Away the Trump Card', 26.
36. Kieran Allen, *Fianna Fáil and Irish Labour: 1926 to the Present* (London: Pluto Press, 1997), 21. It is unfair, though, to label this vision of 'sturdy, self-sufficient farmer[s]' as something vague, as Allen does. It was a vision of Irish life that, for rural Irish men, drew on familiar and strongly felt economic experiences.
37. O'Neil, 'Handing Away the Trump Card', 29.
38. Dunphy, *Fianna Fáil Power*, 125.
39. Terence Dooley, *The Land for the People: The Land Question in Independent Ireland* (Dublin: UCD Press, 2004), 3–4.
40. Dunphy, *Fianna Fáil Power*, 41, 31.
41. Indeed, O'Donnell sought Fianna Fáil's support for the campaign whilst also, incongruously, linking the campaign to the work of the Comintern's Peasant International, Krestintern; O'Neil, 'Handing Away the Trump Card'.
42. On Moore, see Marie Coleman, 'Moore, Maurice George (1854–1939)', in *Dictionary of Irish Biography: From the Earliest Times to the Year 2002*, ed. James McGuire and James Quinn (Cambridge: Cambridge University Press, 2002).
43. It is not clear how Moore reached the calculation that the annuities accounted for one-fifth of the Free State's revenues. While his claim is inaccurate, it does point to the emotiveness of Ireland's economic 'tribute' to the UK Treasury!
44. Moore asserted that it was 'universally recognised that the duty of a Negotiator on behalf of a State is to claim all he can and come back with the best terms he can get out of the rival State'. Thus, Cumann na nGaedheal were failing in one of *the* basic duties of statecraft!

45. So as to make this claim, he seemed to have collapsed the annuities (which were essentially state-backed mortgages) into the overall tax bill. Moore included Irish government payments for the imperial debt as part of his calculations, which included payments for war pensions and debts accrued during the Great War; Maurice Moore, *British Plunder and Irish Blunder: The Story of the Land Purchase Annuities* (Dublin: Gaelic Press, 1928), 22.
46. Ibid., 4, 9, 10–11, 20, 23–24, 27.
47. Owen McGee, 'Harrison, Henry (1867–1954)', *Dictionary of Irish Biography*.
48. Henry Harrison, *The Strange Case of the Land Purchase Annuities* (Dublin: M. H. Gill and Son, 1932), 5. Most of the rest of Harrison's 1932 pamphlet was a summation of the British position that the Free State was strictly bound to hand over the annuities, as well as a historical background to the annuities issue.
49. Henry Harrison, *Spotlights on the Anglo-Irish Financial Quarrel* (Dublin: M. H. Gill and Son, 1934), 3.
50. In the pamphlet, Harrison also pointed out the irony that the people who had been hurt by the Economic War—large cattle farmers—were the ones who were strongest advocates for a close trading partnership between Ireland and the United Kingdom. This had strengthened the hand of nationalists, by which he primarily meant Fianna Fáil.
51. Henry Harrison, *The Game of 'Beggar-My-Neighbour': Who Wins?* (London: Irish News and Information Bureau, 1934), 3–5, 7–8, 22–23.
52. *Cóiriú Fhianna Fáil* [Constitution of Fianna Fáil], National Library of Ireland (hereafter, NLI) LO P103.
53. *Fianna Fáil: Clár an Chéad Árd Fheis*, 24 Nov. 1926, 25 Nov 1926, NLI LO P103. The two proposed amendments came, respectively, from the Ballinalough Branch and the Fintan Lalor Branch, Dublin, of the party.
54. Fianna Fáil pamphlet, *The Wheels are Moving* (n.p, n.d. [1933?]), NLI LO P111, item 10.
55. Open Letter from Oscar Traynor, *To Each Elector of North Dublin* (n.p., n.d. [1932?]), NLI LO P111, item 19; see also Fianna Fáil pamphlet, *The Men for North City* (n.p., n.d. [1933]), NLI LO P111, item 20.
56. Dunphy, *Fianna Fáil Power*, 39–40.
57. Ibid., 97.
58. English, *Radicals*, 117.
59. Memorandum from the Minister for Finance, Land Annuities: Relief for Annuitants, 1932–34, 11 Nov. 1932, NAI TAOIS S/2888.
60. Beatty, *Masculinity*, chap. 6.
61. John M. Regan, *The Irish Counter-Revolution: Treatyite Politics and Settlement in Independent Ireland* (Dublin: Gill and Macmillan, 1999), 213. Emphasis added.

62. Daly, *Industrial Development*, 35–36.
63. Regan, *Counter-Revolution*, 210–11.
64. R. M. Douglas, *Architects of the Resurrection: Ailtirí na hAiséirghe and the Fascist 'New Order' in Ireland* (Manchester: Manchester University Press, 2009), 7–8. As Douglas has said, this was 'perhaps the most asinine statement ever made by an Irish public representative'.
65. Ó Gráda, *Rocky Road*, 5.
66. Eoin O'Duffy, *An Outline of the Political, Social and Economic Policy of Fine Gael* (Dublin: United Ireland, 1934), 4, 7, 10. This pamphlet was a transcript of the opening address delivered at the First Annual Ard-Fheis of Fine Gael in the Mansion House, Dublin, 8 Feb. 1934.
67. Eoin O'Duffy, *The Labour Policy of Fine Gael* (Dublin: Fine Gael/Browne and Nolan, 1934), 4, 5, 9. These are transcripts from two speeches by Eoin O'Duffy in February and March 1934. In an echo of the claims of horseshoe theory, corporatist economics was also presented as the antidote to 'socialist extremism' as well as 'conservative old curmudgeons' and 'plutocratic extremists' who derived 'pleasure' form 'keep[ing] the workers in … their place'; idem, 11. O'Duffy's fascist corporatism was on fuller display in *Why I Resigned From Fine Gael (Blueshirt Series: Pamphlet No. 1)* (Dublin: League of Youth, 1934), which, as the title suggests, marked his break from the more conventionally conservative ideas of Fine Gael.
68. O'Duffy, *Outline*, 4.
69. Regan, *Counter-Revolution*, 364.
70. Ibid., 347.
71. Ciara Meehan, *The Cosgrave Party: A History of Cumann na nGaedheal* (Dublin: Royal Irish Academy, 2010), 146.
72. Jason Knirck, 'A Cult of No Personality: W. T. Cosgrave and the Election of 1933', *Éire-Ireland* 47, nos. 3–4 (2012): 65, 75, 82.
73. Tom Garvin, *Preventing the Future: Why Was Ireland So Poor for So Long?* (Dublin: Gill and Macmillan, 2004), 2.
74. Allen, *Fianna Fáil*, 42.
75. The looming threat of Hitler was perhaps *the* motivating factor for Britain in ending this 'war'. As one commentator observed in the *New Statesman* whilst simultaneously hinting at Irish nationalist concerns, 'The bully remains a bully until he is frightened by a bigger bully'; *New Statesman and Nation*, 20 Aug. 1938, quoted in Ó Gráda, *New Economic History*, 416.
76. Cronin, 'Golden Dreams, Harsh Realities', 162.
77. Mary Daly, *The First Department: A History of the Department of Agriculture* (Dublin: Institute of Public Administration, 2002), 196–97.
78. Daly, *Industrial Development*, 170.

79. As Dooley argues 'Clann na Talmhan did best in areas where Fianna Fáil had failed to deliver upon its earlier election promises of more land acquisition and division'; Dooley, *Land for the People*, 208.
80. Daly, *Industrial Development*, 170.
81. Kevin Hjortshøj O'Rourke has said that little about the Economic War, or the history of Irish economic planning, was surprising; Ireland acted in the manner of other peripheral European states—such as Portugal, Greece, and Spain—that sought to catch up to the industrialised core. O'Rourke thus gives short shrift to any of kind of insular or nationalist explanations; Kevin Hjortshøj O'Rourke, 'Independent Ireland in Comparative Perspective', *Irish Economic and Social History* 44, no. 1 (2017): 19–45. I would add, however, that the legitimising ideologies presented in the various pamphlets discussed here are specifically Irish, even insular.
82. Bryce Evans provides some intimate details of the divisions within Fianna Fáil between Lemass, whose economics leaned towards industrialisation, and Sean MacEntee, who was cut from agrarian cloth; Bryce Evans, *Seán Lemass: Democratic Dictator* (Cork: Collins Press, 2011), 71–110.
83. Ó Gráda, *Rocky Road*, 146.
84. This is part of what Regan has aptly called 'The Consensus of Irish Nationalist Politics'; Regan, *Counter-Revolution*, 373–83.
85. O'Donnell, *There Will Be*, 132; see also Aidan Beatty, 'An Irish Revolution Without a Revolution', *Journal of World-Systems Research* 22, no. 1 (2016): 54–76.

CHAPTER 13

The Irish Tax State and Historical Legacies: Slowly Converging Capacity, Persistent Unwillingness to Pay

Michelle D'Arcy and Marina Nistotskaya

The hallmarks of the modern Irish tax state have been its low yield, narrow base, and instability. In 2016, tax revenue as a percentage of gross domestic product (GDP) was 23 per cent, below the Organization for Economic Cooperation and Development's (OECD) average of 34 per cent.[1] The European Commission has recently again warned about the dangers of the country's narrow tax base. Ireland has faced persistent problems of fiscal sustainability, most recently since the financial crash in 2008.[2]

While proximate factors, like the state of the economy and policy choices around tax types and rates, help to explain the character of the Irish tax state, we argue that historical legacies are also important for understanding contemporary outcomes, as the development of tax states is a path-dependent process.[3] We track the development of the Irish tax state along two main pathways: formal institutions related to the

M. D'Arcy (✉)
Trinity College Dublin, Dublin, Ireland
e-mail: darcym1@tcd.ie

M. Nistotskaya
University of Gothenburg, Gothenburg, Sweden
e-mail: marina.nistotskaya@gu.se

D. Kanter, P. Walsh (eds.), *Taxation, Politics, and Protest in Ireland, 1662–2016*, Palgrave Studies in the History of Finance,
https://doi.org/10.1007/978-3-030-04309-4_13

administrative capacity of the tax authority, and attitudes towards taxation, which are shaped by levels of taxation and fairness in its distribution and revealed through supportive or oppositional popular responses to tax.

Analysing these pathways across three centuries from the origins of the Irish tax state in the late seventeenth century, we argue that Ireland's pre-independence history created two main legacies for the republic: weak tax administration and a population with resistant attitudes towards taxation. As summarised in Table 13.1 and discussed in more detail in the chapter, in 1922 the Free State inherited a tax administration with staffing levels equivalent to the mid-eighteenth century. Pre-independence populations experienced increasing levels of taxation per capita, within a tax structure dominated by indirect regressive taxes. Whereas for most of the period British governments built popular trust in the state and consent to tax,[4] in Ireland tax measures almost unvaryingly provoked opposition and grievance.

Table 13.1 Tax outcomes, structure, and administration, 1700–2015

Year	*Revenue pc, £*	*Revenue, % GDP*	*Indirect taxes, % Revenue*	*Tax officials, #*
1700	0.19		89	700
1750			90	1,325
1800	0.45		90	3,150
1850	0.61		81	
1885	1.56		73	
1922	9.3		64	1,756
1965		25	53	
1980		30	43	
2015		23	33	5,745

Note: Tax data: Duanaire, A Treasury of Digital Data for Irish Economic History, ***Public Revenues and Expenditures of Ireland in the Eighteenth Century***, http://www.duanaire.ie/finances18/ (accessed 13 Aug. 2018); Brian Mitchell, ***International Historical Statistics: Europe, 1750–2000*** (New York: Palgrave Macmillan, 2007); author's calculations based on House of Commons, 'Accounts Relating to Customs, Excise, Stamp Duties and Post Office of Ireland; Abstract of Appropriated Duties; State of Establishment and Charges for Government of Ireland, and State of National Account. Accounts, Presented to the House of Commons, respecting that part of the United Kingdom called Ireland', ***Sessional Papers, 1801*** (22), vol. 5, pp. 183, 34; idem, 'Return of Amount of Assessments under Each Schedule of Income Tax in Ireland, 1853–54', ***Sessional Papers, 1854*** (471) vol. 58, p. 373. Tax officials: Patrick Walsh, 'The Fiscal State in Ireland, 1691–1769', ***Historical Journal*** 56, no. 3 (2013): 634; Seán Réamonn, ***History of the Revenue Commissioners*** (Dublin: Institute of Public Administration, 1981), 124. Population and GDP: Jutta Bolt et al., 'Rebasing "Maddison": New Income Comparisons and the Shape of Long-Run Economic Development', ***Maddison Project Working Paper 10*** (University of Gronigen: Gronigen Growth and Development Centre, 2018)

After independence, the state struggled to transcend this history. Levels of taxation remained low and fundamentally focused on indirect taxes until the 1970s–80s. Attempts at reforms were constrained both by the weakness of the Revenue Commissioners and by public attitudes, as those outside the tax net opposed new taxes and those within it resisted rate increases. Even after successful reforms in the 1990s, which addressed the historical legacy of the administrative weakness of formal institutions, unwillingness to pay has remained a persistent attitude of Irish taxpayers, constraining governments of different ideological colours in their attempts to achieve a sustainable revenue base, even when economic conditions and administrative capacity were no longer obstacles. Overall, this suggests that while historical legacies in formal institutions can, slowly, erode, informal institutions can persist.

The chapter proceeds as follows: first, we provide an overview of the theoretical framework employed to analyse the evolution of the Irish tax state. We then apply this from its origins in the seventeenth century, highlighting the critical juncture after the Act of Union and the subsequent path-dependent developments of the nineteenth century. We then examine the kind of tax state this bequeathed Irish governments and how this influenced tax administration and politics after independence, with particular emphasis on tax politics since the 1960s, when the first significant tax reforms began.

Theoretical Framework

A growing literature suggests that history has long-lasting effects on current formal institutions, and also on values, beliefs, and social norms.[5] Formal institutions are seen as arising from concrete historical circumstances and evolve in a path-dependent manner, affecting present-day institutions. For example, there is a large literature showing the importance of colonial rule on current formal institutions, such as those related to property rights or the financial sector.[6]

The high degree of path dependency in tax systems has long been acknowledged and emphasised again recently.[7] For example, D'Arcy and Nistotskaya show that the extent to which European early modern states evolved into large complex organisations geared for the extraction of resources is consequential for their tax outcomes today.[8] They also process-traced a high degree of continuity in the monitoring capacity of the extremely effective Swedish state: from the seventeenth-century cadastral maps and population statistics to present-day surveillance of individual taxpayers.[9] In a contrasting case, Likhovski showed how the practice of the late Ottoman and British colonial states, to tax with little regard for formal institutions, led the newly established Israeli state to tax not through the reliance on law and bureaucracy but 'by utilizing state-created social norms'.[10]

History also matters by affecting informal institutions—people's attitudes, values, and norms—which then persist over time. Informal institutions are not fully reflective of proximate conditions but are rather a product of interactions between individuals and between individuals and organisations, including the state, over the *longue durée*. The claim that the character of past interactions with the state affects present-day attitudes, values, and norms has strong empirical support.[11] For example, Becker et al. showed that communities in five East European countries that were part of the well-administered Habsburg Empire exhibit higher levels of trust in public institutions today, despite the formal institutions of the empire being long gone.[12] Evidence suggests that such impacts survive over hundreds of years.[13]

The importance of the historically contingent nature of citizen attitudes towards the state becomes clear in the light of a growing literature that points out that such attitudes are an important predictor of citizens' willingness to comply with the state's fiscal demands.[14] This is congruent with the existing cross-disciplinary literature on the fiscal contract, which argues that citizens are more willing to pay taxes if they perceive the distribution of the tax burden as equitable, if the quality of public goods received is of equivalent value to the payments made, and if other taxpayers are not shirking on their fiscal obligations.[15] The insights from these literatures suggest that the absence of a fiscal contract in the past may have long-run effects on norms of compliance that carry on beyond changes in formal institutions.

In the rest of the chapter, we interpret the evolution of the Irish tax state through these theoretical lenses. We analyse the development of formal institutions over time, focusing on critical junctures and path-dependent trajectories, and the historical circumstances relevant to informal institutions, particularly the structure of taxation, as well as visible popular responses to taxation, assessing the presence or absence of a fiscal contract.

The Origins of the Irish Tax State, 1660–1800

In the 1600s, the English authorities in Ireland began to shift away from a medieval system of feudal dues towards the first elements of a modern tax state. In the broader context of the Restoration, Charles II was granted hereditary revenue in perpetuity. Customs and excise, which would be seen today as regressive taxes,[16] dominated the tax structure.[17] Taxes were collected at first through tax farming and then through an expanding but patrimonial state bureaucracy.[18] For most of the period from the late seventeenth century to the Act of Union (1800), the popular experience of taxation was one of pervasive, regressive taxes and of an increasingly professionalised tax administration that was at best reasonably competent and at worst ignorant and corrupt.[19] The institutional origins of the Irish tax state, therefore, lie in an expanding but, in comparative European terms, weak administration and the absence of a meaningful fiscal contract.

Revenue Administration: The Patrimonial Irish Tax State

In terms of administrative structure, unlike in England where the medieval body for revenue collection, the Exchequer, was reformed, the Irish Exchequer was retained and the new taxes were initially farmed, creating a parallel structure that was subsequently layered over the Exchequer.[20] While tax farming was initially a relatively efficient innovation, the Exchequer collected little revenue and was a source of patronage for the King's allies in Ireland, who were granted offices, although they were often absentee and had few responsibilities.[21] The tendency to use the revenue service for sinecures was rife both in Dublin and the provinces.[22]

By the mid-eighteenth century, patrimonial tendencies had become institutionalised. The revenue administration was characterised by non-operative management and, subsequently, poorly supervised lower-level officials who often engaged in bribe taking.[23] Corruption among officials was particularly acute in hearth tax collection and increased across the seventeenth century as collectors' salaries stagnated.[24] Although in general appointees did need to demonstrate some level of ability and egregious transgressions were punished, the high costs of administration were reflective of its inefficiency.[25] Collection costs were 13 per cent of total revenue in 1758, increasing to 16 per cent in 1783 and 18 per cent in 1789.[26] By comparison, in 1778 collection costs in England were 7 per cent.[27] The problems of sinecures and bribe taking were highlighted in a series of commissions established after the Act of Union.[28]

Although by the eighteenth century revenue officials became the largest category of civil state employees and an important point of contact between the centre and periphery, tax administration remained largely centralised and poorly informed about the population's activities relevant to taxation.[29] In contrast to some European countries that were developing fiscal capacity through information gathering—tax registers, cadastral maps, and population statistics[30]—Britain had neither a cadaster[31] nor fine-grained information on the population for the purposes of taxation.[32] While in England the 1692 land tax led to the creation of a complex infrastructure for the collection of direct taxes, comprised mostly of lay assessors and commissioners at the local level and a small central bureaucracy, the absence of this tax in Ireland meant there was no equivalent infrastructure.[33] The hearth tax, collected from the bulk of the population, was administered by a relatively small number of officials and without building durable extractive capabilities at the local level: in 1750, there were eighty-five collectors in the country, each assigned a 'walk' composed of several baronies.[34]

Although the Irish tax state certainly developed during the eighteenth century it did so from a low base and by the end of the century tax collection was less than one-quarter of per capita British levels.[35] While no state in this period was entirely free of patrimonial tendencies, their entrenchment varied, and in some European states, such as Sweden and Denmark, rulers expanded the state's administrative reach by collecting information on their subjects' taxable assets, increasing the number of salaried bureaucrats, and legitimising new tax regimes by underscoring their contractual—taxes in exchange for public goods—nature.[36] Despite collecting revenue adequate to meet expenditure, Irish tax administration fell well short of the 'planned, rationally ordered, hierarchical, routinized and scrutinized roles, practices and spaces' of the British excise, nor were there systematic efforts to gather and apply information on the population and their economic assets for taxation purposes.[37] In comparative terms, Irish tax bureaucracy was weaker than that of England, which in turn lagged behind the frontier tax states of Europe.

Popular Experiences of Taxation: Pervasive, Regressive Taxes

During the period under consideration, the tax structure in Ireland was regressive in a number of ways. First, as part of the bargain with the recalled Irish Parliament, the taxes on Courts of Wards and Liveries, a levy aimed at the rich, were replaced by the hearth tax.[38] Although some population categories, such as poor widows and those living off alms, were exempt, the tax affected most of the population, as evidenced by the fact that hearth returns are a key source for historical population estimates.[39] The hearth tax was much resented in both England and Ireland because it was levied by means of domiciliary visits by tax collectors.[40] When the hearth tax was repealed in England in 1689, the preamble to the act stated that it was 'in itself not only a great oppression to the poorer sort, but a badge of slavery upon the whole people, exposing every man's house to be entered into and searched at pleasure by persons unknown to him'.[41]

While the hearth tax in England was replaced with a number of other personal taxes—on personal estates, public offices, and land in 1692, or the graded window tax in 1696, which was much less onerous for the generally window-less poor—it remained in place in Ireland for another century.[42] Until 1706, the hearth moneys were collected by tax farmers, who were seen to be the most rapacious collectors because of incentives to collect every penny to recoup their initial investment.[43] The subsequent state-administered collection was equally bad, characterised by 'harsh, arbitrary, or corrupt behaviour on the part of local officers', which caused popular disaffection.[44]

Second, if the new taxes of the 1690s in England placed a large (though gradually shrinking) fiscal burden on the rich, in Ireland the tax structure remained regressive.[45] For example, in England the land tax was levied on land value, but in Ireland, the functional equivalent of land tax—quit rents, a tax on land forfeited during the 1641 Rebellion and subsequently granted to the Protestant gentry—was levied as a fixed payment charged by the acre without reference to the land's market value. Consequently, while the English land tax brought to the state's coffers 35 per cent of revenue in the 1690s and about 17 per cent in the 1790s, the contribution of the quit rents depreciated considerably over time: from 32 per cent of revenue in 1664 to only 4 per cent in 1801.[46]

Moreover, as in England, the greatest source of taxation in Ireland was indirect. As shown in Table 13.1, by the end of the period, 90 per cent of revenue came from indirect taxes, particularly customs. As Réamonn noted, the Irish government was mainly 'funded by taxes on consumables such as salt, leather, sugar, tea and, notably, alcohol'.[47] Because such taxes impose a larger burden (relative to resources) on those who are poorer, some have concluded that 'Ireland was not poor because she was overtaxed but overtaxed because she was poor.'[48]

The uses to which tax revenue was put were not visibly beneficial to the population in ways that might have fostered a meaningful fiscal contract. Because of Parliament's limited fiscal powers, much of the revenue was used on patronage—offices granted to English non-residents and pensions to the King's allies and dependents (a practice not tolerated by the English Parliament)—and on supporting a proportionally larger army than in England.[49] Although the Protestant gentry minority supported the use of Irish revenue to maintain a standing army in Ireland, and security was one of the primary public goods of the period, the army was used primarily in defence of England, for example during the Jacobite rising, or in tax collection.[50]

The imposition of regressive taxes on the population, which were then used in ways that were not visibly beneficial, makes it unsurprising that resistance was common, and tax grievances were one of the economic issues cited by the United Irishmen, who promised to redress 'the price of land, unequal taxation, illegal fees, tithes, non-residence of clergy and landlords and the whole of the revenue laws'.[51] The army increasingly assisted revenue collection because taxmen were subject to frequent attacks.[52] Although tax grievances were ubiquitous in Europe, they were less pronounced in countries, such as England or Sweden, where rulers were building strong, durable relationships of negotiated trust and consent around taxation.[53] This process was not in evidence in eighteenth-century Ireland.

Taxation, 1800–1920: Overtaxed, Underdeveloped

The Act of Union was a critical juncture in the evolution of the Irish tax state. The revenue administration was transferred to London, making it more efficient but minimal. During this period, there developed a strong popular perception that the country was taxed beyond its means, and that revenue, rather than being used to the country's benefit or even to alleviate dire need during the Famine, was instead used to fund policies detrimental to the island's economic interests. This created broad-based resistance before the Famine and increasingly politicised grievance and protest after it. Overall, fiscal union did not produce a fiscal contract; rather it created a legacy of distrust and resistance to taxation.

Revenue Administration: Less Patrimonial, but Minimal

Transition to a less patrimonial but minimal revenue bureaucracy marked a pivotal development in the Irish tax state in the nineteenth century. The inefficiency and corruption reported by the Commissioners for Reduction of National Debt[54] and the resistance to taxation among the general population led to the adoption of a highly centralised administration that operated, after the union of Exchequers in 1817, primarily from London. Further amalgamations and consolidations followed and by the 1830s 'the whole of the Irish revenue machinery was managed by United Kingdom departments.'[55]

Although accurate data on the number of revenue officials in Ireland in the nineteenth century is not available, the difference between the figures for the 1810s and 1920s—3,150 and 1,756 correspondingly—suggests that consolidation and rationalisation led to loss of personnel on the ground.[56] The Treasury began 'enforcing severe administrative standards' through its representatives on the island.[57] These measures improved the efficiency of tax administration, as evidenced by the fall in collection costs to 5 per cent in 1854.[58]

This administrative structure defined how taxes were collected over the course of the nineteenth century and beyond. When income tax was introduced in Ireland in 1853, it was collected by a central bureaucracy, while in Britain it was done by local lay assessors and commissioners.[59] Likewise, tax on rental income was not collected, as in Britain, 'at source' from the tenant (who then paid the rent, net of tax, to the landlord), because the Chancellor of the Exchequer, William Gladstone, 'wished to avoid placing tenants in contact with the tax assessors and collectors whenever possible, because he feared that attempts "to levy off the tenants would be hazardous and might lead under given circumstances to a system of passive resistance"'.[60] The use of central government officials who aimed to minimise contact with taxpayers proved to be a necessity for implementing the tax in Ireland, whereas Britain relied on the tradition of local autonomy and the associated administrative system that dated back to the 1692 land tax.[61]

Popular Experiences of Taxation After the Union: Increasing Levels of Taxation and Resistance

Throughout the nineteenth century, there was a strong popular perception in Ireland that the country was taxed beyond its means. Initially, fiscal separation—which continued for the first seventeen years after the Act of Union, ostensibly for Ireland's benefit—set a contribution level that was later calculated by Cormac Ó Gráda, and admitted by the Financial Relations Commission in the 1890s, to be beyond the capacity of the country's economy.[62] From a situation of having lower debt than Britain in 1800, debt levels began to escalate thereafter.[63] Although real levels of taxation are impossible to establish with precision, fiscal unification in response to this imbalance seems only to have exacerbated the situation.[64]

The tax structure continued to be mostly indirect and therefore regressive. Income tax was introduced in Britain, at first temporarily in 1799 and then permanently in 1842, but delayed in Ireland until 1853 due to a number of factors, including administrative capacity and political risk. While Britain utilised the administrative infrastructure of the land tax for the collection of income tax, Ireland lacked equivalent arrangements.[65] As Robert Peel noted, 'it is a tax for the levy of which no machinery exists in Ireland.'[66] There were also political considerations as the first half of the nineteenth century was dominated by the mass movement calling for Catholic Emancipation, the Tithe War—often violent resistance to paying tithes to the Church of Ireland—and Daniel O'Connell's movement to repeal the Act of Union. Under these conditions, income tax could 'not be collected through the use of lay auxiliaries, and the use of government officials would create resentment'.[67] O'Connell took the credit for having 'preserved the country from an income tax'.[68]

The perception of over-taxation in Ireland was not shared in Britain. British politicians such as Gladstone claimed that Ireland was a 'fiscal free-rider'.[69] Despite the difficulties of gauging both real revenue and expenditure, a select committee corroborated this viewpoint by finding that expenditure had exceeded revenue since 1817.[70] This made the exemption of Ireland from income tax increasingly politically problematic in Britain, especially after the Famine, which increased expenditure. Although much Famine relief was funded through loans to be repaid by Irish rate payers, it reinforced the perception that Ireland was an undue burden and made the exemption from income tax increasingly untenable.[71] Critics of the policy countered this by arguing that extending income tax to Ireland was unjust because it amounted to using revenue from an impoverished part of the Union to remit indirect taxes and expand free trade policies that would remove Ireland's preferential access to the British market.[72]

The introduction of income tax in 1853 increased revenue by almost 50 per cent and exacerbated the perception that the country was taxed beyond its means.[73] In 1890, the Financial Relations Commission concluded that the situation was unsustainable: while Irish revenue contributed approximately one-eleventh of the total revenue of Great Britain, the Commission estimated the taxable capacity of the island to be no more than one-twentieth.[74] Furthermore, the overall structure of taxation did not change radically. There was some decrease in the share of customs, as tariffs were lowered, but this was compensated for by excise and thus overall the reliance on indirect taxes remained.

Given the perception of a high fiscal burden, it is unsurprising that taxation provoked resistance and violence, first in localised and unorganised ways and later as part of the nationalist cause. The first half of the nineteenth century witnessed the Tithe War and strong resistance to the enforcement of the Poor Law rates and to attempts to crack down on illicit distillation. Enforcing duties on many small illegal stills throughout the country had long proved difficult: 20,000 illegal stills had been destroyed by the army towards the end of the Napoleonic Wars.[75] The state at first tried a system of fining townlands where illegal stills were found. However, the fines were met with obstructionism—juries refusing to convict and peasants refusing to take in the harvest—and eventually were abandoned.[76] In 1822, an alternative approach was tried with the establishment of a dedicated Revenue Police. The force, which numbered over a thousand in the 1850s, was often met with resistance and sometimes violence.[77]

After the Famine, the tax grievances fuelled by the perception of overtaxation were increasingly harnessed by nationalists, and purposeful political protest replaced the sporadic resistance of the early 1800s. For example, Daniel O'Connell, though he did not use the term 'fiscal contract', made the argument that Ireland was not taxed fairly and did not benefit from taxation proportionately when he pointed out that 'the resources of Ireland have to bear an undue pressure' and the revenue collected went into a collective pot and was spent 'indiscriminately'.[78] Similarly, the criticism that 'British policy-makers were willing to treat Ireland as an integral part of the United Kingdom for the purpose of raising revenue, but refused to do so when disbursing it' mounted in the post-Famine period.[79] Such grievances were also channelled through organised protest, such as the anti-tax campaign of the 1860s and in the context of the home rule movement, which ultimately led to the establishment of the Financial Relations Commission.[80] The commissioners' concession that Ireland had, as nationalists claimed, been overtaxed made it hard to deny the link between fiscal policy and the constitutional question. During the War of Independence, Sinn Féin encouraged supporters to boycott paying tax to the British state and tried to appropriate the collection of local rates.[81]

The lack of a fiscal contract in Ireland contrasted with the situation in the frontier tax states of Europe. The foundations of the formidable fiscal contract observed today in Sweden can be traced back to the sixteenth century when, in exchange for taxes, the state provided the most valuable, in the early modern context, public goods: freedom from foreign rule and internal law and order.[82] Nineteenth-century Britain was designing tax policy that would enable trust in Leviathan.[83] However, tax policy towards Ireland, as in all parts of the empire, was considered through the lens of metropolitan interests in a way that precluded the emergence of a meaningful fiscal contract.

Historical Legacies: Slowly Converging Capacity, Persistent Unwillingness to Pay

Cumulatively, the historical legacy inherited by the Irish state that became independent in 1922 was one of weak administrative capacity and popular experiences of taxation as excessive and unjust. These legacies posed significant challenges for the Free State to overcome. In the first four decades after independence, there was more continuity than change in tax administration and structure. In the initial years after independence, the state failed to create an effective tax collection infrastructure, and freedom did not lead to the emergence of a fiscal contract. From the 1960s onwards, commitment to economic development, as well as fiscal crisis, created the need for tax reform. Historical legacies of weak administration were eventually overcome through reform of the Revenue Commissioners in the early 1990s. However, a persistent unwillingness to pay has shaped tax politics from the 1960s to the present.

Administrative and Attitudinal Continuity, 1921–60

In 1922, the Free State government decided to retain the British model of revenue administration: a Board of Revenue Commissioners was appointed by the Minister for Finance but operated independently on a day-to-day basis.[84] The minimal nature of this inherited administrative structure created immediate challenges for Revenue, most especially in terms of personnel. They initially borrowed experienced officials from Britain's

Department of Inland Revenue, while training the necessary new staff. In some areas, such as customs, 65 per cent of all staff was new and required comprehensive training.[85] Other issues the Revenue faced included: erecting a land border infrastructure; collecting arrears; the destruction of records in the Custom House and the Public Record Office during the War of Independence and Civil War; and the continuation of a tax code that was not appropriate to Irish economic circumstances.[86]

Attitudes towards taxation did not automatically change with independence. The Cumann na nGaedheal government faced pressures from all sides to keep taxes low.[87] The attempts by the Revenue to collect arrears for the taxes not paid to the British government during the War of Independence provoked resentment and resistance. Claims by some TDs that the pursuit of these debts meant sending some of their constituents to their graves contributed to a perception that the Revenue was overly aggressive.[88] Non-compliance remained an issue in some sectors, most especially in farming. Overall, the number of taxpayers remained low: only 75,000 people paid income tax in 1938–39, rising to some 175,000 by the mid-1950s, but out of a working population of 1,112,000 in 1959.[89] Levels of arrears were high: by the 1950s, arrears amounted to half the annual income tax yield.[90]

For the first thirty years, the administration and structure of taxation remained on a path-dependent trajectory, as weak capacity and popular resistance to paying tax created a stable, but low efficiency, equilibrium. The administrative weakness of the Revenue Commissioners and popular attitudes towards taxation constrained the possibility of tax policy change, without which there was limited organisational reform, which further disincentivised policy change. Thus, as in the broader spheres of political and economic life in Ireland in this period, the 1920s, 1930s, and 1940s saw more continuity than change in terms of taxation. As Table 13.1 demonstrates, until the 1980s, the tax structure remained as it had been in the previous 200 years: dominated by indirect taxes, especially customs.[91] Weak administrative capacity and resistance to widening the tax net led to the maintenance of a regressive tax structure with a narrow tax base.

Lagged Administrative Convergence, Persistent Unwillingness to Pay, 1960–2016

From the 1960s onwards, pressures to modernise led to reform but under the continued conditions of weak administration and persistent unwillingness to pay. Consequently, though the number of taxpayers and the amount of revenue generated by income tax increased, the tax base as a whole remained narrow, with Pay As You Earn (PAYE) workers shouldering the greater share of the income tax burden. This created the conditions for the popular unrest and fiscal distress of the 1980s and the eventual reform of the Revenue Commissioners in the 1990s. While the Irish tax state began to converge with European standards at that point, politicians continued to respond to resistant attitudes towards taxation by decreasing taxes throughout the Celtic Tiger period, with serious consequences for the state's fiscal sustainability.

In 1957, as part of a broader political shift towards economic development and modernisation, a Commission on Income Taxation was established to investigate modernisation of tax policy.[92] Its most significant recommendation was for the adoption of PAYE, which led to a considerable increase in income tax intake after its introduction in 1960: by 184 per cent between 1965 and 1972.[93] Further changes in tax policy resulted from Ireland's accession to the European Economic Community in 1973, specifically, the introduction of value added tax (VAT).

While on the surface the structure of taxation began belatedly to resemble other European countries, historical legacies continued to have an effect. First, the policy innovations posed challenges that the weak administration could not deal with effectively, with long-run implications for tax structure and attitudes. The implementation of PAYE tripled the number of cases to be dealt with by Revenue, leading to the computerisation of collection.[94] However, it did not bring capacity to the level required for the administration of a modern tax system. By the 1980s, the Commission on Taxation stated in its Fifth Report that 'the administration of taxation in Ireland has virtually broken down.'[95]

Administrative weakness in turn hampered the broadening of the tax base. While the number of prospective taxpayers increased tenfold from 1960 to 1975, the revenue service failed to address this demographic change to broaden the tax base effectively.[96] As the overwhelming majority of the income tax payers were PAYE workers, the system of assessment for income tax for non-PAYE taxpayers was 'cumbersome and inefficient', as it involved setting high estimates for tax liability, resulting in 70–90 per cent appeal rates and a situation where 'tax finally paid is only about one-quarter of the tax in the original assessments.'[97] Farming income, in particular, remained effectively exempt, and the Commission on Taxation named non-compliance as a major issue.[98] Therefore, the state derived most income tax revenue from the easier-to-administer PAYE workers, leaving many self-employed workers under-taxed or outside the tax net altogether. By the mid-1980s, 816,000 PAYE workers were paying 90 per cent of the total income tax, which, as a percentage of overall revenue, was above the OECD average.[99]

Attempts to broaden the tax base were hampered not only by administrative challenges but also by unwaveringly resistant attitudes towards taxation. From the 1970s onwards, governments tried to increase taxes and broaden the tax base but were met with widespread resistance. The Fine Gael-Labour coalition government, which came to power in 1973 and introduced new taxes on capital gains, capital acquisitions, and wealth, lost power in 1977 to Fianna Fáil, which followed through on election promises by abolishing a plethora of taxes—both the newly introduced wealth and capital gains taxes, and also taxes on cars, and the very unpopular domestic rates charged by local authorities.[100] When Fianna Fáil tried to introduce a new tax themselves in 1979—a 2 per cent levy on farm produce—the Irish Farmers' Association launched a series of protests, and within a year the government was forced to abolish the levy. They tried again with a resource tax in 1980, but compliance was very low, with only £700,000 of the projected £7 million being collected.[101] The government had again to bow to resistance and not only repeal the tax, but also reimburse those who had paid.

The failed attempts to introduce a modern tax system in a context of weak administrative capacity and resistant public attitudes towards taxation created the conditions for crisis in the 1980s. Although overall revenue levels were comparable to other OECD countries, this revenue was being extracted by a weak administration from a narrow base. It was also insufficient to meet expenditure and was not focused on building a welfare state, as was the case in other European countries.[102] PAYE workers in particular were shouldering most of a tax burden that was unfairly distributed, and receiving little in return. In 1979, prior to the budget and provoked by the abolition of the farmers' levy, they were mobilised by trade unions to protest. In a series of demonstrations, an estimated 700,000 employees marched across the country in one of the largest mass protests of the twentieth century.[103] In response, the government promised a new Commission on Taxation to examine the issues.

The crisis continued throughout the 1980s. Industrial unrest around fiscal policy and budget proposals contributed to the fall of two short-lived governments in the early 1980s. This meant that the Commission on Taxation—which proposed wholesale reform of the revenue administration, the lowering of rates, the creation of the widest possible tax base, and self-assessment—was established by one government, reported to another, and consequently was not implemented. Caught between citizens outside the tax net refusing to be brought within it and citizens within it refusing to pay more tax, governments were forced to increase borrowing. By 1987, debt was 11.7 per cent of GDP, which was twice the European average and required the total tax receipts to service it.[104]

In the face of this fiscal crisis, tax reform became unavoidable. In 1987, a minority Fianna Fáil government tried to engage in base broadening and to reform the Revenue Commissioners. In 1988, they introduced a voluntary tax amnesty, and the scale of self-employed under-reporting became apparent through an unexpectedly high yield. The Progressive Democrats, who joined Fianna Fáil in government in 1989, insisted on further reforms.[105] Self-assessment was introduced, as the Commission on Taxation had recommended, and Revenue was given increased powers of enforcement.[106] A second amnesty in 1993 again confirmed widespread non-compliance: the £240 million raised via the amnesty indicated that there were £1.6 billion in hidden funds within the economy.[107] The reform of Revenue continued throughout the 1990s, with its powers and resources being increasingly strengthened.

These reforms succeeded in transforming the administrative capacity of Revenue, turning it into an effective administration with strong powers, comparable to other OECD tax authorities. According to an OECD benchmarking study, Irish Revenue is a highly autonomous agency with the full suite of delegated powers (except for negotiating staff pay), is one of the fastest VAT processing performers in the OECD, has below average collection costs, and has below average levels of outstanding tax debt.[108] The authoritative Doing Business project currently ranks Ireland fourth in the world in terms of ease of paying taxes for small and medium-size enterprises.[109] In other words, the 1990s reforms brought a welcome disruption to the century-long equilibrium of weak tax administration.

The subsidence of the historical legacy of weak formal institutions did not, however, lead to immediate changes in attitudes to taxation, which continued to inform the tax policy responses of politicians and trade unions throughout the 1990s. All governments in the 1990s reduced taxes and narrowed the tax base, though their targets differed. The Rainbow government of 1994–1997 provided tax relief for the lower paid, while the Fianna Fáil-PD governments from 1997–2007 alternated between rich and poor.[110] The latter abolished property tax, halved capital gains tax, and pushed for systematic reductions in income tax rates, as well as increased tax credits and exemptions, delivered through social partnership agreements with the trade union movement and ever greater exemptions from tax liability altogether. The 1997 and 1999 legislation on corporate taxation, driven by Fianna Fáil's Finance Minister Charlie McCreevy, laid the framework that made Ireland one of the largest so-called conduit offshore financial centers, which allows multinational companies to shift profits around the world while 'paying no or little taxes'.[111] These tax optimisation opportunities, together with one of the lowest corporate tax rates in the world (12.5 per cent), make Ireland an attractive destination for foreign multinationals, whose contribution to Ireland's corporate tax receipts is about 80 per cent.[112] With corporate tax receipts comprising about 16 per cent of tax revenue, such a high exposure of the corporation tax base to foreign-based firms is considered to be a risk.[113] Despite this, there has been a conspicuous absence of any meaningful domestic discussion of corporation tax reform.

In the 1990s, rapid economic growth temporarily masked the underlying weakness of the tax system by increasing employment and providing increased revenue from indirect taxes, and from stamp duty on property transactions. By 2007, the average tax burden as a percentage of gross wage earnings for a single person without children was 13.9 per cent, almost half the OECD average of 25.4 per cent.[114]

Rather than taking advantage of the newly reformed Revenue Commissioners and buoyant economic conditions to broaden the tax base in a way that would make it sustainable, governments in the 1990s and 2000s made decisions that eroded the tax base. This underlying weakness became clear again when the recession began in 2008. Excluding debt from the banking crisis, the gap between revenue and public expenditure in 2012 stood at 15 billion euros or 8 per cent of GDP.[115] In addition to cutting expenditure, there have been efforts to fill this gap by introducing a number of new taxes: the universal social charge, the household levy, property tax, water charge, and the pension levy. These taxes have again faced resistance, most particularly in the case of the water charge, which resulted in its suspension in 2016. Public support for low tax policies may also partially explain the conspicuous absence of any meaningful discussion over corporate taxation and corporation tax reform. As the economy has recovered, governments have again begun, modestly, to cut taxes. Resistant attitudes to taxation continue to be a significant constraint on the development of a broad-based, sustainable tax state.

Conclusion

The Irish tax state emerged over the course of several centuries in a non-linear but highly path-dependent process. Our analysis of the evolution of the formal and informal institutions of taxation over 300 years suggests that historical legacies played an important role at every stage of development. Path dependence in formal institutions is evident in the persistent low administrative capacity of the tax administration for most of the period after independence. Only protracted fiscal crisis prompted critical reforms of Revenue, which brought a welcome disruption of this stable equilibrium. If administrative capacity is no longer a weighty obstacle, public attitudes towards increased taxation remain deeply resistant. While there are many factors that may contribute to this, contemporary unwillingness to pay is congruent with historical experiences of taxation as excessive and unfair.

This case study of the development of the Irish tax state contributes to our understanding of the impact of historical legacies on contemporary outcomes by emphasising the differences between formal and informal institutions and, especially, the different rates at which they change over time. The Irish case is particularly instructive in the broader global context as a tax-state building project under postcolonial conditions. Having become independent earlier than most, it allows us to examine these legacies over a longer period. It suggests that while the legacies of weak administrative capacity, common in most postcolonial countries, can be overcome, attitudes towards state authority and social norms of non-compliance may take longer to erode.

Notes

1. OECD, *StatExtracts: Revenue Statistics: Comparative Tables, 1965–2016*, http://stats.oecd.org/Index.aspx?QueryId=21699 (accessed 13 Aug. 2018).
2. European Commission, *European Semester: Assessment of Progress Structural Reforms, Prevention and Correction of Macroeconomic Imbalances, and Results of in-Depth Reviews under Regulation (EU) No 1176/2011. Country Reports, Ireland, 2018*, https://ec.europa.eu/info/sites/info/files/2018-european-semester-country-report-ireland-en_1.pdf (accessed 13 Aug. 2018).
3. For a review, see Edgar Kiser and Steven Karceski, 'Political Economy of Taxation', *Annual Review of Political Science* 20, no. 1 (2017): 75–92.

4. Martin Daunton, *Trusting Leviathan: The Politics of Taxation in Britain, 1799–1914* (Cambridge: Cambridge University Press, 2001).
5. Daron Acemoglu, Simon Johnson, and James Robinson, 'The Colonial Origins of Comparative Development: An Empirical Investigation', *American Economic Review* 91, no. 5 (2001): 1369–1401; Douglass North and Barry Weingast, 'Constitutions and Commitment: The Evolution of Institutions Governing Public Choice in Seventeenth-Century England', *Journal of Economic History* 49, no. 4 (1989): 803–32; Nathan Nunn, 'The Importance of History for Economic Development', *Annual Review of Economics* 1, no. 1 (2009): 65–92; Sascha Becker et al., 'The Empire Is Dead, Long Live the Empire! Long-Run Persistence of Trust and Corruption in the Bureaucracy', *Economic Journal* 126, no. 590 (2016): 40–74; Luigi Guiso, Paola Sapienza, and Luigi Zingales, 'Does Culture Affect Economic Outcomes?', *Journal of Economic Perspectives* 20, no. 2 (2006): 23–48; Nathan Nunn and Leonard Wantchekon, 'The Slave Trade and the Origins of Mistrust in Africa', *American Economic Review* 101, no. 7 (2011): 3221–52; Robert Putnam, *Making Democracy Work: Civic Traditions in Modern Italy* (Princeton, NJ: Princeton University Press, 1993); Guido Tabellini, 'Culture and Institutions: Economic Development in the Regions of Europe', *Journal of the European Economic Association* 8, no. 4 (2010): 677–716.
6. Acemoglu, Johnson, and Robinson, 'Colonial Origins'; Pauline Grosjean, 'The Institutional Legacy of the Ottoman Empire: Islamic Rule and Financial Development in South Eastern Europe', *Journal of Comparative Economics* 39, no. 1 (2011): 1–16.
7. Michelle D'Arcy and Marina Nistotskaya, 'The Early Modern Origins of Contemporary European Tax Outcomes', *European Journal of Political Research* 57, no. 1 (2018): 47–67; Noel Johnson and Mark Koyama, 'Tax Farming and the Origins of State Capacity in England and France', *Explorations in Economic History* 51 (2014): 1–20; Isaac Martin, Ajay Mehrotra, and Monica Prasad, *The New Fiscal Sociology: Taxation in Comparative and Historical Perspective* (Cambridge: Cambridge University Press, 2009); Assaf Likhovski, *Tax Law and Social Norms in Mandatory Palestine and Israel* (Cambridge: Cambridge University Press, 2017); Marina Nistotskaya and Michelle D'Arcy, 'Getting to Sweden: The Origins of High Compliance in the Swedish Tax State', in *The Leap of Faith: The Fiscal Foundations of Successful Government in Europe and America*, ed. Sven Steinmo (Oxford: Oxford University Press, 2018), 33–55; Joseph Schumpeter, 'The Crisis of the Tax State', *International Economic Papers* 4 (1918): 5–38; Sven Steinmo, *The Evolution of Modern States: Sweden, Japan, and the United States* (Cambridge: Cambridge University Press, 2010).

8. D'Arcy and Nistotskaya, 'Early Modern Origins'.
9. Nistotskaya and D'Arcy, 'Getting to Sweden'.
10. Likhovski, *Tax Law and Social Norms*, 6.
11. Becker et al., 'The Empire Is Dead'; Pauline Grosjean, 'The Weight of History on European Cultural Integration: A Gravity Approach', *American Economic Review* 101, no. 3 (2011): 504–8; Putnam, *Making Democracy Work*; Tabellini, 'Culture and Institutions'.
12. Becker et al., 'The Empire Is Dead'.
13. Yann Algan and Pierre Cahuc, 'Inherited Trust and Growth', *American Economic Review* 100, no. 5 (2010): 2060–92; Grosjean, 'The Weight of History'; Nunn and Wantchekon, 'Slave Trade'.
14. For a review, see Nan Zhang et al., 'Willing to Pay? Tax Compliance in Britain and Italy: An Experimental Analysis', *PLoS One* 11, no. 2 (2016): 1–14.
15. Massimo Bordignon, 'A Fairness Approach to Income Tax Evasion', *Journal of Public Economics* 52, no. 3 (1993): 345–62; Ronald Cummings et al., 'Tax Morale Affects Tax Compliance: Evidence from Surveys and an Artefactual Field Experiment', *Journal of Economic Behavior & Organization* 70, no. 3 (2009): 447–57; Michelle D'Arcy, 'Why Do Citizens Assent to Pay Tax? Legitimacy, Taxation and the African State', *Afrobarometer Working Paper No 126* (2011); Bernard Fortin, Guy Lacroix, and Marie-Claire Villeval, 'Tax Evasion and Social Interactions', *Journal of Public Economics* 91, nos. 11–12 (2007): 2089–2112; John Scholz and Mark Lubell, 'Trust and Taxpaying: Testing the Heuristic Approach to Collective Action', *American Journal of Political Science* 42, no. 2 (1998): 398–417; Michael Spicer and Scott Lundstedt, 'Understanding Tax Evasion', *Public Finance* 31, no. 2 (1976): 295–305.
16. Regressive taxes impose a larger burden (relative to resources) on those who are poorer; Encyclopedia Britannica, 'Regressive Tax', https://www.britannica.com/topic/regressive-tax (accessed 13 Aug. 2018).
17. Peter Clarke, 'The Historical Development of the Irish Taxation System', *Accounting, Finance and Governance Review* 21, nos. 1–2 (2014): 5–24; Charles Ivar McGrath, *The Making of the Eighteenth-Century Irish Constitution: Government, Parliament and the Revenue, 1692–1714* (Dublin: Four Courts Press, 2000); Walsh, 'Fiscal State', 629–56.
18. Tax farming is a contractual system of tax collection, involving a private agent who is awarded by the government the right to collect certain revenue in a specified area for a specified period of time, in exchange for a fixed sum paid to the government.
19. Walsh, 'Fiscal State'; Thomas Bartlett, 'From Irish State to British Empire: Reflections on State-Building in Ireland, 1690–1830', *Études Irlandaises*

20, no. 1 (1995): 23–37; David Dickson, Cormac Ó Gráda, and Stuart Daultrey, 'Hearth Tax, Household Size and Irish Population Change, 1672–1821', *Proceedings of the Royal Irish Academy*, section c, 82 (1982): 125–81.

20. John Brewer, *The Sinews of Power: War, Money and the English State, 1688–1783* (London: Unwin Hyman, 1989); T. J. Kiernan, *History of the Financial Administration of Ireland to 1817* (London: P. S. King and Son, 1930), 93–94.
21. Kiernan, *History of the Financial Administration*, 86.
22. Bartlett, 'From Irish State'; Brewer, *Sinews of Power*; David Fleming, *Politics and Provincial People: Sligo and Limerick, 1691–1761* (Manchester: Manchester University Press, 2010).
23. Kiernan, *History of the Financial Administration*, 292.
24. Dickson, Ó Gráda, and Daultrey, 'Hearth Tax', 136.
25. Walsh, 'Fiscal State'.
26. George O'Brien, *The Economic History of Ireland in the Eighteenth Century* (London: Maunsel, 1918), 333.
27. Ibid., 315.
28. R. B. McDowell, *The Irish Administration, 1801–1914* (London: Routledge and Kegan Paul, 1964), 88.
29. Fleming, *Politics and Provincial People*.
30. D'Arcy and Nistotskaya, 'Early Modern Origins'; Nistotskaya and D'Arcy, 'Getting to Sweden'.
31. Although the Down Survey of Ireland was a cadastral map recording property ownership and was incorporated into the Books of Survey and Distribution used in the calculation of quit rents, its primary purpose was land re-distribution rather than taxation. For more information, see Roger Kain and Elizabeth Baigent, *The Cadastral Map in the Service of the State: A History of Property Mapping* (Chicago: University of Chicago Press, 1992), 236–64.
32. Paul Slack, 'Government and Information in Seventeenth-Century England', *Past & Present* 184 (2004): 33–68.
33. J. V. Beckett, 'Land Tax Administration at the Local Level, 1693–1798', in *Land and Property: The English Land Law*, ed. Michael Turner and Dennis Richard Mills (Gloucester: Alan Sutton, 1986); Brewer, *Sinews of Power*, 75–108; Daunton, *Trusting Leviathan*.
34. Dickson, Ó Gráda, and Daultrey, 'Hearth Tax', 132.
35. Fleming, *Politics and Provincial People*, 163–231; Walsh, 'Fiscal State'; idem, 'Enforcing the Fiscal State: The Army, the Revenue and the Irish Experience of the Fiscal-Military State, 1690–1769', in *The British Fiscal-Military States, 1660–c. 1783*, ed. Aaron Graham and Patrick Walsh (London: Routledge, 2016), 131–58; O'Brien, *Economic History*, 331.

36. Thomas Ertman, *Birth of the Leviathan: Building States and Regimes in Medieval and Early Modern Europe* (Cambridge: Cambridge University Press, 1997); Jan Glete, *War and the State in Early Modern Europe: Spain, the Dutch Republic and Sweden as Fiscal-Military States* (London: Routledge, 2002); Nistotskaya and D'Arcy, 'Getting to Sweden'.
37. Miles Ogborn, 'The Capacities of the State: Charles Davenant and the Management of the Excise, 1683–1698', *Journal of Historical Geography* 24, no. 3 (1998): 289.
38. David Dickson, 'Taxation and Disaffection in Late Eighteenth-Century Ireland', in *Irish Peasants: Violence and Political Unrest, 1780–1914*, ed. Samuel Clark and James S. Donnelly Jr. (Madison: University of Wisconsin Press, 1983), 37–63.
39. Dickson, Ó Gráda, and Daultrey, 'Hearth Tax'.
40. Dickson, 'Taxation and Disaffection'; Raymond Gillespie, *Seventeenth-Century Ireland: Making Ireland Modern* (Dublin: Gill and Macmillan, 2006); Walsh, 'Fiscal State'.
41. Andrew Browning, ed., *English Historical Documents* (London: Routledge, 1996), 293.
42. D. E. Schremmer, 'Taxation and Public Finance: Britain, France and Germany', in *The Cambridge Economic History of Europe*, vol. 8: *The Industrial Economies*, ed. Peter Mathias and Sidney Pollard (Cambridge: Cambridge University Press, 1989), 322.
43. Kiernan, *History of the Financial Administration*, 261.
44. Dickson, 'Taxation and Disaffection', 54; Walsh, 'Fiscal State', 636.
45. Rudolf Braun, 'Taxation, Sociopolitical Structure and State-Building: Great Britain and Brandenburg-Prussia', in *The Formation of National States in Western Europe*, ed. Charles Tilly (Princeton, NJ: Princeton University Press, 1975), 284.
46. Mark Pearsall, 'The Land Tax: 1692–1963', https://nationalarchives.gov.uk/documents/the-land-tax-1692-1963.pdf (accessed 13 Aug. 2018); Schremmer, 'Taxation and Public Finance', 328; O'Brien, *Economic History*, 200; Commons, 'Accounts Relating to Customs, Excise, Stamp Duties and Post Office of Ireland', 83, 34, 4.
47. Réamonn, *History of the Revenue*, 24.
48. L. M. Cullen, *An Economic History of Ireland since 1660* (London: B. T. Batsford, 1972), 168.
49. Bartlett, 'From Irish State'; O'Brien, *Economic History*, 315–20; Walsh, 'Fiscal State'; idem, 'Enforcing the Fiscal State'.
50. O'Brien, *Economic History*, 320; Walsh, 'Fiscal State'; idem, 'Enforcing the Fiscal State'.
51. James Quinn, 'The United Irishmen and Social Reform', *Irish Historical Studies* 31, no. 122 (1988): 193–94.

52. Fleming, *Politics and Provincial People*, 174.
53. David Burg, *A World History of Tax Rebellions: An Encyclopedia of Tax Rebels, Revolts, and Riots from Antiquity to the Present* (London: Routledge, 2004); Daunton, *Trusting Leviathan*; Nistotskaya and D'Arcy, 'Getting to Sweden'.
54. Kiernan, *History of the Financial Administration*, 320.
55. McDowell, *Irish Administration*, 94.
56. Ibid., 82; Réamonn, *History of the Revenue*, 124.
57. McDowell, *Irish Administration*, 95.
58. Commons, 'Return of Amount of Assessments', 373.
59. Daunton, *Trusting Leviathan*, 189–91; Douglas Kanter, 'The Politics of Irish Taxation, 1842–53', *English Historical Review* 127, no. 528 (2012): 1153.
60. Kanter, 'Irish Taxation', 1152.
61. Daunton, *Trusting Leviathan*.
62. Cormac Ó Gráda, *Ireland: A New Economic History, 1780–1939* (Oxford: Oxford University Press, 1995), 45.
63. Kiernan, *History of the Financial Administration*, 302.
64. George O'Brien, *The Economic History of Ireland from the Union to the Famine* (London: Longmans, Green and Co., 1921), 471–72.
65. Kiernan, *History of the Financial Administration*, 245–49.
66. *Hansard Parliamentary Debates*, 3rd ser., vol. 61, col. 445 (11 Mar. 1842).
67. Daunton, *Trusting Leviathan*, 191.
68. Kanter, 'Irish Taxation', 1126.
69. Ibid., 1146.
70. Pauric Travers, 'The Financial Relations Question, 1800–1914', in *Ireland, England and Australia: Essays in Honour of Oliver MacDonagh*, ed. F. B. Smith (Canberra: Australian National University, 1990), 49; Kanter, 'Irish Taxation', 1150.
71. Kanter, 'Irish Taxation', 1130.
72. Ibid., 1151.
73. See Kanter in this volume.
74. Travers, 'Financial Relations', 54.
75. O'Brien, *Economic History*, 349.
76. Robert Shipkey, 'Problems in Alcoholic Production and Controls in Early Nineteenth-Century Ireland', *Historical Journal* 16, no. 2 (1973): 291–302.
77. McDowell, *Irish Administration*, 139.
78. Travers, 'Financial Relations', 42.

79. Douglas Kanter, 'The Galway Packet-Boat Contract and the Politics of Public Expenditure in Mid-Victorian Ireland', *Historical Journal* 59, no. 3 (2016): 766.
80. See Kanter in this volume; Clarke, 'Historical Development', 13.
81. See Adams in this volume.
82. Nistotskaya and D'Arcy, 'Getting to Sweden', 43–46.
83. Daunton, *Trusting Leviathan.*
84. Réamonn, *History of the Revenue*, 49.
85. Ibid., 88.
86. Ibid., 102.
87. See Knirck in this volume.
88. Réamonn, *History of the Revenue*, 106.
89. Commission on Income Taxation, *First Report* (Dublin: Stationary Office, 1959), 6; idem, *Third Report* (Dublin: Stationary Office, 1960), 14.
90. Clarke, 'Historical Development', 16.
91. High customs revenue after the 1930s was also due to the Fianna Fáil government's adoption of an economic policy of self-sufficiency, which meant that Irish customs duties were some of the highest in the world; see Ray MacSharry and Padraic White, *The Making of the Celtic Tiger: The Inside Story of Ireland's Boom Economy* (Cork: Mercier Press, 2000).
92. Tom Garvin, *1922: The Birth of the Irish State* (Dublin: Gill and Macmillan, 1996); Réamonn, *History of the Revenue*, 149.
93. Réamonn, *History of the Revenue*, 331.
94. Ibid., 162–63.
95. Commission on Taxation, *Fifth Report* (Dublin: Stationary Office 1985), 21.
96. Niamh Hardiman, 'From Conflict to Co-Ordination: Economic Governance and Political Innovation in Ireland', *West European Politics* 25, no. 4 (2002): 33.
97. Commission on Taxation, *Fifth Report*, 83.
98. Réamonn, *History of the Revenue*, 167; Commission on Taxation, *Fifth Report*, 21.
99. Hardiman, 'From Conflict to Co-Ordination', 42, 31.
100. Tony Farmar, *The Versatile Profession: A History of Accountancy in Ireland since 1850* (Dublin: Chartered Accountants Ireland, 2013).
101. Olivia O'Leary, 'The Farmers and the Land Tax', *Magill*, 1 Oct. 1984.
102. Cedric Sandford, *Successful Tax Reform: Lessons from an Analysis of Tax Reform in Six Countries* (Bath: Fiscal Publications, 1993).
103. Paul Sweeney, 'The PAYE Sector's Perspective of Taxation and Trade Union Demand for Reform', *Journal of the Statistical and Social Inquiry Society of Ireland* 25, no. 1 (1983–84): 27–35.

104. Michael Somers, 'The Management of Ireland's National Debt', *Journal of the Statistical and Social Inquiry Society of Ireland* 26, no. 4 (1991–92): 133–51; Sandford, *Successful Tax Reform*, 180.
105. Sandford, *Successful Tax Reform*, 188.
106. Ibid., 173.
107. Hardiman, 'From Conflict to Co-Ordination', 53.
108. OECD, *Tax Administration: Comparative Information on Advanced and Other Emerging Economies* (Paris: OECD Publishing, 2015), 32, 215, 181, 231.
109. World Bank, 'Doing Business', http://www.doingbusiness.org/data/exploretopics/paying-taxes (accessed 13 Aug. 2018).
110. Hardiman, 'From Conflict to Co-Ordination', 47.
111. Javier Garcia-Bernardo et al., 'Uncovering Offshore Financial Centers: Conduits and Sinks in the Global Corporate Ownership Network', *Nature: Scientific Reports* 7, no. 1 (2017): 2; Mark Paul, 'Ireland Is the World's Biggest Corporate "Tax Haven", Say Academics', *Irish Times*, 13 June 2018.
112. Paul Tancred, *An Analysis of 2015 Corporation Tax Returns and 2016 Payments* (Dublin: Revenue Commissioners, 2017), 14, https://www.revenue.ie/en/corporate/documents/research/corporation-tax-returns-2016.pdf (accessed 13 Aug. 2018).
113. Arthur Beesley, 'Ireland Enjoys Tax Boom but Fears a Reckoning', *Financial Times*, 31 Jan. 2018.
114. OECD, *Taxing Wages* (Paris: OECD, 2010).
115. Government of Ireland, *2013 Estimates of Receipts and Expenditures*: http://www.budget.gov.ie/Budgets/2013/Documents/White%20Paper%20-%20Estimates%20of%20Receipts%20&%20Expenditure%20for%202013.pdf (accessed 20 Aug. 2018).

Index[1]

[1] Note: Page numbers followed by 'n' refer to notes.

D. Kanter, P. Walsh (eds.), *Taxation, Politics, and Protest in Ireland, 1662–2016*, Palgrave Studies in the History of Finance,
https://doi.org/10.1007/978-3-030-04309-4

D

The manufacturer's authorised representative in the EU is Springer Nature Customer Service Centre GmbH, Europaplatz 3, 69115 Heidelberg, Germany. If you have any concerns regarding our products, please contact ProductSafety@springernature.com

Printed and bound by CPI Group (UK) Ltd, Croydon, CR0 4YY

30/09/2026

02225490-0014